Cash Flow

FOR

DUMMIES®

Cash Flow
FOR
DUMMIES®

by Tage C. Tracy and John A. Tracy

WILEY

John Wiley & Sons, Inc.

Cash Flow For Dummies®

Published by
John Wiley & Sons, Inc.
111 River St.
Hoboken, NJ 07030-5774
www.wiley.com

For general information on our other products and services, please contact our Customer Care Department within the U.S. at 877-762-2974, outside the U.S. at 317-572-3993, or fax 317-572-4002.

For technical support, please visit www.wiley.com/techsupport.

Wiley also publishes its books in a variety of electronic formats and by print-on-demand. Some content that appears in standard print versions of this book may not be available in other formats. For more information about Wiley products, visit us at www.wiley.com.

Library of Congress Control Number: 2011939639

ISBN 978-1-118-01850-7 (pbk); ISBN 978-1-118-16392-4 (ebk); ISBN 978-1-118-16391-7 (ebk); ISBN 978-1-118-16390-0 (ebk)

Manufactured in the United States of America

10 9 8 7 6 5 4 3 2 1

WILEY

About the Authors

Tage C. Tracy (Poway, California) is the principal owner of TMK & Associates, an accounting, financial, and strategic business-planning consulting firm focused on supporting small- to medium-sized businesses since 1993. Tage received his baccalaureate in accounting in 1985 from the University of Colorado at Boulder with honors. Tage began his career with Coopers & Lybrand (now merged into PricewaterhouseCoopers). More recently, Tage coauthored with his father, John, *How to Manage Profit and Cash Flow* and *Small Business Financial Management Kit For Dummies*.

John A. Tracy (Boulder, Colorado) is professor of accounting, emeritus, at the University of Colorado in Boulder. Before his 35-year tenure at Boulder, he was on the business faculty for four years at the University of California at Berkeley. He served as staff accountant at Ernst & Young and is the author of several books on accounting and finance, including *Accounting For Dummies, Accounting Workbook For Dummies, The Fast Forward MBA in Finance,* and *How to Read a Financial Report.* He has coauthored two books with his son Tage, *How to Manage Profit and Cash Flow* and *Small Business Financial Management Kit For Dummies.* Dr. Tracy received his BSC degree from Creighton University and earned his MBA and PhD degrees from the University of Wisconsin. He is a CPA (inactive) in Colorado.

Dedication

We would like to dedicate this book to the backbone of the U.S. economy, namely the tens of thousands of business owners, managers, and entrepreneurs that battle every day to make their companies succeed. Remember that while the deck at times may seem stacked against you during these trying economic times, your spirit cannot be deterred. Our simple hope is that for those of you experiencing cash flow problems or just simply looking to understand cash flows a little better, this book can help ease your pain and offer additional insight on how to improve and manage your business interests.

We also want to mention who this book is not dedicated to: the politicians in Washington and across the U.S. and the banksters that have lost sight of what it means to create, launch, build, and operate a business. Simply put, these parties have spent too much time managing other people's hard-earned money and not enough time creating real value, wealth, and opportunity. Think of the Grinch from the wonderful story by Dr. Seuss, *How the Grinch Stole Christmas.* The Grinch attempted to "steal" Christmas by taking all of the trees, presents, decorations, and whatever else was available from Whoville. Yet Christmas still came, and it was then that the Grinch realized that "Maybe, just maybe, Christmas meant a little bit more." When the politicians and banksters finally realize that maybe, just maybe, owning a business and risking everything one has to pursue a dream means just a little bit more, the unparalleled historical disconnect between the twin Ws (Washington and Wall Street) and Main Street America will begin to evaporate, allowing for real growth to resume.

From Tage Tracy: I would like to dedicate this book to my old man and coauthor (or as I refer to him, TOP, or The Old Pro). About seven years ago, my dad, in a manner reminiscent of Vito Corleone of *The Godfather,* made me an offer I couldn't refuse: Take over the family business or else. (Thank goodness we didn't own a horse, but I was concerned about our cat from time to time). In this case, the family business involved carrying on his remarkable and deeply insightful legacy of being able to translate even the most complex and difficult accounting and financial concepts into easy-to-comprehend layman's terms. As for the "else," well let's just say that the old man has threatened to ditch me from his will more than once (a running joke in our family). I am forever grateful for the opportunity to write with and learn from TOP.

Acknowledgments

We are deeply grateful to everyone at John Wiley & Sons, Inc., who helped produce this book. Their professionalism and courtesy were much appreciated. First, we thank Stacy Kennedy, the acquisitions editor. She helped us develop the concept for the book. We appreciate her encouragement. Our editors, Tim Gallan and Caitie Copple, were exceptional. It was a pleasure working with them. We owe them a debt that we cannot repay. So a simple but heartfelt "thank you" will have to do. Every author should have such superb editors.

Publisher's Acknowledgments

We're proud of this book; please send us your comments at http://dummies.custhelp.com. For other comments, please contact our Customer Care Department within the U.S. at 877-762-2974, outside the U.S. at 317-572-3993, or fax 317-572-4002.

Some of the people who helped bring this book to market include the following:

Acquisitions, Editorial, and Vertical Websites

Senior Project Editor: Tim Gallan

Acquisitions Editor: Stacy Kennedy

Copy Editor: Caitlin Copple

Assistant Editor: David Lutton

Editorial Program Coordinator: Joe Niesen

Editorial Manager: Michelle Hacker

Editorial Assistants: Rachelle S. Amick, Alexa Koschier

Cover Photos: © iStockphoto.com / Amanda Rohd

Cartoons: Rich Tennant (www.the5thwave.com)

Composition Services

Project Coordinator: Nikki Gee

Layout and Graphics: Carrie A. Cesavice, Sennett Vaughan Johnson, Lavonne Roberts, Corrie Socolovitch, Christin Swinford

Proofreader: Bonnie Mikkelson

Indexer: Ty Koontz

Publishing and Editorial for Consumer Dummies

  Kathleen Nebenhaus, Vice President and Executive Publisher

  Kristin Ferguson-Wagstaffe, Product Development Director

  Ensley Eikenburg, Associate Publisher, Travel

  Kelly Regan, Editorial Director, Travel

Publishing for Technology Dummies

  Andy Cummings, Vice President and Publisher

Composition Services

  Debbie Stailey, Director of Composition Services

Contents at a Glance

Table of Contents

Part IV: Managing Your Business with Cash Flow in Mind.................................... *239*

Chapter 12: Covering the Basics of Cash and Cash Activity 241

Chapter 13: Preventing Cash Losses from Embezzlement and Fraud 267

Introduction

Cash Flow For Dummies explains how cash flows in the business setting. In broad terms, *cash flow* refers to generating or producing cash (cash inflows) and using or consuming cash (cash outflows). As such, maybe the simplest way to view cash flows are to consider them the blood of the business, and you must keep that blood circulating at all times in order avoid failure or death. So the first rule is that you can't run out of cash, no more than you can run out of blood, and although you might be able to go on cash flow life support for a short time, the outcome of this strategy is almost always extremely painful. In addition to explaining the basics of cash flow, this book then tackles numerous issues on how to improve cash flow and manage this invaluable resource more efficiently. Continuing the analogy of cash flow being the blood of the business, we assist you in keeping your arteries free and clear of any potential blockages to ensure that your blood flows freely and that your business's health is protected at all times.

In large business organizations, cash-flow duties are delegated to finance professionals. In small businesses, and even in many midsize businesses, managers and owners have to take a more direct role in cash-flow affairs, and this area of business management isn't always easy to navigate. That's why we're here to help.

Cash flow is both clear and opaque. Borrowing money from a bank is an obvious source of cash. But when should you borrow money, what payment terms should you negotiate, and what are the risks of debt? Our book provides practical answers for the fundamental cash-flow questions facing every business. We explain the crucial difference between recording a profit, which is an accounting measure, and generating cash flow from that profit. Many business managers confuse profit and cash flow, which can have serious consequences. With this book at hand, you'll be prepared to handle cash flow in an efficient and profitable way.

About This Book

Cash Flow For Dummies aims to help managers and owners of small and midsize business who have direct involvement in the cash flows of their business. We also provide very useful information for business lenders and investors. Although business finance professionals may find fresh insights in this book, this book sticks to essentials, and we don't delve into technical areas.

Business managers are very busy people; they have to carefully budget their time. Small business owners/managers are especially busy people; they have little time to spare. We promise not to waste your time with this book. In every chapter, we cut to the chase and avoid detours. We restrict our discussions to fundamentals — topics you must know to handle the cash-flow affairs of your business.

This book is not like a mystery novel; you can read the chapters in any order. You may have more interest in one chapter than others, so you can begin with the chapters that have highest priority to you. Where a topic overlaps with a topic in another chapter, we provide a cross-reference.

By all means, use the book as a reference manual. Put it on your desk and refer to it as the need arises. It's your book, so you can mark topics with comments in the margins or place sticky notes on pages you refer to often. This book isn't a college textbook. You don't have to memorize things for exams. The only test is whether you improve your skills for managing the cash flow of your business.

Conventions Used in This Book

Throughout this book we use examples to explain cash flow, most of which are illustrated with financial statements or elements of financial statements. We make the examples as true to life as we can without getting bogged down in too many details. Our examples are hypothetical, but they come from the real world of business.

As you may know, financial statements are based on standardized accounting methods and terminology. It's been said many times that accounting is the language of business. You may not be entirely comfortable with financial statements and the methods and jargon of accountants. We understand your predicament. Throughout the book we take care to use plain English in explaining financial statements and accounting methods.

In this book, we distinguish between the internal accountant, who is an employee of your business, and the outside, independent accounting professional who advises you from time to time. A small business employs an accountant who is in charge of its accounting system. The employee's job title may be controller, in-charge accountant, or office manager. In this book, the term *accountant* refers to the person on your payroll. We refer to your independent professional accountant as a *CPA* (certified public accountant).

As for formatting conventions, we use *italic* to introduce new terms that are defined. We also use italic to reference information listed in figures.

What You're Not to Read

We occasionally go off on tangents or offer anecdotes in gray boxes called *sidebars*. These sidebars offer interesting but nonessential information, so you can skip them if you like.

Not every topic may have you sitting on the edge of your seat. For example, you may already have a good grasp on the three primary financial statements of a business — the income statement, the balance sheet, and the statement of cash flows. If so, you may not be terribly interested in Chapter 3, which introduces these three financial statements. (But be sure that you understand the statement of cash flows!) You can skip over topics that aren't immediately relevant or urgent; you won't hurt our feelings.

We suspect that a few topics in the book are more detailed than you're interested in. For example, you may find that the details of the technique discussed in Chapter 6 for analyzing cash flow from profit is not practical for your business because it deviates from the standard methods of accountants. You may simply skim over the technique, and reconsider it at a later time.

Foolish Assumptions

In writing this book, we've done our best to put ourselves in your shoes as a manager of a small or midsize business who has responsibilities for cash flow. Of course, we don't know you personally. But we have a good composite profile of you based on our experience in consulting with small business managers and explaining cash-flow issues to business managers who have a limited background in financial matters.

Perhaps you've attended a short course in finance for the nonfinance manager, which would give you a leg up for reading this book. We should mention that many of these short courses focus mainly on financial statement analysis and don't explore the broader range of cash-flow management issues that owners and managers of smaller-size businesses have to deal with.

However, we take nothing for granted and start our discussions at ground zero. We present the material from the foundation up. The more you already know about the topics, the quicker you can move through the discussion. Whether you're a neophyte or veteran, you can discover useful insights and knowledge in this book. If nothing else, the book is a checklist of the things you ought to know for managing the cash flow of your business.

How This Book Is Organized

This book is divided into parts, and each part is divided into chapters. The following sections describe what you find in each part.

Part I: Fitting Cash Flow into the Big Picture of Running a Business

Part I explains the crucial importance of managing cash flow to avoid running out of cash and to keep your business financially viable. The continued existence of a business depends on a healthy rhythm of cash flow. Cash flow from making profit is the starting point. The first two chapters explain the important difference between accrual basis accounting that's used in recording revenue and expenses and the cash flows of revenue and expenses. Also, the three basic financials statements of a business are reviewed with special emphasis on the statement of cash flows.

Part II: Using Financial Statements to Assess Cash Health

Part II offers chapters that take you on a walk through the balance sheet from the cash-flow point of view. As you probably know, this financial statement summarizes the assets, liabilities, and owners' equity of the business. The cash-flow aspects of assets and liabilities are typically overlooked or not understood well. Business managers need to astutely understand the cash-flow aspects of every asset and liability. Also, we take the particular assets and liabilities from the balance sheet that affect cash flow from profit and use them to build a technique for analyzing the difference between cash flow and bottom-line profit in the income (profit and loss) statement.

Part III: Getting Intimate with Your Company's Cash Flow Needs

To begin this part of the book, we explain the importance of developing a viable and realistic business plan, one that lays the foundation for the business and that serves as the key document in raising capital to start and grow a business. A business has to demonstrate clear thinking when it comes to raising cash from lenders and investors, and its clearheaded thinking must show through in its business plan. This part of our book takes a hard but realistic look at the two basic sources of business capital: debt and equity.

Part IV: Managing Your Business with Cash Flow in Mind

Part IV gets down to the nuts and bolts of managing cash flows. The first two chapters explain the day-to-day management details of keeping cash flowing and preventing cash losses from embezzlement and fraud. The last two chapters explain how to squeeze more cash flow from the two basic cycles of business: the selling cycle and the disbursement cycle. Managers often overlook the potential cash-flow benefits from paying more attention to the cash-related aspects of these two basic operating cycles.

Part V: The Part of Tens

The Part of Tens is a staple in every *For Dummies* book. These chapters offer pithy lists of advice related to the main points of the chapters. One chapter summarizes ten cash-flow management rules for the small business (that apply to larger businesses as well, we should mention). The final chapter in this part of the book tells ten tales of cash-flow woes.

Icons Used in This Book

Throughout this book, you see some little pictures in the margins. These icons highlight the following types of information:

This icon asks you to keep in mind an important point that is central in the explanation of the topic at hand.

This icon serves as a bookmark tagging an extremely significant concept.

As you may surmise, this icon serves as a "yellow light" that the going gets a little heavier here. You may have to slow down and read this stuff more carefully and ponder it more than usual. However, this information isn't critical to understanding the basic concept.

This icon highlights, well, *tips* for understanding, analyzing, and managing cash flow. These pointers and advisories are worth highlighting with a yellow marker so you don't forget them. On second thought, this icon saves you the cost of buying a highlighter pen.

When you see this icon, we're presenting a real-world example of whatever concept or point we happen to be discussing.

This icon calls out terminology that is frequently used in the accounting and finance world.

This sign warns you about speed bumps and potholes on the cash-flow highway. Taking special note of this material can steer you around a financial road hazard and keep you from blowing a fiscal tire. You can save yourself a lot of trouble by paying attention to these warning signs.

Where to Go from Here

Many small business managers and owners are confused (or if not confused, then not entirely sure) about earning profit on the one hand and squeezing out cash flow from profit on the other hand. For that matter, many managers of larger businesses are confused about profit and cash flow. If you are in this state of mind, you should start with Chapter 1, where we distinguish between revenue and expenses that you see in a profit report and the cash flows of revenue and expenses. Chapter 2 is the logical next step, which explains why accrual accounting is necessary for measuring revenue and expenses.

You may need to review business financial statements. If so, then by all means read Chapter 3. You can start with that chapter, but you'll probably get more use out of it after you have absorbed the captivating topics in Chapters 1 and 2. You may already have a solid understanding of accrual accounting (be certain that you do) and you may already have a good understanding of the balance sheet and income statement of businesses. In this case, you may want to charge directly ahead to Chapter 4, which explains the statement of cash flows.

After Part I, you can take a more cafeteria-style approach and read the chapters in Parts II, III, and IV as you prefer. One or more chapters may have particular interest to you, such as Chapter 14, on the "ground rules" for using debt, or Chapter 8, on creating a business plan with cash flow foremost in mind. Feel free to jump around. However, we recommend saving the chapters in Part V for dessert, after enjoying a full meal of other chapters.

Part I

Fitting Cash Flow into the Big Picture of Running a Business

The 5th Wave   By Rich Tennant

"This ledger certainly paints a picture of the company. Edvard Munch's 'The Scream' comes to mind."

In this part . . .

We begin with the first rule of business — you can't run out of cash. Business managers and owners need to understand cash flow. The logical place to start is cash flow from making profit. When you read about revenue and expenses in an income statement (also known as a *profit and loss report*), you aren't reading cash-flow numbers. The cash flows of revenue and expenses are different, and you'd better know why.

Business managers and owners need to know how to read their three basic financial statements from the cash-flow point of view, and that includes having a sure grip on the statement of cash flows and how it connects with the balance sheet and income statement. Ignoring cash flow is not an option in managing a business — unless you have more cash than you know what to do with. Many businesses operate with a razor-thin cash balance, so understanding cash flow should be a top priority.

Chapter 1

Getting in Sync with the Rhythm of Cash

*I*n running a business, you have to follow many rules, but one rule stands above the others: *Don't run out of cash.* As obvious as you may think this rule is, the importance and difficulty of maintaining an adequate cash balance are generally taken for granted in business management books and articles. Many business managers ignore cash until a serious problem pops up. They assume that cash will take care of itself, as if cash could be put on automatic pilot. Nothing is farther from the truth. If you don't pay attention to cash, you may be in for a nasty surprise.

To control cash, you must control cash inflows and cash outflows. To do that, you need cash-flow information, and you need to know how well your current cash balance stacks up against the short-term demands on cash. Managers depend on regular accounting reports for financial information; in particular, their monthly income statement (also called the *profit and loss,* or *P&L, report*). However, the income statement doesn't provide the cash-flow information you need.

You must turn to another financial statement for cash-flow information, appropriately called the *statement of cash flows.* But here is where things get rather befuddling for the business manager. The cash-flow statement lists adjustments to profit to arrive at the cash flow from making profit. It assumes that the reader has a good basic understanding of profit accounting and, therefore, knows why adjustments are necessary to find cash flow. But in our experience, business managers do not fully understand how their accountants measure profit, which makes understanding cash flow and why it's higher or lower than profit very difficult.

This chapter starts by pointing out the catastrophic consequences of running out of cash. Next, we offer a brief review of profit accounting and the assets and liabilities that are used in recording revenue and expenses. Changes in these assets and liabilities are the reasons why cash flow differs from profit. Then the chapter takes the first steps in explaining the cash-flow aspects of making profit and why cash flow is invariably higher or lower than the bottom-line profit or loss number in the income statement. We also explain the cash-flow side of business transactions and the basic classes of cash flows.

Not Letting the Well Run Dry

One morning you arrive at your business. As usual, you're the first person to arrive. But none of your employees come to work. Not one. Who will open the doors for customers? Who will sell your products? Who will start tapping on the computers? This scenario may seem like a nightmare, but it's not the worst thing that can happen to a business.

Here's the real fiasco you should worry about: One day your accountant rushes into your office and tells you that the business's bank account balance is zero. You have $50 in petty cash and a small amount of currency in the cash registers. But that's it. Your checking account is empty. You can't cut any checks to your vendors, who will cut off your credit if not paid on time. You have a sizable payroll to meet in two days. If not paid, your employees will quit. And your bank is sure to notice that your checking account balance is zip and may consider shutting down your credit line. It's not a pretty picture, is it?

A zero cash balance puts you on the edge of a cliff. One false step and you can fall off and be unable to recover. When your suppliers, employees, and sources of capital find out about your cash problems — and they will — your credibility drops to zero. The businesses and various people you deal with depend on your ability to continue as a going business that they can rely on in the future. Running out of cash would pull the rug out from under the reputation of your business that you worked so hard to build up over the years. You could lose your business to creditors or have to declare bankruptcy.

Running out of cash is an extreme, worst-case scenario, although it's a threat many businesses face. The purpose of mentioning it here is to emphasize its disaster potential for a business. Running out of cash is not just a life-changing event for a business; it can be a life-*ending* event. Business managers should never let their guard down regarding cash and cash flows.

Surprisingly, many business managers, small-business owners/mangers in particular, do not take an aggressive, proactive approach toward controlling cash. Instead of learning cash-flow fundamentals and techniques of controlling cash flows, they retreat into a passive mode. But very few businesses have the luxury of sitting on hoards of cash such that they really don't have to worry about the cash balance period to period. Many businesses operate on a razor-thin cash balance.

Outlining Profit Accounting Basics

The best way to avoid cash flow problems and to generate a stream of cash flow is to earn profit. Measuring profit (or loss) is the job of your accountant. Each period your accountant prepares an income statement that summarizes revenue and expenses and profit (or loss) for the period. To understand cash flow emanating from profit, you need to understand how your accountant records revenue and expenses. Otherwise you'll be confused about why your cash flow from profit during the period is different from your profit for the period. You don't have to delve into the technical aspects of revenue and expense accounting — just understand the basics. This section gives you the brief overview you need to go forward with managing cash flow.

We're optimistic that you know that profit is the excess of revenue over expenses (and loss is the excess of expenses over revenue). We mention it simply to stress that *profit* accounting really refers to *revenue and expense* accounting. Profit (or loss) is just the residual number left over after recording revenue and expenses for the period.

The brief discussion of revenue and expense accounting in this section is no more than dipping our toes in the water. Profit accounting involves much, much more than this very brief introduction covers. We go into more details later in this chapter in and future chapters. For a more extensive explanation of accounting methods and problems, see *Accounting For Dummies,* 4th Edition, by John A. Tracy (John Wiley & Sons, Inc.).

Reviewing revenue accounting

When a sale is made for "cash on the barrelhead," to use an old expression, cash increases and the accountant increases the sales revenue account the same amount. At the retail level, most sales are for cash; currency and coins are received by the business, or a credit or debit card is accepted that almost immediately increases the cash account of the business. In contrast, many businesses sell on credit, especially to other businesses. No money is collected from the customer until a month or so after the sale. In those cases, the accountant records the sale immediately by increasing an asset account called *accounts receivable* and increases sales revenue the same amount. When the customer pays later, cash is increased and the accounts receivable asset is decreased. Notice the time lag between the two events — point one when the sale is recorded and point two when the cash is received.

Revenue accounting can be much more complicated than recording simple cash and credit sales. For example, some businesses collect cash from customers before delivering the product or service, such as newspapers that collect subscriptions in advance before delivering the papers, and insurance companies that collect premiums before the insurance period coverage begins. But in any case, recording revenue is coupled with a corresponding increase in an asset or, in some cases, a decrease in a liability.

Examining expense accounting

A business records many expenses by decreasing cash and increasing an expense account, such as paying the monthly utility bill for gas and electricity. This transaction is straightforward enough: Cash decreases and an expense account increases the same amount. But many expenses are more complicated. Perhaps an expense is recorded before cash is actually paid out, or it may be recorded sometime after cash has been paid out.

Recording an expense is coupled with a corresponding decrease in an asset or an increase in a liability. For example, a business receives a bill from its lawyer for work already done. The appropriate expense account (legal fees) is increased, and a liability account called *accounts payable* is increased. When the bill is paid later, cash is decreased and the accounts payable liability is decreased.

When a business buys products that it will sell later to its customers, it increases an asset account called *inventory*. Suppose the purchase is on credit from the vendor. The inventory asset account is increased, and the accounts payable liability account is increased. When the goods are sold — but not until then — the inventory asset account is decreased for the cost of products sold and the expense account cost of goods is sold is increased the same amount.

Usually a business pays its vendor before it sells the products to its customers. However, in some cases a business may sell products to its customers before it pays the supplier of the products.

Here's another example of an important expense: Suppose a business bought a delivery truck three years ago and paid for it then. The cost of the truck is recorded as an increase in an asset account. Then each year the truck is used, a fraction of the total cost of the truck is recorded to expense, which amount is recorded as a decrease in the asset account. That portion of the original cost charged to expense in the year is called *depreciation expense,* and we discuss its cash-flow aspects in the later section "Depreciation expense."

Contrasting cash- and accrual-basis accounting

For most businesses, profit accounting (recording revenue and expenses) involves much more than just recording cash inflows and cash outflows. Recording only cash inflows and outflows is not acceptable for most businesses and, in fact, would be seriously misleading. That type of accounting, called *cash-basis accounting,* doesn't fit how most businesses carry on their profit-making activities or how businesses raise and invest capital.

Under cash-basis accounting, revenue and expenses are recorded when the cash flow happens. Revenue is recorded when cash is received, and expenses are recorded when cash payments are made — not before and not after. Some small businesses that tend to operate through straightforward transactions get by with cash-basis accounting. Federal income-tax law allows cash-basis accounting for businesses that meet certain conditions. Generally, cash-basis accounting is acceptable only for relatively small businesses that don't buy or sell on credit and that don't make investments in operating assets.

Most businesses of any size and complexity buy and/or sell on credit and make sizable investments in long-term operating assets (buildings, machinery, and the like). For these businesses, cash-basis accounting is woefully inadequate. Instead, they use accrual-basis accounting. (How well they use it is another matter.) Fundamentally, *accrual-basis accounting* means that several assets other than cash and several liabilities are used in recording revenue and expenses.

Accrual is not a particularly good descriptive term. In accounting jargon, it doesn't mean accumulation, accretion, growth, or enlargement. In the field of accounting, the term *accrual* refers to recording revenue and expenses (as well as the resultant increases and decreases in assets and liabilities) at the time that economic exchanges and business transactions take place. The cash flows of many transactions occur before or after the transaction — perhaps a few days, maybe a month, or even years before or after recording revenue and expenses. Accrual-basis accounting is on one timetable; cash flows are on another timetable.

Seeing Why Profit and Cash Flow Are Different Bottom Lines

You often hear that a business "made money," meaning that it earned a profit. But earning a profit does not mean that the business's cash balance went up the same amount. In fact, earning profit can sometimes cause the cash balance to decrease. To keep the business healthy, managers need to differentiate the two numbers and understand the importance of each.

The income statement of a business (a key accounting report also called the *P&L report, earnings statement, statement of operations,* and other titles) summarizes the revenue and expenses of a business for a period of time. The last line of the statement is the profit or loss for the period. The cash increase (or decrease) from making the profit is a different matter. Many business managers mistakenly assume that profit reported in this statement means the cash balance increases the same amount — a potentially dangerous misperception.

In this section, we discuss what information you can glean from the income statement, what info you can't, and why you need to keep an eye on more than one bottom line.

Considering what the income statement doesn't say about cash flow

Figure 1-1 presents the most recent annual income statement of your friendly hardware store. We keep the number of lines in this income statement example to a minimum, to focus attention on fundamentals. Also, the dollar amounts are rounded off. (Following common practice, numbers in parentheses mean a decrease by that amount; numbers not in parentheses mean an increase.) The figures for revenue and expenses are in accordance with generally accepted accounting standards, and you can assume that they're free of fraud or deliberate distortion.

The business sells a wide variety of products to retail customers who pay cash or use credit and debit cards, which the business converts into cash almost immediately. The hardware store also sells to other businesses. Its basic business model is to mark up the costs of products (called "goods") it buys to earn enough total gross margin to cover its operating, depreciation, and interest expenses, and to provide profit. As you see in Figure 1-1, the business earned $600,000 bottom-line profit for the year just ended, which equals sales revenue minus all expenses. As an aside, you may notice that profit equals 5 percent of sales revenue ($600,000 profit/$12,000,000 sales revenue = 5%), which means that expenses are 95 percent of sales revenue.

Income Statement for Year Just Ended

Dollar amounts in thousands

Sales Revenue	$12,000
Cost of Goods Sold Expense	($7,500)
Gross Margin	$4,500
Operating Expenses	($3,400)
Depreciation Expense	($200)
Operating Earnings	$900
Interest Expense	($300)
Net Income	$600

Figure 1-1:
Example income statement.

The income statement by itself doesn't report how much of sales revenue was collected in cash during the year. Consider the $12 million sales revenue amount, for instance. This accrual-basis accounting amount may be relatively close to the actual cash inflow from sales during the year — but then again, it may not be. Most of the total annual sales revenue probably has been collected in cash through the end of the year, but some of it probably hasn't been collected in cash yet at that time. In this case, cash flow from sales would be less than sales revenue. (We explain cash flow from revenue in the next section, "Exploring cash flow from profit.")

Likewise, the income statement by itself does not report how much of each expense was paid in cash during the year. You don't see in the income statement the impact of expenses on the particular assets and liabilities used to record the expenses. The amount of an expense may be relatively close to the actual cash outflow for the expense — but maybe not. One expense in particular is important to understand in this regard because it is a noncash expense: *depreciation*. Depreciation recorded on the income statement involves no cash outlay at any point. In contrast, other expenses are intertwined with cash. (We also explain cash flow for expenses in the next section.)

The actual cash flows of revenue and expenses differ from the accrual-basis amounts reported in the income statement for most businesses. Therefore, the bottom-line profit number does not indicate the increase in cash from making profit. Cash flow can be about the same, or can be considerably lower or higher than profit.

Exploring cash flow from profit

Figure 1-2 presents a summary of the cash flows for sales revenue and expenses that are reported in the income statement (refer to Figure 1-1).

Your accountant can prepare this summary in the process of compiling the financial statements of the business at the end of the period.

Revenue and Expense
Cash Flows for Year

Dollar amounts in thousands

Sales Revenue	$11,750
Cost of Goods Sold Expense	($7,800)
Operating Expenses	($3,250)
Depreciation Expense	$0
Interest Expense	($300)
Net Increase in Cash	$400

Figure 1-2: Summary of revenue and expense cash flows.

The cash flows of revenue and most expenses in Figure 1-2 are different from the accrual-basis numbers in the income statement (in Figure 1-1). The income statement reports the correct profit for the period, $600,000 in the example. The cash-flows summary shows actual cash flows of revenue and expenses, and it turns out that net cash flow for the year is $400,000, which is $200,000 lower than profit for the year. This discrepancy isn't unusual and doesn't in any way imply that profit has not been accounted for correctly.

Here's a quick summary of the differences between the income statement amounts and the cash flows of revenue and expenses in thousands.

Sales	($250)
Goods sold	($300)
Operations	$150
Depreciation	$200
Interest	$0
Total cash flow	($200)

A negative number (shown in parentheses) means that cash inflow from revenue is lower than the accrual-basis number in the income statement, or that cash outflow for an expense is higher than the number in the income statement. A positive number (without parentheses) means that cash inflow from revenue is higher than the accrual-basis number in the income statement, or that cash outflow for an expense is lower than the number in the income statement.

Because these numbers are different, business managers need to keep an eye on both cash flows and accrual-basis revenue and expenses. You could say that the business manager needs bifocals — one level for focusing on cash flow and one level for profit — because cash flow can get out of control even when profit performance is acceptable. For example, a business may allow its uncollected receivables from credit sales to balloon way out of proportion to the growth in sales. Or a business may overstock its inventory of products, resulting in slow-moving products (that take too long to sell). Business survival depends both on making profit and controlling the cash flow outcomes of making profit. Like riding a bicycle, a business needs to keep both the cash-flow wheel and the profit wheel turning.

In the following sections, we offer brief explanations for each of the cash-flow amounts in Figure 1-2, explaining why the cash-flow amount differs from the income statement amount.

Cash inflow from sales

The reason cash inflow from sales revenue is $250,000 less than sales revenue for the year is that the company's accounts receivable balance increased $250,000 during the year. The balance in this asset account is the total of uncollected credit sales. The sales were recorded in sales revenue but were not collected in cash by the end of the year. In short, the business made $250,000 in credit sales that it has not yet collected. This amount counts toward profit but won't turn into cash inflow until the customers pay for their purchases next year.

Cash outflow for products

The reason cash outflow for products is $300,000 more than cost of goods sold expense for the year is that the business increased its inventory of products (goods) being held for sale. The inventory asset account holds the cost of products purchased or manufactured until the goods are sold, at which time the business decreases the asset account and records the cost of the items sold. The $300,000 inventory increase was paid for during the year, but the cost of these goods will not be charged to expense until next year when the products are sold.

Cash outflow for operations

Cash outflow for operations is $150,000 less than the amount of operating expenses for the year because the business increased its payables for these costs $150,000 during the year. Many operating costs are not paid for immediately. The expenses are recorded when the obligation to pay becomes fixed on the business (when the business incurs the liability to pay the expense). The expenses are not paid until four to six weeks later. For example, a business records advertising expense as soon as the ads are run in the local newspaper, even though the newspaper will not be paid until weeks later.

The obligations for these expenses are recorded in liability accounts. During the year, the balances in these liability accounts increased $150,000. The business will not pay these liabilities until next year.

Depreciation expense

Depreciation expense is a prime example of accrual-basis accounting — of recording an expense in the period benefited rather than when cash is paid out. The assets being depreciated were bought and paid for sometime in the past. These assets last many years. Thus, the cost of a long-lived asset is recorded as an investment. No expense is recorded until the business starts using the asset in its operations. The costs of these long-term or *fixed* assets are allocated over the years the assets are used. The business doesn't make a second cash payment when recording depreciation expense. Depreciation is not a cash outlay in the period the expense is recorded.

Depreciation accounting methods get rather involved, and this chapter isn't the place to go into a lengthy discussion on depreciation accounting. The main point is that a fraction of the cost of a long-lived operating asset — such as a delivery truck, a building, or a computer — is recorded as a decrease in the asset account and the amount is charged to depreciation expense. The business doesn't write a check for depreciation; no cash is involved in recording deprecation expense. Depreciation is a real expense because the long-term operating assets wear out and lose their economic usefulness. Eventually these assets are traded in, sold, or sent to the junkyard.

From the cash-flow point of view, depreciation is a zero outlay expense. In recording depreciation, the recorded cost value of the asset is decreased and the amount is charged to depreciation expense. Depreciation expense is deducted from revenue like other expenses to determine profit. But from the cash-flow point of view, there is nothing to deduct. So in Figure 1-2, the cash outflow for depreciation is zero.

Don't simply add back deprecation expense to bottom-line profit and call this amount cash flow. This practice may appear to be a convenient shortcut to finding cash flow, but it isn't. In this example, cash flow would be $800,000 because $600,000 net income + $200,000 depreciation expense = $800,000. In fact, cash flow from profit for the year is only $400,000 because of the other factors that determine cash flow (refer to Figure 1-2). You should consider all the factors that impact cash flow from profit.

Interest expense

The cash outlay for interest in the example in Figure 1-2 is exactly equal to the interest expense for the year. No difference between the two amounts means that the business paid the exact interest that was owed on its debt during the year. Interest is one of the few expenses for which cash payments often are equal to (or very nearly equal to) the amount of expense that is recorded in the year. On the other hand, if the business had not paid all its interest that had accumulated during the period, it would record the unpaid amount in a liability account in order to pick up the full amount of interest expense for the year and to recognize its obligation to pay the additional unpaid amount of interest.

Depreciation expense versus losses from nonrecurring write-downs of assets

Depreciation expense is based on a predetermined, systematic method. When a depreciable asset is bought or constructed, its cost is recorded in an asset account. The accountant estimates its future useful life to the business and chooses a method to allocate the cost to each year of expected use. Depreciation is not a cash outlay in the year in which depreciation expense is recorded. The cash outlay occurred in its entirety when the asset was acquired.

In contrast, a business may have to record an unexpected write-down in the recorded value of an asset. The write-down was not predetermined and is not factored according to any systematic plan. For example, a business may suffer irreparable damage to its building from an earthquake. Assuming that insurance doesn't cover this risk, the business records an entry to reduce the recorded value of the asset to zero and records a loss of equal amount. The loss is reported as an extraordinary item in the income statement. The loss reduces the profit of the business, of course, but it doesn't involve cash outlay. Like depreciation, recording the loss does not decrease the cash balance of the business.

Identifying and Reporting Basic Types of Cash Activities

Until a generation ago, explicit cash-flow information was not included in the external financial reports of businesses. Sophisticated financial statement users could do cash-flow analysis, but it was a burdensome and time-consuming process. Under pressure from financial analysts and others, the rule-making body of the accounting profession decided that henceforth a *statement of cash flows* should be included in external financial reports to supplement the income statement and balance sheet.

Cash-flow information is useful to users of financial reports, who are primarily business managers, investors, and creditors. Both public and private companies are required to include a statement of cash flows in their external financial reports. By law, publicly owned corporations must make their financial reports available to the public at large. Private companies, on the other hand, generally limit circulation of their financial reports to their investors and lenders. They treat their financial reports as confidential. Internally, businesses can report information however they want, but in general, internal accounting reports look a lot like the external financial statements of the business.

For external financial reporting, accountants divide cash flows into three groupings or types, which we discuss in the following sections. In fact, these three classes constitute the three parts of the statement of cash flows, as we explain further in Chapter 4.

Cash flow from investing activities

One group of cash flows contains the investing and "disinvesting" activities of the business during the year. As you would think, *investing* refers to the expenditure of cash for investments in different assets. Most years (except in severe downturns), businesses make new investments to replace and expand *long-term operating assets,* such as buildings, building improvements, land, machinery, manufacturing equipment, vehicles, and information-processing equipment. These cash outlays are referred to as *capital expenditures.* The term *capital* is used to stress the long-term commitment of these investments in assets that will be used in the operations of the business.

Companies also invest in intangible assets, such as patents and trademarks. A business may buy all the ownership shares or a controlling interest of another business and pay for a goodwill asset. A business may invest in marketable securities, either short term or long term. Or a business may invest in ownership instruments that are not readily marketable. We suppose a business could even invest in pork-belly futures contracts if it wanted to (and meat processors do). The law allows a business to invest in almost anything (that's legal).

During the year, the business may sell or otherwise dispose of some of its investments. The cash inflows from these disinvestments are included in the investment category. So the category includes both cash outflows and cash inflows. The buying and selling of marketable securities can be a major source of income for a business. In contrast, long-term tangible and intangible assets that are used in the operations of a business are not sold off very often, except when the assets reach the end of their useful lives or when the business has to downsize its scale of operations.

Cash flow from financing activities

The term *financing* refers to securing capital and returning capital to its sources. We discuss capital sources in Chapters 10 and 11. Basically, the two sources of capital to a business are equity and debt. *Equity* refers to ownership capital invested in a business. For example, a business corporation issues shares of capital stock to individuals willing to put their money in the business. The business may or may not be able to pay its shareowners for the use of their money, depending on whether it makes a profit and whether it generates enough cash flow from profit to make a cash distribution. Equity can be simple (just one class of ownership shares) or incredibility complex, and it depends on the legal organization of the business. (We discuss equity sources in Chapter 10.)

Debt refers to money borrowed from banks and other business lenders, and even credit cards used by the business. Businesses pay interest for the use of the debt capital. The debt is either paid back or renewed on the maturity date of the loan. The business signs a note payable or a similar legal instrument to the lender. (Chapter 11 explores debt in more detail.)

Interest paid on debt capital is reported as an expense in the income statement, so the bottom-line profit is after interest expense is deducted. In contrast, a cash distribution from profit that is paid to shareowners for the use of their equity capital is not treated as an expense. (Cash distributions from profit by corporations are called *dividends*.) Bottom-line net income is calculated before making distributions to shareowners. The amount of cash distributions from profit to shareowners is included in the financing category of cash flows.

Cash flow from operating (profit-making) activities

The third class of cash flow is the profit-making activities of the business. Investing and financing activities constitute only a small fraction of the total activities of a business during the year. Over 95 percent, maybe 99 percent, of the action in a business has to do with *operating activities:* making sales, acquiring products for sale, hiring employees, and all the other things that are done to make a profit.

The cash flows of the operating activities during the year can be reported the same way as the summary of cash flows shown in Figure 1-2. In fact, the authoritative rule-making body of the accounting profession prefers this method of reporting the cash flows. However, an alternative method of reporting operating cash flows is permitted, which has become the most popular method. Instead of directly reporting the cash flows of revenue and expenses, the alternative method starts with bottom-line net income and then lists several adjustments to net income in order to work down to the amount of cash flow from profit. (Chapter 4 goes into more detail.) Both ways of presenting cash flow from operating activities report the same cash flow figure; the difference is how you get there.

Putting cash-flow activities together

The change in cash during the period is the sum of the changes in the three types of cash flow:

> ✔ Cash from investing activities
>
> ✔ Cash from financing activities
>
> ✔ Cash from operating activities

For most businesses, investing activities result in a decrease in cash, which is caused by expenditures for new machinery, equipment, buildings, and other long-term operating assets. The old assets disposed of during the year don't produce much cash inflow. Financing activities can have either positive or negative cash impact, depending on whether the business raised new debt and equity capital during the period or reduced its debt and equity capital. Also, it depends on the size of cash dividends paid to shareowners from profit for the year. Ominously, all three activities can be negative, which would probably indicate serious cash-flow problems.

We end this section with a pop quiz to wrap things up: Suppose the net cash result from the investing activities of a business during the year is a $500,000 decrease in cash. Purely by coincidence, the net cash result from its financing activities is $500,000 increase in cash. Therefore, the net effect on cash of these two classes of cash-flow activities is exactly zero for the year (not too likely, of course). Yet the company's cash balance increased $200,000 during the year. Is this cash increase due solely to its cash flow from operating activities for the year?

The answer is yes. In addition to cash flow from investing and financing activities, the only other source of cash to a business is from its operating (profit-making) activities. Therefore, the $200,000 cash increase must be the cash flow from profit. The other two sources and uses of cash are a wash; the increase in one offsets the decrease in the other.

What was the company's profit for the year? Well, you can't tell from the cash-flow figure. Profit could be much more, about the same, or less than the $200,000 cash-flow amount. In fact, the business may have recorded a loss for the year (and still have $200,000 positive cash flow from operating activities). You have to look at the company's income statement for the year, which is based on accrual-basis accounting, to find the profit or loss for the period.

Chapter 2

Why Accrual Accounting Is Essential

*W*hen most people hear the term *accounting,* they first think of *recordkeeping* (or *bookkeeping,* which is the same thing). Accounting certainly does involve a lot of recordkeeping. Why go to the time, trouble, and expense? Recordkeeping isn't done just for the sake of keeping a detailed financial history of a business. Businesses spend money on recordkeeping because it serves the *information needs* of the business.

Every business's information needs include a multitude of financial and other types of information for operating day to day, making decisions, controlling the activities of the business, complying with various tax laws, and preparing financial statements that are essential for securing capital and reporting to the sources of its capital.

Compared with personal accounting, business accounting is much more comprehensive and standardized. Few people, for example, prepare formal financial statements, keep track of the daily balance of their credit cards, or formally list their assets. Most people simply keep a checkbook and save other receipts and documents that are needed for preparing their income tax returns. A business, in contrast, needs a comprehensive accounting system. More specifically, it needs an *accrual accounting system,* which records revenue and expenses at the time of transactions whether or not cash flow takes place at the same time. Recordkeeping through accrual accounting helps businesses keep track of profit or loss more effectively.

This chapter begins with an overview of the main functions of accounting, starting with the recordkeeping that captures and stores this vital information. We then move on to explain accrual accounting and why your business needs it (as opposed to cash-based accounting), and we close by taking a look at common accounting terms that you need to be familiar with to keep successful records of your business's transactions.

Finding Out the Four Functions of Accounting

Accountants do a lot of multitasking. They carry out the four functions described in this section — bookkeeping, management accounting, complying with tax laws, and reporting financial info — all of which have to be done well and under time constraints. Delays cause serious problems. Quite literally, a business can't continue to operate very long without these accounting functions because its managers typically would be in the dark about which bills were due for payment, the amounts of wages and salaries to pay its employees, and whether a bank loan was due.

Accountants should design a business's accounting system to fit the specific needs of the business. Frankly, in our experience, small businesses tend to be too lackadaisical in designing their accounting systems. A company's accounting system should report all detailed expenses that are needed for making decisions and keeping control over operations.

Accountants at small businesses may decide to record revenue and expenses through simple *cash-basis* accounting, which, as the term implies, means recording only cash inflows and cash outflows. Even so, the business has to be careful to distinguish its various cash inflows and outflows. For example, the business must distinguish between cash from sales versus cash from borrowing money.

Cash-basis accounting simplifies recordkeeping, but it puts serious limits on the range of information that is reported to the company's managers. And when a business uses cash-basis accounting, its financial reports may not fully report its financial condition and may not report its correct profit or loss. Cash-basis accounting is adequate only when a business conducts nearly all of its revenue and expense transactions in cash, has very few noncash assets, and has very few liabilities. *Accrual basis accounting,* which we introduce in Chapter 1 and discuss in more detail in the later section, "Examining the Nature of Accrual Accounting," offers many advantages even to very small businesses.

Keeping records (Bookkeeping)

A business can't operate day in and day out without a good recordkeeping system. Accountants capture and store information through the recordkeeping system of the business so that they can complete many critical tasks in the daily operating activities that demand up-to-date, accurate, complete, and readily available information. The lack of information can bring things to a halt or at least cause a costly delay.

Folks may not think much about these back-office activities of accountants, but they would sure notice if those activities didn't get done. On payday, a business had better not tell its employees, "Sorry, but the accounting department is running a little late this month; you'll get your checks later." And when a customer insists on up-to-date information about how much he owes to the business, the accounting department can't very well say, "Oh, don't worry, just wait a week or so and we'll get the information to you then."

An army marches on its stomach, and a business marches on information. To give you an idea of the various types of information that the recordkeeping system of a business has to gather and make accessible, consider the following tasks the accounting department of a business is responsible for:

- **Payroll:** The total wages and salaries earned by all employees every pay period, which are called *gross wages* or *gross earnings,* have to be calculated. Based on detailed private information in personnel files and earnings-to-date information, the correct amounts of individual income tax, Social Security tax, and several other deductions from gross wages have to be determined, and all this information is reported to each employee every pay period. The total amounts of withheld income tax and Social Security taxes, plus the employment taxes imposed on the employer, have to be paid to federal and state government agencies on time. Retirement, vacation, sick pay, and other benefits earned by the employees have to be updated every pay period.

- **Cash collections:** All cash received from sales and other sources has to be carefully identified and recorded, not only in the cash account but also in the appropriate account for the source of the cash received. The accounting department makes sure that the cash is deposited in the correct checking accounts of the business and that an adequate amount of coin and currency is kept on hand for making change for customers. Accountants balance the checkbook of the business and control who has access to incoming cash receipts. (In larger organizations, the *treasurer* is responsible for some of these functions.)

- **Cash payments (disbursements):** In addition to payroll checks, a business writes many other checks during the course of a year — to pay for a wide variety of purchases, to pay property taxes, to pay on loans, and to distribute some of its profit to the owners of the business, for example. The accounting department prepares all these checks for the signatures of the business officers who are authorized to sign checks. The accounting department keeps all the supporting business documents and files to know when the checks should be paid, makes sure that the amount to be paid is correct, and forwards the checks for signing.

✔ **Procurement and inventory:** Accounting departments usually are responsible for keeping track of all purchase orders that have been placed for *inventory* (products to be sold by the business) and all other assets and services that the business buys, from postage stamps to forklifts. A typical business makes many purchases during the course of a year, many of them on credit, which means that the items bought are received immediately but paid for later. So this area of responsibility includes keeping files on all liabilities that arise from purchases on credit so that cash payments can be processed on time. The accounting department also keeps detailed records on all products held for sale by the business. When products are sold, the accountant determines the cost of the goods sold, which is recorded as an expense.

✔ **Property accounting:** A typical business owns many different substantial long-term assets collectively called *property, plant, and equipment,* including office furniture and equipment, retail display cabinets, computers, machinery and tools, vehicles, buildings, and land. Except for relatively small-cost items, such as screwdrivers and staplers, the accounting department maintains detailed records of the business's property, both for controlling the use of the assets and for determining personal property and real estate taxes.

To keep its wheels turning, a business needs a *complete* and *reliable* recordkeeping system that can organize and protect many different things: formal accounting records (mainly accounts and journals), supporting schedules, files, purchase orders, cancelled checks, correspondence, legal documents, and so on. Businesses have the choice of many customizable computer-based recordkeeping programs, and they may hire certified public accountants or certified public bookkeepers to advise in selecting, designing, and updating a system.

Giving company management the information it needs

Another main function of accounting in a business is to provide its managers with the financial information they need. This function is generally called *management accounting* or *managerial accounting*. Business managers need financial information for developing strategy and policies, planning and constructing budgets for the coming period (assuming they do budgeting), and controlling the activities and performance of the business.

The laundry list of financial information that managers need is long and diverse, but the info falls into the following three basic categories:

- ✔ **Profit or loss performance:** Did the business earn a profit for the period or suffer a loss, and why?

- ✔ **Financial condition:** Is the business in a healthy and viable situation, or is it in trouble and facing disruption?

- ✔ **Cash flows:** What amount of cash flow was realized from profit, and what were other sources and uses of cash?

Not every manager in a business gets all three types of financial information. For example, the vice-president of production may get only cost reports for manufacturing. In designing internal financial reports for managers, accountants follow the organizational structure of the business to provide only information for the sphere of activity that the manager is responsible for. In a small business, the owner/manager may be responsible for all aspects of the business, which means she gets all types of financial information.

The three separate audiences that receive accounting reports are the *managers* of the business, *tax authorities* (principally the IRS), and the *investors* and *lenders* of the business. Internal financial reporting to managers, which tends to be more detailed as well as sensitive and confidential, is not bound to the financial statements and formats that are required in income tax returns and issued to the investors and lenders. Nevertheless, in actual practice, accountants generally use the same templates for all three audiences even though they divulge different information.

A business has to decide on the accounting methods that it will use to measure profit period by period and to record its assets, liabilities, and owners' equity. The IRS, which you know cannot be ignored, requires that most businesses that produce or sell merchandise or that have annual sales revenue of $5 million or more use accrual, not cash-basis, accounting. (See the sidebar "IRS and accounting methods.") The cash basis of profit accounting may be adequate for certain smaller businesses, such as a barber shop, computer repair business, law firm, or real estate agency. However, for the reasons we explain in "Examining the Nature of Accrual Accounting," accrual accounting is necessary for businesses of any size and complexity.

Managers need to understand the cash-flow consequences of earning a profit. Unfortunately, accrual accounting can obscure the cash flows of revenue and expenses. This chapter isn't the place for jumping into a detailed examination of accounting reports to managers, but we do advise accountants to pay particular attention to reporting the cash flows of revenue and expense to managers in a manner they can understand. (We discuss this topic more in Chapter 4.)

IRS and accounting methods

Some people view the IRS as a blood-sucking ogre intent on harassing businesses. Actually the IRS has quite reasonable rules regarding business accounting methods for determining annual taxable income. Businesses with annual sales revenue of more than $5 million are required to use accrual-basis accounting methods for revenue and expenses. One main exception: Personal service corporations (in which 95 percent or more of revenue is from rendering personal services) may elect to use cash accounting. Also, farmers can use cash-basis accounting. Smaller businesses (less than $5 million annual sales revenue) can elect to use cash accounting — except for those businesses that produce, purchase, and sell merchandise. They must use accrual accounting for inventory, cost of goods sold, and sales revenue; they can use the cash basis for other income and expenses. So they may use a hybrid accounting system that includes elements of both cash and accrual accounting.

The IRS stresses *consistency* of accounting methods year to year, which is a fundamental pillar of accounting theory and standards. Changes in accounting methods from one year to the next are anathema — to be avoided unless absolutely necessary. The IRS does allow changes in accounting methods, but a business has to jump through hoops to do it. See IRS Publication 538 *Accounting Periods and Methods* for more details. To download this publication, go to www.irs.gov and navigate to forms and publications for businesses.

Complying with tax laws

A saying in business is that if something *can* be taxed, it *is* taxed. Even in a relatively small business with just a few employees, one accountant can keep busy just filing all the tax returns and forms that are required. The federal income tax is the 500-pound gorilla, but many other types of taxes are imposed on businesses.

Businesses that are employers pay taxes on their payroll, including Social Security, Medicare, and unemployment taxes. Some states levy a tax on inventory (goods being manufactured and products being held for sale). Most states and local jurisdictions tax the real estate owned by the business. International trading has its own types of taxes, such as import and export duties. Then they have to deal with sales taxes, for which a business acts as a collection agent for the taxing authority. Furthermore, a business has license fees to pay, and some companies have to pay franchise fees.

The accounting department has the responsibility of keeping up with changes in all the tax laws the business is subject to and filing all the forms and reports required under the various tax laws and regulations. Failure to pay the proper amounts of taxes or filing tax returns after their deadlines can result in heavy fines and penalties. Furthermore, the accounting department is expected to keep managers informed about major changes in tax laws and to advise them on tax strategies.

The sticky business of tax evasion

You probably are aware that some businesses engage in illegal practices to evade taxes, and we don't mean just the federal income tax. One well-known tactic for evading income tax is *sales skimming*, in which the manager or owner doesn't record all sales revenue in the accounts of the business. Instead, some amount of the cash flow from sales goes directly into the pocket of the owner/manager without being recorded on the books. Another example of illegal evasion of taxes concerns payroll taxes. A business may deliberately misclassify certain persons as being independent contractors when in fact they are employees, in order to avoid paying Social Security and Medicare employer taxes on their salaries.

Most accountants work with the implicit assumption that the business is not engaging in illegal tax-evasion tactics. They assume that the business managers want all revenue to be recorded and want all expenses to be legitimate costs of operating the business, which may not be entirely true, of course. The accountant should be careful regarding whether he could be held liable as a coconspirator in a tax-evasion scheme. And business investors and lenders should understand that when a business engages in tax evasion, its financial reports as well as tax returns are fraudulent and misleading. Furthermore, all involved parties should be aware of the risk that tax authorities may find out the business, which can lead to major penalties and collapse.

Reporting financial information

Financial reporting refers to the preparation and delivery of reports about a business's financial activities. Financial reports that accountants prepare for equity shareowners and debt holders consist of certain basic financial statements that are accompanied with footnotes and other disclosures. We explore financial statements in depth in Chapter 3 but give you an overview in the following sections.

Accountants also have to decide how to present financial information to managers, how often to present it (daily, monthly, quarterly), and who gets what information. (See the previous section "Giving company management the information it needs" to review the types of financial information that may need to be reported.) Different managers get different information based on their sphere of responsibility. The top-level president and chief executive get global information for the business as a whole. Likewise, the board of directors should receive high-level comprehensive financial reports for the business as a whole.

Financial statements

Following are the three primary financial statements, prepared by accountants, that are included in the financial report of a business:

- ✔ **Income statement:** This statement (commonly called the *P&L* within a business) reports total sales revenue and other income for the period and expenses and losses for the period. The total amount of expenses and losses is deducted from total revenue to get the bottom line, which is the net profit or loss for the period.

- ✔ **Balance sheet:** This statement lists the assets of the business at their recorded values, the business's liabilities, and the amounts invested from its equity shareowners and accumulated retained earnings (profit earned but not distributed to equity shareowners).

- ✔ **Statement of cash flows:** The cash flow from operating activities (that is, profit-making activities) and other sources and uses of cash during the period are reported in this financial statement.

Don't forget that the three financial statements are supplemented with footnotes and other disclosures in the financial report. Not all relevant information can be contained within the boundaries of the three financial statements. Each financial statement is somewhat of a skeleton of information, not a full explanation.

External reporting

Accountants have to provide financial reports to people or organizations outside the business that have provided the business with *capital,* money to acquire the various assets for operating and achieving the business's objectives. Capital comes from two basic sources: debt and equity.

Debt is money loaned to the business by banks, other types of financial institutions, and individuals. Debt has a finite life; it has to be paid at maturity (or rolled over and renewed for an additional period). Interest has to be paid on debt, so it's accounted for as an expense of the business.

Equity refers to the ownership capital of a business, which is divided into shares (for example, capital stock shares of a corporation). Equity capital is committed for the long run; the business has no obligation to redeem or return equity capital to its shareowners. (Mutual funds are an exception to this rule.) The shareowners take the risk that a business may suffer a loss (which diminishes their equity in the business), may not earn enough profit to justify the amount of capital they have invested in the business, or may not generate enough cash flow from profit to allow the business to distribute some of its profit to the equity shareowners of the business.

The equity shareowners and debt holders of a business demand to be kept informed about the financial performance and condition of the business. Therefore, a business prepares financial reports for its sources of capital.

The equity shareowners and debt holders who receive financial reports from a business are treated as outsiders who are not active members of management. They're entitled to fair and adequate disclosure about the financial performance and condition of the business, but they're not entitled to all the information that the managers of the business know. Most recipients of an annual financial report, for instance, can't get back to the accountant and ask for more information or for a different explanation. However, members of the board of directors, acting in their capacity as representatives of all equity shareowners, as well as major lenders or shareowners, can usually ask the accountant for more explanation about what's in the standard financial report. But in general, financial reports are presented on the newspaper model — only one paper for all readers is released outside the business.

Businesses, contrary to popular belief, do not keep two sets of books. The formats in externally reported financial statements of a business are generally the same frameworks used for internal accounting reports to its managers. Businesses rarely adopt a completely different format and structure for the internal financial statements to their managers. The profit or loss reported in the financial report issued to shareowners is the same number that managers use inside the business. However, managers have a better idea regarding to what extent revenue and expenses have been massaged (manipulated) to boost or dampen the profit number that is reported outside the business.

Examining the Nature of Accrual Accounting

As we mention in Chapter 1, the term *accrual* is not a particularly helpful word for understanding accrual accounting. *Accrual* suggests accumulation, accretion, addition, or growth. These meanings are wide of the mark. *Accrual accounting* refers to the recording of revenue and expenses when these economic events take place, whether or not cash flow takes place at the same time.

A good example of the difference between accrual and cash accounting is when a business makes a sale on credit. The sale takes place today, but the customer doesn't pay the business until, say, 30 days later. The products and/or services are delivered to the customer at the time of sale. Accrual accounting records the sale immediately and also records the cost of goods sold at the same time so that the expense is matched with the sales revenue in the same period. Cash-basis accounting waits to record the sales revenue until the cash is collected from the customer. That type of accounting gives good numbers for cash flows but poor numbers for profit (or loss).

Uncovering the inadequacy of cash-basis accounting

In cash accounting, sales revenue is recorded when cash is received, and expenses are recorded when paid. Profit or loss equals the net increase or decrease in cash from making sales and paying expenses. Simple? Yes. Correct? No. For one thing, profit shown by using the cash method depends on when you write checks for expenses. You can improve profit by simply not writing checks to pay for certain expenses until next year.

Accrual accounting provides a more realistic picture of revenue and expenses. You get a better matching of expenses against revenue to determine profit or loss. Accrual accounting captures the economic reality of what's going on. Cash-basis accounting looks only at what's going on in the cash account. The business of making profit involves much more than just cash flows — although cash flows are very important, of course.

Cash accounting is tolerated as "good enough" for small businesses that don't sell on credit and don't sell products from inventory. The cash-basis numbers for sales revenue and expenses are reasonably close to the accrual-basis numbers for these businesses, assuming that the business doesn't deliberately time cash payments for expenses in order to manipulate profit for the period. The IRS allows, but does not require, certain small businesses to use cash accounting (see the sidebar "IRS and accounting methods").

Though the accrual-accounting method is best for measuring profit for the period, it comes with some additional baggage, which we examine in the next section.

Recognizing accrual accounting in financial reports

Financial report readers are entitled to assume that accrual accounting is being used to prepare the financial statements in the report unless stated otherwise. In other words, accrual accounting is taken for granted unless the financial report makes clear that some other basis of accounting is being used. (We explain financial statements in Chapter 3.)

You can't tell whether accrual accounting is being used by a business from its income statement. Both the cash- and accrual-accounting methods report sales revenue and expenses in the income statement. (Different amounts are reported between the two accounting methods). If you want to know for sure whether accrual accounting is being used, look in the balance sheet of the business. This statement of financial condition, which we discuss in more detail in the following section, lists the assets and liabilities of the business (and other information as well).

Cash-basis accounting — in which only cash transactions are recorded for sales and expenses — doesn't record several assets and liabilities that are employed in accrual accounting. Accrual accounting uses several noncash asset and liability accounts in recording sales and expenses. These additional elements "complicate" the balance sheet. On the other hand, the additional assets and liabilities improve the informational value of the balance sheet and give a superior measure of profit or loss.

The telltale balance sheet items that reveal the use of accrual accounting in recording revenue and expenses include the following assets and liabilities. Only their names are mentioned here. The next section explains these assets and liabilities in the context of a balance sheet example.

✔ **Assets**:

  • Accounts receivable

  • Inventory

  • Prepaid expenses

  • Property, plant, and equipment

✔ **Liabilities**:

  • Accounts payable

  • Accrued expenses payable

When you see these assets and liabilities in a company's balance sheet, you know that it is using accrual accounting, because they're the devices and means to carry out accrual accounting. The accounts are necessary to record revenue and expenses when the transactions occur, regardless of when cash flows take place.

Even when the financial reports tell you that accrual accounting is being used, they don't reveal how *well* it's being done by the business. A business may be cutting corners regarding how it applies accrual-accounting principles. For instance, a business should, according to accrual-accounting principles, record the accumulation of vacation and sick pay earned by its employees each pay period. However, the business may wait to record this cost until employees are paid when they take sick leave or their vacations. The business is using the cash method for this particular expense.

Many businesses do not strictly observe every principle of accrual accounting. They take practical shortcuts to reduce the amount of entries that have to be recorded. Such deviations from accrual accounting are understandable, and as long as the amounts involved aren't significant, accountants and CPA auditors don't object to these departures from the letter of the law. But a business can go too far and stray off the path of acceptable accrual-accounting standards. One troublesome area, for instance, concerns expenditures on minor renovations and refurbishment of buildings. The amount should be recorded in a property, plant, and equipment asset account and then gradually charged to depreciation expense over the estimated future useful life of the improvement. But a business may simply record the cost immediately to expense instead of going to the trouble of recording it in an asset account and depreciating the cost over many years.

Reporting Assets and Liabilities in the Balance Sheet

The assets and liabilities of a business are reported in a financial statement called the *balance sheet*, which lists the total assets on one side and balances them on the other side with the total liabilities and owners' equity. (It is also called the *statement of financial condition* or *statement of financial position*.) We explain the balance sheet and the other financial statements issued by businesses in Chapter 3. In this section, we focus on the key assets and liabilities that are used in accrual accounting.

Balance sheets follow certain rules regarding the placement of assets and liabilities. On the asset side, cash is listed first, and then accounts receivable, inventory, and so on. Accounts payable and accrued expenses payable are placed before other liabilities. Figure 2-1 shows an example of a balance sheet with cash and the other assets and the liabilities that are used to record revenue and expenses shown "in place" (that is, in their typical positions in a balance sheet).

Balance Sheet at End of Most Recent Year

(Dollar amounts in thousands)

Figure 2-1:
Accrual-accounting assets and liabilities in a balance sheet.

Assets		Liabilities & Owners' Equity	
Cash	$300	Accounts Payable	$200
Accounts Receivable	$550	Accrued Expenses Payable	$240
Inventory	$750		
Prepaid Expenses	$40	Debt	$800
Property, Plant, and Equipment	$800	Owners' Equity	$1,200
Total Assets	$2,440	Total Liabilities & Owners' Equity	$2,440

The assets and first two liabilities in the Figure 2-1 balance sheet are explained briefly as follows:

✔ **Accounts receivable:** When a sale is made on credit, this asset account is increased and sales revenue is increased. Cash accounting involves no accounts receivable asset account because sales on credit are not recorded until cash is received from customers.

✔ **Inventory:** The cost of products manufactured or purchased is entered as an increase in this asset account, and remains in the asset account until the products are sold, at which time the cost of the items sold is removed from the asset and is recorded as cost of goods sold expense. No inventory account is used in cash accounting.

✔ **Prepaid expenses:** A business makes certain expenditures today for operating costs that will benefit several future months. One example is a 12-month fire-insurance policy on a building and its contents. Such paid-in-advance amounts are first entered in this asset account. The asset account is gradually decreased month by month over the beneficial life of the prepayment and the amounts are recorded in an expense account. Cash accounting charges the entire cost of the insurance policy immediately to expense. Cash accounting doesn't involve a prepaid expense asset account.

✔ **Property, plant, and equipment:** This asset group includes buildings and land, land improvements (parking lots and landscaping), machinery, tools, office equipment, computers, and vehicles. These assets are used by a business for many years. The assets are held not for sale but for use in the operations of the business; hence the name *fixed assets.* The cost of these assets (except land) is spread over the estimated useful lives of the assets. Each period a fraction of the cost is taken out of the asset and entered in the *depreciation* expense for the period. In cash accounting the costs of such assets are recorded to expense immediately and, therefore, no such assets are recorded.

✔ **Accounts payable:** This *liability* account is used to record unpaid expenses of the business. When a business gets an invoice for an operating cost — such as a utility bill, a bill from its lawyers for services provided, or from the local TV station for ads that have already run — it records the cost in this liability, and the amount is entered in the appropriate expense account. When a bill is paid, cash is decreased and this liability account is decreased. In cash accounting, no such liabilities are recorded. Expenses are not recorded until actually paid.

✔ **Accrued expenses payable:** Certain operating costs are recorded that will not be paid until a month or more later. An expense account is increased and this liability is increased. One example is the estimated cost of future warranty and guarantee work on products that have already been sold. Another example is the accumulated amount of interest that has been earned by the lender but not yet paid by the business. In cash accounting, this liability isn't recorded; expenses are recorded only when they're actually paid.

In Figure 2-1, the balance sheet is in balance because it includes the company's sources of capital. We explain in the earlier section "External reporting" that business capital comes from two basic sources: interest-bearing debt and owners' equity. We show just one account labeled *debt* for all the company's interest-bearing debt, but in actual balance sheets, short-term debt is separated from long-term debt. Also, we show just one account for owners' equity. As we explain in Chapter 3, owners' equity is actually divided into two (or more) different accounts. (If you want to see a more complete and less simplified balance sheet, flip to Chapter 3.)

Debt and owners' equity accounts aren't involved in recording revenue and expenses. The cash inflow from borrowing money isn't revenue, and the cash outflow for paying down a debt balance isn't an expense. Keep in mind, however, that the interest on debt is recorded as an expense. Likewise, when owners invest money in a business, the cash inflow isn't revenue, and when a business returns equity capital to its owners, the cash outflow isn't an expense. At the end of every year the final amount of profit (or loss) for the year is entered as an increase (or decrease) in the owners' equity account *retained earnings*.

The Figure 2-1 example doesn't have any extraneous assets or liabilities. All the assets and the first two liabilities are directly involved in the profit-making operating activities of the business. These several balance sheet accounts are increased or decreased in recording revenue and expenses. Knowing the balance sheet accounts that are used in recording revenue and expenses is extremely important for understanding cash flow from profit because changes during the period in the noncash assets and liabilities that are used in recording revenue and expenses determine the cash flow from profit (operating activities) for the period.

For example, suppose accounts receivable increases $100,000 during the year. Using accrual accounting, during the year the business records $100,000 sales revenue that it hasn't yet collected in cash. Accounts receivable increases $100,000 because the cash hasn't arrived yet. Sales revenue, which is used to measure profit, is $100,000 higher than the cash inflow from customers during the year. (If you want to find out more about cash-flow analysis of profit, turn to Chapter 4.)

Chapter 3

The Big Three Financial Statements

*O*ne of the main functions of accountants in a business is to prepare its *financial statements.* This chapter takes a look at the three primary financial statements of a business: the balance sheet, the income statement, and the statement of cash flows. Together, these three documents provide a comprehensive summary of the financial condition and performance of the business. The *income statement* reveals whether the business earned a profit or suffered a loss during the period. The *balance sheet* stacks up the company's assets against its liabilities at the end of the period. The *statement of cash flows* explains the difference between bottom-line profit and the cash flow from profit-making operations, and the business's other cash sources and uses during the period.

Which of the three financial statements is most important? If you had time to read only one, which one would give you the best understanding of the business's situation? Accountants would find these questions rather odd. The three financial statements fit together like pieces in a puzzle. Profit performance may look good in the income statement, but the balance sheet may reveal that the business is on the edge of bankruptcy. And if you didn't read the statement of cash flows, you might not notice that the business didn't generate much actual cash during the period. In short, the three financial statements are designed to be read in conjunction with one another. You've heard the expression, "It takes two to tango." With financial statements, tangoing takes all three.

The accountant who prepares the financial statements of a business needs to be knowledgeable and up-to-date on the "rules of the game." The content, format, and reporting of financial statements are governed by generally accepted standards. Most important, financial statements should be based on correct accounting methods. And it should go without saying that financial statements should be fair and honest. As you probably suspect, financial statements can be deliberately false and misleading. Some of the biggest business scandals in recent memory involved fraudulent financial statements (does Enron ring a bell?).

In this chapter we focus first on the balance sheet. It's the "financial anchor" of a business. Revenue and expenses pass through the balance sheet, as do cash flows. The assets, liabilities, and owners' equities reported in a balance sheet are called *real accounts*. The amounts reported in the other two financial statements are total flows for the period, whereas the amounts in the balance sheet are net balances (excess of increases over decreases) at the end of the period. After examining the balance sheet, we next look into the structure of the income statement from the top line to the bottom line and see how revenue and expenses are connected with the balance sheet. Finally, we introduce the statement of cash flows, which is more fully explored in Chapter 4.

Why Financial Statements Are Essential

Are financial statements really necessary? Must a business prepare regular financial statements? Is it a crime not to prepare financial statements? For most businesses, the answer to these questions is yes. (Well, strictly speaking, you may not be breaking the law if you don't prepare financial statements, but you get our meaning.) However, you may be surprised to hear that many small privately owned businesses that use cash-basis accounting don't bother to regularly prepare financial statements. We were surprised to see a 2003 study by the U.S. Federal Reserve System and Small Business Administration that found that the large majority of small business firms don't use financial statements for managing the business.

Being accountants, we believe in the importance and usefulness of financial statements. But preparing financial statements costs some money — the business has to hire a competent accountant and have an adequate accounting system to prepare financial statements, so many small, private businesses don't go to the trouble. To keep track of the profit or loss performance of the business, the owner/manager may simply look at his or her monthly bank statement to track profit — after sorting out nonrevenue sources of cash and non-expense uses of cash. If cash increases, then according to cash-basis accounting the business made a profit. (We explain cash and accrual accounting in Chapter 2.)

However, modest-size and larger businesses need to prepare financial statements on a regular basis. They use accrual accounting to capture all the information needed for preparing financial statements. Financial statements are needed for the following reasons:

- ✔ **Business income tax returns require income statement information (to determine taxable income) and a balance sheet.** The accounting system has to be designed to record and accumulate this financial information (as we explain in Chapter 2).

- ✔ **The managers of a business need the financial information in the statements for making decisions and controlling the financial affairs of the business.** They can't make decisions and identify problems without a broad range of financial information, and financial statements provide that key information in a reasonably compact and summarized format — not all the information they need, but a good part of the information.

- ✔ **Sources of debt capital and major creditors typically want to see the financial statements of a business before they are willing to loan money to the business or to extend other forms of credit to a business.** Money put into a business by lenders and investors is at risk to one degree or another. Lenders want to see the latest financial statements to assess the risk of the business defaulting on the interest and debt repayment requirements of their loans. Investors want the information to assess the ability of the business to stay financially healthy and to earn a return on their capital invested in the business.

- ✔ **Financial statements are the bedrock information for business valuation.** When the owners of a business put it up for sale, or when a company is approached with an offer to buy the business, its financial statements are the main source of information to both sides.

- ✔ **"Outside" shareowners use financial statements to keep informed about their investment in the business.** The larger a business becomes, the more likely it is that one or more of its equity owners (shareowners) are not active members of the management team running the business. Sending them financial statements is the most practical way of communicating with them.

Financial reports are also used for several other secondary purposes in business. For example, financial statements serve as the financial archives of the business and are its historical financial trail. And many companies operate a franchise, and the contract may require that financial statements be provided to the franchisor.

Who gets financial statements and why

The managers of a business are the first people to get the business's financial statements, which they use for decision making and controlling the financial performance and condition of the firm. However, exactly which managers get which financial statements depends on the organizational structure of the company. Generally, the higher up you go in the management hierarchy, the more likely a manager is to get all three financial statements, or at least the balance sheet and income statement. We explain how managers analyze their financial statements in Chapters 5, 6, and 7.

Beyond its managers, who else get the financial statements of a business? The first thing to keep in mind is that the financial statements of a business are *privileged information*. A business doesn't publish its financial statements in the local newspaper or put a copy in the library. You could call a business and ask for a copy of its latest financial report that includes its financial statements, but don't expect the business to comply — unless the business is a *publicly owned* corporation.

Roughly speaking, businesses fall into two groups: privately owned companies and publicly owned corporations. The availability of financial information to the public depends largely on which type of business it is.

- ✔ **Publicly owned companies:** The ownership shares of public companies are traded in markets open to the public, such as the New York Stock Exchange and NASDAQ. Stockholders of a public company, such as IBM, GE, or Apple, are entitled to receive a copy of the company's latest financial report. Public corporations also have to make regular filings with the Securities and Exchange Commission (SEC), which is the federal agency that oversees the federal laws that govern the original issue and subsequent trading in corporate securities (bonds and stocks).

  In addition, public companies are required by law to make their financial reports available to the public at large. Most public companies today put their financial reports online, so you can go to their websites and retrieve their financial reports. Also, mutual funds and other financial institutions are subject to federal laws; their financial reports are available to anyone who wants to see them.

- ✔ **Privately owned companies:** These businesses are a different kettle of fish altogether regarding the circulation of their financial reports. Generally speaking, a private business is one that isn't covered by federal securities law. A private business has to be careful regarding whether or not federal (or state) laws apply to reporting its financial statements.

If not required by specific legal requirements, private businesses generally limit the distribution of their financial statements to their current shareowners and lenders. Usually, though not always, banks and other sources of debt capital ask to see the financial statements of a private business in the loan-application process. The loan may or may not include a provision that the business provides up-to-date financial statements on a regular basis over the life of the loan. In addition, a private company may release particulars about its business to credit-rating agencies and in response to business surveys by state agencies, local business groups, and academics doing research.

Who doesn't get financial statements and why

Think about range and number of individuals and other businesses that a company deals with. By and large, a private business doesn't send its financial statements to any of these people or businesses. A private business certainly doesn't send a copy of its financial statements to its competitors, but it also doesn't release its financial statements to customers or vendors.

In fact, a private business doesn't even provide its financial statements to its own employees, who obviously have a stake in the stability of the company. On the other hand, a private business may have a profit-sharing plan for its employees, in which case it releases some information about its profit performance to its employees. Even in this situation, a private company generally doesn't provide balance sheet or cash-flow information to its employees who are participating in its profit-sharing plan.

Overall, most private businesses keep their financial statements private and away from prying eyes of those who may want to take advantage of some weakness or vulnerability of the business revealed in its financial statements. Private companies take the attitude that people who want to see financial statements are up to no good and that sharing the statements would only harm the business. This attitude may seem a little paranoid, but it's undeniable that many private businesses have weaknesses that would be noticed by someone reading their financial statements.

The restricted availability of the financial reports of private businesses contrasts sharply with the open distribution of financial reports by public businesses. As we explain in the preceding section, public companies make their financial reports available to the public; anyone can get their financial reports. And public companies provide financial reports to their lenders and shareowners, of course. In addition, public companies must file financial reports with the Securities and Exchange Commission (SEC). So the financial problems of these companies are more out in the open. We should add, however, that many public companies resort to inadequate and opaque disclosure in their financial reports to obscure their problems.

Facing Off: The Balance Sheet

The *balance sheet* shows how a company's assets and liabilities stack up at the end of the period, as well as the sources of its owners' equity. Balance sheets are presented either in a horizontal (landscape) layout, with assets on the left and liability and owners' equity on the right, or in a vertical (portrait) layout, with assets on top and liability and owners' equity below. Segregating assets from liabilities and owners' equity indicates a face-off of sorts: Liabilities and owners' equity have claims and rights against the assets. Cash and assets that will be converted into cash in the future are used to satisfy the claims of liabilities and shareowners.

We present a prototype balance sheet with a horizontal layout in Figure 3-1.

Assets	At Close of Year Just Ended	At Close of Preceding Year	Liabilities & Owners' Equity	At Close of Year Just Ended	At Close of Preceding Year
Cash	$2,345,675	$2,098,538	Accounts Payable	$2,537,232	$2,180,682
Accounts Receivable	$3,813,582	$3,467,332	Accrued Expenses Payable	$1,280,214	$1,136,369
Inventories	$5,760,173	$4,661,423	Income Tax Payable	$58,650	$117,300
Prepaid Expenses	$822,899	$770,024	Short-Term Debt	$2,250,000	$1,765,000
Total Current Assets	$12,742,329	$10,997,317	*Total Current Liabilities*	$6,126,096	$5,199,351
			Long-Term Debt	$7,500,000	$5,850,000
Property, Plant, and Equipment	$20,857,500	$18,804,030	*Total Liabilities*	$13,626,096	$11,049,351
Accumulated Depreciation	($6,785,250)	($6,884,100)	Capital Stock (422,823 and 420,208 shares)	$4,587,500	$4,402,500
Cost less Accumulated Depreciation	$14,072,250	$11,919,930	Retained Earnings	$8,600,983	$7,465,396
			Total Owners' Equity	$13,188,483	$11,867,896
Total Assets	$26,814,579	$22,917,247	*Total Liabilities and Owners' Equity*	$26,814,579	$22,917,247

Figure 3-1: A balance sheet example.

Strolling through the balance sheet

If you count the number of assets, liabilities, and owners' equity in the Figure 3-1 balance sheet example, the total comes to 13 accounts. Subtotals and totals are not included in this count. Compared with most actual balance sheets, this number of accounts is a little low; according to our experience, a typical balance sheet reports roughly 15 to 20 accounts. But for the purposes of this example, we keep it simple by not jamming in too many accounts. For instance, we don't include an asset account for investments or for loans to employees. We also omit "other assets," which many balance sheets include to cover who knows what.

The question concerning how many accounts are included in a balance sheet raises a very important issue. How much detail should a balance sheet disclose about the company's assets and liabilities? For example, the accounts receivable asset account can include amounts seriously overdue from customers, which raises the question whether the past-due balances will be collected in full. Should the overdue amounts be reported in a separate asset account?

The property, plant, and equipment asset account includes the cost of the land owned by the business. The cost of land is not depreciated, whereas the costs of the other assets in this balance sheet account are depreciated. Should the cost of land be reported separately in the balance sheet? Usually it isn't.

The accountant faces many disclosure questions in preparing a balance sheet. On the one hand, a financial statement should provide *adequate disclosure*. On the other hand, too much detail can defeat the very purpose of a financial statement. A balance sheet with 40, 50, or more accounts becomes unwieldy and takes too much time to read. The accountant must compromise between reporting too much information versus too little, which can be a tough call. Furthermore, in many situations, the managers and directors of a business intervene and put pressure on the accountant not to disclose certain information that would make the business look vulnerable or reveal losses from bad decisions. So the accountant "buries" the negative information in one of the accounts in the balance sheet without calling attention to it.

One of the calls an accountant has to make is how to treat accumulated depreciation on property, plant, and equipment. In the Figure 3-1 balance sheet example, the accumulated depreciation account balance is deducted from the balance of the property, plant, and equipment asset account. Accumulated depreciation is a *contra* account, meaning its negative balance is subtracted from the positive balance of its companion account. Original historical costs are recorded in the property, plant, and equipment asset account, and the depreciation expense recorded each year is accumulated in the contra account. The *book value* of these long-term operating assets (also called *fixed assets*) is the net amount after deducting accumulated depreciation. In the example, the book value of the company's property, plant, and equipment assets is $14,072,250 at the close of the year just ended. This is the amount included in the $26,814,579 total assets of the business at that date.

Some businesses report only one line for their property, plant, and equipment assets, which is the net amount after deducting the accumulated depreciation on the assets. The original costs of the assets and the accumulated deprecation on the assets are relegated to the footnotes that accompany the financial statements of the business. So rather than the three lines for these long-term assets, shown in Figure 3-1, only the following line is reported:

> Property, Plant, and Equipment, net of Accumulated Depreciation $14,072,250

This alternative illustrates the desire to keep the balance sheet as brief as possible and include only truly relevant information. Is reporting original cost and accumulated depreciation really necessary? That's the $64,000 question. Do readers of financial reports really need to know the original costs and accumulated depreciation of a company's long-term operating assets? Would their assessment of a company's financial condition be any different if only the book value (net of accumulated depreciation) is reported in the main body of the balance sheet?

Accountants don't object to reporting only one line for a company's property, plant, and equipment (book value net of accumulated depreciation). This alternative doesn't violate generally accepted financial reporting standards. But at the same time, most accountants are probably a little uncomfortable with this alternative and prefer that both original cost and accumulated depreciation be included in the balance sheet. In the old days, the prevailing practice was to report both original cost and accumulation depreciation. Old habits die hard. Accountants know that the newer method of reporting just one line for cost minus depreciation is okay, but accountants are generally conservative and prefer to stick to traditional ways in financial reporting.

Accountants do not allow *offsetting,* or netting off a liability against a related asset. It's a definite no-no. For instance, the amount of accounts payable for inventory purchases is never deducted from the cost balance of the inventories asset account with only the net difference reported. Long-term debt may a have a mortgage on the property, plant, and equipment of a business. The debt is never deducted from the balance of the assets.

Putting accounts in their right places

Assets, liabilities, and owners' equity components are grouped into certain classes in a balance sheet. Liabilities are not intermingled with assets, nor are owners' equity accounts. These three basic types of accounts are clustered together in their own neighborhoods.

Assets and liabilities are separated into current and longer-term categories. *Current* basically means one year or less, although the technical rule for this classification doesn't put a strict and definite time limit on what's reported as current. In our balance sheet example, total current assets and liabilities equal $12,742,329 and $6,126,096, respectively. We explain in Chapter 5 that current assets are compared with current liabilities to get an important indicator of the short-term solvency of the business.

The Figure 3-1 balance sheet example includes 13 accounts for assets, liabilities, and owners' equities. In addition, subtotals and totals take up seven lines. The subtotals for current assets and current liabilities are always presented. The total of assets on the one side and the total of liabilities plus owners' equity on the other side are always given. Otherwise, reporting practices vary somewhat. For instance, Figure 3-1 includes a subtotal for all liabilities ($13,626,096). Many balance sheets do not include this line, which is acceptable.

When you see that total assets exactly equals the total of liabilities and owners' equity, you are reassured that the accounting system of the business must be okay — the books are in balance. However, even when the books are in balance, serious accounting errors or even outright accounting fraud can be taking place, resulting in a balance sheet that is seriously misleading.

Most balance sheets are presented in a two- or three-year comparative format so that readers can compare the balances a year and two years ago with the balances at the end of the most recent year. The Figure 3-1 example is a two-year presentation. Notice, however, that the changes in each account are not included in the Figure 3-1 balance sheet example. The changes can be included but are not in most financial reports.

The account balances in a balance sheet can be rounded off to the nearest thousand, or nearest million for very large businesses. So the balance of cash at the close of the year just ended can be reported as $2,346 thousand (rounded). Rounding off account balances is fairly common. It puts less strain on the eyeballs. No one raises any objection to rounding off.

Figure 3-2 is the same example as in Figure 3-1 except that the dollar amounts are rounded to the nearest thousand and changes in the accounts during the year, as well as changes in the subtotals and totals, are included. (Note that this balance sheet is in the vertical format — assets on top and liabilities and owners' equity on bottom.)

A balance sheet can be prepared at any point in time (assuming that the company's accounting system is up-to-date). However, balance sheets take time to assemble and to make available in print form or put online. Generally, a business doesn't prepare a balance sheet any more often that it has to. The standard time for preparing a balance sheet is at the close of business on the last day of the profit period. Profit (or loss) is reported in the income statement (see the later section "Making Profit: The Income Statement"). If, for example, the income statement is for the year ending September 30, 2012, the balance sheet is prepared as of midnight on that date.

Dealing with the limitations of the balance sheet

Financial statements don't include interpretative comments or indicators of what's most important. The premise is that financial statements "speak for themselves." Or, rather, we should say that the financial statements are presented on the premise that readers know how to understand and interpret financial statements. Financial reporting assumes that the readers of these accounting statements are persons who are fairly knowledgeable about business, financial terminology, and accounting methods. Quite a presumption, isn't it?

Dollar amounts in thousands	At Close of Year Just Ended	At Close of Preceding Year	Change During Year
Assets			
Cash	$2,346	$2,099	$247
Accounts Receivable	$3,813	$3,467	$346
Inventories	$5,760	$4,661	$1,099
Prepaid Expenses	$823	$770	$53
Total Current Assets	$12,742	$10,997	$1,745
Property, Plant, and Equipment	$20,858	$18,804	$2,054
Accumulated Depreciation	($6,785)	($6,884)	$99
Cost less Accumulated Depreciation	$14,073	$11,920	$2,153
Total Assets	$26,815	$22,917	$3,898
Liabilities & Owners' Equity			
Accounts Payable	$2,537	$2,181	$356
Accrued Expenses Payable	$1,280	$1,136	$144
Income Tax Payable	$59	$117	($58)
Short-Term Debt	$2,250	$1,765	$485
Total Current Liabilities	$6,126	$5,199	$927
Long-Term Debt	$7,500	$5,850	$1,650
Total Liabilities	$13,626	$11,049	$2,577
Capital Stock (422,823 and 420,208 shares)	$4,588	$4,403	$185
Retained Earnings	$8,601	$7,465	$1,136
Total Owners' Equity	$13,189	$11,868	$1,321
Total Liabilities and Owners' Equity	$26,815	$22,917	$3,898

Figure 3-2:
An alternative balance sheet layout that includes changes during the most recent year, with balances rounded to the nearest thousand.

You should understand that a balance sheet reports *recorded values*. The dollar amounts you see in the asset, liability, and owners' equity accounts are the result of the amounts recorded in these accounts. Some of the balances are the result of recent transactions and some are from transactions that took place years ago. However, the balance sheet doesn't disclose how old the balances in each account are. You, the reader, are expected to understand that some balances are driven mainly by recent activities and other balances include amounts recorded 5, 10, or 20 years ago (or even longer).

The balance sheet does not report up-to-date market values for its assets. (A few exceptions exist, but they don't apply in our example.) For instance, the assets included in property, plant, and equipment are the original costs of these resources, which very well may be considerably lower than current replacement values of the assets.

A balance sheet also does not report what the business would be worth if it were for sale, either as a thriving going concern or as an entity that might be liquidated. In other words, the *net worth* of the business reported in its balance sheet — its assets minus its liabilities — may or may not be a good indicator of what a buyer would be willing to pay for 100 percent ownership of the business. The business may be worth much more than the book value of its owners' equity, or much less. Until the shareowners actually put their shares up for sale, the business's worth is anyone's guess. (For more on business valuation, you can go to our book *Small Business Financial Management Kit For Dummies* [John Wiley & Sons, Inc.].)

Every day that a company is open for business, it engages in transactions and carries on operating activity of all sorts. All these transactions and activities are recorded in the balance sheet accounts of the business. Therefore, the balance sheet is constantly changing. Though the balance sheet is prepared as of the last day of the income statement period, the preparation normally takes a few weeks or longer. Suppose, for instance, that the balance sheet is prepared at the close of business on September 30, 2012, because the income statement is for the year that ends then. The financial report of the business may not be ready until, say, November 15, 2012. (Six weeks' delay is not unusual.) So by the time the balance sheet is ready for distribution, it's already somewhat out of date. Things may have changed for the better or for the worse.

The accountant must decide whether or not the balance sheet at the last day of the income statement period is misleading compared with the more recent up-to-date financial condition of the business. Developments between the official balance sheet date (the last day of the income statement period) and the date of distribution of the balance sheet are called *subsequent events.* If the subsequent events substantially change the financial condition of the business, the changes should be disclosed in the footnotes to the financial statements of the business so that readers are not lulled into false impressions based on the balance sheet at the previous date.

Tracing revenue and expenses in the balance sheet

Chapter 2 explains accrual-basis accounting for measuring profit or loss — that is, for recording revenue and expenses. (Other types of income and gains may be recorded, as well as losses, to determine the final profit or loss for the period.) Understanding which accounts in the balance sheet are the result of recording revenue and expenses is very helpful because these accounts are inextricably linked with making profit. In fact, the accounts connected with recording revenue and expenses are a large part of the balance sheet.

To "size up" assets and liabilities, or to determine whether the balances of assets and liabilities are too high or too low, you compare the balance of the asset or liability with the revenue and/or the appropriate expense reported in the income statement. For example, in the Figure 3-2 balance sheet, the accounts receivable asset at the end of the most recent year is about $3.8 million. Is this amount about right, or is it out of whack? Well, the only way to answer is to compare it with sales revenue for the year. If sales revenue were, say, only $10.0 million for the year, an ending balance of $3.8 million of accounts receivable is way too high and should raise alarm. Why should such a large percent of annual sales revenue still be uncollected at the end of the year?

Cash is like the Grand Central Station of the balance sheet. More or less everything passes through the cash account sooner or later. Not just revenue and expenses, but investing and financing activities also pass through the cash account. One exception is depreciation expense, which consists of writing down the long-term operating assets of the business that are reported in property, plant, and equipment. (A business may record noncash gains and other kinds of noncash expenses, such as amortization of the cost of its intangible assets.)

So which balance sheet accounts in addition to cash do revenue and expenses drive? Quite a few, as it turns out. The following list summarizes the balance sheet accounts that are part and parcel of recording revenue and expenses:

- **Accounts receivable:** Sales made on credit are first recorded in this asset account. The balance in this account is the amount of uncollected sales revenue at the balance sheet date.

- **Inventories:** When products are manufactured or purchased, their costs are recorded in this asset account, and when the products are later sold, the cost is taken out of this asset account and charged to cost of goods sold expense. The balance in this account is the total cost of unsold products at the balance sheet date.

- **Prepaid expenses:** Certain operating costs have to be paid in advance of when the amounts should be recorded as expenses, and the amounts are first recorded in this asset account. Over time, the costs are allocated to the months in which the company benefited from the prepaid expense. The balance in this asset account is the amount of prepaid operating costs that have not yet been charged to expense at the balance sheet date.

- **Property, plant, and equipment (PP&E) and accumulated depreciation:** The costs of long-term operating resources (that are not held for sale but are for use by the business) are recorded in the PP&E asset account. The cost of each item, except land, is allocated over the estimated useful life of the asset. A fraction of the cost is charged to each period as depreciation expense. The amounts of depreciation are not directly deducted from the asset account but rather accumulated in the contra account called *accumulated depreciation*. The book value of the asset (cost minus accumulated depreciation) is the amount of cost that has not yet been written off to depreciation expense at the balance-sheet date. The book value will be charged to depreciation in future periods unless the business disposes of such assets before they reach the end of their estimated useful lives.

✔ **Accounts payable:** When a business makes a purchase on credit, the amount is recorded in this liability account, which is reduced later when the amount is paid. These purchases are for products to be sold, raw materials used in manufacturing, utilities, various services, office supplies, and so on, which are charged to expense. The balance in this account is the cost of things the business has not yet paid for at the balance sheet date.

✔ **Accrued expenses payable:** To recognize the gradual accumulation of certain expenses over time, for which the business does not receive a bill, certain expenses are recorded in the correct period by increasing this liability account. These liabilities are paid at a later time. For example, each period, the cost of employee vacations is recorded in this liability even though they don't take their vacations until later. The balance in this account is the accumulated amount of expenses that have been recorded but have not been paid for at the balance sheet date.

On the balance sheet, if you were to cross out cash and the accounts just listed, you would end up with only the two debt accounts (short-term and long-term) and the two owners' equity accounts (capital stock and retained earnings). These accounts are not involved in recording revenue and expenses. Rather, the accounts have to do with where the business gets its *capital* from, which we turn to next.

Managing capital

One reason for reading a balance sheet is to determine the business's *capital structure,* the mix of sources of capital. We're sure that you've heard the comment that it takes money to make money. It does. Before opening its doors, a business needs to raise enough capital to invest in the assets it needs for its operations. Being undercapitalized is the kiss of death. Many businesses gamble that they can get by with too little capital, but this is a bad bet. They may have a great business plan and model, but without sufficient capital, it's just a pipe dream.

The assets show how the capital is deployed, and the other half of the balance sheet shows where the capital came from. So in the Figure 3-2 example, how much total capital does the business have at its disposal at the end of its most recent year? The answer is the total of liabilities and owners' equity — in other words, the part of the balance sheet below assets.

Identifying sources of capital

The first three liabilities in Figure 3-2 — accounts payable, accrued expenses payable, and income tax payable — in one sense are not sources of capital. They are the *operating liabilities* of the business and arise naturally from carrying on the profit-making operations of the business. The business doesn't borrow money from these sources of credit. These short-term liabilities are non–interest bearing. The business has no explicit or determinable interest cost on these liabilities — although accounts payable and income tax payable typically include late payment penalties that tack on an interest charge beyond the interest-free credit period.

When people speak of raising capital, they aren't talking about operating liabilities. They're talking about borrowing money, having owners invest money in the business, or having the business itself plow back profit (by not distributing cash dividends from profit to shareowners). Therefore, you may often hear discussions about debt versus equity and the advantages and disadvantages of each source of capital. Operating liabilities more or less get lost in the shuffle. Nevertheless, operating liabilities are usually a fairly significant source of the total assets of a business — as they are in the Figure 3-2 business example (14.5 percent of total capital).

Using the same example, the capital structure of the business at the close of its most recent year is summarized in Figure 3-3. Three sources of capital are reported: operating liabilities, interest-bearing debt, and owners' equity. As you can see, debt is separated between short-term (one year or shorter maturity date) and long-term (longer than one year). Details about the maturity dates, interest rates, and significant provisions of the debt instruments are disclosed in the footnotes to the financial statements.

Total owners' equity (refer to Figure 3-1 or 3-2) is separated into two quite distinct types. The first account, *capital stock,* keeps track of the amounts invested in the business for which the owners receive capital stock shares (assuming that the business is a corporation). The second owners' equity source is *retained earnings* and equals the cumulative profit earned by the business over the years that has been retained instead of having been distributed as cash dividends to shareowners.

From the information in Figure 3-3, you can say that this business is moderately leveraged. *Leverage* refers to the use of debt capital on top of equity capital. The basic strategy is to magnify your equity capital by adding debt so that the business has more total capital to work with. If the business earns a higher percent of operating profit than the interest rate on its debt, it boosts the earnings on its equity capital. *Leverage* may refer to the total of both operating liabilities and interest-bearing debt. In other words, the term can refer just to debt or to all liabilities. Another term you may hear is the *debt load* of the business. Generally this term refers just to the interest-bearing debt of a business, which in the example is $9,750 thousand (both short-term and long-term).

Accounts Payable	$2,537		
Accrued Expenses Payable	$1,280		
Income Tax Payable	$59		
Total Operating Liabilities		$3,876	14.5%
Short-Term Debt	$2,250		
Long-Term Debt	$7,500		
Total Interest Bearing Liabilities		$9,750	36.4%
Capital Stock	$4,588		
Retained Earnings	$8,601		
Total Owners' Equity		$13,189	49.2%
Total Liabilities and Owners' Equity		$26,815	100.0%

Figure 3-3:
Sources of
capital.

We extend the explanation of various sources of capital in Chapters 10 and 11, and we go into more detail about reading the balance sheet in Chapter 5.

Figuring out what to do with capital when you have it

The whole point of raising capital is for the business to make good use of the money by investing in the assets needed for operating and making profit. Capital has a cost; interest is paid on debt capital, and the business needs to earn an adequate bottom-line profit (after interest) to justify the use of its owners' equity capital. Capital supplied by the operating liabilities of a business has no explicit cost. In the example in Figure 3-3, 14.5 percent of the total capital of the business is from its operating liabilities. This amount can be viewed as "free capital" on which the business does not pay a cost for using the money.

From Figure 3-3, you can also see that the business has raised about $27 million total capital (rounded) as of the close of its most recent year. The asset side of a balance sheet reveals how the company has invested its capital. The listed assets reveal how much money the business has invested in each kind of asset. Referring back to Figure 3-2, you can see, for example, that the business has invested $5,760 thousand in products being held for sale to customers (labeled *inventories* in the balance sheet). The business has invested $2,346 thousand in cash, which may seem odd to you. How do you invest in cash? Well, by not spending the money.

A business needs to maintain an adequate cash balance for day-to-day operations. Letting the cash balance hover around zero isn't practical. If a business did, it might have to wait for cash to come in from collections of accounts receivable or from cash sales to be able to pay its bills and cut payroll checks for its employees. The cash balance is a buffer against unexpected delays in cash inflows. Having cash on hand allows the business to take advantage of opportunities that demand quick cash payment.

The investment in fixed assets (property, plant, and equipment) needs a comment or two here. The balance sheet (refer to Figure 3-2) shows that the total original cost of these long-term operating resources is $20,858 thousand at the close of the year just ended. This amount was invested in the assets at the times of acquisition. The accumulated depreciation recorded on the assets is $6,785 thousand. This amount is the portion of original cost that has been recovered by the business. A business sets sales prices high enough to cover its depreciation expense (as well as the cost of goods sold, other operating expenses, interest, and income tax.). In this way, a business gradually "sells off" some of its fixed assets to its customers over the years. Each year part of the original cost is converted back into cash. So at the close of the year just ended, the business has only $14,073 thousand still invested in its fixed assets.

Making Profit: The Income Statement

A business earns profit by making sales and controlling expenses. Thus, the financial statement that reports profit performance starts with sales revenue and then deducts the expenses of making the sales and operating the business. Figure 3-4 shows the latest annual income statement of the business whose balance sheet is explained in the previous sections in this chapter.

Note: If the balance sheet reports assets, liabilities, and owners' equity rounded to the nearest thousand, then the income statement follows suit.

Two basic financial benchmarks that tie together the income statement and the balance sheet can be used to judge a company's financial performance. First, annual sales revenue is compared against total assets to test whether the business is making good use of its assets (because assets are used to make sales). The business in our example reports about $27 million total assets (refer to Figure 3-2). The company reports about $40 million annual sales (see Figure 3-4.) Second, annual net income is compared against owners' equity, which gives a measure of return on investment earned for the shareowners. The business in our example reports about $13 million total owners' equity at the end of the most recent year (shown in Figure 3-2), and it earned about $1.6 million bottom-line net income for the year (shown in Figure 3-4).

Sales Revenue	$39,661,250
Cost of Goods Sold Expense	$24,960,750
Gross Margin	$14,700,500
Selling, General, and Administrative Expenses	$11,466,135
Earnings before Interest and Income Tax	$3,234,365
Interest Expense	$795,000
Earnings before Income Tax	$2,439,365
Income Tax Expense	$853,778
Net Income	$1,585,587
Earnings Per Share	$3.75

Figure 3-4: The income statement for the year just ended.

Publicly owned corporations disclose earnings per share (EPS) in their income statements just below bottom-line net income. The market value per share is the most closely watched figure of a publicly owned company, and market value depends mainly on the earnings (net income, or profit) performance of the business. Therefore, generally accepted financial reporting standards require that EPS be reported by public companies.

In contrast, privately owned business corporations don't have to report earnings per share. The ownership shares of a private business aren't actively traded in a public market, so the market value per share is not readily determinable. The EPS of a private company can't be compared to any reference point, so financial reporting standards don't require that private companies report their EPS.

Truth be told, the income statement presented in Figure 3-4 contains minimal disclosure. Take out the subtotals — gross margin, earnings before interest and income tax, earnings before income tax, and bottom-line net income — and you're left with only five lines of "hard information": sales revenue and four expenses. The managers of the business need much more information about expenses; for that matter, they need more detailed information about sales revenue as well.

The disclosure in the income statement example in Figure 3-4 is for *external* financial reporting to the lenders and shareowners of the business. The extent of disclosure of expenses in Figure 3-4 meets minimum financial reporting standards. Many public businesses disclose research and development expenses separate from selling, general, and administrative expenses. In contrast, external income statements don't disclose management compensation or marketing expenses as separate expenses.

Moving from the revenue top line to the profit bottom line

The income statement can be read from the top down or from the bottom up. You can start with the sales revenue line and then work your way down to the bottom line. Or you can start with the bottom line and work your way up to the top line. One professional football player who is a very successful businessman was quoted as saying that the first thing he looks for in his company's income statement is whether the bottom line has parentheses around it, meaning that the bottom line is a loss (negative number) rather than a profit (positive number). Suffering a loss is said to be "in the red," and earning a profit is said to be "in the black."

The income statement example shown in Figure 3-4 includes four profit lines: gross margin, earnings before interest and income tax (also called *operating earnings*), earnings before income tax, and net income. As shown in Figure 3-4, businesses that sell products should disclose gross profit (also called *gross margin*), which equals sales revenue less the cost of goods (products) sold. Many public businesses don't report earnings before interest and income tax or earnings before income tax. Because private companies limit the distribution of their financial reports, we don't know whether they generally report those profit lines.

Earnings before interest and income tax (abbreviated EBIT) is compared with sales revenue to see whether the company has been able to maintain its *operating margin* (as a percent of sales revenue). Financial analysts consider this performance measure very important, so they would be upset if the business didn't provide the EBIT in its income statement.

Deciding which is more important: Revenue or expenses

Revenue and expenses act like the two blades on scissors. The final cut of profit is the result of both revenue and expenses. Quite clearly, both factors determine profit for the period. So in one sense, asking which is more important is nonsensical. Yet at the same time, experienced business managers argue that making sales and generating sales revenue is more important than controlling expenses — keeping in mind that both are important, of course.

Why is revenue more important? Without revenue, there can be no profit. In other words, the starting point for making profit is making sales. Of course, a business may let its expenses get out of control relative to its sales revenue. But for a given level of sales revenue, a rock-bottom level of expenses has to be incurred to make the sales and operate the business. A business can only cut costs to a certain point before hurting sales in the process.

On the other hand, sales have no theoretical limit; with smart marketing a business can keep increasing its sales (assuming it can raise enough capital). The upside potential of sales is limitless, but the downside limit of reducing expenses is definitely limited. For these reasons, financial analysts are generally more concerned with the direction of sales year to year. Sales downturns are more likely to kill a business than costs that are out of control.

Summarizing Cash Flows: The Statement of Cash Flows

In 1987, the accounting rule-making body in the United States decided that a statement of cash flows should be included in financial reports to supplement the income statement and to help explain changes in the financial condition as reported in the balance sheet. The concept of this statement is rather straightforward: It summarizes the sources and uses of cash during the year.

From the very first page of this book, we emphasize the importance of cash flows. Our purpose here is to simply introduce the statement of cash flows. Figure 3-5 illustrates this financial statement for the same business example for which we present a balance sheet (Figures 3-1 and 3-2) and income statement (Figure 3-3).

Note: If the balance sheet and income statement figures are rounded to the nearest thousand, then the statement of cash flows follows suit.

The purpose of the statement of cash flows is to give the reader a road map of the reasons for the change in cash during the year. You can see in the example in Figure 3-5 that cash increased $247,137 during the year. But remember, the increase in cash is not a measure of the profit performance of the business. You must look in the income statement for profit performance.

Frankly, the first section of the statement of cash flows is a bearcat to get a grip on. For this reason, we spend a good part of Chapter 4 on understanding and interpreting *cash flow from operating activities,* or the cash result from earning profit. Chapter 2 explains that the cash impact from the profit-making activities of a business is invariably different from the bottom line of the business. Chapter 4 offers a more in-depth explanation of the reasons for the difference between cash flow and profit. In the following sections of this chapter, we introduce the three categories of cash flows that are reported in the statement of cash flows.

Cash Flow from Operating Activities	
Net Income	$1,585,587
Changes in Operating Assets and Liabilities:	
Accounts Receivable	($346,250)
Inventories	($1,098,750)
Prepaid Expenses	($52,875)
Depreciation Expense	$768,450
Accounts Payable	$356,550
Accrued Expenses Payable	$143,845
Income Tax Payable	($58,650)
Cash Flow from Operating Activities	$1,297,907
Cash Flow from Investing Activities	
Investment in Property, Plant, and Equipment	($3,186,250)
Proceeds from Disposals of Property, Plant, and Equipment	$265,480
Cash Used in Investing Activities	($2,920,770)
Cash Flow from Financing Activities	
Net Increase in Short-Term Debt	$485,000
Increase in Long-Term Debt	$1,650,000
Issuance of Capital Stock Shares	$185,000
Cash Dividends to Stockholders	($450,000)
Cash from Financing Activities	$1,870,000
Cash Increase during Year	$247,137
Cash Balance at Beginning of Year	$2,098,538
Cash Balance at End of Year	$2,345,675

Figure 3-5: A statement of cash flows for the year just ended.

Showing cash flow from operating (profit-seeking) activities

The first section in the statement of cash flows explains why cash flow from profit is a different amount than the bottom-line profit (net income) for the period. As you can see in Figure 3-5, this section of the statement of cash flows is called *cash flow from operating activities*. A better title might be cash flow from *profit-making* activities. In any case, this section begins with the net income reported in the income statement, which in the example is $1,585,587 for the year. Next, several adjustments are made to the net income figure in order to arrive at the cash flow from operating activities amount, which in the example is $1,297,907.

You may question the difference between net income and cash flow from net income (or cash flow from operating activities). Cash flow is $287,680 lower than net income for the year: $1,585,587 net income – $1,297,907 cash flow from operating activities = $287,680 difference. This gap is due to a combination of factors, in particular depreciation expense and changes in the assets and liabilities used in recording revenue and expenses. The net result of all these factors is a reduction in cash flow from net income for the year. Chapter 4 carefully explains each of the cash-flow adjustments to net income.

Listing other sources and uses of cash

The remainder of this financial statement divides cash flows between investing activities and financing activities (refer to Figure 3-5). _Investing_ refers to making capital expenditures for expanding, updating, and replacing the long-term operating assets of the business, which are reported as property, plant, and equipment in the balance sheet. A business may also make other types of investments, for example in intangible assets, marketable securities, and capital stock shares in other businesses. (The example in Figure 3-5 doesn't include any of these other types of investments.)

The investing activities section of the statement includes any cash inflows from disposals of the assets classified in the investment activities section. In the example, the business realized $265,480 cash proceeds from disposing of some of its fixed assets.

In the example, the business spent $2,920,770 cash (net of the cash inflow from disposals) on capital expenditures, or about $3 million. Where did it get this $3 million? Cash flow from profit (operating activities) was only about $1.3 million, and its cash balance increased during the year. Therefore, the business must have raised additional cash from its sources of capital.

Sure enough, the third section of the statement reports that the business raised $1,870,000 cash during the year through _financing activities_ — in this case, by increasing its short-term and long-term debt and by issuing additional stock shares to its owners. This cash increase figure is net of the $450,000 cash dividends paid to its stockholders during the year. Cash dividends are placed in the financing section of the statement of cash flows. (More on this in Chapter 4.)

Chapter 4

Getting a Grip on the Statement of Cash Flows

....

In This Chapter

▶ Defining the different kinds of cash flows

▶ Determining what the statement reveals about changes in financial condition

▶ Checking out different cash-flow situations

▶ Realizing the faults of the statement of cash flows

....

*T*he statement of cash flows is the youngest of the three primary financial statements reported by businesses. In 1987, the high priests that mandate financial reporting standards decided that this statement should be included alongside the balance sheet and income statement in financial reports of businesses.

Despite being one of the "big three" financial statements, the statement of cash flows doesn't draw the attention from financial analysts, creditors, and investors that the balance sheet and income statement do. The top line (sales revenue) and the bottom line (net income, or profit) in the income statement get the most focus, and the balance sheet also gets a fair amount of consideration, especially if the business is on the ropes and faces a serious risk of bankruptcy.

However, the statement of cash flows is the dominant financial statement when a business isn't generating enough cash flow or is hemorrhaging cash from operations, and has gotten itself in a precarious situation regarding its ability to pay its debt obligations on time. In these stressful situations, the statement of cash flows takes center stage.

Even for financially healthy and prosperous companies, the statement has several important uses, so don't limit your attention to the statement to dire situations. At the same time, be cautioned that reading this financial statement presents certain challenges. In this chapter, we explain the statement's important uses and advise you on how to read and understand it.

Distinguishing Cash Flows

Figure 4-1 presents a basic example for the statement of cash flows, presented according to generally accepted financial reporting standards of course. (If you read Chapter 3, note that this example is different.) The statement of cash flows doesn't stop with the change in cash during the year, a $25,000 decrease in the example. The statement also includes the beginning balance and the ending balance (as you see in Figure 4-1).

Cash Flow from Operating Activities
(Dollar amounts in thousands)

Net Income	$350	
Cash-Flow Adjustments to Net Income:		
Accounts Receivable Increase	($70)	
Inventories Decrease	$60	
Prepaid Expenses Increase	($5)	
Depreciation Expense	$85	
Accounts Payable Decrease	($20)	
Accrued Expenses Payable Increase	$15	
Income Tax Payable Increase	$5	
Cash Flow from Operating Activities		$420

Cash Flow from Investing Activities

Expenditures for Property, Plant, and Equipment		($400)

Cash Flow from Financing Activities

Net Decrease in Short-Term Debt	($50)	
Increase in Long-Term Debt	$50	
Issuance of Capital Stock Shares	$25	
Cash Dividends to Stockholders	($70)	
Cash Flow from Financing Activities		($45)
Cash Decrease during Year		($25)
Cash Balance at Beginning of Year		$460
Cash Balance at End of Year		$435

Figure 4-1:
Example of a statement of cash flows.

In this financial statement, cash flows are classified into three categories:

✔ **Cash flow from operating activities:** The first section in the statement of cash flows lists the adjustments to net income for determining the net cash increase or decrease from the profit-making operating activities of the business during the period. In the example in Figure 4-1, net income is $350,000 for the year, but this amount isn't the cash flow for the year. Cash flow for the year is $420,000. In other words, the total cash inflow from revenue during the year was $420,000 more than the total cash outflow for expenses during the year. This first section leaves the trail you follow to see why cash flow was higher than net income for the year.

✔ **Cash flow from investing activities:** The second section in the statement of cash flows lists outlays called *capital expenditures.* They include cash expenditures to replace, upgrade, and expand the long-term operating assets of the business, including its buildings, land, machinery, equipment, tools, and so on. Also, a business may make other investments in marketable and nonmarketable securities, intellectual property (patents and secret processes, for example), and in other businesses. A business may make an "investment" by loaning money to one or more of its key executives. This section of the statement includes proceeds from the sale or disposals of investment assets. In the example in Figure 4-1, the business made capital expenditures of $400,000 during the year. It had no sales or other disposals of investments.

✔ **Cash flow from financing activities:** The third section in the statement of cash flows reports dealings between the business and its sources of capital, which are interest-bearing debt and owners' equity. It does not include changes during the year in its non-interest-bearing, short-term operating liabilities: accounts payable, accrued expenses payable, and income tax payable. Changes in these three operating liabilities are included in the first section, cash flow from operating activities. The third section focuses on changes during the year in the short-term and long-term debt of the business, whether the business raised additional capital from its owners or returned capital to them, and cash dividends paid to its shareowners.

Chapters 1 and 2 explain the differences between accrual-basis accounting for revenue and expenses versus the cash flows of revenue and expenses. The following section explains in detail how to get from the accrual-basis profit number for the period (net income) to the increase or decrease in cash resulting from the profit-making activities for the period. The profit-making operating activities change the balances in those assets and liabilities that are used to record revenue and expenses. These changes are the stepping-stones from net income to cash flow from operating activities.

Adjusting your way to cash flow from operating activities

Think of the first section in the statement of cash flows as the route from one side of the river (the accrual-accounting shore) to the other side (the cash-basis shore). Net income, the bottom line of the income statement and the first line in the statement of cash flows, is the first steppingstone and the connecting link between the two documents. Be warned: The trip is across choppy waters. It's like crossing the Mississippi, not jumping over a puddle. The other two sections of the financial statement are more intuitive and straightforward (which is why we devote less discussion to them in the next section).

Assuming that you have a basic understanding for why revenue and expense cash flows are different from their accrual-basis amounts, you could simply skip down to the line for cash flow from operating activities ($420,000 in the example in Figure 4-1). However, you might miss an important piece of information about the business. For example, suppose that during the year there was a huge increase in its inventory of products held for sale. This increase caused a corresponding decrease in cash flow. Also, the inventory buildup could force the business to sell products below normal prices.

Referring back to Figure 4-1, net income is $350,000 for the year just ended. This amount isn't the same as cash increase (or decrease) from earning profit for the year. To get from net income to the amount of cash flow, you have to make several adjustments to net income. These adjustments to net income, explained in the following sections, are usually presented in the same order that the assets and liabilities connected with revenue and expenses are listed in the balance sheet. So the first adjustment is the change during the year in accounts receivable.

Accounts receivable increase

In the example in Figure 4-1, accounts receivable causes a $70,000 *negative* adjustment to net income. This asset account, which is used to record sales on credit, increased $70,000 during the year. (To find out more about asset accounts and effect on cash flow, you may want to refer to the sidebar "Understanding adjustments to net income.") The increase means that $70,000 less cash was collected during the year than the amount recorded in sales revenue.

Cash inflow from credit sales was $70,000 less than the sales revenue amount used to determine profit for the year. An easy way to think about this is to assume that the business started the year with zero accounts receivable and has $70,000 accounts receivable at the end of the year. The ending balance is the amount of uncollected receivables from customers. The business won't collect this amount until early next year. For the year being reported, the cash had not been collected.

Understanding adjustments to net income

Many (probably most) readers of financial statements find that the most difficult part of the statement of cash flows to understand is the first section — cash flow from operating activities. This section starts with net income and then lists several adjustments to net income. In addition to cash, several other asset accounts as well as several liability accounts are used in recording revenue and expenses In accrual accounting.

Changes in these asset and liability accounts during the year help or hurt cash flow, causing cash flow from profit (operating activities) to be higher or lower than the amount of profit. The rules are fairly straightforward:

✔ An increase in an asset decreases cash flow.

✔ A decrease in an asset increases cash flow.

✔ An increase in a liability increases cash flow.

✔ A decrease in a liability decreases cash flow.

In summary, asset changes work in reverse direction on cash flow, and liability changes work in the same direction.

Inventories decrease

In the example in Figure 4-1, the change in inventories results in the $60,000 *positive* adjustment to net income. The balance in this asset account (the cost of products awaiting future sale) decreased $60,000 during the year, which means that the business didn't replace all the products it sold during the year. It allowed its stockpile of products held in inventory to drop. The implication is that the business started the year with too much inventory and reduced the size of its inventory during the year.

In this situation, the business is said to have *liquidated* part of the amount invested in its inventories asset. In other words, it sold some products without replacing them, reducing cash outflow. Suppose, for instance, that the business sold 100,000 units of product during the year but replaced only 95,000 of units. Therefore, the business avoided cash outlay for the 5,000 units it did not replace. In short, the business spent $60,000 less cash on purchasing products than the amount of cost of goods sold expense recorded in the period. Therefore, the $60,000 inventories decrease is added to net income, as you see in Figure 4-1.

Prepaid expenses increase

Usually the change in the prepaid expenses asset account during the year is relatively small compared with changes in accounts receivable and inventories. In the example, the prepaid expenses asset account increased $5,000 during the year. This increase had to be paid for, of course. Basically, the business spent $5,000 more for prepaid costs than was charged to expense during the year.

For instance, suppose the balance in this asset was $70,000 at the start of the year. This amount would have been charged to various operating expenses during the year. The business would end the year with $75,000 in the asset, which means it would have paid out $5,000 more than the amount charged to expenses. Therefore, the increase in the asset is shown as a negative adjustment to net income (as you can see in Figure 4-1).

Accumulated depreciation increase

Like almost all companies, the business in the example in Figure 4-1 recorded depreciation expense to the year. Depreciation accounting in actual practice is somewhat controversial. The influence of the federal income tax law has caused deviations from what accountants should theoretically record as depreciation expense period by period over the actual useful lives of fixed assets. Speaking broadly, the useful lives over which assets are depreciated are too short, and, for no good reason, depreciation is front-loaded. The federal income tax law gives businesses rapid depreciation options as incentives to invest in long-term operating assets. Be that as it may, the concern here is with the cash-flow aspects of depreciation.

In Figure 4-1, the business recorded $85,000 depreciation expense for the year. This amount is one of the expenses deducted from sales revenue to determine net income for the year. In recording depreciation, a business increases the contra account *accumulated depreciation* instead of reducing the asset account property, plant, and equipment. The balance in the accumulated depreciation account is deducted from the balance in the property, plant, and equipment asset account, and the difference, which is called the *book value* of the asset, is the value reported in the balance sheet.

The recording of depreciation does not require cash outlay. For this reason, it's sometimes called only a *book entry*. The business paid cash when it originally purchased or constructed its fixed assets (property, plant, and equipment). It does not have to pay a second time when using its fixed assets. But depreciation is real and factual, and fixed assets wear out over time or otherwise lose their usefulness to the business. Except the cost of land, which is not depreciated, all fixed assets are on the march to the junkyard. Because depreciation is not a cash outlay expense, the amount of depreciation for the year is a positive adjustment to net income.

Accounts payable decrease

A business makes many purchases on credit (unless it has a lousy credit rating and no vendors will extend it credit). Also, a business receives many bills (invoices) from a variety of sources — for utility costs, wireless and landline telephone and Internet services, property taxes, renewal of insurance policies, and so on. These short-term liabilities generally have to be paid in a month, give or take a little. Until paid, the amounts sit in the liability called *accounts payable*.

Although not entirely correct in a technical sense, the practical way to think about accounts payable is that when recording an increase in this liability account, an expense account is also increased. When payments are made on this liability, cash decreases and the liability decreases. If the business starts and ends the year with the same balance of accounts payable, the cash outflow equals the amount of expenses recorded during the period. But usually the ending balance of accounts payable is higher or lower than the beginning balance, so net income needs a cash-flow adjustment.

In the example in Figure 4-1, the accounts payable balance decreased $20,000. In other words, the business paid down its accounts payable during the year. Cash outflow was $20,000 more than the amount of expenses that are deducted from sales revenue to determine net income for the year. Therefore, the $20,000 pay down on accounts payable is a negative cash-flow adjustment to net income.

Accrued expenses payable increase, and income tax payable increase

Changes in accrued expenses payable and income tax payable have the same impact on cash flow as the change in accounts payable. Both these operating liabilities increased during the year, whereas accounts payable decreased. Therefore, as you should expect, the cash-flow adjustment to net income is opposite to that caused by the decrease in accounts payable. The changes during the year in these liabilities are *positive* adjustments to net income (refer to Figure 4-1 for an example). Cash flow is higher because these two operating liabilities increased during the period.

When an operating liability increases during the period, the amount of cash outlay associated with the liability is less than the amount charged to expense in the period. The full amount of the expense is deducted from sales revenue to determine profit (net income). The $15,000 increase in the accrued expenses payable liability means that this amount of expenses for the year was recorded by an increase in the liability, not by cash outlay. Likewise for the increase in income tax payable: The company's actual cash outlay for income tax expense during the year was $5,000 less than the amount recorded to the expense for the year.

The final cash-flow tally from operating activities

In Figure 4-1, the cash flow from operating activities, after making several adjustments, is $420,000 for the year, which is considerably higher than the $350,000 net income for the year. In a particular situation, cash flow can be about equal to net income, or it can be much higher or lower than profit for the period. The difference depends on changes in the assets and liabilities used to record revenue and expenses. We examine different cash-flow scenarios in the later section "Comparing Cash-Flow Scenarios."

Cogitating on cash flow from investing activities

If you made it through the last section, you can breathe easier now. You made it over the hump — the cash-flow adjustments to net income. The remaining two sections of the statement of cash flows are relatively straightforward, and you can navigate though the next part of the statement, cash flow from investing activities, without much guidance. But in this section we deal with a few potholes on the road through this type of cash flows. (If you want to review the difference between *investing* cash flows and the other two types, refer to "Distinguishing Cash Flows.")

In one sense, every asset is an investment. In the broad sense of the term, a business "invests" in accounts receivable by making sales on credit that generate the receivables. Under this inclusive definition, a business "invests" in inventories and prepaid expenses.

Keep in mind, however, that the changes in accounts receivable, inventories, and prepaid expenses are not included in the investing activities section of the statement of cash flows. Instead, the changes are treated as adjustments to net income to determine cash flow from operating activities. Changes in other assets are reported in the *cash flow from investing activities* section of the statement of cash flows. In the example in Figure 4-1, the business has only one other asset — *property, plant, and equipment.* In other situations, a business may have investments in marketable securities or intangible assets.

In the example, the business didn't make any disposals of investments during the period. It had no cash inflow from this source. On the other hand, it spent $400,000 in *capital expenditures* during the period to replace, upgrade, and expand its building, machines, tools, and equipment. By the way, the $400,000 outlay during the period does *not* include repair and maintenance costs on the company's fixed assets. These routine upkeep costs are recorded to expense in the period. This particular expense is not disclosed in the external income statement of a business, but it must be reported in its federal income tax return.

Considering cash flow from financing activities

The last part of the statement of cash flows deals with financing activities. A business relies on certain short-term non-interest-bearing liabilities to *finance,* or provide part of the total capital it needs. Typically, the total of a company's accounts payable, accrual expenses payable, and income tax payable may be 10 or 20 percent or more of its total assets. In other words, these three liabilities provide a small but significant fraction of the total capital of a business. Changes in these three operating liabilities are not reported as financing activities in the statement of cash flows. Instead, these changes are treated as adjustments to net income in order to determine cash flow from operating activities. Refer to Figure 4-1 to see an example.

Changes in debt borrowings, in other liabilities, and in the company's owners' equity are reported in the *cash flow from financing activities* section of the statement of cash flows. In the example, the business has short-term and long-term debt and reports two owners' equity sources. In some situations, a business may record unusual types of long-term deferred liabilities that arise from recording certain expenses or losses. Changes in these special types of liabilities during the year are reported in the cash flow from operating activities section, even though the placement of these long-term liability accounts is close to long-term debt liabilities in the balance sheet.

Reporting cash flows from financing activities may appear to be rather straightforward. But appearances can sometimes be deceiving. The purpose of this section in the statement of cash flows is to summarize changes during the period in the debt and equity capital of the business, but in many situations, disclosure problems are lurking under the surface.

Detailing debt changes

One issue concerns the turnover of short-term debt that came due during the year. Often a business doesn't actually pay off its debt. Instead it *rolls over* (renews) the debt. The interest rate and other terms of the loan may change. Should only the net increase or decrease of short-term and long-term debt be reported? Or should the statement also disclose the gross turnover, which includes the totals for renewal of old loans as well as new loan activity? Different companies follow different reporting practices.

Because businesses want to keep the statement to a page in length, they don't have all that much room in the statement of cash flows to go into a lot of detail. To clarify, a business should include relevant details in the footnotes of its financial statements. In the example in Figure 4-1, the business decreased its short-term debt a net $50,000 and increased its long-term debt $50,000. The two changes may be independent of one another, or maybe not. Perhaps the business persuaded its lender (say a bank) to stretch out the term of its short-term notes payable to make them long term. The particulars aren't apparent.

Explaining equity changes

A business keeps two distinct types of accounts for owners' equity. One is for capital activity between the business and its owners, which refers to the putting in and taking out of capital by its shareowners. For example, a business may issue additional ownership shares or redeem some of its shares during the year. In the example in Figure 4-1, the business issued new shares for $25,000 and did not redeem any of its capital stock during the year. As you see in Figure 4-1, the cash inflow from issuing capital stock (or other ownership shares) is reported in the cash flow from financing activities section in the statement of cash flows.

Business owners tend to be sensitive to increases in the number of shares because they dilute ownership, reducing power per owner and potentially decreasing the cash dividend per share. For that reason, a business should comment on the reasons for issuing additional ownership shares, probably in the footnotes to its financial statements.

The other basic type of owner's equity account is typically called *retained earnings.* Net income for the period increases the balance of this account (or, a loss for the period decreases the balance). (Net income is also the leadoff figure in the cash flow from operating activities section of the statement of cash flows.) The $350,000 net income for the year (refer to Figure 4-1) increased the balance in the account.

Cash dividends paid to stockowners are also reported in the cash flow from financing activities section. Businesses have to decide whether to retain all the cash flow from operating activities (which may be done to help fund the growth of the business or to shore up its cash position) or to pay a cash dividend from profit to its shareowners. In the example in Figure 4-1, the business decided to distribute $70,000 in dividends to its shareowners, which equals 20 percent of its net income.

> $70,000 cash dividends ÷ $350,000 net income = 20%

The business retained 80 percent, or $280,000 of its net income for the year. Therefore, its retained earnings increased $280,000 during the year.

There is no agreed-upon benchmark regarding the percent of net income that "should" be distributed as cash dividends from net income. One factor is the cash flow from operating activities. Obviously a business must have enough cash flow to pay cash dividends. Other demands on the cash flow are also a factor. For example, a business may need every cent of its cash flow for desperately needed upgrades and expansion of its fixed assets. Every business is a relatively unique case. Indeed, a business may be in entirely different cash circumstances year to year.

Some businesses have abundant cash flow but don't pay cash dividends; instead they hoard cash. For many years, Microsoft didn't pay a cash dividend — until it did. The absence of cash dividends in the financing activities section of the statement of cash flows reveals that the business did not pay cash dividends. However obvious that may seem, readers may not note the omission.

For clarity, businesses can explain their cash dividend policy in the footnotes or elsewhere in their financial reports. But in fact, such disclosure is not required by generally accepted financial reporting standards. Public companies have to be careful in what their press releases and chief executives say about their cash dividend plans. Market prices of their stock shares depend on many factors, but anticipated cash dividends is one of the most important. A public company does not want to be accused of misleading investors about its future dividend plans, which can change abruptly because of changing business conditions. Private companies can be more relaxed about making comments concerning their cash dividend plans.

Getting to Know the Dual Personality of the Statement of Cash Flows

The name itself — *the statement of cash flows* — would lead you to think that its purpose is limited to reporting cash flows and explaining the increase or decrease in cash during the period. The statement does serve this objective. However, reporting cash flows is not the whole and only purpose of the statement. Cash is not the end of the story told by this financial statement — not at all. In some respects, cash flows aren't even the most important information being reported in the statement, despite the title and organization of information in the statement of cash flows.

The statement has a dual nature and twofold purpose: to summarize cash flows and to summarize changes in the financial condition of the business during the period. The changes in the financial condition of a business are very important and should not be overlooked. Cash flow may be satisfactory, but it doesn't guarantee that changes in the financial condition of a business are satisfactory. Make the effort to read the statement of cash flows twice, as it were — first focusing on cash flows, and then focusing on changes assets, liabilities, and owners' equity.

Spotting changes in financial condition

Cash is king, as the saying goes. But the managers of a business should pay close attention to its overall financial condition. Cash is just one piece in the financial-condition chess game of a business, and putting on blinders and watching only cash can lead to catastrophic results. A business's managers should keep a careful eye on all assets as well as the liabilities and owners' equity. Cash flow may be the most pressing problem facing a business, but after it gets its cash flow under control, it still has to keep its financial condition healthy, under control, and out of harm's way.

After evaluating the statement of cash flows in terms of, well, cash flows, concentrate on the changes in the assets, liabilities, and owners' equity of the business during the period. Ask whether there are any "outsize" changes during the year. In other words, did any relatively large changes signal a major shift in the policies or predicament of the business?

Suppose the business in the example had increased its long-term debt by $750,000 during the year. (In the example shown in Figure 4-1, the business increased its long-term debt by only $50,000.) The obvious questions are: Why did the business take on so much additional debt, and what did it do or will it do with this money? You should look for an explanation in the footnotes or in other communications from management that explain such a large step-up in the company's long-term debt. The business may have a very good reason for it. Then again, taking on so much additional debt may be too risky and ill advised.

In the Figure 4-1 business example, the changes in assets, liabilities, and owners' equity appear more or less in a normal range. The biggest change is the $400,000 additions to property, plant, and equipment. These capital expenditures are typically large amounts. Ideally, the financial report should include commentary by management on the reasons for the relatively large outlay for capital expenditures.

To interpret the changes in assets, liabilities, and owners' equity that are reported in the statement of cash flows, you need to compare the amounts of the changes with the balances in the company's assets, liabilities, and owners' equity, which are reported in its balance sheet. As a matter of fact, the statement of cash flows provides a bridge from the balance sheet at the start of the period to the balance sheet at the end of the period.

Building the year-end balance sheet

The statement of cash flows is presented as a stand-alone statement, as are the balance sheet and income statement. Because each financial statement is presented on a separate page, you may lose sight of the fact that the three financial statements are tightly interwoven. For example, the balance in the accounts receivable asset is connected with sales revenue amount in the income statement, and the statement of cash flows provides the connecting links between the beginning and the ending balance sheets.

Figure 4-2 shows the beginning balance sheet of the business in the left column. The changes in assets, liabilities, and owners' equity that are reported in the statement of cash flows are in the middle column, and these changes lead over to the ending balances in the right column. Note that two changes affect the ending balance of the owners' equity account *retained earnings:* Net income is an increase in this account, and cash dividends are a decrease.

Dollar amounts in thousands	At Start of Year	Changes During Year – See Statement of Cash Flows	At End of Year
Assets			
Cash	$460	($25)	$435
Accounts Receivable	$345	$70	$415
Inventories	$675	($60)	$615
Prepaid Expenses	$70	$5	$75
Total Current Assets	$1,550		$1,540
Property, Plant, and Equipment	$965	$400	$1,365
Accumulated Depreciation	($365)	($85)	($450)
Cost less Accumulated Depreciation	$600		$915
Total Assets	$2,150		$2,455
Liabilities & Owners' Equity			
Accounts Payable	$185	($20)	$165
Accrued Expenses Payable	$265	$15	$280
Income Tax Payable	$85	$5	$90
Short-Term Debt	$250	($50)	$200
Total Current Liabilities	$785		$735
Long-Term Debt	$350	$50	$400
Total Liabilities	$1,135		$1,135
Capital Stock	$600	$25	$625
Retained Earnings	$415	$280 *	$695
Total Owners' Equity	$1,015		$1,320
Total Liabilities and Owners' Equity	$2,150		$2,455

Figure 4-2: Using the statement of cash flows to get from beginning to ending balance sheets.

* [$350 net income – $70 dividends = $280 net increase]

The changes in assets, liabilities, and owners' equity taken all together can be thought of as the collection of decisions made by managers during the year. These changes are the outcomes of their actions (or perhaps not taking actions when they should have). Change is constant. A business is always doing things that change its financial condition. For instance, the business in

Figure 4-2 allowed its accounts receivable to increase $70,000 during the year. In contrast, it reduced its inventory level $60,000. Hopefully, these changes were the results of carefully thought-out decisions to improve profit performance and to keep the financial condition of the business in good order.

You'll never see a situation in which all assets, liabilities, and owners' equity accounts of a business remain unchanged or nearly so during the year. You'll be confronted with many changes in the balance sheet accounts. To evaluate the year overall, the trick is to look at the changes in their entirety and ask whether the business is better or worse off (or perhaps simply about the same) because of the changes.

Businesses do not include a supplementary explanation like Figure 4-2 in their financial reports. We show Figure 4-2 as a teaching tool to illustrate the tie-ins between the changes during the period in assets, liabilities, and owners' equity and the amounts reported in the statement of cash flows. Including a summary like Figure 4-2 in the financial report of a business wouldn't be objectionable. However, financial reports don't explicitly integrate or connect the three primary financial statements to make the connections between the statements more obvious. Each financial statement is reported as a tub standing on its own feet.

Comparing Cash-Flow Scenarios

One of the scariest comments business managers can hear from their accountant or CPA is "You have a cash-flow problem." It's like the famous line from *Apollo 13,* "Houston, we have a problem." Of course, business managers should plan and closely monitor cash flow so that they don't have to go into a panic mode to deal with it. But cash-flow problems have a habit of sneaking up on a business. If a business is earning profit, many business managers simply assume that cash flow is satisfactory. Earning a profit means making money, doesn't it? We hope you know better by now. Even if profit is good, cash flow can be bad.

Savvy business managers demand quarterly or monthly accounting reports on cash flows. They keep a close watch on the variables that drive cash flow from profit, which are the changes in the assets and liabilities used in recording revenue and expenses. If accounts receivable, for example, takes a big jump, the experienced manager knows that this increase hurts cash flow during the period. The manager understands that a part of the sales revenue used in calculating profit has not been actually received as cash inflow by the end of the period. If inventories creep up, the perceptive manager knows that cash was spent to build up the inventory, which reduces cash flow during the period.

If your bank pulls the plug

If your business has an existing loan come due and all of a sudden the bank refuses to roll it over, you're facing a serious cash-flow problem. The bank, in addition to refusing to renew the loan, may even demand immediate payment of all loans. Of course, this situation would put the business into a real bind, and not just because of the lost capital from the bank. After word got around that the bank had stopped lending money to your business, you'd find convincing another source of debt capital to loan you money that much harder. The business probably would find it difficult, if not impossible, to raise equity capital on short notice to replace its debt capital. Scrambling for more equity capital is a worst-case scenario. Your business may find a source, but the price it would be asked to pay for the new equity capital would probably be steep.

If your bank senses that you're not doing a good job managing your cash flow, the loan officer will probably become very nervous. Try to avoid any blunders, such as making a late interest payment, because a single incident may cause the bank to reach its tipping point and refuse to renew your loan. It's extremely important to keep your debt sources convinced that you know what you're doing in managing cash flow.

A cash-flow problem can arise out of the blue (as discussed in the sidebar "If your bank pulls the plug"). As we address in Chapter 11, securing and managing debt capital, which are necessary for good cash flow, can be tricky. When a business is said to have a cash-flow problem, most often the meaning is that the business isn't generating enough positive cash flow from profit (operating activities) or that its cash flow is negative. We explain the calculation of cash flow from operating activities in the earlier section "Adjusting your way to cash flow from operating activities." But if your calculations turn up an ugly truth about your situation, you'll need to know what to do to fix it. This section explores different cash-flow scenarios, good and bad.

Starting with cash flow in a steady state

Suppose that over the last few years, a business has been in a relatively steady state. Its sales revenue and profit have been relatively constant year to year. Its managers keep accounts receivable, inventories, and prepaid expenses under control, which means that the balances in these assets are consistent with sales revenue and operating costs. The managers also control accounts payable, accrued expenses payable, and income tax payable. The balances in these liabilities are in line with its total expenses and profit for the year. In this steady-state scenario, what's the story with cash flow?

In this situation, the cash-flow adjustments to net income are close to zero — not significant — except one, depreciation. Other than depreciation, the cash-flow adjustments to net income are negligible because the assets and liabilities didn't change during the year (or the changes were minor so as not to matter much). However, depreciation has to be added to net income to determine cash flow.

To illustrate the steady-state scenario, we modify the example shown in Figure 4-1. Assume that the company's accounts receivable, inventories, prepaid expenses, accounts payable, accrued expenses payable, and income tax payable did not change during the year. Their ending balances are equal to their beginning balances. Therefore, depreciation is the only cash-flow adjustment to net income. In this scenario, the company's cash flow is as follows (refer to Figure 4-1 for data):

$350,000 net income + $85,000 depreciation expense = $435,000 cash flow

Therefore, the company has $435,000 cash available for general purposes, such as replacing fixed assets and paying dividends to shareowners.

Now, instead of earning $350,000 profit in the steady state, suppose the company breaks even. In other words, its net income for the period is zero (expenses equal revenue). The company's cash flow from operating activities would be

$0 net income + $85,000 depreciation expense = $85,000 cash flow

Despite earning no profit, the business would have $85,000 cash flow, all of it attributable to depreciation. The break-even scenario isolates attention on depreciation, which is not a cash outlay in the period the expense is recorded. The story isn't over, however. The cash inflow from sales revenue each period includes an amount toward the recovery of the capital invested property, plant, and equipment, or fixed assets. In the break-even scenario, the business recoups $85,000 of the money invested in its fixed assets in past years.

Almost all businesses record depreciation every year, but that recordkeeping may not be the end of the story for cash-flow adjustment in stable conditions. A business may record other kinds of noncash expenses, such as amortization on intangible assets, that are first cousins to depreciation. Also, a business may record noncash gains and losses in the year. For example, a business may record a loss due to an uninsured flood loss that destroyed one of its warehouses. The asset is written off and the loss is recorded; no cash outlay is caused by the loss (other than the cost of removing the rubble). In these situations, you have to add back the noncash losses and subtract noncash gains (writing up the market value of investments, for example).

Assessing cash-flow effects of growth and of decline

To assess your cash-flow scenario, start with profit plus depreciation and then ask, why is the company's cash flow higher or lower that this bench-mark? You know the answer, don't you? (If you have no idea, here's a hint: Refer to the earlier section "Adjusting your way to cash flow from operating activities.") The changes during the period in the assets accounts receivable, inventories, and prepaid expenses, as well as the changes in the liabilities accounts payable, accrued expenses payable, and income tax payable, help or hinder cash flow. To remind you: Asset increases and liability decreases hurt cash flow, and asset decreases and liability increases help cash flow.

The amount of depreciation is not driven by current events or recent transac-tions; it's largely historical. The calculation of depreciation is based on a pre-determined schedule that reaches back to the earliest years in which the fixed assets were acquired. In most situations, the bulk of a company's fixed assets were acquired some years ago. In sharp contrast, the changes in the other cash-flow factors — accounts receivable, inventories, and so on — are driven by recent transactions.

In the example scenario way back in Figure 4-1, the changes in assets and liabilities cause a $15,000 net negative adjustment to cash flow. (Do the arith-metic to check our calculation if you like.) Taking into account these several changes, cash flow is calculated as follows:

> $435,000 cash flow from net income and depreciation – $15,000 net change in other cash flow factors = $420,000 cash flow

When a business experiences rapid sales growth, its accounts receivable and inventories grow rapidly also. Sizable increases in these two areas can put a big dent in current cash flow. These negative cash-flow effects can be partially offset with increases in accounts payable and accrued expenses payable, but only in part. Rapid growth causes a cash-flow penalty as the business pumps up its receivables and inventories. In extreme cases, the increases in accounts receivable and inventories can get very large and cause a negative cash flow for the year.

When a business has a rapid decline in sales, its cash flow, ironically, may improve because the business's accounts receivable and inventory assets decline as rapidly as sales. However, a business may not be able to reduce expenses as quickly as its drop in sales, which results in a loss. In these situa-tions, a business may suffer a negative cash flow: Cash inflow from sales may be significantly less than cash outflow for expenses. See the next section for more info.

Suppose, for example, that sales revenue increases 30 percent over last year. You would then expect a corresponding increase in accounts receivable and inventories (usually the two biggest cash-flow adjustments to net income). Alternatively, if sales revenue drops 30 percent, these two assets probably drop more or less the same percent. However, life is not so simple. The actual changes in receivables and inventories may be out of step with the change in sales revenue, and there may be good business reasons for the deviations. Managers should know the reasons, of course. However, discrepancies between changes in accounts receivable and inventories and the growth or decline in sales revenue are generally not commented on in the financial reports.

Understanding negative cash flow

A negative cash flow means simply that the first section of the statement of cash flows (refer to Figure 4-1) reports a *decrease* in cash flow from the operating activities of the business during the period. Unless the decrease is offset with cash increases from investing activities (possible but not too likely) or increases from financing activities, the business suffers a decrease in its cash balance during the year.

Mention that a business has negative cash flow, and most people have a knee-jerk reaction: The business must be in deep trouble and on the edge of bankruptcy. Not so fast. In reading a financial report, look for the reasons behind the numbers, which can tell you the real story. The causes of a negative cash flow for the year may be temporary and unlikely to repeat in later years. Then again, the reasons may be systemic and likely to continue until drastic action is taken by the business.

The starting point is looking at why cash flow from operating activities is negative. The worst-case scenario is when a business records a large net loss for the year and the cash-flow adjustments don't mitigate the loss. Suppose, for example, that a business reports $2,000,000 bottom-line loss for its most recent year. It recorded $300,000 depreciation expense for the year. So its negative cash flow is $1,700,000 before looking at the changes in its other assets and liabilities. Decreases in accounts receivable and inventories combined with increases in accounts payable and accrued expenses payable may be large enough to overcome the negative $1,700,000 cash flow, but probably not. In fact, the changes in the assets and liabilities may be in the wrong direction and aggravate negative cash flow.

When a business has negative cash flow, financial analysts pay particular attention to its cash *burn rate*. The amount of negative cash flow per month is divided into its available cash balance to see how long the business can survive before it runs out of cash. During their start-up phases, new businesses typically have relatively large negative cash flow until they get over the hump and start bringing in enough sales revenue to get the company into the profit column. The cash burn rate is a rough measure of how long they have to get their sales up to speed.

It hardly needs mentioning that a business should quickly solve its negative cash-flow problem. If it's caused by a one-time extraordinary event that won't be repeated (for example, a business may have been forced to make a huge expenditure to remove asbestos in its plant and offices), then the loss won't be repeated next year and the managers have nothing to worry about. On the other hand, the problem may be that the business's sales prices are too low and/or its expenses are too high. In that case, unless things are turned around, the business is on a negative cash-flow death march.

Recognizing Problems with the Statement of Cash Flows

As we note in the opening to this chapter, the statement of cash flows has been around for about a quarter of a century. At the time of writing this book, generally accepted financial reporting standards — which include the requirement that a statement of cash flows be included with financial reports — apply to all businesses, public and private and large and small. However, some facts about the statement of cash flows make it a less-than-ideal tool for understanding the cash-flow situation of your own business and that of other businesses. The primary problems occur when small businesses skip creating the statement altogether and when businesses include too much or not enough information in the statement.

Getting skipped by small businesses

Practicing CPAs would admit off the record that private companies are cut a lot of slack in financial reporting. Some private companies don't even include the statement of cash flows in their financial reports. They include a balance sheet and an income statement, but not a cash-flows statement. In contrast, public companies, without exception, include a statement of cash flows in their external financial reports, because failing to do so would jeopardize the trading in their securities. Their CPA auditors would find fault and the Securities & Exchange Commission would take action to force the business to report a statement of cash flows.

Smaller businesses may find preparing a cash-flow statement difficult. Many small businesses do not employ a full-time qualified accountant. Their book-keeper may not know how to prepare this financial statement. The small business may decide not to hire a CPA or other trained person who knows how to prepare the statement of cash flows. This statement isn't prepared in a straightforward manner from the accounts kept by a business; the cash-flow figures reported in the statement have to be "backed out" from the information in the accounts of the business and the comparative balance sheet of the business at the start and end of the period. We don't go into the accounting techniques for preparing the statement of cash flows, because preparing this statement is a demanding "extra step" that many private businesses evidently either cannot do or don't bother to do. We've even talked to CPAs who aren't sure footed regarding the preparation of this statement. Accountants are not cash-flow people.

As of 2011, a movement is underway to allow private businesses to make exceptions and modifications to generally accepted financial accounting standards, but nothing has been set in concrete yet. We would be surprised if private businesses were allowed to skip reporting a statement of cash flows. But you never know.

Providing too much or too little information

Another problem with the statement of cash flows concerns the number of lines of information in the statement. Many cash flow statements have 30, 40, or more lines of information. (The cash flow statement in Figure 4-1 is relatively simple, with only 18 lines of information.) Therefore, this financial statement can be very demanding on the reader. Should a business expect readers to spend 30 minutes or more reading the statement? In short, all too many statements of cash flow suffer from information overload. Therefore, readers have to pick and choose what information they want to absorb; most won't take time to pore over every line.

Despite the sometimes overwhelming amount of information in the statement of cash flows, it doesn't really lay bare the cash-flow strategy and policies of a business. You can (and theoretically should) read the statement line by line. But after reading all the lines, getting a clear picture of the financial strategy of a business is still difficult. What's needed is management commentary and explanation concerning cash flow and the company's long-run cash-flow plan in the context of its overall financial strategy. Here's one example: If a business is sitting on a large cash balance and has a strong cash flow, it would be helpful for the CEO or president to explain what's going on. But you don't usually find explanatory comments about cash flow in financial reports.

Another complicating detail is that in many statements of cash flows, one or more amounts reported in the statement cannot be reconciled or matched up with their corresponding changes during the year that are reported in the balance sheet. For example, the amount of the adjustment to net income for the change in accounts receivable may not tie out with the difference between the beginning and ending balances that are reported for accounts receivable in the balance sheet. Many readers may not care about such loose ends. But the lack of clear-cut connections between the comparative balance sheet and the amounts in the statement of cash flows is frustrating to financial analysts and others who do a close reading of a company's financial report.

Business managers definitely should understand and control cash flow. However, the design of the statement of cash flows for external reports is not necessarily the best layout for internal reporting to managers. Business managers, working with their accountants, should devise a report design that is most useful for their planning and controlling of cash flows. The statement of cash flows that is included in external financial reports should not be a straitjacket for the internal reporting of cash flows to managers. (We explore cash-flow reporting for managers in Chapter 7.)

The role of cash flow in business valuation

When a company's owners decide to put the business up for sale, and in certain other situations, they need to put a value on the business. The number one factor in determining a value of a business is its cash flow from operating activities, which typically is called simply *cash flow*. Other factors come into play, including the debt load of the business, continuity or replacement of management, long-run business trends, the location(s) of the business, and many other considerations. But in most situations, the dominant factor is the business's potential to generate future cash flow.

The topic of business valuation is beyond the scope of this book. If you want to delve into the topic, we recommend our book *Small Business Financial Management Kit For Dummies* (John Wiley & Sons, Inc.).

Part II
Using Financial Statements to Assess Cash Health

The 5th Wave   By Rich Tennant

"Sorry, Cedric the King cut my budget for additional fools. He said the project already had enough fools on it."

In this part . . .

The three chapters in this part of the book explain techniques and methods for getting the most cash-flow information from your basic financial statements. Chapter 5 explains how to read the balance sheet for "hidden" cash information — information that isn't always apparent and doesn't jump out at you. Chapter 6 offers a useful technique for analyzing cash flow from profit, which avoids the time-consuming task of reading a formal statement of cash flows. Chapter 7 clarifies the very important distinction between liquidity and available cash. Confusing these two critical aspects of cash flow when running a business is a major mistake we help you avoid.

Chapter 5

Mining the Balance Sheet for Cash

. . . .

In This Chapter

▶ Understanding what the balance sheet does and doesn't tell you

▶ Going through the balance sheet with a fine-toothed comb

▶ Removing any white lies from the balance sheet

▶ Finding money you didn't know you had

. . . .

*I*n the good old days, before the financial crisis that started to engulf the world's capital markets and economies in 2007, business owners and managers tended to focus on the financial statement with the highest degree of perceived value: the income statement. With capital plentiful (whether it was debt or equity), the focus of most businesses was to drive top-line revenue and improve bottom-line profitability. This approach was far and away one of the easiest, most reliable (or so they thought), and most tried-and-proven methods for company owners and managers to evaluate the performance of their businesses (not to mention to assure their year-end bonuses). As for managing the balance sheet and statement of cash flows (the two forgotten financial statements), well, that's what bean counters were for, because the financial information provided from these reports was deemed simply too complicated or less important than sales and profitability. But over the past three years, business owners and managers learned very quickly and painfully that if their business wasn't liquid with readily available access to cash and capital, which at its heart is a strong balance sheet, life was going to be very difficult.

One of the best descriptions offered about the so-called "Great Recession" experienced in the United States was provided by a number of economists who simply stated the obvious. Past recessions were basically income-statement driven in that sales levels decreased, resulting in lower profits being earned and thus the need to reduce expenses, including eliminating employees where needed. What separated the recent recession from others, as noted by Richard Koo (of the Nomura Research Institute) among others, is that it was a *balance sheet* driven event, centered in the unavailability of capital, cash, and liquidity to businesses. To companies that had strong balance sheets with ample cash and liquidity, a once-in-a-lifetime opportunity was presented to capitalize on the marketplace turmoil by taking market share. And for the companies that didn't (like AIG and GM, which benefited enormously from the generosity of the government), unfortunately, weak balance sheets proved catastrophic.

The essence of a financially strong business resides not just in how much profit is generated but also, more importantly, in how much financial muscle and capital resources reside in the balance sheet. So this chapter is designed first to provide tools to assist you with understanding what the balance sheet is really saying and then to let you know how the balance sheet can be worked with, managed, and controlled to improve cash flows and financial strength.

Reading the Balance Sheet from a Cash-Flow Perspective

The balance sheet is most often viewed from a relatively simple perspective of assessing what assets a company owns compared to its obligations or liabilities. The difference between those numbers is the company's net equity (which hopefully is a positive number for most businesses). If you are evaluating the balance sheet from only this perspective, however, you miss a much larger and more important concept: understanding the balance sheet from a cash-flow point of view. This perspective is focused not on the stated value of a company's assets and liabilities but rather on how quickly assets can be converted into cash (that is, sources of cash) and how soon liabilities will consume cash (the uses of cash). The basic structure of almost all company balance sheets is centered on this one all-important concept: the proper ordering of assets and liabilities.

The balance sheet must balance! That is, total assets must equal total liabilities plus net equity. This concept is so simple, you may ask why we even bother to mention it, and the reason is simple. For non-accounting/financial types, this simplest of equations is often the most difficult to comprehend.

The standard balance sheet structure used by most businesses is very straightforward and is based on the following ordering concepts:

✔ **All company assets are listed on the left side of the balance sheet** (when the balance sheet is presented in a side-by-side format, as in Figure 5-1).

✔ **The assets are classified as either current or long term.**

  • A *current asset* classification assumes the asset will either be converted into cash within one year (as is the case with trade receivables) or, conversely, the asset will be consumed within one year (like a prepaid insurance policy).

  • *Long-term assets* represent assets that will convert into cash past a year period (like a note receivable due in three years) or will be consumed over an extended period of time (for example, equipment used to manufacture products).

✔ **All company liabilities are listed on the right side of the balance sheet** (when the balance sheet is presented in a side-by-side format, as in Figure 5-1).

✔ **The liabilities are classified as either current or long-term.**

• A *current liability* classification assumes that the liability will either consume cash within one year (like trade payables) or will be worked off within one year (a customer deposit which turns into a sale, for example).

• *Long-term liabilities* will consume cash past a year period (for instance, a note payable due in three years) or will be worked off over an extended period of time (like a settlement on a lawsuit that will be repaid over three years).

✔ **The company's equity accounts are presented on the right side of the balance sheet, after the liabilities and clearly segregated from them, with no distinction made between current and long term.** Equity is generally considered a long-term or permanent commitment to support business operations.

Figure 5-1 represents an example of a standard balance sheet for a distribution company that we use as an example throughout this chapter.

In the title of the balance sheet in Figure 5-1 is the word *Unaudited,* which is a clue to the reader to be aware of the chance of mistakes, omissions, or irregularities. As we address throughout this chapter, the difference between audited and unaudited financial information is as significant as the difference between night and day. Audited financial statements indicate that an independent and qualified third party (most commonly a certified public accountant) has examined, tested, reviewed, and evaluated the financial statements in accordance with GAAP (generally accepted accounting principles) and rendered an opinion on the quality of the financial statements (in an attached report). Unaudited financial statements generally are prepared internally by the company's management without any third-party verification, so obviously they carry higher levels of risk than audited financial statements in terms of assessing the financial health of a business and basing a decision on the assessment (such as extending credit to a customer).

How assets are listed in the balance sheet in relation to generating cash

Upon close review of the ordering of assets in the balance sheet in Figure 5-1, you can see that the flow is very logically based on the nearness of turning assets into cash (or being consumed internally). We take a look at each category of asset in this section.

ACME Distribution, Inc. — Unaudited Balance Sheet as of 12/31/2010				
Assets	**Amount**	**Liabilities**	**Amount**
Current Assets:		Current Liabilities:	
Cash and Equivalents	$265,000	Trade Payables	$385,000
Trade Receivables	$750,000	Accrued Liabilities	$150,000
Inventory	$500,000	Line of Credit Borrowings	$350,000
Prepaid Expenses	$75,000	Current Portion, Long-Term Debt	$0
Shareholder Advances	$150,000	Other Current Liabilities	$75,000
Total Current Assets	$1,740,000	Total Current Liabilities	$960,000
Long-Term Assets:		Long-Term Liabilities:	
Property, Plant, and Equipment	$2,240,000	Notes Payable, Less Current	$1,000,000
Less: Accumulated Depreciation	($900,000)	Capital Leases, Less Current	$150,000
Net Property, Plant, and Equipment	$1,340,000	Subordinated Debt	$250,000
Other Assets:		Total Long-Term Liabilities	$1,400,000
Affiliate Note Receivable	$285,000	Total Liabilities	$2,300,000
Intangible Assets, Net	$250,000	Equity:	
Deferred Income Taxes	$185,000	Common Equity	$100,000
Other Long-Term Assets	$50,000	Retained Earnings	$990,000
Total Long-Term and Other Assets	$2,110,000	Current Earnings	$400,000
		Net Equity	$1,490,000
Total Assets	$3,850,000	Total Liabilities and Equity	$3,850,000

Figure 5-1: Sample of an unaudited balance sheet showing assets, liabilities, and equity.

Trade accounts receivables

Trade accounts receivable represent the final stage of the selling cycle before the sale actually turns into cash. Generally, trade accounts receivable are listed right after cash because this asset class tends to turn over and convert to cash relatively quickly. Although the actual conversion time (that is, from the point of which credit is extended to the point cash is received) varies between different types of businesses, a range of 30 to 45 days is very commonplace for companies that extend credit terms to customers. This calculation is known as the *days sales outstanding* in receivables.

Inventory

Next up in the asset-ordering structure is inventory, which is usually comprised of three subcomponents including raw materials, WIP (work in process, or partially completed products), and finished goods. Inventory takes longer to turn into cash, because it first must be produced or purchased, and then sold (with a trade receivable generated), and finally turned into cash. No set standard tells you how much inventory a company should keep on hand to support ongoing operations because the numbers vary wildly by different industries. For companies that manufacture goods, the inventory levels tend to be higher as a result of having to support the three primary types of inventory (raw, WIP, and finished goods). For distribution companies that generally only carry finished goods, the amount of inventory tends to be lower (in relation to the revenue level of the company), and for retail companies such as Walmart, the amount of inventory is even less (because the goal is to quickly turn over inventory.

Prepaid expenses

Prepaid expenses generally consist of insurance policies that cover a period of time (for instance, a general liability insurance policy that covers the company for a year), rents for facilities and equipment (which are usually paid in advance in the preceding month), advertising programs to reserve space in different media forms such as the Internet and magazines, and various other expenses paid for in advance.

Unlike trade accounts receivable and inventory, which a company strives to turn into cash, prepaid expenses are not likely to be turned into cash. These expenses are consumed over a period of time to support continued company operations. But this doesn't excuse management from properly controlling and monitoring these types of assets, as your vendors, whether it's your landlord or advertising agency, would like nothing more than for you to pay in advance so they can use your cash.

In order to proactively manage prepaid expenses to limit tying up cash, active negotiation is critical. If the landlord wants two months of rent on deposit, offer one (especially if it's a tenant's market). If a law firm or advertising agency wants a large retainer to start work, offer a hint that you need to obtain a competitive bid from another firm but would get started if the upfront cash requirement was reduced. If the insurance company wants your general liability policy for the year paid in advance, request quarterly installments. In most cases, the parties requesting the cash have the room to be flexible.

Other current assets

The final type of asset located in the current asset section of the balance sheet is generally reserved as a catchall for "other" current assets. These assets may include a temporary advance provided to an employee, a short-term deposit or retainer paid, other non-operational-based receivables such as an income tax refund expected to be received within one year, and so on. Some of these assets may in fact turn into cash, while others may not. But both demand the same level of management support, because, similar to prepaid expenses, other current assets can quickly consume cash.

Various strategies are available to help manage other current assets (in terms of consuming cash), such as establishing a clear company policy where employee advances are limited to 50 percent of an employee's monthly compensation and must be repaid within 30 days and making sure that estimated income tax payments are as accurate as possible (to avoid overpaying).

Some types of current assets lumped into "other" may be separately presented if they are deemed material or if multiple immaterial assets are grouped together. In the accounting world, the use of the words *material* and *immaterial* is very important to understand. If an asset is deemed to be immaterial in size, then it tends to get lumped together with other smaller assets and classified in the catchall "other current assets." If an asset is deemed material, then it's presented separately in the financial statements. Of course, the ultimate decision as to what is material or immaterial has led to more than a few lively discussions between management, auditors, and other external parties.

Property, plant, and equipment

Property, plant, and equipment is the primary category for long-term assets. This grouping of assets includes basically all types of production equipment, machinery, facility leasehold improvements, autos, buildings, land, furniture, fixtures, and so on — everything owned by the company and anticipated to be used/consumed in its regular operations over an extended period of time (ranging from at least 1 year to as long as 30 years). Similar to prepaid expenses, these assets aren't turned into cash directly but rather provide an investment basis for a business to deliver its products or services to the market in the most efficient and cost-effective manner possible. Furthermore, these assets are depreciated over the time period during which the asset is anticipated to be consumed. Some assets, such as computers, have a very short depreciation time period of just a few years. For other assets, such as a building, a time period of 25 years may be used to depreciate the asset. The accumulation of depreciation of all asset types is summed and reflected as a reduction to the original cost of this group of assets to produce a net asset value.

Other assets

All other assets owned by the company that are long term in nature (that is, their values will take more than a year to be realized) are the last items presented in the asset section of the balance sheet. Common types of other assets include company-owned intellectual property (such as patents, trademarks, and software development costs), deferred tax assets, permanent deposits, and notes receivable (greater than a year due). Similar to other current assets, some of these long-term types of assets may eventually turn into cash, such as a long-term note receivable, whereas others are consumed in the business, such as company intellectual property.

The long-term asset segment of the balance sheet is subject to the same concept of material versus immaterial as the current asset segment. As a company becomes older, grows larger, and undertakes more complex transactions, more long-term assets may be deemed material and disclosed separately on the balance sheet. You see more separate disclosures for other long-term assets than for other current assets.

How liabilities are listed in the balance sheet in relation to consuming cash

As with assets, the ordering of liabilities in Figure 5-1 is based on the relative closeness of when the liability has to be satisfied and consume or use cash.

Trade accounts payable

To start, the liability that will most likely consume company cash in the shortest time period is generally trade accounts payable. *Trade accounts payable* represents valid claims against the company for the purchases of goods or services that have been formally presented to and approved by the company. For most companies, trade accounts payable require payment anywhere from 15 to 60 days of the date of the balance sheet.

One of the most effective ways to generate extra cash for a company is to request that vendors and suppliers offer extended payment terms for paying invoicing. For example, a jewelry retailer that generates a large percentage of its annual sales during the Christmas holiday season needs to secure inventory well in advance of the actual selling season to make sure the proper type and amount of products are available. Requesting an additional 60 days of time to remit payment to manage seasonal cash-flow pressure is more than acceptable, and the inventory may be ordered and purchased in the summer but not paid for in cash until December. Countless other situations are utilized by companies to extend payment terms, but the point remains the same. Using the cash of other businesses to support your operation can be a very inexpensive source of capital.

Accrued liabilities

After trade accounts payable, accrued liabilities are generally the next item listed in the current liability section of the balance sheet. Accrued liabilities consist of obligations a company knows it has incurred but doesn't yet know a final amount or due date for. Obligations for future commissions, property taxes, product warranties, employee vacations, and so on all fall into this category and are quite often based on estimates (initially) to ensure that a reasonable calculation of the obligation due is reflected in the financial statements.

Most accrued liabilities eventually consume cash in one fashion or another but may take slightly longer than traditional trade accounts payable. For example, a vendor invoice provided from a supplier with net 30-day payment terms will consume cash in approximately 30 days. Commissions accrued for a sales representative that are due and payable based on when the sale is actually received in cash may not be paid out for 45 to 60 days.

Line of credit borrowings

Line of credit borrowings represent the amount of borrowings a company utilizes from a working capital lending agreement established with a bank or other lender. The working capital lending agreement is almost always collateralized by either a company's trade accounts receivable or inventory. For a more detailed understanding of how these agreements are structured, see Chapter 11. Generally, the term for most of these agreements is one year in length, indicating that a current liability is present.

One controversial way to improve the current ratio of a business is to make sure the working capital lending agreement has an expiration date greater than one year. For example, if your fiscal year ends on 12/31/10 and your working capital lending agreement expires on 6/30/12, then most auditors consider this a long-term liability because it expires 18 months after the year-end. By moving the liability from current to long-term, a business's current ratio calculation appears stronger. But at issue is the fact that the lending agreement, which may be considered long-term because of its expiration date, is secured by current assets that generally will turn into cash in well less than a year. Or looking at it from another perspective, if the assets securing the lending agreement, such as trade receivables, are substantially collected within four months, then the outstanding balance on the lending agreement needs to decrease to stay in compliance.

So is this really matching current assets with current liabilities? Well, we leave that discussion to the auditors. What's important to remember is that even though the lending agreement may be classified as long-term in the financial statements, an understanding of how that liability may consume short-term cash flows should be clear.

Current portion of long-term debt

Unlike line-of-credit borrowings, the current portion of long-term debt represents the portion of note-payable borrowings that's due within one year. For example, if you borrow $1 million to finance equipment purchases and the loan must be repaid in 60 equal principal payments of $16,666.67 each, then the $200,000 you pay in cash in the first 12 months is considered a current liability. This system of apportioning applies to all forms of long-term debt, including formal notes payable, capital lease obligations, issued bonds, and others.

Other current liabilities

As you may have guessed, *other current liabilities* are basically the opposite of other current assets. Other current liabilities may include deferred revenue (like an annual license fee billed to customers in one installment but earned over a 12-month period), customer deposits, and other miscellaneous current liabilities. Similar to prepaid expenses, certain other current liabilities tend to be earned back into the business and ultimately don't consume cash.

Guaranteed debt commitments

This group covers basically all long-term liabilities that have set payment terms and that are subordinated by a legally binding agreement such as notes payable, loans, capital lease obligations, and other forms of debt. As previously discussed, the portion of the debt commitments that is due within 12 months is classified as current liabilities, leaving the balance to be treated as long-term liabilities.

Other long-term liabilities

The classification of *other long-term liabilities* captures various other long-term business obligations including commitments, contingencies, deferred revenue earned past 12 months, and others. For most businesses, other long-term liabilities are generally fairly small in size. However, an example of a large long-term liability is an accrual for the restoration of a mining site to its original state by a mining operation after the mineral has been extracted. Over a period of time, the mine operator estimates how much restoring the property (after the mining activities are completed) will amount to, realizes an expense in the current financial statements to account for this cost, and then records the future long-term liability to properly disclose the anticipated obligation. Eventually, well out in the future, the mine is closed and money is then spent to reclaim the property.

What the balance sheet doesn't disclose about cash flows

Despite all the information the balance sheet does provide on cash flows, it only represents part of the cash-flow story. Valuable information must be harvested from other sources to truly understand a business's complete cash-flow picture. In this section, we give you an overview of the balance sheet's limitations.

Capturing only a moment in time

Remember that the balance sheet is based on a snapshot of a company's financial condition at a point in time. It's very different from the income statement and the cash-flow statement, which measure the performance of a business over a period of time (monthly, quarterly, or annually). The balance sheet is a great tool to help understand where cash has been invested/committed and what source provided the cash, but it doesn't offer an explanation of the entire cash-flow cycle.

Reflecting history more accurately than the present

The balance sheet provides a historical perspective on the cost or book value of the assets and the amount of liabilities or obligations owed by a business. The balance sheet doesn't provide a proper picture of what the assets may actually be worth in the market if an asset needs to be liquidated outside the normal course of business. For example, if a company needs to raise cash relatively quickly, it may be forced to sell assets at a discount to cost or the net book value. In the same breath, a building or piece of land purchased decades ago may be grossly understated in value as a result of long-term appreciation in commercial real estate.

Any company that experienced pain during the Great Recession and had to pledge assets against a loan quickly became familiar with the acronym *FLV*. *FLV* stands for *forced liquidation value* and is a tool used by lenders that estimates the value of an asset in the worst possible scenario (that is, a forced or fire sale of the asset required in a hostile market). They use this figure to calculate the amount of a loan they're willing to extend to make sure that at any point in time, if the company can't repay the loan, then the asset offered as collateral for the loan can be liquidated and the lender will be covered. A mistake businesses often make is assuming that just because they paid X dollars for an asset means that the asset still has a reasonable value compared to the original cost and can borrow against this value. Management's somewhat overly optimistic perception of asset values may lead them to believe they have more assets available to pledge as collateral and thus can borrow higher amounts.

Failing to help with future plans

When analyzing a company's cash flow, a simple historical evaluation of the financial statements most likely doesn't suffice, especially for companies that are undergoing a significant change in the operating model or are new and anticipate rapid growth. As much as a business's historical financial information may support the "hows" of cash flow (that is, how much cash has been consumed by asset growth? how much cash was burned to support the launch of a business? and so on), it doesn't support management's future plans. If managers need to know what source of cash is available to support future operations or know when the company will run out of cash at its current growth rate, they need to be fully engaged in the company's strategic planning process and have access to and understand all critical reports, goals, or objectives.

Offering internal information

The balance sheet cannot tell a company how much cash may be available from external business sources to support its operations. Debt and equity markets are constantly changing. One year may provide more financing options than you can shake a stick at, and another year you may find that basically every available option has been eliminated. For an example, look no farther than the period of 2006, when capital was readily available, to 2009, when the debt and equity markets basically ceased to operate.

In order to gain a complete understanding of a business's cash-flow cycle and properly manage cash resources, you need to digest and understand all relevant information, from additional internal financial statements, such as the income statement, to available external data on the state of capital markets.

Banks tend to have far more capital/cash to support your business when you least need it. And conversely, when your business is in greatest need of capital/cash, the banks seem to have little to offer. This drives home the importance of planning, planning, and more planning (covered in Chapters 8 and 9) and the need to always save for a rainy day.

Giving the Balance Sheet a More Thorough Examination

In the health industry, as a patient becomes older, his health risks tend to increase, and, as a result, more thorough examinations commonly are required. Well, the same logic holds for the balance sheet. When companies get older and begin to mature, their balance sheets tend to become more complex as, over time, the volume and diversity of transactions increase. As a result, the aging of the company and its financial statements often trigger the accumulation of excess baggage (from years of neglect) on the balance sheet, which, if left unchecked, can quickly mislead management as to the company's financial health and strength.

The goal of this section is to provide a clear understanding of how to perform a basic financial analysis on the balance sheet to help you identify where problems may reside, when assets are lying to you, and why your liabilities may not be telling the truth.

Just because an asset is stated at "cost" on the balance sheet doesn't mean that the value of the asset if sold or liquidated will match. Market value is often quite different from the original cost when you have a need to turn the asset into cash in a timely manner. More than a few business owners and managers have experienced reverse sticker shock when the need arises to liquidate an asset in a less-than-favorable economic climate. Unless your business is TBTF (too big to fail), don't expect freely operating capitalists to feel your pain.

Using key balance sheet performance-measurement tools

The best way to begin to evaluate and understand your balance sheet is by applying the most commonly used financial performance measurement tools utilized by accounting and financial professionals throughout the country.

Note that these measurement tools are focused on evaluating a company's financial strength at a point and time (for example, as of 12/31/10) rather than over a period of time (for the three-month period of 10/1/10 through 12/31/10). As such, these financial performance measurement tools are geared toward evaluating a company's strength as measured by its solvency and liquidity.

In addition to the financial performance measurement tools we discuss in this section, countless others are available and utilized by professionals operating in different industries, but they're beyond the scope of this chapter. However, the goal of applying all financial performance measurement tools remains the same: to complete an independent and objective evaluation on the company's financial statements to assess its financial health, strength, and stability.

Using the same sample company as presented in Figure 5-1 (the balance sheet), Figure 5-2 shows the six measurement tools we discuss in this section.

ACME Distribution, Inc. — Unaudited Business Performance Measurement Tools as of 12/31/2010				
Net Working Capital:	Amount	Days Sales Outstanding in Trade Receivables:		Amount
Current Assets	$1,740,000	Annual Sales		$8,043,750
Current Liabilities	$960,000	Average Monthly Sales		$670,313
Net Working Capital	$780,000	Trade Accounts Receivable Balance		$750,000
Current Ratio:		**Average Months Outstanding in A/R**		1.12
Current Assets	$1,740,000	Average Days Outstanding in A/R		40.00
Current Liabilities	$960,000	Days Costs of Goods Sold Outstanding in Inventory:		
Current Ratio	1.81	Annual Costs of Goods Sold		$6,032,813
Quick Ratio:		Average Monthly Costs of Goods Sold		$502,734
Current Assets	$1,740,000	Inventory Balance		$500,000
Less: Inventory	($500,000)	Average Months Inventory O/S		.99
Less: Prepaid Expenses	($75,000)	Average Days Inventory O/S		29.84
Less: Other Current Assets	($150,000)	Debt-to-Equity Ratio:		
Adjusted Current Assets	$1,015,000	Total Debt or Liabilities		$2,360,000
Current Liabilities	$960,000	Net Equity		$1,490,000
Quick Ratio	1.06	Debt-to-Equity Ratio		1.58

Figure 5-2: Using measurement tools to assess business performance.

GIGO, or *garbage-in, garbage-out,* is a simple concept that's extremely important to understand. If the financial information you apply the financial performance measurement tools to is "garbage" (in other words, unreliable, inaccurate, incomplete, or otherwise bad), then the results produced from applying the measurement tools will also be "garbage" (and should not be relied on). Don't bother applying financial performance measurement tools to unreliable financial information.

Net working capital

To determine net working capital, total current liabilities are subtracted from total current assets. Generally speaking, a positive figure should be present for most businesses. If this ratio is negative, it implies that the business doesn't have enough short-term or liquid assets to cover its short-term liabilities.

Current ratio

Taking the company's total current assets and dividing them by its total current liabilities determines the current ratio. A current ratio of greater than one to one should be present, because a ratio below that level implies a possible liquidity problem.

Quick or acid-test ratio

This ratio represents an extension of the current ratio. It's calculated by taking the total current assets, less inventory and other current assets (such as prepaid expenses), and then dividing this adjusted figure by total current liabilities to produce the quick, or acid-test, ratio. The higher the ratio, the better. However, having a ratio of less than one to one is common, especially for companies with significant levels of inventory. The idea with this ratio is to evaluate just the company's most liquid assets (generally cash and trade accounts receivables) in relation to its current liabilities to drill down into another measurement of liquidity.

Days sales outstanding (DSO) in trade accounts receivable

Trade receivables divided by average monthly sales multiplied by 30 days produces the days sale outstanding in trade accounts receivable figure. Lower numbers with this calculation are usually positive, because they indicate a company is doing a good job of managing this asset and not consuming excess capital. Again, although the DSO will vary by industry, keeping receivable turnover rates lower than 30 days or one month is generally very positive.

If your company is growing rapidly or has significant seasonal sales, don't use average monthly sales for this calculation, because your numbers won't accurately reflect the state of affairs. Instead, use an average monthly sales figure that is more representative of more recent business activity. For example, if your business sells cold-weather gear such as snow shovels and snow blowers, you stock up on these items starting in the fall so your business probably has a peak selling period of August through December and then a falloff starting in the spring. So when applying this calculation, your days sales outstanding in trade accounts receivable balance is best measured against the seasonal sales peak versus average monthly sales for the year.

Days costs of goods sold outstanding in inventory

The *days costs of goods sold outstanding in inventory* figure is found by dividing inventory by average monthly cost of goods sold and multiplying by 30. You usually want a lower number with this calculation because it indicates that your company is doing a good job of managing this asset and not consuming excess capital.

Note: If your company is growing rapidly or has significant seasonal sales, average monthly costs of goods sold can be misleading. Instead, you want to use an average monthly costs of sales figure that is more representative of more recent business activity. For example, if your company has recently doubled the size of product offerings to the market by tapping new sales channels (such as selling products on QVC), the period of time the new products have been sold offers a better comparison to your inventory levels (as it is only logical that inventory levels are higher to support increased sales activity).

Debt-to-equity ratio

Total debt (current and long term) divided by the total equity of the company equals the debt-to-equity ratio. Higher ratios indicate that the company has more financial leverage (refer to "Unlocking Hidden Cash from the Balance Sheet," later in this chapter, for a discussion on financial leverage), which translates into more risk being present.

Evaluating your assets

In my (Tage Tracy's) 20 years of professional experience with financial statements, I've yet to see a balance sheet that isn't lying in one form or another. Most companies aren't intentionally committing fraud and/or the willful intent to deceive; the financial statements presented have simply not been properly evaluated and adjusted to make sure that all balance sheet accounts have been classified correctly and that the assets' net realizable value are, in fact, accurate.

The problem with properly accounting for and valuing assets isn't so much based in understanding what the stated value of the asset should be. If inventory was purchased for $100 per unit, then it should be valued at $100 per unit. Likewise, if a customer sale amounted to $750, then that amount should be the receivable due from the customer. Accounting for the original cost or value of a transaction is fairly straightforward and easy to understand, so you may be wondering what the problem is. The answer is simple: age and intent.

On the age front, as most assets get older, they naturally depreciate and lose value as the asset is consumed over the ordinary course of business. A perfect example is the purchase of machinery used to manufacture a product.

Over time, the machine slowly depreciates as it's worn out through repeated use or becomes outdated. This same concept also holds for just about every other type of asset, including trade accounts receivable, inventory, intangible assets, and others. As the assets get older, the risks of obsolescence and eventual recoverability increase, directly reducing the value of the asset. For most business assets, aging carries the greatest single risk to value impairment.

As for the intent issue, well, we'll just say that this is where business owners and managers can really start to get creative. It's not that they deliberately lie about the value of their intellectual property being intact or about their intentions to pay back the advance they provided themselves over the next 12 months. As George Costanza says in an episode of *Seinfeld* when Jerry asks him how to beat a lie detector test, it's not a lie if you believe it's the truth. Business owners truly believe that various assets do, in fact, hold the original value paid. However, believing it doesn't make it true on the balance sheet, as we explore in the following sections.

More times than not, those little white lies that business owners and managers start with innocently enough (to support asset value) can quickly turn into all-consuming black holes as the owners and managers really start to believe the horse you-know-what they're shoveling. Business owners and managers are not intentionally trying to inflate asset values and commit fraud, but over time they lose objectivity in making sure that all assets are properly valued.

Determining real cash availability

The balance sheet is not always clear about what assets are readily available to turn into cash. For the most part, cash is cash and can be utilized freely in the business. However, various types of cash need to be clearly segregated and classified when the cash is not freely available for use in normal company operations. Examples of cash that need to be properly classified as other current or long-term assets include certificates of deposits pledge as collateral (like for a facility lease), cash allocated to employees in deferred compensation programs (and generally invested in marketable securities), cash earmarked for the payments of specific obligations (such as deductibles on insurance programs), and so on. A simple rule of thumb is that if cash is restricted to its use, then it needs to be classified appropriately so that it isn't improperly factored into or assumed to be available for general business needs.

Considering whether trade accounts receivables are collectible

Are all receivables really collectible? This question can be answered very concisely: No! And not just for the obvious reason of receivables not being collectible because the customer can't pay. Clearly, bad debt represents one of the largest valuation impairments related to receivables, and most businesses have to deal with some level of it. Bad debt must be proactively managed to limit related losses and must be accounted for in the business's economic profitability model. But in addition to bad debt, the net realizable value of receivables can be impacted by numerous other factors, including the following two examples:

✔ **Allowance for returns and discounts:** In today's economy, sales channels have never been more aggressive in pushing back unsold merchandise to the supplier. So though sales may have taken place, the real question is what potential is present for the return of unsold merchandise after a set period. Making sure that a proper allowance has been established to account for expected sales returns represents a high-profile management task.

Likewise, properly accounting for future discounts needs to be addressed. In certain industries, a sale may occur, but if a competitor offers the same product at a reduced price, your customer may look for a discount (in order to preserve the original sale). If providing discounts after the fact is relatively common practice, then in order to capture the real net value of trade receivables, the business needs to establish a reserve to account for potential or estimated customer discounts that will eventually be provided (after the sale).

✔ **Trade payable offsets:** Numerous businesses both sell products to and purchase material from the same party, creating both a customer and vendor relationship. Quite often, settlements on the accounts are addressed by offsetting the balances owed rather than by remitting payment. The net effect of the offset on the income statement is zero, but a balance sheet impact is present as a result of reducing both trade accounts receivables and trade accounts payable.

Accounting for the true value of inventory

Businesses are required to value inventory at cost based on generally accepted accounting principles (GAAP). However, the inventory's value must also be based on the concept of *lower of cost or market* (LCM). This concept states that any inventory for which the net market value is lower than cost must be recorded on the balance sheet as reflecting the lower net market value (where net market equals the anticipated selling pricing less any direct expenses incurred to support the sale).

The problem with valuing inventory isn't so much based in these two simple concepts but rather in management's ability and willingness to apply these two concepts in a timely and impartial manner. Businesses must be willing to develop and implement disciplined accounting policies and procedures to properly evaluate and account for obsolete, slow moving, lost, and/or market-price-impaired inventory. Inventory maintenance and management are expensive (keep reading to find out why), and, similar to bad debts realized on sales, periodic losses on inventory represent a normal and recurring expense that must be accounted for on a periodic basis to ensure that a business's profit and loss are properly reported.

Continuing to carry and stock obsolete and slow-moving inventory can be very expensive for a business because a number of added expenses are incurred to support the inventory (including leased space, utilities, insurance, taxes, personnel to manage the inventory, and so on). Although these expenses vary by business, a general rule of thumb is that for every dollar of inventory supported, the carrying costs may be as high as 10 percent. So if a business has $1 million in inventory, the annual maintenance and carrying costs are $100,000. By managing inventory appropriately, not only are carrying costs reduced, thus improving a businesses' profitability, but also, more important, cash is not tied up in excess inventory levels. Business owners and managers must not be fooled by a common pitfall based on the thinking, "This is what the inventory costs, so this is what it has to sell for in order to make a profit." For slow-moving, obsolete, and value impaired inventory, liquidating the inventory in bulk is often more profitable than continuing to carry the inventory in the hopes that it will sell some day.

Providing for property pitfalls

The term *property* refers here to all equipment, machines, buildings, land, leasehold improvements, furniture, fixtures, and other fixed assets owned. Significant variations in property market values compared to the net book value are generally present for most companies and can work in both directions. For instance, most tangible personal property, such as machines, equipment, computers, furniture, and autos, tend to have a lower *fair-market value* (the value that could be obtained in the open market if liquidated) than the net book value stated on the balance sheet. This difference is due to the fact that when new equipment becomes used equipment on day one of ownership, a significant decrease in value is realized. And because most companies use the straight-line method of accounting to record depreciation expense, the fair-market value of the property is usually below the net book value of the property for the first 60 to 70 percent of the ownership life. Conversely, other types of real property, such as land and buildings, may actually increase in value, especially if held for an extended period of time.

Numerous opportunities are present to save money and properly manage risk with business property. For example, making sure that all tangible personal property such as computers, equipment, and machinery that are no longer in use are properly relieved from the accounting records can help reduce property taxes and insurance costs. Businesses often forget to remove the cost of property when filing property tax returns and completing insurance coverage applications, which drives taxes and premiums higher.

Dealing with other problem assets

The list of problems that can be encountered with other assets is about as long and varied as the Yellow Pages. So rather than attempt to list every possible scenario, here are two real-life scenarios that illustrate how some business owners and managers can stretch the truth on their balance sheets:

- **Capitalized start-up costs:** A company incurs $250,000 in start-up expenses to start a new business unit. The company elects to capitalize the cost as an intangible asset rather than record it as a direct expense, because by recording the cost as an expense, the company would incur a net loss and thus violate the covenants established with its bank.

- **Owner advances:** One of the oldest and most common tricks used by businesses is to reduce owner compensation levels and instead allow the owners to take loans from the business which will eventually (yeah, right) be paid back during years of strong profitability. The loans are then treated as an asset on the balance sheet, giving the appearance of a stronger company. Be warned that everyone (from outside financing sources to auditors) looks right through this scheme and treats owner advances as an expense on the income statement and a reduction to net equity.

Taking a closer look at your liabilities

If your assets are lying to you, then it should come as no surprise that your liabilities may not be telling you the entire truth either. When businesses implement proper accounting procedures, liabilities tend to suffer from management neglect, poor understanding (of the core issue), and/or plausible deniability.

The following sections take a closer look at a business's liabilities to make sure they're coming clean with management. The overriding issues in whether liabilities are telling the truth are really completeness and accuracy. Have all liabilities of a business been accounted for and been accurately presented in the balance sheet? From an auditor's perspective, auditing what's there (assets) is much easier than auditing what's not there but should be (liabilities).

Examining payable and receivable relationships

Similar to cash, trade payables are just what they sound like (see the earlier section "Trade accounts payable" for an overview) and should be classified as a current liability. However, various trade accounts payable scenarios warrant further discussion:

- As noted with the discussion on trade accounts receivables, certain trade accounts payable owed may be offset against trade account receivables due if a business has a customer that is also a supplier.

✔ Vendor balances that are past due may indicate that a dispute is present between the company and its supplier (for example, concerning defective products that were returned). If material, the balance owed may need to be extracted from the trade accounts payable classification.

✔ If a large balance due has accumulated with a key supplier that is a related or affiliated party, a better understanding of the expected payment terms for the balance due should be obtained (and if needed, properly recorded).

Properly accounting and accruing for all liabilities

Businesses often struggle to make sure that all liabilities are properly accounted for and accrued at the end of each period. Most notably, businesses tend to have problems with accrued liabilities that arise from having to use estimates for calculating future obligations due (which are not necessarily invoiced to the business for payment). A perfect example of this uncertainty is businesses that provide warranties for products and/or services. Though a business doesn't know what sale will eventually result in a warranty claim, it should have enough information to estimate what future claims will arise based on sales levels. Other accrued liabilities are somewhat easier to calculate, such as interest expense on outstanding debt, property taxes on real and personal property, income tax obligations due (based on net profit levels), and employee commissions and bonuses, but the same accounting principle holds for all these problem areas: matching.

The accounting matching principle states that all revenue and expenses should be properly matched in the same period to ensure that a company's true financial performance is reported. A perfect example is employee commissions paid in arrears when cash is received. The commissions earned should be accrued and expensed in the period during which they were generated as opposed to when they're paid. Although paying commissions in arrears based on when the cash from the sale is received represents a solid cash-management strategy, if sales of $800,000 were realized in the third quarter and generated a commission of 10 percent, or $80,000, then the income statement for the third quarter should reflect an $80,000 commission expense.

Classifying debt as current or long term

Properly classifying liabilities between current and long term is extremely important. On the surface, this classification may appear straightforward to you (for example, the next 12 months of principal payments on a note payable get classified as current). But careful classification is often overlooked by businesses with areas that are not quite as clear cut, such as accrued liabilities that cover multiple years. You also need to keep in mind that a liability that was considered long-term a year ago may change based on economic conditions or your company's financial performance and now need to be classified as a current liability for the current year. For example, if your business has a note payable extended from a bank with specific financial covenants attached that were met in a prior year, then the note is most likely accounted for with both a current portion and long-term portion. However, if the business violates the terms of the note-payable agreement by not meeting a covenant, then the note may be in default and become due and payable immediately (requiring 100 percent of the balance due to be classified as current).

Handling risks with other liabilities

The importance of properly accounting for and classifying other liabilities has been highlighted recently by the accounting community in relation to recognizing earned revenue. This issue has been centered in the technology industry as a result of how technology licensing agreements are structured and when revenue is actually earned. I won't go into the specifics because they can get very complicated, but the key issue is based in an agreement that is billed in advance and that covers a period of time (such as an annual license that provides the customer with free future updates and technical support). If for any reason a business is obligated to support a customer over a period of time and potentially incur future expenses to support the customer, then a portion of the revenue billed to the customer will need to be deferred and recognized appropriately — the matching principle.

Remembering off-balance-sheet obligations and transactions

Off-balance-sheet obligations result from transactions or events that are not required to be recorded in the financial statements per GAAP but carry risks to a business in one fashion or another. One simple example is the practice of providing a business guarantee, which has become more commonplace over the past three years. If a business, for any reason, guarantees the obligations of another entity, then an off-balance-sheet obligation is created. Though the other entity may be fully capable of supporting the repayment of the obligation that was guaranteed, if for any reason it can't, the impact on the business providing the guarantee may be significant.

Off-balance-sheet obligations and transactions have been one of the hottest topics with corporate America for the past ten years. From Enron's accounting fraud and eventual implosion in the early 2000s to the current uncertainties facing the banking and financial industry in accounting for exposures to derivatives, understanding a business's risks with these types of transactions is absolutely essential. For most small businesses, this issue may not seem to be all that important, but it can bite very hard and very fast for the unsuspecting.

Scrubbing the Balance Sheet Clean for Its Users

"Scrubbing" the balance sheet means exactly what it sounds like. Every balance sheet account, asset, liability, and equity, is "scrubbed" clean of all the financial and accounting dirt, garbage, grime, and grit (such as old inventory purchased 2 years ago at $10 per unit but which hasn't sold in 12 months) that tends to build up over time. The process of scrubbing the balance sheet is often completed at the end of a quarter or fiscal year end and involves applying strict internal policies and procedures to ensure that the financial information is as accurate and reliable as possible.

After walking you through a case study, we explain some of the reasons why scrubbing is important to both internal management and outside investors.

A case study: Scrubbing the balance sheet of ACME Distribution, Inc.

In this section, we walk you through a review of the assets and liabilities of a fictitious company called ACME Distribution, Inc.

Reviewing the assets

First, we scrub the company's assets as presented in its balance sheet to see if any are lying. Figure 5-3 shows the adjustments being made. This document is nothing more than the asset side of the balance sheet extracted into a separate management analysis tool (or Excel worksheet, in this case) for additional evaluation purposes.

Note: The *amount* column represents the original asset value presented in the company's balance sheet. The *adjustment* column indicates the reduction in the asset's value to properly account for the real value of the asset. The *adjusted amount* column is the new, correct asset value.

Here are some issues with this balance sheet that were adjusted:

✔ In *cash and equivalents,* a certificate of deposit for $35,000 is being used as security for a long-term company office/warehouse lease. Even though the certificate of deposit represents cash (and is an asset of the company, because if the terms of the lease are met, the cash would be returned to the company), it needs to be reclassified as a long-term asset given that its use is restricted. This is a simple asset-misclassification issue that needs to be corrected.

✔ In *trade receivables,* no allowance for potential bad debts has been accounted for. An estimate of 2 percent of outstanding trade receivables was determined based on historical data (so the adjustment here is 2 percent × $750,000, resulting in a $15,000 bad-debt reserve being required). In addition, a 3 percent reserve for sales returns was established based on the previously three months sales of $1,000,000 to account for historical return rates. (The adjustment here is 3 percent × $1,000,000 of sales over the past three months, resulting in a $30,000 reserve for sales returns.) The combination of these two reserves amounts to $45,000. The percentage reserve amounts for both bad debts and sales returns would primarily be based on evaluating the company's historical operating and sales trends by evaluating the number of adjustments to previously recorded sales that occur over a period of time after the sale.

✔ Under *current assets: inventory,* obsolete inventory of $50,000 is calculated and written off as being worthless.

✔ Shareowner advances provided in a past year were not supported by proper documentation and were determined at the time of the creation of the balance sheet to represent a dividend.

✔ Under *long-term assets: property, plant, and equipment* and *less: accumulated depreciation,* fully depreciated and disposed of equipment is removed from the accounting records.

✔ The note receivable from an affiliated operation wasn't properly reconciled for over two years, and the discrepancy wasn't supported. In the adjustment, management confirmed with the affiliated operation that a $100,000 reduction in the value should be realized based on support provided by affiliated operations, agreed to by all parties.

✔ Amortization of intellectual property wasn't recorded in the current year. The intellectual property's total value was $250,000, which management determined should be written off or amortized over a 60-month period (5 years). A full year's amortization expense amounts to one-fifth of the total, or $50,000.

✔ The *deferred income taxes* needed to be fully reserved for at the end of the year due to future uncertainty over profitability. Although the company properly calculated the value of a deferred income tax asset (which can be used to offset potential future profits and reduce taxable income), at the point and time the balance sheet was prepared, the future profitability of the company was in question, so if no future profits are generated, the deferred income tax asset has no value.

Reviewing the liabilities

Next, take a look at Figure 5-4, which lists the company's liabilities, to make sure they're all telling the truth.

ACME Distribution, Inc. — Scrubbing the Assets as of 12/31/2010			
Assets	Amount	Adjustment	Adjusted Amount
Current Assets:			
Cash and Equivalents	$265,000	$35,000	$230,000
Trade Receivables	$750,000	$45,000	$705,000
Inventory	$500,000	$50,000	$450,000
Prepaid Expenses	$75,000	$0	$75,000
Shareholder Advances	$150,000	$150,000	$0
Total Current Assets	$1,740,000	$280,000	$1,460,000
Long-Term Assets:			
Property, Plant, and Equipment	$2,240,000	$100,000	$2,140,000
Less: Accumulated Depreciation	($900,000)	($100,000)	($800,000)
Net Property, Plant, and Equipment	$1,340,000	$0	$1,340,000
Other Assets:			
Affiliate Note Receivable	$285,000	$100,000	$185,000
Intangible Assets, Net	$250,000	$50,000	$200,000
Deferred Income Taxes	$185,000	$185,000	$0
Other Long-Term Assets	$50,000	($35,000)	$85,000
Total Long-Term and Other Assets	$2,110,000	$300,000	$1,810,000
Total Assets	$3,850,000	$580,000	$3,270,000

Figure 5-3:
Adjusting
the assets
of ACME
Distribution,
Inc., by
"scrubbing."

The liabilities and equity in the balance sheet had these problems:

✔ The note payable requires $200,000 of principal be repaid each year. In addition, the amortization schedule for the capital lease obligation indicates that $50,000 of principal will be repaid over the next 12 months. So in total, $250,000 of short-term debt-repayment obligations are present and have been reclassified under the heading *current portion, long-term debt*. This term is generally used to capture all debt or loan principal payments due within the next 12 months (for loans that have been structured to be repaid over a longer period of time, such as 5 or 10 years). Although in total the liability amounts reflected in the balance sheet are correct, the classification between short-term and long-term liabilities is incorrect because readers need to understand what portion of debt is due within the coming 12 months.

✔ Accrued interest due in 90 days on the subordinated debt was not recorded during the year. The error was noted from evaluating two sources of information. First, the subordinated debt agreement stated that interest of 10 percent per year was due, but it was noted in the income statement that this interest expense was never recorded. Second, when loans, notes payable, and/or other similar types of liabilities are recorded in the balance sheet as an obligation, associated interest expense should be present in the income statement. When the income statement was evaluated, the interest expense was deemed to be unusually low (resulting in further investigation and identification of the error) and needed to be increased to properly reflect the company's real interest expense (which decreased the company's profits).

✔ The company didn't record the limited warranty is offers for product replacements. An estimate of $40,000 for warranty repairs and service is determined based on an analysis of historical product returns and repairs (for defects and malfunctions), so when combined with the accrued interest adjustment of $25,000, the total increase in accrued liabilities is $65,000.

Furthermore, both of these adjustments to accrued liabilities reduce the company's profits because interest expense was understated (as previously discussed), in addition to understated product warranty expense. According to the matching principle, if a warranty is provided, then the estimated costs associated with fulfilling the warranty must be matched in the same period as the product sales (even if the eventual cost incurred for the warranty repair occurs five months later).

Completing the scrubbing

Many small businesses (like the fictional ACME Distribution, Inc.) do not receive audited financial statements and subsequently have somewhat weak accounting policies and procedures. More times than not, our experiences in these cases have generally resulted in having an independent party, such as a CPA or financial consultant, perform rather intensive "scrubbings" of the balance sheets originally prepared by the company's internal management team or accounting firm retained to assist with basic accounting and taxation related matters.

The balance sheet in Figure 5-5 displays the final adjusted balance sheet (in the traditional format, with assets on the left side and liabilities and equity on the right side) for our fictitious company after the asset scrubbing in Figure 5-3 and liability scrubbing in Figure 5-4 are taken into consideration.

Now that the balance sheet shown in Figure 5-5 is scrubbed, you can revisit the balance sheet performance measurement tools (described in the earlier section "Using key balance sheet performance-measurement tools") to really evaluate the company's financial strength. Check out Figure 5-6 to take a look, paying particular attention to the company's financial measurements tools that changed significantly, including net working capital, the current ratio, and the debt-to-equity ratio.

ACME Distribution, Inc. — Scrubbing the Liabilities and Equity as of 12/31/2010			
Liabilities	**Amount**	**Adjustment**	**Adjusted Amount**
Current Liabilities:			
Trade Payables	$385,000	$0	$385,000
Accrued Liabilities	$150,000	($65,000)	$215,000
Line of Credit Borrowings	$350,000	$0	$350,000
Current Portion, Long-Term Debt	$0	($250,000)	$250,000
Other Current Liabilities	$75,000	$0	$75,000
Total Current Liabilities	$960,000	($315,000)	$1,276,000
Long-Term Liabilities:			
Notes Payable, Less Current	$1,000,000	$200,000	$800,000
Capital Leases, Less Current	$150,000	$50,000	$100,000
Subordinated Debt	$250,000	$0	$250,000
Total Long-Term Liabilities	$1,400,000	$250,000	$1,150,000
Total Liabilities	$2,360,000	($65,000)	$2,425,000
Equity:			
Common Equity	$100,000	$0	$100,000
Retained Earnings	$990,000	$435,000	$555,000
Current Earnings	$400,000	$210,000	$190,000
Net Equity	$1,490,000	$645,000	$845,000
Total Liabilities and Equity	$3,850,000	($105,000)	$3,270,000

Figure 5-4: Scrubbing the liabilities of ACME Distribution, Inc., to find the real story.

With this new and improved information (at least from a reliability standpoint), the scrubbed information really sheds new light on the company and its financial strength. On the unaudited performance analysis in Figure 5-2, the net working capital was $780,000, and in Figure 5-6 it's reduced to $185,000 with the current ratio also decreasing from a relatively healthy 1.81 to a very slim 1.15 (and the quick ratio decreasing to .73 from 1.06). All these measurements indicate that the company is not nearly as liquid and financially strong as first presented. Furthermore, the company's debt-to-equity ratio decreases from 1.58 to 1.00 all the way to 2.87 to 1.00, indicating a much higher degree of financial leverage (and associated operating risk).

ACME Distribution, Inc. — Scrubbed Balance Sheet as of 12/31/2010			
Assets	**Amount**	**Liabilities**	**Amount**
Current Assets:		Current Liabilities:	
Cash and Equivalents	$230,000	Trade Payables	$385,000
Trade Receivables	$705,000	Accrued Liabilities	$215,000
Inventory	$450,000	Line of Credit Borrowings	$350,000
Prepaid Expenses	$75,000	Current Portion, Long-Term Debt	$250,000
Shareholder Advances	$0	Other Current Liabilities	$75,000
Total Current Assets	$1,460,000	Total Current Liabilities	$1,275,000
Long-Term Assets:		Long-Term Liabilities:	
Property, Plant, and Equipment	$2,140,000	Notes Payable, Less Current	$800,000
Less: Accumulated Depreciation	($800,000)	Capital Leases, Less Current	$100,000
Net Property, Plant, and Equipment	$1,340,000	Subordinated Debt	$250,000
Other Assets:		Total Long-Term Liabilities	$1,150,000
Affiliate Note Receivable	$185,000	Total Liabilities	$2,425,000
Intangible Assets, Net	$200,000	Equity:	
Deferred Income Taxes	$0	Common Equity	$100,000
Other Long-Term Assets	$85,000	Retained Earnings	$555,000
Total Long-Term and Other Assets	$1,810,000	Current Earnings	$190,000
		Net Equity	$845,000
Total Assets	$3,270,000	Total Liabilities and Equity	$3,270,000

Figure 5-5:
A scrubbed-clean balance sheet for ACME Distribution, Inc.

ACME Distribution, Inc. — Scrubbed Business Performance Measurement Tools as of 12/31/2010			
Net Working Capital:	Amount	Days Sales Outstanding in Trade Receivables:	Amount
Current Assets	$1,460,000	Annual Sales	$6,750,000
Current Liabilities	$1,275,000	Average Monthly Sales	$562,500
Net Working Capital	$185,000	Trade Accounts Receivable Balance	$705,000
Current Ratio:		Average Months Outstanding in A/R	1.25
Current Assets	$1,460,000	Average Days Outstanding in A/R	37.60
Current Liabilities	$1,275,000	Days Costs of Goods Sold Outstanding in Inventory:	
Current Ratio	1.15	Annual Costs of Goods Sold	$3,500,000
Quick Ratio:		Average Monthly Costs of Goods Sold	$291,667
Current Assets	$1,460,000	Inventory Balance	$450,000
Less: Inventory	($450,000)	Average Months Inventory O/S	1.54
Less: Prepaid Expenses	($75,000)	Average Days Inventory O/S	46.29
Less: Other Current Assets	$0	Debt-to-Equity Ratio:	
Adjusted Current Assets	$935,000	Total Debt or Liabilities	$2,425,000
Current Liabilities	$1,275,000	Net Equity	$845,000
Quick Ratio	0.73	Debt-to-Equity Ratio	2.87

Figure 5-6:
More accurate performance measurement from a scrubbed balance sheet.

Aiding internal business management

The concept of CART is discussed in detail in Chapter 8, but it's also worth mentioning in this discussion of scrubbing. CART stands for complete, accurate, reliable, and timely financial information that's available to internal management and used to make business decisions. To operate a business effectively (not to mention profitably), all financial statements, including the balance sheet, *must* adhere to CART. The following real-world example highlights just how important having a CART-based balance sheet is:

Looking to avoid violating a debt covenant that required the company to remain profitable, a service company decided it would "capitalize" certain start-up costs associated with a new business unit and then amortize the costs over 60 months. (Management convinced themselves that this was appropriate accounting.) This maneuver had the effect of inflating the balance sheet with assets of limited value, which, in turn, helped the company achieve profitability (because expenditures that should have been recorded as expenses were in fact treated as assets). Of course, the bank questioned this transaction, and the company had to restate its financial statements. The outcome was not pleasant because not only did the company now show a loss and violate the lending covenant, but also the bank lost faith in management, reduced the lending facility (further restricting already tight cash availability), and basically demanded that the company find a new lending source.

Because they didn't have an accurate and reliable balance sheet, the company's internal managers had formalized growth plans assuming that financial resources would be available from the bank. When these resources were reduced and eventually eliminated, the company faced a number of very uncomfortable and unpopular decisions as damage control became the primary focal point (as opposed to being able to grow the business).

Providing confidence to outsiders

The concept of CART — making complete, accurate, reliable, and timely financial information available — applies not only to internal business management needs but also, more importantly, to outside parties. Outside parties come in all shapes, sizes, and forms and range from financing sources such as a bank, to the owners of a business undertaking estate planning and in need of a company valuation, to public and governmental agencies looking to obtain a vast range of info. The goal when providing info to outsiders, however, remains the same: Eliminate unnecessary questions and concerns by instilling confidence that financial information provided is accurate and reliable.

Most external users of business financial data are not consuming the information in an effort to help you run your business. Rather, they are reviewing it to help make a decision in their best interest (not yours). Did the company collect and remit the appropriate amount of sales and use tax? Does the company's performance warrant a loan to be extended that they'll make money on? The more confidence the outsiders have in the business financial information, the fewer questions and issues that will be raised, which translates into reduced management time and effort being expended on managing compliance-related matters.

In any economic environment, the importance of providing CART business information to external parties is essential. But since 2007, this issue has reached an entirely new level of importance based on one of the hottest terms used during this period — *transparency*. Business credibility is so critical in today's uncertain economic environment that any indication that a business is not being honest, forthright, open, and professional leads to almost-certain rejection from outsiders. When providing financial statements, reports, and forecasts to external parties, you have no room for error.

Unlocking Hidden Cash from the Balance Sheet

Data mining has become one of the most important tools and management functions businesses must perform today in order to remain competitive in the global economic marketplace. From knowing everything about your existing and target customer base to scheduling production from engineering design through final delivery to the warehouse, having access to your company's information and thoroughly understanding it is critical. This same concept applies to a company's balance sheet as well, because if business owners and managers understand the vast amount of data available, in plain sight, they can use it to unlock cash.

Though countless examples on how to use individual assets and liabilities to unlock cash from the balance sheet can be offered, we like the following four key strategies for improving cash flow: turning over current assets, investing in long-term assets, leveraging suppliers and vendors, and using notes payable, loans, and leases. In this section we explore all four methods.

Turning over current assets

The most important (and perhaps most obvious) method for improving cash flow is converting current assets into cash. This concept is related to what we discuss in "Using key balance sheet performance-measurement tools" about using business measurement tools to evaluate how quickly a company can turn over current assets, including trade receivables and inventory. The quicker these assets can be turned over, the lower balances these assets retain on the balance sheet, which in turn drives cash balances higher. For example, if a company generates $10 million a year in revenue and has an average days sales outstanding of 45 days, a balance of $1,250,000 of trade receivables is outstanding. However, if the company can reduce the days sales in trade accounts receivable to 35 days, the trade receivables balance will amount to roughly $975,000 (which translates into increased cash of $275,000).

Investing in long-term assets

When cash is plentiful, you probably have no trouble making a decision to simply purchase long-term assets such as equipment, machinery, computers, furniture, and even buildings. (After all, why would a business borrow and pay interest when it has ample cash available to support the purchase?) Of course, when cash isn't plentiful, the question is, "Why did we purchase everything for cash when we need it to operate the business? Or simply put, why didn't we set aside some cash for a rainy day and just get a loan?" And to add insult to injury, if your business then needs to secure cash from these assets (by using them as collateral for a loan or selling the assets), you have to be prepared for sticker shock if the value has decreased.

Avoid the common pitfall of consuming cash needed for short-term operating needs in long-term, illiquid assets. When investing in long-term assets, consider the purchase in the context of your business plan and make a careful and thorough evaluation of financing options available (at the point of purchase). For example, a lease for equipment may be priced by using an 8 percent per annum interest rate when the equipment is new with 90 percent of the original cost available to be financed. Compare this to attempting to secure lease financing against the same equipment (but now used, even if it's just six months old), which may cost twice as much in terms of the interest rate charged with only 50 percent of the original purchase price available to be financed. What looked expensive at the point of purchase could quickly become the bargain of the century down the road.

Leveraging your current liability friends

The suppliers and vendors a business uses on a regular basis can quickly turn into cash-generating friends if managed properly. If you need a little extra credit or require extended time to make payments, looking to suppliers and vendors to offer better terms during a period of short-term cash-flow pressure is more than reasonable. Over time, if vendor and supplier payment terms (whether stated or accepted/assumed) can be pushed out an extra week to ten days, your cash resources can be increased.

Vendors and suppliers clearly understand the importance of customer relationships. The vendors and suppliers have worked hard to secure their customers and don't want to lose them to the competition. If they have to bend a little to provide more credit, most will be receptive to strong and long-lasting relationships. Chapter 15 discusses this strategy in more detail.

The concept of leveraging liabilities goes well past the more traditional trade payables. You can improve cash balances by lengthening the time period in which cash is remitted by using accrued liabilities, appropriately structured employee compensation programs, and other current liabilities (like requiring customer deposits or prepayments). And the final perk is that a number of these strategies can be implemented without incurring any type of interest, carrying costs, and/or related expenses (as long as the requests are kept reasonable).

Using notes payable, loans, and leases appropriately

When notes, loans, and leases are used and structured appropriately, they can offer a great and efficient source of cash. However, that tip comes with a caveat: When these methods aren't used appropriately, cash resources can quickly be consumed, weakening the business's financial strength.

Businesses must understand that using debt in the form of formally structured notes payable, loans, and leases should be done only when appropriate. Chapter 10 evaluates when this type of debt is most appropriately used, but the general rule of thumb is easy to follow: Structured debt is best used when a company has positive earnings and cash flow and the debt can be secured against an actual asset. Structured debt is not well suited to and generally should not be used to support continued operating losses or to support investments in relatively high-risk business assets (such as unproven technology, patents, developing new markets, and so on). An asset should be able to generate or "throw off" enough cash to support the associated debt principal and interest payments.

In addition, notes payable, loans, and leases should always be structured to make sure a proper balance is maintained between the current portion and the long-term portion. A common problem businesses can encounter is inappropriately structuring the liability section of the balance sheet by using too much short-term debt to finance long-term assets (or vice versa). For example, a line of credit loan or lending facility established to be used to finance increases in trade receivables should not be used to purchase fixed assets.

Chapter 6

Digging Deeper into Cash Flow

· ·

In This Chapter

▶ Reviewing cash flow through financial statements

▶ Analyzing cash flow from operating activities

▶ Being on guard for accounting high jinks

· ·

This chapter explains useful techniques and tricks for analyzing cash flow. If you recall that the statement of cash flows is one of the primary three financial statements, you may anticipate, therefore, that this chapter focuses on that statement. However, analyzing cash flows requires looking beyond the statement of cash flows to the other two financial statements: the income statement and the balance sheet.

The cash flows reported in the statement of cash flows depend on the profit-making activities reported in the income statement and the changes in the assets, liabilities, and owners' equity reported in the balance sheet. Trying to analyze cash flows without the income statement and balance sheet would be like watching a ballet without music: You could see the moves of the dancers (the amounts in the statement of cash flows), but you couldn't hear the music that energizes their movements (the related amounts in the other two financial statements).

This chapter starts with what you could call the basic training or boot camp for reviewing the cash flows of a business. Then we move on to more incisive cash-flow analytical techniques that managers, lenders, and investors can use for making their business decisions and evaluations.

Tying Up Cash Flow in a Neat Bundle

Money constantly flows into and out of a business. Cash flows, as we stress in virtually every chapter of this book, pose an unending challenge to business managers because they have to be carefully managed. Business managers need to clearly understand the dynamics of cash inflows and cash outflows. Savvy business lenders and investors, who are very concerned about how well managers are controlling the cash flows of the business, also need a solid understanding of cash-flow dynamics. The trick is to connect the dots between the drivers of cash flow in the balance sheet and income statement with the cash-flow outcomes in the statement of cash flows.

Presenting financial statements for analyzing cash flows

In this book, we focus on businesses that make profit by selling products. Many businesses sell services rather than products; examples include utility companies, cellphone network providers, professional sports organizations, and financial institutions that make a profit by investing and lending. We don't have the space in this book to explore all the differences in financial statements between product-based, service-based, and other types of businesses. The variety is simply too large. But the financial statements of product-based businesses are a good example for all types of businesses.

Figures 6-1 and 6-2 introduce an example business's financial statements (borrowed from *How To Read A Financial Report* by John A. Tracy [John Wiley & Sons, Inc.]). Figure 6-1 presents the income statement for the company's most recent year, and Figure 6-2 presents its balance sheet at the end of the year. From Figure 6-1, you can tell that the business sells products. Note the relatively large cost of goods sold expense, which is the cost of products sold that's deducted from sales revenue to determine gross margin. Also, note the relatively large inventory asset account in the balance sheet. Most businesses provide services for the products they sell. The costs of these services are not in cost of goods sold expense; the costs are lodged in the broad category of selling, general, and administrative expenses.

Both financial statements are free of nuisance elements that would divert attention from analyzing cash flow. The income statement doesn't include extraordinary gains or losses, which are a dreadful distraction from the mainstream information. And, mercifully, the balance sheet doesn't include "other assets" (which can be almost anything) or long-term liability deferrals resulting from the recording of certain types of expenses. In short, the examples are financial statements that are free of distracting elements.

We don't include the statement of cash flows for the business. The company would, of course, include this statement in its financial report, but we don't need this statement for explaining and analyzing cash flows. As we mention at the start of the chapter, the cash flows of a business are driven by the sales and expense activities of a business and the changes in its assets, liabilities, and owners' equity.

Sales Revenue	$ 52,000
Cost of Goods Sold Expense	33,800
Gross Margin	$ 18,200
Selling, General, and Administrative Expenses	12,480
Depreciation Expense	785
Earnings before Interest and Income Tax	$ 4,935
Interest Expense	545
Earnings before Income Tax	$ 4,390
Income Tax Expense	1,748
Net Income	$ 2,642
Earnings Per Share	$3.30

Figure 6-1: Income statement for most recent year (amounts in thousands, except earnings per share).

TIP

Try to always keep the possibility of accounting and financial-reporting fraud in the back of your mind. In this case, you can assume that the business has not engaged in accounting or financial-reporting fraud in the preparation of its financial statements. The statements are presented according to generally accepted financial reporting standards. The company is private, so it doesn't have to report earnings per share, but the business decided to provide this vital statistic to save its shareowners the trouble of calculating it.

Cutting the balance sheet down to size

For analyzing cash flow, working with a formal, full-blown balance sheet is very clumsy. It has too many numbers to deal with, which compete for attention against the key metrics of the business. A useful technique is to condense and rearrange the balance sheet information.

The balance sheet in Figure 6-2 is in "formal dress" and conforms to generally accepted financial reporting standards. In contrast, Figure 6-3 presents the company's balance sheet in "work clothes," which is much easier to work with. Figure 6-3 also includes the two columns on the right side for reviewing the cash rules of a business. Increases in assets and decreases in liabilities and owners' equity result in a cash decrease. Conversely, decreases in assets and increases in liabilities and owners' equity result in a cash increase.

Assets

Cash		$ 3,265
Accounts Receivable		5,000
Inventory		8,450
Prepaid Expenses		960
Current Assets		$ 17,675
Property, Plant, and Equipment	$ 16,500	
Accumulated Depreciation	(4,250)	12,250
Intangible Assets		5,575
Total Assets		$ 35,500

Liabilities & Owners' Equity

Accounts Payable		$ 3,320
Accrued Expenses Payable		1,515
Income Tax Payable		165
Short-Term Notes Payable		3,125
Current Liabilities		$ 8,125
Long-Term Notes Payable		4,250
Total Liabilities		$ 12,375
Capital Stock (800,000 shares)	$ 8,125	
Retained Earnings	15,000	
Stockholders' Equity		$ 23,125
Total Liabilities & Stockholders' Equity		$ 35,500

Figure 6-2: Balance sheet at end of most recent year (amounts in thousands, except number of shares).

Figure 6-3 introduces a new item: The company's short-term operating liabilities are deducted from its short-term (current) noncash operating assets, which renders an amount called *net short-term operating position*. The acronym for this key financial metric is NSTOP, which doesn't exactly roll off the tongue, does it? But compared with other financial acronyms such as EBITDA (earnings before interest, tax, depreciation, and amortization), EPS (earnings per share), and GAAP (generally accepted accounting principles), NSTOP isn't that bad.

Assets		Cash Rules	
Cash	$3,265	–	+
Net Short-Term Operating Position*	$9,410	+	–
Property, Plant, and Equipment	$12,250	+	–
Intangible Assets	$5,575	+	–
Total Capital Deployed	$30,500		
Sources of Capital			
Debt (Short-Term and Long-Term)	$7,375	–	+
Capital Stock	$8,125	–	+
Retained Earnings	$15,000	–	+
Total Capital Available	$30,500		

Figure 6-3: Condensed balance sheet for analyzing cash flows (amounts in thousands).

* Equals [Accounts Receivable + Inventory + Prepaid Expenses] – [Accounts Payable + Accrued Expenses Payable + Income Tax Payable].

TIP

The three short-term operating liabilities (accounts payable, accrued expenses payable, and income tax payable) are deducted from the three noncash short-term operating assets (accounts receivable, inventory, and prepaid expenses). These six accounts are transformed into one net amount, which is on the asset side. Short-term operating liabilities of a business are almost never more than short-term operating assets. *Netting,* or offsetting short-term operating liabilities against their cousins on the asset side, helps you to better understand the common characteristics of these assets and liabilities and provides a clearer picture of the capitalization of the business. By netting, you can analyze the following aspects:

✔ **Behavior of accounts:** The short-term operating liabilities (accounts payable, accrued expenses payable, and income tax payable) tend to march in tandem with the short-term operating assets of a business. These liabilities are close working partners with the assets, though on different sides of the street. For example, a good fraction of the accounts payable liability balance is for recent purchases of products held in the inventory asset account. The cadence of the liabilities and assets are not in perfect unison, but by and large, the two sides dance together.

✔ **Non-interest nature of accounts:** The short-term operating liabilities are non-interest bearing liabilities that are distinct and substantially different from the short-term debt of a business. They arise from the expense activities of the business, not from borrowing money on the basis of formal loan procedures and signing a negotiable instrument (such as a promissory note payable). Short-term noncash operating assets, accounts receivable and inventories being the prime examples, do not earn interest income. The business doesn't earn investment income from inventories, for example. Both the short-term operating assets and the short-term liabilities have high turnover of activity.

✔ **Capitalization structure:** The capitalization of a business usually refers to the mix of its debt (interest-bearing liabilities) and owners' equity. You can more easily focus on the capitalization structure of a business by deducting short-term operating liabilities from short-term operating assets. In the example in Figure 6-3, for instance, the company's largest source of capital is its retained earnings, and its capital stock is larger than its total indebtedness. At a glance, you can see that the business has a conservative (low debt/high equity) capitalization structure.

One key advantage of reducing the formal balance sheet into its condensed version is that you can more easily see and focus on where the business has invested its capital. The business has $30.5 million total capital to work with, which it deploys among the assets it needs to operate. The company is holding more than $3 million cash (deposited in banks or invested in very short-term marketable investments that can be immediately converted into cash). It has $9.4 million in net short-term operating position.

The business has invested $12.25 million over the years in fixed assets. Money invested in these long-term operating assets has to be recovered through future sales revenue or by disposing of the assets. As we explain in Chapter 4, a business should set its sales prices high enough to generate enough revenue to recoup the cost of its depreciable assets. In doing so, the business recovers part of the total cost of these assets year by year.

The business has invested almost $6 million in intangible assets. The cost of intangible assets may or may not be written down annually and charged to amortization expense. In the example, the business did not record any amortization expense in the year, which is permissible if the assets didn't suffer impairment in value during the year. (The writing-down of intangible assets and recording of amortization expense is a long story that we don't have space to go into here.)

The balance of the net short-term operating position, or NSTOP, is the net cash invested by the business in its high turnover short-term assets minus its high turnover short-term liabilities. Collapsing the assets and liabilities into one net amount and leaving the details to the day-to-day management of the business simplifies the balance sheet. This technique is particularly handy in analyzing the cash flow from profit (operating activities), which we discuss in the next section.

By the way, don't confuse NSTOP with a similar term in financial analysis that you may come across, net working capital. *Net working capital* equals all current assets, including cash, minus all current liabilities, including short-term notes payable. NSTOP does not include cash in the assets and does not include short-term debt in the liabilities.

Reviewing sources and uses of cash

Figure 6-3 has two columns titled *cash rules.* Most of the rules need just a quick comment: If debt had been higher, cash would be higher. That is, if the company had borrowed more from its lenders, then its cash would have been higher, *ceteris paribus* (all other factors being equal). If the capital stock source of owners' equity had been lower, cash would have been lower. In other words, if the shareholders had put less capital in the business, the company would have a lower amount of cash to work with, holding all other assets, liabilities, and retained earnings the same.

If the business had invested less over the years in its property, plant, and equipment or in its intangible assets, then its cash balance would be higher. However, investing a smaller amount may not have provided enough production or sales capacity to carry on its current level of activities. In the example, the business paid $750,000 cash dividends to its stockholders, which decreased its retained earnings. If it had not made any cash distributions from profit to shareowners, its cash balance would have been $750,000 higher (and retained earnings would be this much higher). The shareowners may have been very dissatisfied and restive if no dividends had been paid. They might have even gone after the scalps of the president or CEO.

Zeroing in on changes in financial condition from making profit

Now for a tough question. The business reports $2,642,000 bottom-line profit, or net income for the year just ended (refer to Figure 6-1). How did the company's financial condition change as the result of earning this profit? You can answer part of this question from the income statement, which reports bottom-line profit and depreciation expense for the year.

The company's profit of $2,642,000 increased the *net worth* of the business — its assets minus its liabilities — without any additional capital investment by shareowners. To be more specific, profit increases the owners' equity account *retained earnings,* which is one of the two types of owners' equity of a business. The shareowners are $2,642,000 better off from earning profit. What about the assets of the business? Its assets also increased $2,642,000. But which assets? Did cash increase this amount?

During the year, the company's fixed assets (property, plant, and equipment) decreased $785,000. This amount of depreciation expense is reported in the company's income statement (refer to Figure 6-1). The business didn't record any amortization expense during the year, so its intangible assets were not affected by profit for the year. Therefore, the decrease stems from the remaining two assets shown in Figure 6-3 — cash and net short-term operating position. The change in cash depends on the change in the net short-term operating position (NSTOP).

Figure 6-4 presents three scenarios for the change in NSTOP during the year. If by chance NSTOP did not change during the year (not too likely, of course), cash would increase by the amount of net income plus the amount of depreciation, as you see for Scenario A in Figure 6-4. In this scenario, cash increases $3,427,000. But in almost all situations, NSTOP increases or decreases during the year. In Scenario B, NSTOP increases $500,000 during the year, and in the Scenario C, it decreases $200,000 during the year.

Figure 6-4: Changes in financial condition from earning profit for three scenarios.

	Scenario		
Assets	A	B	C
Cash	$3,427	$2,927	$3,627
Net Short-Term Operating Position	$0	$500	($200)
Property, Plant, and Equipment	($785)	($785)	($785)
Change in Total Assets	$2,642	$2,642	$2,642
Sources of Capital			
Retained Earnings	$2,642	$2,642	$2,642
Change in Total Capital	$2,642	$2,642	$2,642

Figure 6-4 is a useful template for summarizing and analyzing cash flow from operating activities. However, it requires that several assets and liabilities be collapsed into one neat number: net short-term operating position (as we explain in "Cutting the balance sheet down to size"). Unfortunately, NSTOP is not reported in financial statements. The "outsiders" who read financial statements (lenders and shareowners) don't have the time or savvy to condense the balance sheet as shown in Figure 6-3. Perhaps stock analysts go to the trouble of condensing a company's balance sheet in this way. But calculating NSTOP doesn't appear to be a commonly used technique.

On the other hand, business managers can "order up" from their accountant the condensed version shown in Figures 6-3 and 6-4 for analyzing cash flow from operating activities (instead of plowing through the more detailed formal statement of cash flows). As long as the change in NSTOP is reasonably consistent with the change in sales revenue over last year, it probably isn't worth the time and attention of top-level managers to go into details. On the other hand, if the change in NSTOP were wildly out of step with the change in sales revenue, this discrepancy would serve as a red flag to top management to look into the reasons more closely. This approach illustrates the "management by exception" principle. Managers should assiduously allocate their time to the most important problems and issues, not waste their valuable time on the trivial and unimportant.

Developing Benchmarks for Cash Flow

A large number of ratios and other benchmarks are used in analyzing profit performance and financial condition, which are reported in the income statement and balance sheet. We explain many of these yardsticks in other chapters (see Chapters 5 and 7 in particular). You may be surprised to discover that ratios and benchmarks are used sparingly for analyzing the cash flows of a business. The statement of cash flows is in a kind of no man's land for financial analysts.

Nevertheless, you do see with some regularity certain ratios and other types of interpretation in the financial analysis literature. How widely they're actually used by financial analysts is hard to tell. The handful of cash-flow ratios is nothing like the manifold ratios and benchmarks used for analyzing profit performance and financial condition. But these cash-flow ratios and comparisons are useful for understanding cash flow, and business managers would be well advised to consider using these analytics.

Comparing cash flow with sales revenue momentum

To explore how sales revenue affects cash flow, in this section we rely on the business example introduced earlier in the chapter and illustrated with the income statement (Figure 6-1), condensed balance sheet (Figure 6-3), and the changes in financial condition from earning profit (Figure 6-4). These statements constitute the point of departure for looking ahead to the coming year.

Suppose sales revenue surges 25 percent in the coming year, which is a sizable rate of growth, to be sure. (We make the increase in sales revenue fairly dramatic in order to arrest your attention and to make the impact on cash flow from operating activities sizable.) Of course, the first thing most business managers, lenders, and investors would do is look at the growth in profit at the 25 percent–higher sales level.

Profit does not move in lock step with increases and decreases in sales revenue. Or putting it another way, expenses seldom change by the same exact percent as sales revenue. Therefore, profit probably would increase more or less than 25 percent. (You can read more about profit behavior in our books *How To Manage Profit and Cash Flow* and *Small Business Financial Management Kit For Dummies* [both published by John Wiley & Sons, Inc.].)

However, to keep the business example simple, assume that its net income also increases 25 percent, from $2,642,000 to $3,302,500 in the coming year. And assume depreciation expense in the coming year is $825,000, which is higher than for the most recent year. (The company increased its investment in property, plant, and equipment, causing depreciation expense to increase.) So far, you have two of the three critical factors you need to compute cash flow from profit (operating activities) in the coming year; that is, profit and depreciation. The missing factor is the change in NSTOP (net short-term operating position).

In general terms, NSTOP should move in close relationship with the change in sales revenue. Think about it: Accounts receivable should keep at about the same percent of annual sales revenue, so if sales increase 25 percent, accounts receivable should increase about 25 percent — unless the company makes substantial changes in its customer credit terms or customers begin paying sooner or later than normal. And inventory should change at about the same percent as sales, unless the business changes its inventory policies. Likewise for accounts payable and accrued expenses payable. These two short-term operating liabilities should march in close formation with the change in sales. Therefore, assume in the example that NSTOP increased 25 percent in the coming year:

> $9,410,000 NSTOP from Figure 6-3 × 25% = $2,352,500 increase in net short-term operating position

You now have all the information you need to determine cash flow from operating activities for the coming year. The projection for the next year's cash flow is shown in Figure 6-5. Cash flow from profit (operating activities) would be $1,775,000, just a little more than half the $3,302,500 net income for the year. The gain in profit from sales growth causes a serious reduction in cash flow for the year.

In a high-growth scenario such as this one, the net short-term operating position of a business tends to grow as fast as the growth in sales. This increase puts a big dent in cash flow, at least in the short-run, as you can see in Figure 6-5. The company needs a larger investment in its net short-term operating position to support the higher sales level, and this increase has a big impact on cash flow in the year of the increase. Business managers, lenders, and investors should clearly understand the cash-flow "price" of rapid growth.

Financial report readers should compare the change in NSTOP against the change in sales revenue. The two changes should be reasonably consistent with one another. This doesn't mean that a 10 percent drop in sales, for example, should lead to an exact 10 percent decrease in NSTOP. But NSTOP should follow sales downward by roughly the same percent. A lag in the decrease in NSTOP can indicate that management doesn't yet have the sales decline under full control. For example, the business may not have reduced its inventory down to the lower sales level, which means that too much money is tied up in excessive inventory.

Assets

Cash	$1,775,000
Net Short-Term Operating Position	$2,352,500
Property, Plant, and Equipment	($825,000)
Change in Total Assets	$3,302,500

Figure 6-5: Projected cash flow for 25 percent sales revenue increase next year.

Sources of Capital

Retained Earnings	$3,302,500
Change in Total Capital	$3,302,500

Deducing the business's true state of affairs from the statement of cash flows is difficult. Lenders and shareowners would appreciate if a business explained the change in its net short-term operating position so that they could make informed decisions about the creditworthiness and investment value of the business. However, in their financial reports, companies generally don't include commentary on their cash flow. Instead, only the statement of cash flows is presented.

Using other tools for cash-flow analysis

Cash flow from operating activities is money that the business generates itself without having to go to outside sources (lenders and shareowners). A business depends on its cash flow from profit (operating activities) for several absolutely critical purposes. Without adequate cash flow from profit, a business is severely restricted and may end up in a downward spiral that is hard to reverse.

Cash flow from profit provides the seed capital for growth. It provides cash for replacing long-term operating assets as they wear out over time. It provides cash for paying dividends to shareowners. It supplements the capital the business raises from debt and equity sources. As important as it is, however, analyzing cash-flow profit is not the whole of cash-flow analysis. Business managers, lenders, and investors can use other tools to help them in interpreting the cash flow of a business.

Putting cash flow on a per share basis — or not

For public companies, earnings per share (EPS) is an extraordinarily important number. For example, the current market value of the company's capital stock shares is divided by its EPS to determine the *price/earnings ratio*. Fundamentally, EPS equals total bottom-line net income, or earnings divided by the total number of capital stock shares outstanding (in the hands of shareowners). For many corporations, the calculation of EPS is anything but simple; they may have to report not one, but two EPS amounts — the second one being *diluted earnings per share* that takes into account additional shares that the company is committed to issue in the future. Anyway, the basic idea of EPS is to put profit on a per-share basis.

You may suppose that cash flow from profit (operating activities) is also put on a per-share basis. Suppose that NSTOP increased $322,000 during the year. For this scenario, suppose that $2,642,000 net income + $785,000 depreciation – $322,000 increase in NSTOP = $3,105,000 cash flow from operating activities. The computation of cash flow per share would be as follows:

> $3,105,000 cash flow ÷ 800,000 capital stock shares (from Figure 6-2) = $3.88 cash flow per share

However useful this calculation may seem, you won't find cash flow per share in financial reports. For one thing, the rule-making body of the accounting profession has decreed that this particular financial statistic should not be reported, at least not in the formal financial statements. The worry was that financial statement readers might think that cash flow per share is a better measure of profit than the measure of profit according to accrual-basis accounting (which is in conformity with generally accepted practices and standards). The rule-making body doesn't want more than one profit measure to appear in the financial statements. Of course financial statement readers can compute cash flow per share, but they should understand that it's not a measure of profit.

Expressing cash flow as a ratio to net income, or operating income

Financial analysts track cash flow over time by measuring cash flow from operating activities as a ratio to bottom-line net income or, alternatively, to operating income before interest, income tax, and extraordinary gains and losses. The thought behind this ratio is that cash flow should be reasonably stable as a ratio to profit. An unusual dip or jump in the ratio may have a perfectly logical explanation. But abrupt changes in the ratio of cash flow to net income should be investigated.

A sudden drop in the ratio of cash flow to net income may be a red flag that raises questions about the company's accounting practices. For example, a business may be recording revenue or other income that's not being converted into cash inflow. The revenue or income may consist of a buildup in a noncash asset in the balance sheet. The actual cash conversion value of the asset compared with the value reported for the asset in the balance sheet may be contingent on future events that may or may not take place on time.

Comparing dividends to cash flow

Financial analysts measure dividends as a percent of net income to see what proportion of bottom-line profit is distributed to shareowners instead of being retained in the business. Alternatively, dividends can be expressed as a percent of cash flow from operating activities, which is logical because the payment of dividends in cash requires cash, of course. The decision about paying dividends is always "competing" with alternative demands on the cash flow of a business.

Cash flow from operating activities may be needed for building up the cash balance of a business, for increasing its net short-term operating position (NSTOP), for investing in its long-term operating assets, for reducing its debt, and for returning capital to its shareowners. The complement of the percent of cash dividends to cash flow tells you what percent was used for other purposes. If cash dividends were, say, 30 percent of its cash flow, then the business used the remaining 70 percent for the other uses. You can trace these uses of the cash flow from operating activities that was not paid out as cash dividends in the statement of cash flows. For example, the amount spent on capital expenditures for new fixed assets is in the investing activities section, and the amount used for redeeming capital stock shares is in the financing activities section.

Looking at free cash flow and other concepts and measures

Many financial analysis books, articles, and editorials discuss *free cash flow*. *Free cash flow* refers to cash flow from operating activities minus one or more "claims" against the cash flow. For example, free cash flow may be used to refer to cash flow from operating activities minus capital expenditures during the year. (Recall that capital expenditures are new investments to replace, expand, or modernize the long-term operating assets of a business.) The amount of cash flow remaining after deducting capital expenditures is thought to be "free" for any other use. Financial analysts sometimes also use other definitions of free cash flow, so you have to be careful to determine which particular meaning of free cash flow is being used.

All of a company's cash flow from operating activities is free in the sense that the business has broad discretion regarding what to do with it and is under no constraints or legal requirements (by and large) regarding how to use its cash flow. After all, the whole point of generating cash is having the freedom to do what you want to with it. So to us, frankly, free cash flow doesn't seem to be a terribly useful measure. In one scenario, however, a measure of free cash flow can be very helpful. A business may fall into dire financial straits and come under loan restrictions that kick into effect because it's in default on paying interest or principal on its loans. A major portion of its cash flow from operating activities may be controlled by the demands of its creditors. Only the remaining balance, if any, would be free for the business to use.

When a business is struggling through one or more periods of losses, especially large losses, very likely its cash flow is negative. This negative number simply means that the business's total cash outlays for expenses is more than its cash inflow from revenue. In these circumstances, carrying on operating activities burns up its cash. Financial analysts employ a rather drastic measure called the cash *burn rate* in these situations. The negative cash flow per month is calculated and divided into the company's cash balance. The result is a rough estimate of how long the business can survive before it uses up all its cash.

The struggling business may be able to raise additional capital and extend its survival time. Or the business may be able to break into the profit column without going bankrupt. Most start-up ventures go through an initial period of losses before they can move up to sustainable profit performance. During this period, the managers can use the burn rate to estimate how long they have to get the business in the black.

Another cash-flow based number gets a lot of press, though it doesn't have great importance. This number is not reported in financial reports. In fact, financial analysts have to go to some trouble to calculate it. It's called *EBITDA*, which is the acronym for *earnings before interest, tax, depreciation, and amortization*. Depreciation and amortization expenses are not deducted from revenue and income. Part of the reason is that these expenses are arbitrarily determined based on crude estimates that are under the control of the company's managers. Furthermore, neither expense involves a cash outlay during the period. Not deducting these two expenses may make some sense if the assets being depreciated and amortized did not in fact lose any value during the period. But in the large majority of cases, assets are depreciated and amortized because they do lose value over time.

By not recognizing several expenses, EBITDA is a dangerous and misleading "alter ego" of profit. In addition to ignoring real depreciation and amortization expenses when calculating profit, another problem with EBITDA is that interest and income tax are disregarded, despite certainly being expenses.

Frankly, the usefulness of EBITDA as a tool in financial analysis is of doubtful validity. However, it may have some value in special situations. But keep in mind that it's far off the beaten path of generally accepted accounting standards and practices for reporting profit performance. If you have a lot of money at stake in a particular business, this alternative profit measure may be worth calculating and comparing with the bottom-line net income in the income statement. You would then have two tracks of profit to follow over time. Divergences between the two may provide a tip-off to radical changes you should know about.

Massaging Cash-Flow Numbers

Managers of a business have certain control over the financial statements that the business's lenders and shareowners, who are on the outside looking in, do not. The president or CEO (and perhaps other managers as well) may override the regular accounting methods and practices of the business. The manager may order the company's accountant to make changes in how certain assets or liabilities are recorded instead of sticking to the company's established accounting procedures. Such intervention by managers is referred to as *massaging the numbers*. It's also described as *doctoring the numbers, management of earnings, accounting shenanigans, fiddling with the figures,* and, as authors' grandfather and father-in-law (a very successful business owner/manager in his day) used to call it, "fluffing the pillows."

However negative the connotation of the term, *massaging the numbers* should not be confused with *cooking the books,* which refers to the deliberate falsification of the company's accounting records. Cooking the books amounts to accounting fraud. Massaging the numbers can be compared to telling a white lie, whereas cooking the books is like committing perjury. Using terms from Catholicism, massaging the numbers is like committing a venial sin, whereas cooking the books is like a mortal sin. You can go to jail if convicted of cooking the books.

The main reasons for massaging the numbers are to make bottom-line profit look better and to smooth the trend of reported profits year to year. Also, a business may want to make its short-term liquidity look stronger by manipulating its reported profit. The income statement and balance sheet are not the only two financial statements subject to accounting manipulation. A business may massage some of the numbers reported in its statement of cash flows.

The statement of cash flows reports cash flow from operating activities, as we explain in Chapter 4 and in this chapter. Business lenders and investors watch this key number, so managers know the importance of this cash-flow metric. Unsurprisingly, then, many managers are tempted to manipulate cash flow to make it look better than it really was for the year.

Massaging the cash flow numbers can be done through a wee bit of *window dressing.* For example, the recording of cash receipts from customers in payment of their amounts owed to the business may be kept open for a few days after the actual close of the year. Suppose a company's year-end is December 31. But the business continues to record cash receipts for the first few days of January, as if the money had been received by December 31. This maneuver artificially inflates cash flow from operating activities for the year and decreases the accounts receivable balance reported at year-end.

You may assume that CPA auditors prevent the manipulation of its accounting numbers by a business. But keep in mind that although public corporations are legally required to have their annual financial reports regularly audited by an independent CPA firm, private businesses in general are not legally required to have audits (but many do). And although CPA auditors don't encourage or condone the practice, truth be told, auditors tolerate massaging of the numbers by a business — but only up to a certain extent. Unless the effect is judged to be material, such that it would cause substantially misleading interpretations by readers of the financial statements, the CPA auditor doesn't demand that the business correct the effects of massaging its numbers. The CPA auditor gives the business a clean opinion on its financial statements even though some numbers in the statements have been "manhandled" to some extent.

Our bottom-line advice to financial report readers is that they shouldn't simply assume that the numbers in financial statements, including the statement of cash flows, are the gospel truth. Management may have, as they say, "put a little lipstick on the pig."

Frankly, finding red flags in financial statements that may signal major massaging of the numbers is very difficult for the typical financial report reader. The only realistic option is to rely on the CPA auditor not to allow massaging of the numbers to get out of hand. In contrast, members of the company's board of directors, its lenders, and its major shareowners have closer contact with the business and they may have reasons to be suspicious about the business and its managers. They can hire a forensic accounting specialist to go in and do an investigation, but this is done only in extreme situations.

Chapter 7

Understanding Liquidity versus Available Cash

*T*he life of a business owner is often fraught with so many pitfalls, road-blocks, speed bumps, detours, and just about any other obstacle one can (or can't) think of that it's no wonder that on average, approximately 80 percent of all small businesses fail within the first five years of operations. On top of the endless series of day-to-day business-management issues that must be addressed, ranging from internal staff to customers to the endless sea of government regulations (just to name a few), a business must constantly maintain and manage an appropriate level of available capital resources to ensure that ongoing operations don't miss a beat. That is, a business must always ensure that it has enough *liquidity* — access to cash or the ability to quickly turn assets into cash — to pay the bills, cover payroll, remit taxes, repay debt, and/or be ready to cough up cash to address whatever surprise may come down the road. Due to the Great Recession, being liquid has taken on an entirely new meaning and has become an extremely powerful and effective competitive tool and advantage.

Being liquid doesn't necessarily mean the same thing as being *solvent,* or able to pay all debts. Though the two concepts are closely related and tend to be highly correlated (as higher levels of solvency typically go hand in hand with increased levels of liquidity), one does not guarantee the other. Understanding both concepts is critical when managing a business's financial affairs.

When times are good, businesses tend to have enough capital available from both internal sources and external partners (such as a bank providing a loan) because everyone wants to jump on the bandwagon and share in the success. But when the times turn, profits suddenly become losses, and internal financial pressures mount, you find that your financial partners may begin to demand that you perform before they commit. It's the ultimate Catch-22, because before your business can perform, you need them to commit. So remember, implementing proper business-planning efforts is the foundation to ensuring that your business will always remain solvent and have ample liquidity to manage through both good times and bad.

In this chapter we explore the significance of two simple concepts that help you maintain necessary levels of cash:

- ✔ Solvency and liquidity are different and have different implications.
- ✔ Liquidity doesn't equal available cash (but rather, cash is a component of liquidity).

We've yet to see a small to medium-size business *not* have a major liquidity squeeze at some point. So in this chapter we also provide tools, insights, and strategies on how to manage and improve both liquidity and solvency.

Before you dive into the material in this chapter, we want to quote the late Ted Knight in his role as the ever-popular Judge Smealls in the movie *Caddyshack:* "It's easy to grin when your ship comes in and you have the stock market beat. But the man who's worthwhile is the man who can smile when his shorts are too tight in the seat." Trust us, remembering this simple quote when dealing with liquidity and solvency squeezes can be helpful.

Defining Business Solvency and Liquidity (Hint: Not the Same Thing)

On the surface, the concept of keeping a business solvent appears to be relatively simple if you only consider that the business needs enough capital available to meet current obligations and commitments. Though this notion isn't entirely untrue, the problem is that business solvency isn't so much based in managing short-term financial issues and obligations as in how a business manages its long-term business plan in relation to ensuring that the appropriate amount and type of capital is readily available to protect its business interests.

To truly understand whether a business is solvent, the idea of liquidity must be addressed simultaneously. These two financial concepts are highly interdependent, though one doesn't guarantee the other. A business may appear to be solvent yet not have the necessary liquidity to operate another month. Or a business may appear to be insolvent yet have more than adequate resources available to support ongoing operations.

Examining a thorough explanation of each term can help your understanding:

- ✔ *Solvency* is best determined by evaluating the apparent (and we use this term with caution) financial strength of a business *at a point in time* to measure whether it has the ability to pay or cover all just debts. Are current assets greater than current liabilities? Are debt levels reasonable compared to equity levels? Are the most liquid assets, including cash and trade receivables, greater than trade payables? Answering yes to these questions suggests solvency, but it doesn't tell the complete solvency story (which can't fully be understood until available liquidity is addressed).

- ✔ *Liquidity* is best measured by evaluating all business financial information, data, facts, resources, and so on available to calculate how much total capital resources a company has, in order to determine if a business can continue to operate *over a period of time* (as opposed to just at a point in time). Has the company properly structured a lending facility to support ongoing operations? Have internal business policies, procedures, and/or strategies been changed to improve internal cash flow? Again, the desired answer to these questions is yes, but the liquidity question is dependent on far more information than just the current financial statements. Liquidity includes having access to all company plans, projections, financial disclosures, critical third party documentation and agreements, and so on.

A company's available cash does not — repeat, does not — equal a company's available liquidity. Cash represents just one component of a company's total available liquidity, which generally includes multiple other sources of, or access to, cash. For example, an unused line of credit lending may be available, which provides access to cash when needed (but with no current borrowings).

Although providing definitions of business solvency and liquidity is helpful, as the old saying goes, a picture is worth a thousand words. So to illustrate the concept of liquidity versus solvency, Figure 7-1 summarizes the financial results of a fictitious company, ACME Distribution, Inc., during the past three years.

ACME Distribution, Inc.			
Summary Balance Sheet	Year-End 12/31/2008	Year-End 12/31/2009	Year-End 12/31/2010
Current Assets:			
Cash and Equivalents	$16,674	$54,131	$230,000
Trade Receivables	$886,364	$635,870	$705,000
Inventory	$750,000	$400,000	$450,000
Other Current Assets	$100,000	$275,000	$75,000
Total Current Assets	$1,753,038	$1,365,001	$1,460,000
Long -Term Assets:			
Property, Plant, and Equipment, Net	$1,840,000	$1,590,000	$1,340,000
Other Assets	$535,000	$500,000	$470,000
Total Fixed and Other Assets	$2,375,000	$2,090,000	$1,810,000
Total Assets	$4,128,038	$3,455,001	$3,270,000
Current Liabilities:			
Trade Payables	$350,000	$500,000	$385,000
Accrued Liabilities	$225,000	$250,000	$215,000
Line of Credit Borrowings	$750,000	$300,000	$350,000
Current Portion of Long-Term Liabilities	$250,000	$250,000	$250,000
Other Current Liabilities	$90,000	$100,000	$75,000
Total Current Liabilities	$1,665,000	$1,400,000	$1,275,000
Long-Term Liabilities:			
Notes Payable, Less Current	$1,200,000	$1,000,000	$800,000
Capital Leases, Less Current	$200,000	$150,000	$100,000
Subordinated Debt	$0	$250,000	$250,000
Total Long-Term Liabilities	$1,400,000	$1,400,000	$1,150,000
Total Liabilities	$3,065,000	$2,800,000	$2,425,000
Equity:			
Common Equity	$100,000	$100,000	$100,000
Retained Earnings	$751,463	$963,038	$555,001
Current Earnings	$211,575	($408,038)	$190,000
Total Equity	$1,063,038	$655,001	$845,000
Total Liabilities and Equity	$4,128,038	$3,455,001	$3,270,000

Summary Income Statement	Year-End 12/31/2008	Year-End 12/31/2009	Year-End 12/31/2010
Revenue	$9,750,000	$7,312,500	$8,043,750
Costs of Goods Sold	$7,068,750	$5,630,625	$6,032,813
Gross Profit	$2,681,250	$1,681,875	$2,010,93 8
Gross Margin	27.50%	23.00%	25.00%
Selling, General, and Administrative Expenses	$1,950,000	$1,715,000	$1,445,000
Depreciation Expense	$250,000	$250,000	$250,000
Interest Expense	$140,000	$125,000	$125,938
Other (Income) Expenses	$0	$250,000	$0
Net Profit Before Tax	$341,250	($658,125)	$190,000
Income Tax Expense (Benefit — Carry-Back)	$129,675	($250,088)	$0
Net Profit (Loss)	$211,575	($408,038)	$190,000

Summary Cash Flow Statement	Year-End 12/31/2008	Year-End 12/31/2009	Year-End 12/31/2010
Operating Cash Flow:			
Net Income (Loss)	$211,575	($408,038)	$190,000
Depreciation Expense	$250,000	$250,000	$250,000
Net Operating Cash Flow	$461,575	($158,038)	$440,000
Working Capital:			
(Increase) Decrease in Trade Receivables	($110,000)	$250,494	($69,130)
(Increase) Decrease in Inventory	($75,000)	$350,000	($50,000)
(Increase) Decrease in Other Current Assets	$0	($175,000)	$200,000
Increase (Decrease) in Trade Payables	$50,000	$150,000	($115,000)
Increase (Decrease) in Accrued Liabilities	$25,000	$25,000	($35,000)
Increase (Decrease) in Current Debt	$100,000	($440,000)	$25,000
Net Working Capital Cash Flow	($10,000)	$160,494	($44,130)
Financing Capital:			
Equity Contributions	$0	$0	$0
Additions to Long-Term Debt	$0	$0	$0
Deletions to Long-Term Debt	($200,000)	($250,000)	($250,000)
Fixed Asset Additions	($2 50,000)	$0	$0
Change to Other Long-Term Assets	$0	$35,000	$30,000
Change to Other Long-Term Liabilities	$0	$250,000	$0
Net Financial Capital Cash Flow	($450,000)	$35,000	($220,000)
Beginning Cash	$15,099	$16,674	$54,131
Ending Cash	$16,674	$54,131	$230,000

Figure 7-1:
A comparison of unaudited financial statements.

By applying business-solvency measurement tools (discussed in detail in the next section), you can easily come to the conclusion that ACME Distribution, Inc., is basically insolvent as of 12/31/09. The company's current ratio is less than one-to-one and stands at .98 with an even worse quick ratio of .49, only $54,131 in cash is available, the company realized a loss of roughly $408,000 during the year, and only $655,000 of equity remains — compared to total liabilities of $2,800,000. All relatively poor signs (no doubt) to an external party attempting to understand the financial performance of the company and evaluate if ACME has a chance to survive.

But this point in the evaluation is where business-solvency measurements stop and business-liquidity measurements start. Business liquidity not only looks at the current financial position of a company (which looks bleak for ACME) but also captures financial information and data that aren't clearly presented in the basic financial statements. For ACME, the following additional company information would be present in footnotes documenting all material and/or critical business relationships and agreements impacting the company's operations. This info needs to be evaluated to determine if enough liquidity is available to survive:

- ACME has structured a line of credit facility that allows the company to borrow up to 80 percent of eligible trade receivables and 50 percent of inventory. As of 12/31/09, the company can borrow a total of roughly $709,000 (80 percent of $636,000 of receivables plus 50 percent of $400,000 of inventory) compared to an outstanding balance of just $300,000 (the current balance outstanding on the line of credit borrowings). These calculations reveal an additional $409,000 of borrowing capacity left to support the company's operations.

- ACME has successfully secured extended payment terms with its vendors and suppliers. The primary shareowner of the company has provided a personal guarantee (see Chapter 11 for further information on PGs) to key vendors and suppliers, which has allowed the company to move its payment terms from net 30 days to net 90 days. Vendors and suppliers accepted the personal guarantee due to the shareowner's high personal net worth. These terms can be extended to 180 days and provided an additional $85,000 of extra liquidity as of 12/31/09.

- The financial performance of ACME in 2009 was negatively impacted by the company's decision to expand its product offerings into a high-volume, low-price/profitability product line at the exact same time a severe economic recession began. Both sales and gross profits decreased as a result of a drop in demand; gross margins suffered significantly as too much of the product was purchased and had to be sold at discounted prices (to move the inventory). In addition, the company was not able to reduce its selling, general, and administrative expenses in relation to declining sales levels. By 12/31/09, the company's "sins" finally were addressed by management as the product line was discontinued. This step drove sales lower but allowed gross margin to recover from 23 to 25 percent in 2010 (as well as allowing selling, general, and administrative expenses to be reduced). However, the company had to take a one-time write-down of $250,000 (reflected in other expenses) for obsolete inventory with the product line that could not be sold. By cleaning house and refocusing the company's efforts in 2010, ACME had to sacrifice its current financial statements to position the company for future growth.

Although the company has struggled the last two years, negatively impacting its current business solvency, ACME secured additional capital to ensure that it has enough liquidity to survive and prosper in the coming years. Also, you may note that no income tax expense or benefit is present in 2010. The reason for this is that the company had net operating loss carry-forwards from previous years to offset tax liabilities.

Applying Business-Solvency and Liquidity Measurement Tools

The previous section jumped ahead a little bit in terms of presenting Figure 7-1 and applying both liquidity and business-solvency measurement tools so that you could see the big picture first. In this section, we delve into a more complete examination of standard business solvency and liquidity measurement tools.

Measuring and monitoring solvency

Business-solvency measurements tend to evaluate data as of a point in time (for instance, the fiscal year-end for ACME). This data is then subjected to numerous analyses to evaluate how well a company is performing and how strong it is financially (including measuring the businesses solvency). Figure 7-2 presents basic business-solvency measurement tools that all business executives should clearly understand.

ACME Distribution, Inc.			
Ratio	Year-End 12/31/2008	Year-End 12/31/2009	Year-End 12/31/2010
Net Working Capital:			
Total Current Assets	$1,753,038	$1,365,001	$1,460,000
Total Current Liabilities	$1,665,000	$1,400,000	$1,275,000
Net Working Capital	$88,038	($34,999)	$185,000
Current Ratio:			
Total Current Assets	$1,753,038	$1,365,001	$1,460,000
Total Current Liabilities	$1,665,000	$1,400,000	$1,275,000
Current Ratio	1.05	0.98	1.15
Quick or Acid-Test Ratio:			
Total Current Assets	$1,753,038	$1,365,001	$1,460,000
Less: Inventory and Other Current Assets	$850,000	$675,000	$525,000
Net Current Assets	$903,038	$690,001	$935,000
Current Liabilities	$1,665,000	$1,400,000	$1,275,000
Quick or Acid-Test Ratio	0.54	0.49	0.73
Debt-to-Equity Ratio:			
Total Liabilities	$3,065,000	$2,800,000	$2,425,000
Total Equity	$1,063,038	$655,001	$845,000
Debt-to-Equity Ratio	2.88	4.27	2.87
Days Sales O/S in Trade Receivables:			
Total Trade Receivables	$886,364	$635,870	$705,000
Average Monthly Sales	$812,500	$609,375	$670,313
Days Sales O/S in Trade Receivables	32.73	31.30	31.55
Days Costs of Goods Sold O/S in Inventory:			
Total Inventory	$750,000	$400,000	$450,000
Average Monthly Costs of Sales	$589,063	$469,219	$502,734
Days Costs of Goods Sold O/S in Inventory	38.20	25.57	26.85
Debt Service Coverage Ratio:			
Net Income (Loss)	$211,575	($408,038)	$190,000
Interest Expense	$140,000	$125,000	$125,938
Depreciation Expense	$250,000	$250,000	$250,000
Adjusted Debt Service Cash Flow	$601,575	($33,038)	$565,938
Interest Expense	$140,000	$125,000	$125,938
Note Payable Principal Payments Due, 1 Yr.	$250,000	$250,000	$250,000
Current Balance of Line of Credit, Due in 2 Yrs.	$375,000	$150,000	$175,000
Total Debt Service Payments, 1 Yr.	$765,000	$525,000	$550,938
Debt Service Coverage Ratio	0.79	(0.06)	1.03

Figure 7-2:
Business-
solvency
ratio
analysis.

The list of business solvency measurements presented in the figure is by no means complete, as the boys on Wall Street would attest (as they have a much larger arsenal of measurements available). However, the following measurements represent the basics in understanding business solvency:

- **Net working capital:** Total current assets less total current liabilities equals the *net working capital* of a business. Generally speaking, businesses want a positive figure.

- **Current ratio:** Total current assets divided by total current liabilities equals a company's *current ratio*. A ratio of greater than one-to-one is desirable.

- **Quick or acid-test ratio:** Total current assets is reduced by inventory and other current assets (such as prepaid expenses and deposits) and then divided by total current liabilities to produce the *quick* or *acid-test ratio*. The higher the ratio, the better, but having a ratio of less than one-to-one is common, especially for companies with significant levels of inventory.

- **Debt-to-equity ratio:** Total debt (current and long term) divided by the total equity of the company equals the *debt-to-equity ratio*. Higher ratios indicate that the company has more financial leverage, which translates into more risk being present. (Check out the final section of this chapter for a discussion on financial leverage.)

- **Days sales outstanding in trade accounts receivable:** Trade receivables divided by average monthly sales multiplied by 30 days produces the *days sale outstanding in trade accounts receivable* figure. Lower numbers with this calculation are usually positive because they indicate that a company is doing a good job of managing this asset and not consuming excess capital. *Note:* Companies that are growing rapidly or that have significant seasonal sales need to use an average monthly sales figure that's more representative of more recent business activity.

- **Days costs of goods sold outstanding in inventory:** Inventory divided by average monthly costs of goods sold multiplied by 30 days produces the *days costs of goods sold outstanding in inventory* figure. Lower numbers indicate a good job of managing this asset and not consuming excess capital. *Note:* Again, companies that are growing rapidly or that have significant seasonal sales need to use an average monthly costs of sales figure that's more representative of more recent business activity.

- **Debt service coverage ratio:** Interest and depreciation expense are added back to the net income (or loss) of a company, which is then divided by the current debt service (defined as interest expense plus the current portion of long-term debt plus any outstanding balance with a current line of credit facility) to produce the *debt service coverage ratio*. A ratio of greater than one-to-one is desirable because it indicates that a company generates enough free cash flow to cover its debt service.

Keeping tabs on liquidity

Unlike solvency measurements, which look at a certain point in time, business liquidity measurements are meant to evaluate a business's total liquidity by using both data as presented at a point in time as well as resources available to a business (but not necessarily presented in the basic financial statements) either today or in the future. The following three liquidity measurement tools are illustrated in Figure 7-3:

- ✔ **Available current working capital:** Add the current net working capital (defined in the preceding section) to available capital that can be accessed during the next 12 months. Then adjust the figure to account for any other factors that impact the company's liquidity (such as extended vendor terms), and the result is the *available current working capital.*

  In the example provided in Figure 7-3, two points are important. First, in 2008, the available borrowing capacity was reduced to account for $250,000 of obsolete inventory. In this example, the bank became concerned about the value of this inventory and decided to eliminate it from the company's ability to borrow. Second, in 2009, $85,000 was added back to account for the fact that the company was able to secure extended payment terms from vendors for the coming year. In effect, the company secured a "permanent" source of capital for the year from the vendors providing extended terms (and thus providing more capital to operate the business).

- ✔ **Cash burn rate:** This rate calculates the average negative cash flow (defined as net income or loss plus depreciation and other noncash expenses) the company is experiencing on a periodic basis (usually monthly). Burn rates represent key data points for investors attempting to understand how long it takes until a company becomes cash-flow positive. This indicator then drives how much capital is needed to support the company during the negative cash burn periods.

  For ACME, the company's cash burn rate was approximately $13,000 a month in 2009 (the worst performing year over the past three).

- ✔ **Liquidity availability analysis:** Calculating the potential available liquidity that can be tapped from company assets and comparing it to the total current outstanding debt (secured with the assets) lets you evaluate if any "untapped" sources of capital are available on the balance sheet.

  In the example provided for ACME in Figure 7-3, roughly $439,000 of potential and actual liquidity is available (even though the solvency measurements paint a much more difficult situation). (See the second highlighted line.)

ACME Distribution, Inc.

Ratio	Year -End 12/31/2008	Year -End 12/31/2009	Year -End 12/31/2010
Available Current Liquidity:			
Net Working Capital	$88,038	($34,999)	$185,000
Available Borrowing Capacity	$209,091	$408,696	$439, 000
Extended Vendor Terms Benefit	$0	$85,000	$85,000
Available Current Liquidity	$297,129	$458,696	$709,000
Cash Burn Rate:			
Net Income (Loss)	$211,575	($408,038)	$190,000
Depreciation Expense	$250,000	$250,000	$250,000
Monthly Cash Burn Rate	$38,465	($13,170)	$36,667
Liquidity Availability Analysis:			
Trade Receivables	$886,364	$635,870	$705,000
Borrowing Rate	80%	80%	80%
Available Liquidity	$709,091	$508,696	$564,000
Inventory, Net of Obsolete Items	$50 0,000	$400,000	$450,000
Borrowing Rate	50%	50%	50%
Available Liquidity	$250,000	$200,000	$225,000
Total Available Liquidity	$959,091	$708,696	$789,000
Current Borrowings — Line of Credit	$750,000	$300,000	$350,000
Net Available Liquidity	$209,091	$408,696	$439,000
Total Potential and Actual Available Liquidity	$959,091	$708,696	$789,000
Total Borrowings, Line of Credit	$750,000	$300,000	$350,000
Net Potential and Actual Available Liquidity	$209,091	$408,696	$439,000
Current Borrowing Utilization Rate	78%	42%	44%
Available Borrowing Capacity Rate	22%	58%	56%

Figure 7-3:
Business
liquidity
ratio
analysis.

These three liquidity measurement tools represent just a small sample of the entire list of potential liquidity measurements, tools, and analyses available. Unlike the business-solvency measurements noted in the preceding section, liquidity measurements tend to be customized for specific company and industry issues (in order to properly manage and understand liquidity at any point in time). The key concept, however, is the same for both types of measures: You must always have a clear understanding of what capital and liquidity is available to your company (at any time) in order to properly manage your business interests.

Looking at the actual results of ACME, the company's strongest year over the period (as measured by profitability) for the period of 2008 through 2010 was 2008, during which it earned a net pre-tax profit of $341,000, yet as of 12/31/08, the company had the least amount of liquidity ($297,000 compared to $709,000 at 12/31/10; see the first highlighted row). Now, this added liquidity didn't come without a price — the $85,000 of extended vendor terms required a personal guarantee, and $250,000 of subordinated debt (from the owners) was secured to strengthen the balance sheet. But the important fact is that the company was able to secure ample amounts of liquidity in 2010 to operate the business and hopefully grow in future years.

Understanding both business-solvency and liquidity measurements concepts is important when managing your business. Solvency measurements by themselves don't often tell a company's entire story or indicate whether it has the ability to survive as a going concern.

The fictitious financial performance provided for ACME in Figures 7-1 through 7-3 presents a company that appears to be insolvent. But upon further review of the company's operations (information derived from analyzing the footnotes attached to the financial statements and from undertaking management inquiries), we find that the company has additional liquidity to operate the business and has implemented operational changes to support its return to profitability. Conversely, we could have just as easily presented a company that's highly profitable with strong solvency measurements but that, as a result of poor planning, has run out of cash (with no borrowing facilities structured to support continued growth) and has pushed its vendors and suppliers to the limit. Due to the lack of understanding of liquidity and poor planning, this company could even be at greater risk of failing (as the vendors and suppliers may cut off the flow of products to sell, thus causing a chain reaction of events causing the company to implode). This scenario is discussed in more detail in "Avoiding Liquidity Traps" later in this chapter.

Finding out where cash fits into liquidity equation

This book is focused on managing cash, but we haven't yet addressed where cash fits into the discussion on business solvency and liquidity. Well, the answer is easy — cash represents just one component of business-solvency measurements and liquidity calculations. As discussed in the previous sections, cash is one of the four primary components comprising working capital (the others are trade receivables, inventory, and other current assets), and working capital represents a critical element in measuring business solvency. Likewise, net working capital (including cash) represents a critical element of calculating available liquidity.

Unlike a company such as Apple, which sits on billions of dollars of cash with basically no liabilities and is constantly trying to figure out what to do with all its riches, the cash component of working capital is usually relatively small (20 percent or less of current assets) for most businesses. It's kept small by numerous factors, ranging from lack of access to anywhere near the capital markets large corporations have, to the need to constantly deploy cash in the business to finance growth. As such, simply focusing on only a company's available cash balance to evaluate its financial strength and ability to support continued operations is generally very misleading and can quickly lead to incorrect conclusions. Cash is king, no doubt about it, but having ample liquidity to support your business is, as they say, priceless.

Avoiding Liquidity Traps

After you know the basics of business liquidity and solvency, why it is important, and how to measure it (all discussed in the previous sections), your attention can turn to how businesses tend to get into trouble and unintentionally find themselves in liquidity traps. Liquidity traps come in a variety of shapes, sizes, and forms and to a certain extent result from business- or industry-specific factors. However, when the liquidity traps are viewed from a generalized perspective, the primary liquidity traps are typically in the following areas: tying up cash in company assets, using debt inappropriately, assuming that growth is always good, and assuming that shrinking is " always bad.

As we discuss in the following sections, the volume and complexity of liquidity traps are extensive and vary from business to business. You would be amazed at how many liquidity traps can occur and how quickly they can consume your business. One day everything is fine, and then 180 days later the market's turned, new product releases have been delayed, sales have softened, and the bank is all over you. (The words of Cousin Eddie in the movie *Vacation* come to mind: "The bank's been after me like flies on a rib roast.") To be quite honest, having to manage a liquidity trap is more a matter of *when* than *if,* so the better prepared you are to deal with liquidity traps (and understand the primary causes of the liquidity traps), the better you will be at managing a problem when it arises.

Having access to capital (whether debt or equity) represents one of the most important elements of executing a business plan, especially when a business is turning the corner and is ready to grow rapidly, because this is the point when the demand for capital is the greatest. As one of our business mentors says, "I don't need access to capital going into a recession or downturn, but I sure as heck need access to capital as I come out of a recession and begin to grow quickly again." Not managing the liquidity traps discussed in the following sections can prevent you from positioning a business to pursue new market opportunities. And this blunder often leads to one of the largest losses a company will ever realize (but never see): lost market opportunity.

Tying up cash in company assets

A company needs assets on which to execute its business plan and generate revenue. Some assets are highly liquid and represent attractive vehicles through which to secure financing (for example, trade accounts receivable that a bank may use as collateral to extend a loan or new equipment that a leasing company may use as collateral to provide a long-term lease).

Other assets, however, are not nearly as attractive to a lender, including certain inventory, prepaid expenses, intangible assets, and the like. The main reason for this lack of interest is the difficulty the lender will face when liquidating the asset (and repay the loan) in the event the company doesn't survive. The more liquidation value the asset has, the higher lenders' interest is in providing financing. The following list of asset-investment liquidity traps are examples of when "good assets go bad":

- ✔ **Trade receivables:** Trade receivables are usually very liquid assets that can be utilized to secure financing. Certain trade receivables, however, are not as attractive to financing sources. For example, trade receivables that are 90 days past due often are excluded by a lender from being able to borrow against because the age of the receivable indicates that the customers are having trouble paying their bills. Whether or not this is the case, the lender usually assumes the worst and excludes the trade receivable.

  In addition to old trade accounts receivable, other receivables that can create problems include receivables generated from foreign customers, governmental entities, and related parties/entities. Also (and as strange as this may sound), receivable concentration issues may produce problems if too many of your company's trade receivables are centered in too few accounts. In this case the lender gets nervous because if one big customer tanks, it may take the entire company down.

  Make sure that you have a complete understanding of what comprises your trade accounts receivable balance to have a clear understanding of what is available to borrow against at any point in time. Though the balance sheet may state that your company has $1,000,000 (of which the company can borrow 80 percent, or $800,000), you may find that $400,000 of the receivables are *ineligible* (meaning the company can't borrow against them). In this case, only $600,000 of good receivables are left to borrow against, meaning only $480,000 of financing is available.

- ✔ **Inventory:** You may think that inventory is a sound asset on which to secure financing because if a company's product has a readily available market, there should be no problem liquidating the products in case the worst should happen. Right? Nope. Financing sources tend to be very nervous and skittish about lending against inventory, because if the worst happens, taking possession of the inventory and attempting to sell or liquidate it lead to all kinds of problems. Financing sources are just not prepared to handle this function.

  When all potential liquidation factors are considered with inventory, including identifying and disposing of obsolete items, having to pay a liquidator to sell the inventory, watching the market hammer the value of the inventory as it becomes available (that is, the going-out-of-business sale), and so on, the lender will be lucky to receive 40 to 50 percent on the dollar. Hence, lenders tend to shy away from extending loans against inventory, and when they do extend loans, lending rates are usually well below 50 percent.

Besides potentially draining a business's liquidity, tying up cash in excessive inventory can also create problems on numerous other fronts.

- For every dollar of inventory increase, a lending source may only provide 40 percent of the cash necessary to support the added investment (leaving 60 percent to be supported by internal resources). So cash that could be invested in other business operations, such as research and development, is left sitting in inventory.

- The risk of inventory obsolescence increases because the slower the inventory moves, the older it becomes, which generally forces the company into taking inventory write-off "hits" on the financial statements. As most business owners know, in today's rapidly changing market, inventory can become obsolete in as little as three months.

- Excessive inventory is expensive to maintain because it must be stored, insured, tracked, protected from theft, and so on. Quite often, inventory maintenance expenses can run up to 10 percent of the inventory's cost on an annual basis.

✔ **Property, equipment, and other fixed assets:** The concept of consuming liquidity in fixed assets is similar to purchasing a new car (but even worse). The day you purchase a new car and drive it off the lot, it may lose up to 25 percent of its value. For fixed assets such as new equipment, computers, furniture, and fixtures, within 90 days of purchase the value is based on a "used" status (and you will be lucky to get 50 percent on the dollar). Compounding this problem is that if you do need to secure financing against the fixed assets (which are now used), the financing will be expensive (that is, have higher interest rates) compared to acquiring the fixed assets when new.

The time to obtain financing with fixed assets is at the point of purchase. At this point, the asset value is the highest and the most financing sources are available to obtain competitive pricing and terms. When the equipment becomes used, the market for financing sources shrinks and becomes much more expensive.

Using debt inappropriately

The second major liquidity trap is at its core centered in not keeping your balance sheet in balance. The imbalance we're referring to comes from using short-term debt, such as a line of credit structured to support trade accounts receivable, to finance a purchase of a long-term asset. The following example explains how this issue can create significant problems for a company.

A company had structured a line of credit financing agreement or loan where it could borrow up to 80 percent of eligible or qualified receivables. The company was growing quickly and had increased its trade accounts receivable to roughly $2 million in total, of which 90 percent were eligible to borrow against. Altogether, the company borrowed $1.4 million, which was within the financing-agreements limit ($2 million of total accounts receivable, of which $200,000 were ineligible to borrow against, leaving a net borrowing base balance of $1.8 million, producing a total borrowing capacity of $1.44 million). Of the $1.4 million, $400,000 was used to purchase fixed assets and $1 million was used to support the trade accounts receivable.

Within six months, the company's trade accounts receivable decreased to $1.5 million, while at the same time the ineligible percent increased to 20 percent (as a result of certain trade accounts receivable becoming 90 days past due). This change reduced the company's ability to borrow to $960,000 ($1.5 million of trade accounts receivable times 80 percent eligible times 80 percent advance rate). Unfortunately, the company used the cash generated from the $500,000 decrease in trade accounts receivable to reduce trade payables and cover operating losses (as well as pay down the loan). The company was only able to pay down the loan by $200,000, leaving an outstanding balance of $1.2 million against an available borrowing of $960,000. Needless to say, the financing source requested the company "cure" this over-advanced position, but the company could not (leading to a very interesting round of discussions and the financing source placing additional restrictions on the company). By not properly financing the fixed-asset purchase, the company fell into a very common and painful liquidity trap.

The exact opposite problem can happen as well, if, for instance, a loan payable with a repayment term of three years is used to support a current asset (such as trade accounts receivable). Although the asset (trade accounts receivable) may be growing as a result of increased sales, the debt is being reduced over a three-year period. Just when the company needs capital to finance growth, capital is flowing out of the organization to repay debt.

A proper balance of capital to asset type must be maintained to better manage the balance sheet. The following three very simple rules guide matching capital or financing sources with asset investments:

  ✔ **Finance current assets with current debt.** Current assets, such as trade accounts receivable or inventory, should be financed with current debt, such as trade vendors or suppliers and a properly structured lending facility.

✔ **Match the cash-flow stream to the financing stream.** The general concept here is that a fixed asset produces earnings or cash flow over a period of greater than one year. Therefore, fixed assets, such as equipment, furniture, computers, and technology, should be financed with longer-term debt, such as term notes payable (having, for example, a five-year repayment period) or operating or capital leases.

✔ **Use debt financing sources to provide capital for tangible assets and use equity financing for losses or "soft" assets.** Assets that are considered "soft" (including intangibles such as patents, trademarks, certain investments, and prepaid expenses) and company net losses need to be supported from equity capital sources, including the internal earnings of the company.

Assuming that business growth is always good

Now we come to one of the most common, but least understood, liquidity traps:

> **Congratulations on your business's rapid revenue growth, but remember: Growth does not always translate into business success!**

Remember that rapidly growing businesses require significant amounts of capital to support ongoing operations (because the balance sheet tends to expand relatively quickly). As revenue (and hopefully profitability) levels grow, so do assets and the need to finance the assets. Further compounding this event is the additional problem that rapidly growing companies run into with getting caught up in the seemingly endless new-market opportunities being presented and the need to "invest" earnings from profitable operations into the expansion of the new operations (which tend to lose money during the start-up phase). This strategy, if properly managed, can be very effective as long as management keeps a keen eye on the distribution of earnings between supporting new operations versus strengthening the balance sheet.

No set rule dictates how much of your earnings should be used to reinvest in new operations versus strengthening the balance sheet. The real key lies in the ability to keep your debt-to-equity ratio (refer to "Measuring and monitoring solvency," earlier in this chapter) manageable so that if the company hits a speed-bump or pothole, resources are available to see you through the difficult times. One thing is for sure, however: Pushing your company to the limit by leveraging every asset (with debt financing) and reinvesting internal earnings in new operations (that lose money during start-up) is a recipe for failure. Businesses must constantly manage the growth versus available capital trade-off issue to ensure that its interests are not exposed to unnecessary risks that quite often carry extremely expensive outcomes.

In the business world, you may hear the saying that someone is "growing himself out of business." This expression means that rapidly growing businesses may fail as a result of running out of liquid assets (cash or access to cash) if a proper plan has not been developed to support the growth. Business assets such as trade receivables, inventory, and equipment can increase so quickly in a rapidly expanding business that before you know it, all the company's cash has been consumed and vendors and suppliers have begun to cut off credit (effectively killing the business).

Assuming that a shrinking business always represents trouble

Another very common but little-understood liquidity event represents the alter ego of a rapidly growing business.

> **Wow, your business revenue levels have decreased during the year, resulting in a small loss, so you must be in financial distress. Nope! Most businesses, at one point or another, experience losses that should not be interpreted as a failure.**

A rapidly growing business usually is accompanied by an expanding balance sheet because both assets and liabilities tend to increase (with assets generally increasing faster than liabilities, thus consuming cash). The opposite occurs when a business shrinks via decreasing revenue, closing a division, selling a business unit, closing stores, and/or undertaking similar types of transactions. When a company shrinks, it usually is the result of either a poor economic environment (case in point, the period from 2008 through 2010) or a management decision to exit underperforming markets and/or focus on the most profitable operations. The second scenario carries the following dual benefits:

✔ First, even though revenue levels may be decreasing, the company's operating performance generally improves as expenses are eliminated and management focuses on more lucrative opportunities with stronger profit potential. These changes have the effect of improving internal operating results, profits, and hopefully cash flows to improve liquidity and strengthen the balance sheet.

✔ Second, and of greater assistance to improving business liquidity, downsizing a business has the effect of contracting the balance sheet at both the asset and liability levels. So as long as the asset contraction is greater than the liability contraction, cash is freed up, which should (if properly managed) improve business liquidity levels.

Obviously, in a number of situations, shrinking revenue levels do represent a significant problem, especially if expenses can't be reduced fast enough in relation to lower revenue levels, resulting in accumulating losses that may eventually lead to severe financial distress. However, jumping to the conclusion that a decrease in a company's top line must mean financial troubles is inappropriate. Management may be very well ahead of the game and actually undertaking a plan to improve the financial strength of the business.

Discovering Untapped Sources of Liquidity

If you've read all the previous sections in this chapter, you now understand what liquidity is, why it's so valuable, how to measure it, and where the traps are. But you may be thinking, "Great, but to be quite honest, Authors, your chapter is a little too late. I've run out of cash, have no more ability to borrow, and my suppliers are breathing down my neck." Well, now the real fun begins. It's now up to the executive management team to identify sources of capital to work through the troubled times. The purpose of this section is to identify potential capital sources (to provide liquidity) that can assist your business in times of need.

Liquidating assets

The first option is relatively straightforward but easier said than done. Liquidating assets is often proposed by management as a quick and easy method to raise capital. This practice makes sense because if a company has unneeded or underutilized assets, selling them can help ease a cash crunch. Following are some examples of prime assets that can be liquidated:

✔ **Old trade accounts receivable:** Certain older, problematic trade accounts receivable can possibly be sold to collection companies to secure cash. Various companies specialize in this area, with some of the largest and most successful operations purchasing past-due consumer debt such as credit cards, auto loans, and so on (which, needless to say, has been very big business since 2008). But be prepared to take a significant discount when selling receivables, because these operations don't come cheap.

- ✔ **Slow-moving or obsolete inventory:** Slow-moving and obsolete inventory is often targeted for liquidation for two reasons. First, it's tying up cash that could be used for other business purposes. Second, managing and maintaining inventory (that is, paying rent to store it, providing insurance coverage, and other necessary measures) is expensive, reaching up to 10 percent or more of the inventory value on an annual basis. Bulk buyers of obsolete or slow-moving inventory have developed into a large industry (as evidenced by Overstock.com) over the past decade, with specialty business models developed for different types of products.

- ✔ **Property, equipment, furniture, and so on:** There's probably not a company operating that doesn't have some type of property, equipment, or furniture that's not being used and can possibly be turned into cash. The issue with this asset class is not supply or availability but rather price, demand, and obsolescence (ever try to sell a computer that's three years old?). That is, since 2007, supply has been excessive and demand limited, which has driven the value of this asset class very low. However, you may be surprised by what businesses are willing to purchase; an entire cottage industry has developed that does nothing but facilitate the liquidation of business fixed assets.

- ✔ **Other assets:** Depending on a company's operating situation, various other assets may be available for sale, including any intellectual property the company may own (such as patents or trademarks), cash value that has built in certain life insurance policies, securities or investments held, and others. The pros and cons of liquidating each asset should be weighed prior to determining the feasibility of selling the assets (especially related to intellectual property).

Liquidating assets does represent a viable alternative, but be careful of the following pitfalls with this strategy:

- ✔ **Values received:** If you plan on moving older, slow-moving inventory in bulk or selling some old equipment that's not being used, be prepared to take some significant value hits (well below cost). Although the cash received is great, the losses taken will have to be explained (to investors, lending sources, and others).

- ✔ **Collateral support:** Remember that certain assets represent collateral for loans extended to the company. If you liquidate the assets, not only may you be violating your loan agreement, but you may also be reducing your ability to borrow (as the asset base is reduced, so is the borrowing capacity).

✔ **Future growth:** Liquidating assets that may not be needed in the short term but will be needed to support longer-term growth objectives can be very expensive. This cost is especially high in the event crucial intellectual property is sold that represents a critical component of the business's ability to generate future sales and profit.

✔ **Management time:** Liquidating assets often takes much more time and effort than anticipated, which means that the parties responsible for this function are being distracted from their regular duties.

Leveraging assets

As an alternative to selling assets, another option is to leverage the inherent value in certain assets to generate cash. The biotechnology industry provides a classic example. Biotechnology companies in an early development stage often retain the rights to very promising research but lack the current capital and/or access to funds to continue to support the development through to selling the final product to consumers. These companies look to larger, well-established pharmaceutical organizations to structure a licensing agreement whereby in exchange for an upfront payment (and potentially future milestone payments), the pharmaceutical organization secures an exclusive right to market the drug per terms and conditions established (with future revenue split).

A company that leases prime real estate but doesn't currently use all the space (and tenant improvements associated with the space) can be another good example of leveraging an asset. In order to reduce overhead costs and free up cash, a portion of the space can be subleased to another company. An underutilized asset (unused space) then generates positive cash flow.

Countless other opportunities and situations exist to leverage assets. In most cases, the leveraged asset tends to be intangible in nature. And in almost any asset-leveraging transaction, multiple parties are involved, which makes execution more complicated and time consuming. Therefore, you must be creative and flexible and have the ability to think outside the box when structuring deals to leverage assets for cash.

When pursuing a strategy of leveraging assets, always remember to secure proper professional counsel and support to structure the agreements. This counsel normally includes both financial and legal experts in addition to subject-matter experts when needed. The damage associated with not structuring a deal correctly can be extremely expensive.

A company that designs, manufactures, and regionally retails fine jewelry is looking to structure a design agreement with a large product supplier to address the needs and resources of both parties. The product supplier gets access to a high-quality designer with ample resources to produce a private-label product for sale in non-overlapping and international markets (thus not having to invest capital in a design studio, which would take both substantial time and money). The jewelry designer generates an upfront fee to produce the initial designs by leveraging its previous investments made in the company's internal design studio capabilities and equipment (with no additional cost outlays) and tap years of jewelry design experience and knowledge (or trade secrets). Furthermore, the jewelry designer has the ability to generate future "evergreen" revenue streams from receiving a royalty on product sales it designed.

Relying on available lending sources

Your company's primary lending sources, such as banks, asset-based lenders, leasing companies, and the like, represent a potential source of quick capital if needed. The key in approaching these sources is to have solid information available for review and a clear action plan on how the additional capital will be repaid (in a reasonable time frame). But of course, as the old saying goes, "There's no such thing as a free lunch," so be prepared to pay when requesting changes to lending agreements.

In general, because these groups have a vested interest in seeing your business survive, you should be able to leverage the relationship. The following three examples show how capital can be squeezed from these sources to obtain added liquidity:

- **Loan advance rates:** Lenders base your borrowing capacity on the value of the asset the loan is secured with. For example, banks commonly advance 80 percent on eligible trade accounts receivable. During a particularly tight period (for example, your business is dealing with increased seasonal demand), you may be able to get the lender to advance 85 to 90 percent of the eligible receivables (to free up some capital). If your bank doesn't want to work with you, then an asset-based lender may be a better financial partner. As covered in Chapter 9, asset-based lenders offer more-aggressive loan facilities in exchange for higher rates and tighter reporting (to compensate for the higher risk present). Asset-based lenders understand the importance of having access to capital in relation to businesses operating in challenging times.

- **Asset sale lease-back:** Asset sales may represent a source of quick capital to your business but come with a number of potential problems. You may want to consider executing an asset sale lease-back in which you sell the asset to a leasing company that in turn immediately leases it back to you. You achieve your goal of freeing up short-term liquidity, and the leasing company doesn't have to worry about finding a new lessee for the asset.

Similar to working with an asset-based lender, leasing companies that support these types of transactions are more expensive.

✔ **Restructure notes payable:** You may want to consider restructuring any long-term notes payable with the lender to lengthen the repayment period (thus reducing the current monthly payment), move it to an interest-only note for a short period (like 12 months), stagger principal payments to be lower in early years and higher in later years, or request a reduction in the fees and interest rates being charged. The goal is to reduce the capital outflow with the note agreement to better match it with the ability for your company to generate internal cash flows (to service the debt).

If you find that your company has to work with financing sources that aren't traditional banks or low-risk leasing companies, you can expect to be charged higher interest rates and more fees. Although there are no set rules, on average you can expect to pay at least 3 to 6 percent more in overall interest costs. If the bank is charging prime rate plus 1 percent, then you can expect to pay at least prime rate plus 4 percent. In addition, be prepared to incur additional costs for asset appraisals, collateral examinations, and administrative fees, which can quickly increase your borrowing rate to the low teens (a range that is not uncommon for risk-based financing sources).

With that higher cost in mind, if the difference between your business making money and losing money is 4 percentage points, then you probably have deeper rooted problems present than just a short-term liquidity squeeze. Access to the capital is the key, so paying 4 percent more (on the capital) should be far cheaper than the alternative, which includes lost business growth opportunities or, worse yet, having the business fail.

Approaching creditors, customers, and other partners

Your vendors, suppliers, and yes, even your customers can be "tapped" from time to time to assist your business with managing potential liquidity issues. After all, these parties are already in bed with you and stand to lose the most if your company fails. In addition, vendors and suppliers stand to gain quite a bit if your business continues to grow and prosper (which means more business for everyone).

✔ **Customers:** Having customers step up with an advance payment, deposit on a large project, or similar payment can help ease a liquidity squeeze. Also, providing customers with incentives to pay quicker (for example, giving a 1 percent discount if paid within ten days) can also be used. If customers have ample cash resources available that are earning them a measly 1 percent, why not offer an incentive that provides a chance to save three times that much? This type of strategy has some pitfalls, but in certain situations customers can be leveraged to accelerate payment delivery (thus providing capital to your business).

✔ **Vendors and suppliers:** If you haven't figured this out by now, vendors and suppliers offer a relatively cheap and easily accessible source of capital to your company. Various strategies are available and range from requesting extended payment terms during a high sales period to "terming out" a portion of the balance due the vendors to be repaid over a longer period (for instance, instead of paying the entire balance in 60 days, paying it over 12 months in equal installments with a nominal interest rate attached).

✔ **Internal employees:** When needed, your internal employees can be evaluated to determine if added liquidity can be secured. In tight times, you may ask your senior management team to defer a portion of their compensation, which will then be paid when the company hits certain milestones. If they are resistant to this suggestion, at least you know where they stand in terms of their commitment to the company. Also, if you pay commissions on sales when they're booked, you may want to restructure this program to pay commissions when the sales are actually received (in cash) to better match cash outflows with cash inflows.

You must remember to be careful when using customers, vendors, and suppliers to provide some additional capital resources. Pushing these sources within the normal course of business is acceptable, but be careful not to appear desperate. If you convey desperation, you may actually find that payment terms tighten up and customers get nervous (thus delaying orders), which then produces the exact opposite of what you were trying to achieve.

Using equity and off-balance-sheet sources of capital

The previous sections help you look for additional capital from internal relationships and sources — assets you can leverage or tap, relationships you can push, and so on, to free up capital. But remember that a number of external capital sources are also available to provide additional liquidity during a bind. Following are a few examples of outside options (but they really only scratch the surface of potential sources):

✔ **Owner personal financial strength:** Business owners and key executives are sometimes asked to step up and provide additional capital to support their business. If your lenders, vendors, suppliers, customers, and employees are all onboard, why not the owners of the business? Business owners with ample personal wealth are often asked to pledge some of this wealth for the benefit of the company. Since the Great Recession that began in late 2007 to early 2008, this source of capital has become one of the most widely utilized, as credit availability contracted at near record rates.

✔ **FF&CBAs:** Chapter 10 identifies FF&CBAs (family, friends, and close business associates) as natural sources to secure capital for a business. During a liquidity squeeze, these sources may be able to provide a "bridge" loan to get the company through a tight period. Though nobody likes to have to ask family members for money, when your business life depends on it, you may have no other choice available.

✔ **Off-balance-sheet assets:** Your business may have various assets that aren't included in the balance sheet or are restricted in nature. For example, the building your company leases may actually be owned by a group of investors with close ties to the company (including the owners of the company). Over a period of time, the building may have appreciated in value and thus can be refinanced, with the proceeds then loaned to your company from the legal entity that owns the building. Conversely, if the legal entity that owns the building has the resources, the lease payments from your company can be reduced or deferred for a period of time to free up cash.

Business owners and key executive management team members have the most to gain if a business succeeds and the most to lose if it fails. Stepping up on the capital front provides for much more than simply helping with a liquidity squeeze. Rather, it displays creditability to other parties that the management team and business owners believe in the business and are willing to stand behind it (in good times and in bad).

Financial Leverage: The Good, the Bad, and the Downright Ugly

Financial leverage is best measured by a business-solvency measurement tool: the debt-to-equity ratio (as discussed earlier in "Measuring and monitoring solvency"). That is, the higher the amount of debt your company has in relation to your equity, the higher the ratio is, which indicates that your company is operating with a greater degree of financial risk. As such, financial leverage can be broken down into the good, the bad, and the downright ugly.

The good

If properly managed, financial leverage can enhance your company's profitability and improve earnings per share. These increases allow the company to secure less equity-based capital (because the appropriate amount and type of debt-based capital is secured), providing the business owners with greater ownership control of the entity. In order to achieve the good, you must remember to keep the balance sheet in balance and avoid leveraging your assets too high. Companies always need to remember to keep a war chest available to manage both business problems and opportunities. The challenge is to find the ideal balance between equity and debt capital sources.

The bad

Financial leverage can often produce a certain amount of business and personal stress during the down times. The creditors of your company tend to be more interested in getting repaid during the down times than providing additional capital (to support a new growth opportunity). Companies that have strong equity levels can afford some missteps along the way and, therefore, have more leeway in pursuing new markets than companies operating under heavy debt loads. Although you may survive a down period and manage to get your company's debt under control, a stronger competitor may have seized the moment and captured new market opportunities that you didn't have the resources to pursue.

The downright ugly

Financial leverage gets downright ugly when it's so excessive (or high) that you've tapped out every asset and have nothing left to work with. In this scenario, your debt-financing sources may push the company into bankruptcy or, worse yet, into an involuntary liquidation (covered in our book *Small Business Financial Management Kit For Dummies* [John Wiley & Sons, Inc.]). Basically, you reach a point of no hope in terms of being able to repay the debt and turn around your operations. The remaining option is then to lose control of your company and watch others dismantle it to settle the obligations due.

So in order to avoid becoming the downright ugly poster child, adhere to three pieces of advice: Have a clear understanding of your company's financial condition at all times (translation: Understand your financial statements), always have a strong business plan and a clear understanding of where your business is headed, and always use debt and equity appropriately.

Part III

Getting Intimate with Your Company's Cash Flow Needs

The 5th Wave   By Rich Tennant

"Hi, I'm Bob Darrel. I'm here to perform the audit of your books. Don't mind the vultures. They follow me everywhere."

In this part . . .

This part of the book gets down to the nitty-gritty of managing cash flow in the present "real world" of business — which is characterized by capital sources applying tighter and tighter scrutiny and tougher and tougher standards to businesses. If a business comes across as inexperienced or superficial about its cash-flow management skills, its chances of getting a loan or equity capital quickly drop to zero.

The four chapters in this part follow a logical path along the road to business success, starting with formulating a realistic and convincing business plan (Chapter 8), using proven practices for forecasting and planning cash needs (Chapter 9), raising cash from equity (ownership) sources (Chapter 10), and persuading lenders to loan money to your business (Chapter 11).

Chapter 8

Creating a Business Plan to Secure Cash

To start this chapter, we make a statement that should resonate loud and clear: No Plan = No Cash. Looking at the point from a different perspective, if you were a potential investor or lending source, would you provide cash (in the form of a purchase of stock or by providing a loan) to a company without having a clear understanding of the amount and when and in what structure or form the cash is required? Or would you, as a CEO or division president, commit cash to support a growing business segment without knowing how much is required and how the cash will be deployed? The answer to these questions (hopefully) is no. Whether a business is a start-up or a mature operation, developing a clear and concise business plan represents an essential tool to assist businesses with securing cash, managing their operations, and protecting their business interests.

This chapter provides the basic understanding and tools needed to develop a viable business plan, which is translated into economic value via the production of financial forecasts and projections. The planning process described in this chapter includes numerous elements ranging from obtaining current market information (on the potential demand for a new product and what price the market will support) to evaluating personnel resources (to ensure that proper professionals are available to support a business) to determining how great operational constraints (like manufacturing space availability or environmental regulations) may be in terms of expanding into a new geographical location.

The overall planning process, including the production of projections or forecasts, does not represent a "chicken or the egg" riddle. From a financial perspective, the preparation of budgets, forecasts, and projections (all terms that are used interchangeably throughout this chapter) represent the *end result* of the entire planning process. Hence, you must first accumulate the necessary data and information on which to build a forecasting model prior to producing projected financial information. Trying to create a forecast before looking at past performance, present conditions, and future expectations will result in a budget that doesn't capture your company's true economic structure.

Outlining the Basic Business Plan

Before aspiring entrepreneurs and corporate-ladder climbers can effectively pursue their business interests, they must develop a business plan. All too often, companies proceed with strategies of "We've always done it like that" or "This is how the industry has operated for the past umpteen years" instead of really evaluating and investigating the economic markets in which they operate. The business plan represents management's foundation and justification for birthing, growing, operating, and/or selling a business based on the economic environment present. Without it, management is left to operate a business in the dark, attempting to guess or use their intuition about the best course of action to pursue.

Business plans come in a variety of shapes, sizes, forms, and structures and often take on the characteristics of the business founder(s). No, the business plan won't be brunette or enjoy hiking, but it can resemble its creators by emphasizing certain traits or areas of expertise the founders may have. For instance, a type-A personality may use a number of bold adjectives to describe the massive, huge, unlimited, exceptional (you get the point) potential of the market opportunity present. As for unique areas of expertise, different sections of the business plan may be developed in depth, whereas other sections may be presented in quasi-summary format because the needed information isn't readily available (for presentation).

Herein lies the first lesson of developing a business plan: The business plan should be built from the outside looking in so that any reasonable party can clearly and quickly understand the business concept.

The business plan can come in a multitude of formats and include all types of information, data, graphs, charts, analyses, and more. The basis of every business plan, however, is in four main sections, which we cover in the following sections.

The executive summary

First and foremost in a typical business plan is the presentation of the executive summary. The *executive summary* is a brief overview of the business concept in terms of the market opportunity present, the operational logistics required to bring a product and/or service to market, the management team that's going to make it happen, and the eventual potential economic return available, including the amount of capital needed to execute the plan. This section of the business plan is really nothing more than a condensed summary of the entire business concept, presented in a neat and tidy overview of usually not more than five pages (and hopefully fewer). The general idea is that the executive summary should capture the critical content of each of the three primary areas of the business plan in a very efficient and easy to digest manner.

Although the meat of the business plan resides in the remainder of the document, this section is the most critical in terms of attracting interest from capital sources and/or management. Basically, the reader of the business plan must be able to conceptualize, understand, and justify the business concept from the information presented in the executive summary. This section must gain the reader's interest, generate some type of excitement, and move him with a sense of urgency to pursue the business opportunity at hand.

The market assessment

The second section of the business plan is generally dedicated to the market for the product or service being offered. Yes, we know that you may have trouble believing that the authors of this book, being accountants, would place marketing above finance and accounting issues. But the fact of the matter is that without a viable market, the only thing to account for is losses (and you know how much capital/financing sources and management love these). The marketing assessment segment of the business plan is often the most important because it substantiates the need for a product and/or service that's not being filled in the current economic environment.

You support the business concept by quantifying the size of the market in coordination with qualifying the market need, but that step is only half the battle (and often the easier of the two halves). Beyond providing information and supporting data on the market size, characteristics, and trends, the market assessment must also present a clear understanding of the business's competitive niche, target market, and specific marketing strategies. Identifying the specific niche and target market and developing an effective marketing strategy to capitalize on the opportunity present is often more challenging and critical to the future success of the business. And to top it all off, locating reliable and meaningful data essential to supporting your conclusions on the market opportunity can often be difficult.

All marketing sections should include a summary of the competition that savvy entrepreneurs or business managers can use to their advantage in several ways:

✔ By including an overview of the competition, the business establishes credibility with the readers (because it indicates that you've done your homework).

✔ By reading in-depth competitor assessments, managers may identify weaknesses in competitors' plans that can be exploited.

✔ By evaluating competitors' strengths and weaknesses, managers can better understand business risks.

The operational overview

Following the market segment of the business plan is a well-developed company operating overview. This segment of the business plan addresses a number of operational issues, including personnel requirements, technological needs, locations (for offices, production/manufacturing, warehouses/distribution centers, and so on), company infrastructure requirements, international considerations, professional/expert counsel resources, and the like. This segment drives various business-operating elements in terms of the resources needed to implement and execute the business plan. For example, if a company is planning on expanding into new foreign markets where the local government still "influences" the distribution channels, then the operating segment needs to address how the product will be distributed and what international partners will be essential to the process.

Business plans often dedicate a large portion of the operational overview to providing an overview of the management team in terms of the members' past credentials as well as their responsibilities with the new business concept moving forward. The market may be ripe and capital plentiful, but without a qualified management team, the business concept will, more times than not, sink. In today's challenging economic environment, management qualifications and credibility have taken on an entirely new level of importance, given the heightened sensitivity to management accountability and transparency.

The management team responsible for executing the business plan *is,* in effect, the business plan. Initially, financing and capital sources are lured in by business plans and may turn over any concept in the plan to a slew of professionals for further due diligence, reviews, evaluations, and critique. For example, if a capital source has concerns over the technological basis within a biomedical company, then medical- or technology-based professionals can be brought in to complete additional due diligence and either approve or can the idea. However, the management team standing behind the business plan and its execution is really what the capital and financing sources invest in. The integrity, qualifications, experience, determination, passion, and commitment displayed by the management team are of utmost importance. Any concerns in this area, and the capital and financing sources have their out.

The financial summary: Performance and required capital (Cash)

Finally, the financial segment of the business plan is developed. In a sense, the financial summary brings all the elements of the business plan together from an accounting and/or financing perspective. In the financial summary, financial forecasts are prepared to project the anticipated economic performance of the business concept based on the information and data presented earlier in the business plan:

- ✔ The market segment tends to drive the revenue portion of the forecasts, because the information accumulated and presented there substantiates items such as potential unit sales growth (in relation to the size of the market), pricing, and revenue sources by product and service.

- ✔ The operational overview drives the expense element of the forecast because it addresses the business cost structure in terms of personnel, assets, company infrastructure, and so on.

When all the elements of the business plan are put together in this segment, not only is the forecast profit and loss or income statement produced but, just as importantly, the projected balance sheet and cash-flow statement are generated as well. And you guessed it: With all this information now in hand, the capital (or cash) required to execute the business plan should be readily quantifiable.

Developing a Business Plan

As coauthor John has pointed out on many occasions (and in numerous books he has published), accounting represents more of an art than a science. This concept also holds true with the planning process, and more than a few accounting Picassos and Rembrandts have been created during the preparation of a business plan. We dive into some more-complex forecasting concepts in Chapter 9, but for now we stick to planning basics. We start by determining where you begin the process of creating a business plan.

The preparation of business plans should not be reserved for new companies just starting out or an existing business looking at launching new products. All companies should implement formal business-planning processes to ensure that their business interests are properly managed and protected.

Outlining your plan by using BOTE, WAG, and SWAG

The real start of developing any business plan is coming up with the initial concept, idea, or thought. This starting point applies equally to a long-standing business evaluating the costs and benefits of outsourcing a product manufacturing process and to a newly launched social-media company targeting the aging Baby Boomer population.

Okay, so what do the acronyms in the preceding heading stand for?

- ✔ BOTE: Back of the envelope
- ✔ WAG: Wild-ass guess
- ✔ SWAG: Scientific wild-ass guess

These terms represent the progression many business plans go through as they are developed. We offer these acronyms on developing business plans and projections somewhat in jest, but at the same time, they do help you understand the evolution of a business plan and projection model from how an idea is born to how the idea is communicated in an economic format/fashion to various parties.

Whether you apply these acronyms and follow this logic or rely on another creation and development cycle, the same key concept holds. Business plans and projection models should continue to evolve, improve, and strengthen over time as more and more effort is invested to bring the idea to life.

BOTE

BOTE usually represents the very first financial projection developed for a business plan: back of the envelope (or maybe in this day and age of advanced technology a more appropriate acronym would be 4GSS, or fourth-generation screen shot). Yes, even the majority of the most astute and experienced business professionals and entrepreneurs can attest to jotting down the basic concepts, needs, potential sales, costs, and profits of a business idea or concept on a random piece of paper (or with a simple mobile communication device application). Sometimes you need to get it out of your head and down in writing just to see if it makes any sense to begin with. You would be amazed at how often BOTE estimates are used.

WAG

If the idea passes the BOTE test, the next step in the evolution of the planning process is the ever-present *WAG* (or wild-ass guess). The WAG is somewhat more sophisticated than the BOTE in that it tends to incorporate more thought and some basic research. WAGs are usually produced using software tools such as Excel and incorporate the basic economic structure of the business, starting with sales and then moving through the remainder of the income statement by capturing costs of sales, operating expenses, and overhead or general and administrative costs. You can then draw two simple conclusions:

- ✔ How profitable the idea will be

- ✔ More importantly, how much capital or cash the idea needs in order to achieve success

These conclusions aren't overly sophisticated, but they're a very early attempt to put some financial logic behind the idea.

SWAG

If your idea has passed both the BOTE and WAG stages, congratulations are in order because you now can use the much more powerful tool, *SWAG* (scientific wild-ass guess) to further the development of your business plan. In other words, the business plan and supporting projection model are actually getting some serious attention and logical consideration. The idea can actually start to be substantiated and corroborated by external sources (or from third-party data/information). The first real form to the business plan and projection models are taking shape. You may be incorporating the use of technology tools to draft the business plan (for example, Microsoft Word), to build version 1.0 of the projection model (perhaps with Microsoft Excel), and to begin to prepare a presentation to summarize the plan (for example, with Microsoft PowerPoint).

Getting the process going

After the business's executive management teams or new company founders have decided that the concept for the new business endeavor has merit (which is by no means a small task), drafting of the business plan can begin. You can prepare a draft by following four simple steps:

- ✔ **Delve into historical business information.** In order to start the budgeting process, you should have a very good understanding of your company's prior financial and operating results. Review as much history as is available and relevant to the current idea, whether it stretches back three months, one year, five years, or longer. Of course for newly formed businesses, the availability of internal historical information is limited, but plenty of external information is usually available from like businesses and competitors and can be utilized to develop a business plan.

Remember that although the history of a company may provide a basic foundation on which to develop a budget, it by no means is an accurate predictor of the future.

✔ **Involve key management.** You must ensure that all key management team members are involved in the planning process, covering all critical business functions, to produce a projection that can be relied upon. The accounting and financial departments actively participate in the planning (and rightfully so, as these are the people who understand the numbers the best) and they produce the final forecast. But the data on which the projection model is based comes from numerous parties, sources, and business functions. Just like you wouldn't have a regional sales manager prepare a fixed asset schedule (tracking all asset additions, disposals, and depreciation expense), you wouldn't have your accountant estimate sales volumes by product line during the holiday season (and what prices the products may fetch). Critical business data comes from numerous parties, all of whom must be included in the planning process to produce the most reliable information possible.

✔ **Gather reliable data.** The availability of quality market, operational, and accounting data represents the basis of the budget. A good deal of this data often comes from internal sources. For example, when a sales region is preparing a budget for the upcoming year, the sales manager may survey the direct sales representatives on what they feel their customers' demand for products and services will be in the coming year (after all, who better to accumulate this information than the people in the field with the direct relationships?). With this information, sales volumes, personnel levels, wages rates, commission plans, and so on can all be determined.

The internal information will certainly be of value, but it represents only half the battle because external information and data are just as critical to accumulate. Having access to quality and reliable external third-party-produced information is absolutely essential to the overall business planning process and the production of reliable forecasts. Market forces and trends that aren't apparent in internal data may be occurring and set to impact your business over the next 24 months.

✔ **Coordinate the planning timing.** Most companies tend to start the planning process for the next year in the fourth quarter of their current calendar year. This way, they have access to recent financial results on which to support the budgeting process moving forward.

The nearer-term the projection, the more detailed the information and results being produced. If you prepare a budget for the coming fiscal year, then you can reasonably include monthly financial statement forecasts (with more detailed support available). Looking two or three years out, you can produce quarterly financial statement projections (with more summarized assumptions used), and so on.

GIGO, or *garbage in, garbage out,* definitely applies to the planning process. If you don't have sound data and information at the core of the planning process (or if the data and information are poor in quality), the output produced will be of little value to the management team. When preparing your company's budgets, try to use data and information that's as complete, accurate, reliable, and timely as possible. Though you can't be 100 percent sure about the data and information accumulated for your plan (because by definition, you're attempting to predict the future with a projection), with proper resources (including appropriate internal management, external subject-matter experts or consultants, and allocating financial resources to secure critical information that's not readily available or free) dedicated to the process, you can avoid large information "black holes."

All too often, we come across budgets and forecasts that were prepared from an outdated business economic model. Just ask any retailer that formerly relied on brick-and-mortar stores and print-based advertising campaigns how the Internet and e-commerce have reshaped the business models. Though management has put forth the effort to restructure the company's operations in a changing market environment, a plan based on an old projection model with outdated assumptions doesn't capture the essence of the new economic realities. Remember, the planning process represents a living, evolving thing that must constantly be updated and adapted to changing market conditions. What worked two years ago may not provide management with the necessary information today on which to make appropriate business decisions.

Using two simple but powerful tools: SWOT and KISS

As described in the preceding sections, the heart of the planning process is the initial business idea or concept (that the plan is being developed around), which is then substantiated by accumulating what may seem like never-ending volumes of information and data. If you're not careful, the data-accumulation process can engulf the entire planning effort; if you get too much data, you can't digest it or draw any type of meaningful conclusion. But fret not, friends, because two simple but powerful planning tools are available to help manage data overload: SWOT and KISS.

The SWOT analysis

Strengths, weaknesses, opportunities, and threats: A SWOT analysis is a very effective planning and budgeting tool used to keep businesses focused on critical issues that may lead to wonderful successes or horrible failures. The SWOT analysis should be as comprehensive as possible and capture both relevant information for the specific idea as well as incorporating more broad-based data about the company, the industry, and the competition. The simple SWOT analysis (or matrix) in Figure 8-1 provides a better understanding of how it works.

Year 2012 Business Plan
Data Worksheet

Internal	**Strengths** (What you do well, competitive advantages)	**Weaknesses** (What you don't do well, competitive disadvantages)
External	**Opportunities** (Potential marketplace openings, new ventures, and ideas to grow your business)	**Threats** (Potential competitive, economic, or environmental factors that may hurt your business)

Figure 8-1:
A SWOT
analysis.

A SWOT analysis is usually broken down into a matrix containing four segments. Two of the segments are geared toward positive attributes (for instance, what are our strengths and what are the opportunities) and two towards negative attributes (what are our weaknesses and what are the threats). In addition to illustrating these categories, Figure 8-1 makes reference to the terms *internal* versus *external*. This distinction highlights the fact that certain attributes tend to come from internal company sources (namely, strengths and weaknesses) and other attributes from external, or outside of the company sources (typically opportunities and threats).

If used correctly, a SWOT analysis not only can provide invaluable information to support the planning process but also (and more importantly) can help identify what type of management a business has in place. The responses received from the management team engaged in the planning process provide invaluable information as to whether the party completing the SWOT analysis is nothing more than a frontline manager (that is, a captain needing direction)

or a bona fide business person (the colonel leading the charge). When business plans are developed and launched, ultimately their success is dependent on having the right leaders driving the bus to take the opportunity from a concept to reality. Frontline managers can assist with this process but are generally not qualified to lead.

SWOT analyses may be completed by a variety of different parties. In a larger or well-established business, the SWOT analysis may be delegated to the management team assigned a project or opportunity to complete. The SWOT analysis is then evaluated and interpreted by the company's executives, who consider whether it's viable and whether the right people are in place. On the other hand, two founders just starting a business may complete a SWOT analysis (so the concept of senior management evaluations is not relevant, although external investors may have a keen interest in the SWOT analysis). The key concept here is that the parties responsible for preparing the SWOT analysis should be heavily vested in the opportunity and be willing to take possession and responsibility.

Remember to KISS

You know what KISS stands for: Keep it simple, stupid. Used in the marketing world for years, the concept of KISS also applies to the planning process every bit as much. Key company management should be involved in the process of planning, but these executives tend not to be well educated in the world of accounting and finance. So rather than confuse these poor souls with technical accounting and financial jargon, the goal should be to provide guidance and support that allows them to accumulate the information that can easily be translated into accounting and financial results.

If you're an executive or owner of a business, you must be able to understand the big picture and your company's key economic drivers in order to prepare proper business plans, strategies, and, ultimately, forecasts. The ability to understand and positively affect the key economic drivers of your business and empower the management team to execute the business plan represents the end game. Getting lost in excessive amounts of detail ("Why did you spend an extra $500 on the trip to Florida?") is generally not the best use of senior management's time, because every level of detail adds more and more complexity to the plan, which can get overwhelmed with TMI (too much information).

Incorporating Third-Party Information into Your Plan

When building reliable and credible business plans, the importance of accumulating data and information from reliable (and we want to emphasize *reliable*) independent third parties (including various trade and industry sources) cannot be underestimated. In this section, we expound on this subject to clarify why it's so important.

Gathering the info

To start, the process of actually gathering independent third-party information, data, and reports needs to be addressed. The Internet is, without question, one of the most powerful data- and information-gathering tools available. In the dark ages, valuable market, industry, and technological information was gathered via such archaic methods as researching in a library, subscribing to trade journals and magazines, and attending seminars or educational trade shows. Today, most of the information you need is available electronically over the World Wide Web, which has improved the efficiency of accumulating information significantly. Most industries' trade organizations now regularly produce and provide content via the web, but you have to be prepared to pay for it, because quality and reliable information costs money.

 Incorporate trade shows, seminars, and educational events into your efforts to accumulate third-party data. Not only can these events offer a great source of information, but they also (and potentially more importantly) can be places to make contacts with potential future employees, vendors, customers, and funding sources who can assist with the execution of the business plan.

The third-party information you gather should cover multiple aspects of your business. Following are three examples of data sources for a jewelry company:

- ✔ The World Gold Council provides an excellent overview of consumer gold-buying trends and patterns by price points, types of jewelry, and different sales channels. This information can support the marketing segment of the business plan.

- ✔ If the production of jewelry is required, then information on available manufacturing sources is needed. Because a large majority of jewelry is produced globally (from Southeast Asia to Europe to Central America), the company needs to make sure that it has a good handle on the political, social, and economic stability of any foreign suppliers.

- ✔ In addition, if the jewelry company is going to sell products through retail storefronts, then an overview of commercial real estate rental rates, trends, and so on can be incorporated (for a specific geographical area) to support a critical expense driver in the business.

Using only reliable info

A significant additional benefit of obtaining and incorporating independent and reliable third-party information is that it carries added weight/credibility with readers. Readers see proof that the management team isn't just making up the story in the business plan. In fact, hard facts are available from independent sources supporting the objectives and conclusions of the business plan.

We can't emphasize enough the importance of securing *reliable* third-party or external information. The quality and reliability of your data is way more important than quantity. While the web has become an incredibly powerful data-accumulation and distribution tool, it also has become just as powerful in distributing worthless and/or distorted information. Face it, 99 percent of the information available on the web is just noise or clutter and must be properly evaluated to ensure that the most appropriate and reliable information is accessed. So beware of the data source, because nothing is more embarrassing than finding out you've referenced unreliable third-party information in your business plan.

Any party reading your business plan expects you to be an industry expert, so if you're not an industry expert, you had better become one very fast. You don't need to have an answer for every question and understand every business topic from top to bottom (professional advice can be secured for additional support), but the management team responsible for the business plan should have strong knowledge of at least 80 percent of the topics presented in the plan.

Riding the CART Concept: Complete, Accurate, Reliable, and Timely

During the whole planning process, you'll do well to remember the importance of data that is CART: complete, accurate, reliable, and timely. Actually, the concept of CART should be applied to all business segments; whether you're developing a business plan, analyzing periodic operating results, or evaluating a employee benefit plan, business owners and managers must have complete, accurate, reliable, and timely information to make appropriate business decisions. Whether the information and data is coming from internal or external sources, from the marketing or manufacturing departments, and is presented in terms of the number of "heads" needed or by the total wages to be paid, the basis of the budget is having access to complete, accurate, reliable, and timely information.

✔ **Complete:** When financial statements are produced for a company, they include a balance sheet, income statement, and a statement of cash flows. All three are needed in order to understand the entire financial picture of a company. If a projection model is incorporating an expansion of a company's manufacturing facility in a new state (to keep up with rising demand), all information related to the new facility needs to be accumulated to prepare the budget. This info includes the cost of the land and facility, how much utility costs run in the area, what potential environmental issues may be present, whether a trained workforce is available and, if not, how much the training cost will be, and so on. Overkill is not the objective; having access to all "material" information and data is.

✔ **Accurate:** Incorporating accurate data is absolutely essential for preparing the business plan. Every business plan needs to state the price your company charges for the goods or services it sells, how much employees are paid, what the monthly office rent is, what evolving patterns exist in sales channels, and every other relevant detail. Accumulating accurate information, whether from internal sources or external third parties, represents a critical and ongoing management endeavor.

✔ **Reliable:** The concepts of reliability and accuracy are closely linked, but they differ as well. A piece of information may be accurate without being reliable. For example, you may conduct some research and find that the average wage for a paralegal in San Diego, California, is $24 per hour. This data sounds accurate, but if the business model you're developing requires paralegals with special training who demand $37 per hour, the information is not reliable.

✔ **Timely:** Finally, the information and data must be accumulated in a timely fashion. Data provided six months after it was needed doesn't do management much good. Companies live and die by having access to real-time information on which to make business decisions and change course (and forecasts) if needed.

An old phrase that's often quoted, "Put the cart before the horse," means to reverse the accepted order of things. However, the CART principle is a case in which the "cart" always needs to come first. You must put the CART information and data before the horse (the business plan). If you attempt to offer a business plan that hasn't been created through CART data, the end result will be nothing short of disastrous.

Chapter 9

Building Best-in-Class Projection Models to Manage Cash

In This Chapter

▶ Getting people and software in place to build financial forecasts

▶ Determining your approach to structuring a plan

▶ Creating a basic projection

▶ Putting your forecasts to good use

Chapter 8 focuses on developing a business plan to substantiate an opportunity and, for all intents and purposes, to identify how much capital (cash) is needed to execute the opportunity. The financial summary segment of the business plan pulls together all the parts of the plan from an economic perspective via the preparation of financial forecasts or projections. In this chapter, we now turn our attention to building financial forecasts, or projection models, to quantify the business plan.

The forecasting process is much easier to undertake (and ultimately understand) if the majority of the relevant data needed is accumulated beforehand because you'll have the big picture in mind. Remember the Boy Scouts' motto and "be prepared." The better prepared you are with the basics of the business plan and key assumptions, the easier it is to build financial projection models that are credible and reliable.

Rounding Up Resources to Build Financial Forecasts

The first thing you want to consider in preparing financial forecasts is identifying and securing the appropriate resources: personnel to complete the projections and software to prepare flexible and adaptable projection models. On the personnel front, the budgeting task tends to fall on the accounting and finance department because these are the people in the organization who seem to work best with "the numbers."

The accounting and finance department may prepare the actual budget, but the base information required for completion of the budget comes from all the critical operations of the organization.

On the software front, the following two choices are readily available to complete company projections:

- **Stand-alone software:** The ever-popular Microsoft Excel is very flexible and relatively easy to use, for both nonfinancial types who simply want to do addition and multiplication and financial types who use the program's more-sophisticated features, like macros and lookup tables. Excel is extremely versatile and can be found in use in companies as small as the local deli to billion-dollar-a-year organizations. If a little more sophistication is desired, then financial-forecasting software is available, such as Alight Planning Enterprise and Budget Maestro (which tend to be geared toward the middle market or companies with annual revenues in excess of $100 million).

- **The budgeting component of accounting software:** Most accounting software packages (QuickBooks, Great Plains, and others) include a budgeting module to support this function, but in general these modules aren't as flexible as Excel (and are a little more difficult to use). *Note:* Most accounting software packages easily interface with Excel, so a combination of strategies may be used. For example, you may create the base projection model in Excel and export the results into the accounting software module.

Planning with the Big Picture in Mind

After getting your personnel and software resources in place, one last task needs to be tackled before a basic financial projection model can be structured. You need to take a step back from the mounds of information of data that's been accumulated and take a look from the 20,000-foot level at what you're attempting to accomplish. In other words, make sure that the financial projection model will give you the critical output needed in order to clearly and concisely summarize the economic proposition presented in the business plan.

Deciding on a top-down versus bottom-up projection strategy

Financial forecasts are usually built on one of two logic structures — from the top down or the bottom up.

Top-down projection models build the logic in the model from sales and revenue expectations first (as in the income statement, sales are always listed first), which then drive the cost structure of a business. Key sales information related to unit volumes, price points, different types of revenue (for example, for a technology company, sales can be driven from technology licensing, system integration fees, and other related fees), different sources of revenue (a technology company may sell technology to the government market, which is very different from a manufacturing company), and other factors. This information is then used to build out the cost structure of the business as various expenses are calculated or determined based on projected revenue levels. The following example shows how a top-down projection works:

> **Top down:** In the business plan, the long-term objective of a sales team is for each sales representative to be responsible for generating $1 million per year in sales, starting at $500,000 in year one and growing to $1 million by year three. So the projection model calculates the number of sales representatives needed based on the revenue being generated during a given period. If sales of $6 million are expected in year two and the average sales representative is responsible for $750,000 of sales, eight sales representatives are needed. If each sales representative is paid a base salary of $50,000 and earns a commission of 5 percent of sales, then the total sales representative compensation expense of $700,000 can be easily calculated from the logic in the projection model. The math is as follows:
>
> 8 sales representatives × $50,000 salary = $400,000
>
> 5% commission × $6 million in sales = $300,000
>
> $400,000 in salaries + $300,000 in commissions = $700,000 in total compensation

This example is rather simplistic, as it assumes that all sales representatives would be working from day one for the entire year. In reality, sales and related expenses tend to build over time and not in a linear fashion. So when building a financial projection model, a clear understanding of variable, semivariable, and fixed expenses needs to be obtained and incorporated to produce more accurate output.

So if a top-down projection focuses on sales and revenue levels, then you can probably guess that a bottom-up projection model is driven by cost/expense information first, which then predicts sales and revenue results. Though this type of financial projection model isn't as widely used as the top-down variety, a number of businesses and industries rely on it, as in the following example.

> **Bottom up:** Government defense contracting businesses usually generate revenue from one of two types of contracts — fixed fee or cost plus. In a cost-plus contract, all costs associated with a specific project (as supported by a contract executed with the government) are accumulated and then billed to the government with overhead rates applied and a contract profit margin attached. Hence, revenue is determined based on the actual costs incurred, which are accumulated and billed to the government on a periodic basis. But before the government executes a contract,

it needs an estimate of the anticipated total cost of the contract, which is often based on a financial projection. So in this environment, costs need to be accumulated first to assist with calculating the total value of the contract (that the government will be responsible for paying). Or in other words, the costs drive the sales.

More-sophisticated financial projection models often incorporate elements of both top-down and bottom-up strategies. Certain components of the financial projection model may very well be built on top-down assumptions (such as sales and direct costs of sales, which vary directly with sales levels), whereas various fixed-cost functions within a business are built from the bottom up.

In the end, both projection-modeling strategies end up focusing on the most critical element of every business plan: sales. That is, without sales, the business isn't going to last very long because nobody wants to support a money-losing operation for very long. And of course, the need for sales ties back to the business plan, which at its heart addresses how your business's products or services will satisfy a market need or demand.

Identifying your critical business economic drivers

Most businesses or business units/divisions of larger companies have numerous moving parts that on first glance may appear to be very complex and overly detailed. Looking at all the information from these different areas and then attempting to build a financial projection model to capture every line item of detail can, needless to say, be a very daunting task. So when you get overwhelmed, remember to revisit your 20,000-foot view by taking a step back and identifying and understanding what the key economic drivers of your business are.

Key economic drivers vary from business to business. What may be a key driver in the personnel staffing industry (which is very sensitive to employee wages) is very different from what drives a technology manufacturing company (which is very sensitive to supporting a high fixed-cost manufacturing facility). But though the drivers may be different, the big picture is basically as follows:

✔ For most companies, economic life or death is usually centered on a half dozen or fewer critical economic drivers. Roughly four to six key items determine whether you make money or lose money.

✔ The critical economic drivers account for the majority of financial activity, transactions, and management attention within the business. This point should make perfect sense because there's no point investing countless hours tracking down every credit card receipt supporting an employee expense report to confirm whether an $18 charge was valid.

> Rather, time and effort should be invested in areas that have the best chance to improve operating results.

> ✔ The allocation of key economic drivers is usually split 50/50 between sales and expenses. For example, in a professional service firm (such as a law firm), billable hours per period represents a critical operating metric at the sales level. On the expense side of life, the average wage paid to each professional is extremely important. If the firm charges a market-accepted bill rate, then if the professional has billed enough hours, the firm generates profits.

A high-technology manufacturing company made a significant investment in its production facility to support large volumes of low-cost technological products (through the year 2000). Over the course of the next five years, market conditions changed, with low-cost, high-volume production moving to cheaper foreign markets, leaving only the advanced-technology, higher-cost, and lower-volume products to be produced in the United States. During this transition period, the company's investment in its production facility did not change, because it represented a fixed cost that doesn't vary with production levels.

In order to survive and generate profits on lower sales volumes, significant price increases were required on a per-unit basis to offset the loss in revenue and profits. So the key economic drivers for this business boiled down to two primary items: what price was needed per unit (based on lower volumes) to cover the company's high production-facility fixed costs, and what costs (generally variable or semivariable in nature because they're easier to reduce over a shorter time period) could be decreased to help the company lower its break-even point and improve profitability. As for the first item, the company's average price per unit increased by over 300 percent over a five-year period to drive additional earnings. As for the second item, unproductive personnel (related to the older business model) were eliminated to reduce expenses.

As this example helps illustrate, each business owner or manager has the responsibility of clearly understanding what really drives the company's financial performance. When these drivers are clearly understood, top business owners and managers can quickly decipher and translate this data to determine whether a company made money or lost money. If you know your revenue level (over a period of time, such as a month) by types of products and services sold, you should already know whether you made money or lost money.

Well-run businesses often use the periodic production of financial statements to simply confirm what they already know or suspect rather than gain new info. If you're relying on monthly financial statements to relay the performance of your company, which is always something new, unexpected, and/or a surprise, then you're behind the curve.

Building the Basic Projection Model

The best way to dive into preparing a projection is to start by reviewing Figure 9-1, which represents a yearly budget for ACME Distribution, Inc.

When reviewing the projection prepared for the company, take note of the following key issues (which correspond to the topics discussed in this chapter):

- ✔ **The most recent year-end financial information is included in the first column to provide a base reference point to work from.** As noted in Chapter 8 on planning, gaining a thorough understanding of your company's historical operating results is an important factor in forecasting the future. Also, by having this base information, a consistent reporting format can be developed so that the format of your financial statements is consistent with your projections (for ease of understanding).

- ✔ **The projections are "complete" from a financial statement perspective.** That is, the income statement, balance sheet, and statement of cash flows are all projected to assist management with understanding the entire financial picture of the company. The forecasts prepared for ACME Distribution, Inc., indicate that the line of credit will be used extensively through the third quarter, because between having to finance increases in trade accounts receivable and inventory levels (to support high seasonal sales levels in the third quarter) and reducing trade accounts payable levels, the company will need to ensure that its line of credit is large enough to handle the expected "cash demand" for the third quarter. By the end of the fourth quarter, borrowings on the line of credit are substantially lower because the balance sheet contracts after the seasonal sales rush.

- ✔ **The projections are presented with quarterly information.** We normally recommend that projections for the next fiscal year be prepared on a monthly basis to provide management with more frequent information. However, for ease of presentation (in this book), quarterly information was prepared. If we continued, looking several years or more out, we would use annual projections because longer projections mean less precision. A good general rule of thumb to use is to prepare monthly projections for the next 12-month operating period, quarterly projections for the two years after the first 12-month operating period, and then annual projections thereafter.

✔ **The projections are prepared and presented in a summary format.** Instead of including a lot of detail, groups of detail are combined into one line item. For example, sales may originate from ten different company divisions or branches. Individual budgets are prepared to support each division or branch, but when a companywide forecast is completed, all the sales are rolled up onto one line item.

Budgets prepared in a summary format are best suited for review by external parties and top company executives, who all tend to be big-picture people who want to first start with understanding the macro-level forecasts to complete a quick sanity check on whether they make sense or not. Furthermore, in revealing too much detail to external parties, you may risk disclosing confidential information that's not appropriate for external consumption. And providing too much information to outside parties can sometimes result in the outside parties asking too many questions (so remember to KISS — keep it simple, stupid).

✔ **Certain key or critical business economic drivers are highlighted in the projection model.** First, the company's gross margin is called out, because it increases from 22.5 percent in the first quarter to 28 percent in the third quarter. The increase was the result of the company increasing prices in the second quarter and then accelerating the increases in the third quarter to capture higher anticipated demand from customers ramping up for the holidays. Second, the company's pre-tax net income, for the entire year, improves significantly because the company's fixed overhead and corporate infrastructure (expenses) didn't need to increase nearly as much to support the higher sales (as a result of realizing the benefits of economies of scale). In addition, the company didn't have to absorb an inventory write-off of $50,000 (as with the preceding year).

You may ask why the company has no income tax expense forecast, despite having positive net pre-tax profits. In this example, ACME identified a deferred tax asset the previous year, which was of no value as of the end of that year. (We discuss this scenario in Chapter 5.) Because the company was able to generate a profit in the most recent year, the deferred tax asset now is anticipated to be of value, and any income tax expense anticipated can be offset against the deferred tax asset (producing a net income tax expense of zero for the year). For cash-flow planning purposes, this concept is very critical because the last thing you want to do is overpay income taxes, unnecessarily consuming cash.

The basic budget presented in Figure 9-1 is fairly simplistic but nevertheless very informative. It captures the macro-level economic structure of the company in terms of where it is today and where it expects to be at the end of next year.

Summary Balance Sheet	Actual Year-End 1/1/15	Forecast Quarter-End 4/1/15	Forecast Quarter-End 7/1/15	Forecast Quarter-End 10/1/15	Forecast Quarter-End 1/1/16	Forecast Year-End 1/1/16
Current Assets:						
Cash and Equivalents	$230,000	$54,375	$137,750	$290,375	$199,250	$199,250
Trade Receivables, Net	$705,000	$725,000	$1,150,000	$1,500,000	$937,500	$937,500
Inventory	$450,000	$540,000	$635,000	$525,000	$500,000	$500,000
Other Current Assets	$75,000	$75,000	$75,000	$75,000	$75,000	$75,000
Total Current Assets	$1,460,000	$1,394,375	$1,997,750	$2,390,375	$1,711,750	$1,711,750
Fixed and Other Assets:						
Property, Plant, and Equipment, Net	$1,340,000	$1,337,500	$1,332,500	$1,325,000	$1,315,000	$1,315,000
Other Assets	$470,000	$452,500	$435,000	$417,500	$400,000	$400,000
Total Fixed and Other Assets	$1,810,000	$1,790,000	$1,767,500	$1,742,500	$1,715,000	$1,715,000
Total Assets	$3,270,000	$3,184,375	$3,765,250	$4,132,875	$3,426,750	$3,426,750
Current Liabilities:						
Trade Payables	$385,000	$450,000	$525,000	$600,000	$425,000	$425,000
Accrued Liabilities	$215,000	$225,000	$250,000	$275,000	$200,000	$200,000
Line of Credit Borrowings	$350,000	$350,000	$750,000	$750,000	$250,000	$250,000
Current Portion of Long-Term Liabilities	$250,000	$250,000	$250,000	$250,000	$250,000	$250,000
Other Current Liabilities	$75,000	$75,000	$75,000	$75,000	$75,000	$75,000
Total Current Liabilities	$1,275,000	$1,350,000	$1,850,000	$1,950,000	$1,200,000	$1,200,000
Long-Term Liabilities:						
Notes Payable, Less Current Portion	$800,000	$750,000	$700,000	$650,000	$600,000	$600,000
Capital Leases, Less Current Portion	$100,000	$87,500	$75,000	$62,500	$50,000	$50,000
Subordinated Debt	$250,000	$250,000	$250,000	$250,000	$250,000	$250,000
Total Long-Term Liabilities	$1,150,000	$1,087,500	$1,025,000	$962,500	$900,000	$900,000
Total Liabilities	$2,425,000	$2,437,500	$2,875,000	$2,912,500	$2,100,000	$2,100,000
Equity:						
Common Equity	$100,000	$100,000	$100,000	$100,000	$100,000	$100,000
Retained Earnings	$555,000	$745,000	$745,000	$745,000	$745,000	$745,000
Current Earnings	$190,000	($98,125)	$45,250	$375,375	$481,750	$481,750
Total Equity	$845,000	$746,875	$890,250	$1,220,375	$1,326,750	$1,326,750
Total Liabilities & Equity	$3,270,000	$3,184,375	$3,765,250	$4,132,875	$3,426,750	$3,426,750

Summary Income Statement	Actual Year-End 1/1/15	Forecast Quarter-End 4/1/15	Forecast Quarter-End 7/1/15	Forecast Quarter-End 10/1/15	Forecast Quarter-End 1/1/16	Forecast Year-End 1/1/16
Revenue	$8,043,750	$1,450,000	$2,300,000	$3,000,000	$2,250,000	$9,000,000
Costs of Goods Sold	$6,032,813	$1,123,750	$1,702,000	$2,160,000	$1,687,500	$6,673,250
Gross Profit	$2,010,937	$326,250	$598,000	$840,000	$562,500	$2,326,750
Gross Margin	25.00%	22.50%	26.00%	28.00%	25.00%	25.85%
Selling, General, and Administrative Expenses	$1,395,000	$325,000	$350,000	$400,000	$350,000	$1,425,000
Depreciation and Amortization Expense	$250,000	$65,000	$67,500	$70,000	$72,500	$275,000
Interest Expense	$125,938	$34,375	$37,125	$39,875	$33,625	$145,000
Other (Income) Expenses	$50,000	$0	$0	$0	$0	$0
Net Profit Before Tax	$190,000	($98,125)	$143,375	$330,125	$106,375	$481,750
Income Tax Expense (Benefit)	$0	$0	$0	$0	$0	$0
Net Profit (Loss)	$190,000	($98,125)	$143,375	$330,125	$106,375	$481,750

Summary Cash Flow Statement	Actual Year-End 1/1/15	Forecast Quarter-End 4/1/15	Forecast Quarter-End 7/1/15	Forecast Quarter-End 10/1/15	Forecast Quarter-End 1/1/16	Forecast Year-End 1/1/16
Operating Cash Flow:						
Net Income (Loss)	$190,000	($98,125)	$143,375	$330,125	$106,375	$481,750
Depreciation and Amortization Expense	$250,000	$65,000	$67,500	$70,000	$72,500	$275,000
Net Operating Cash Flow	$440,000	($33,125)	$210,875	$400,125	$178,875	$756,750
Working Capital:						
(Increase) Decrease in Trade Receivables	($69,130)	($20,000)	($425,000)	($350,000)	$562,500	($232,500)
(Increase) Decrease in Inventory	$50,000	($90,000)	($95,000)	$110,000	$25,000	($50,000)
(Increase) Decrease in Other Current Assets	$200,000	$0	$0	$0	$0	$0
Increase (Decrease) in Trade Payables	($115,000)	$65,000	$75,000	$75,000	($175,000)	$40,000
Increase (Decrease) in Accrued Liabilities	($35,000)	$10,000	$25,000	$25,000	($75,000)	($15,000)
Increase (Decrease) in Current Debt	$25,000	$0	$400,000	$0	($500,000)	($100,000)
Increase (Decrease) in Other Current Liabilities	$0	$0	$0	$0	$0	$0
Net Working Capital Cash Flow	($44,130)	($35,000)	($20,000)	($140,000)	($162,500)	($357,500)
Financing Capital:						
Equity Contributions	$0	$0	$0	$0	$0	$0
Additions to Long-Term Debt	$0	$0	$0	$0	$0	$0
Deletions to Long-Term Debt	($250,000)	($62,500)	($62,500)	($62,500)	($62,500)	($250,000)
Fixed Asset Additions	$0	($50,000)	($50,000)	($50,000)	($50,000)	($200,000)
Change to Other Long-Term Assets	$30,000	$5,000	$5,000	$5,000	$5,000	$20,000
Change to Other Long-Term Liabilities	$0	$0	$0	$0	$0	$0
Net Financial Capital Cash Flow	($220,000)	($107,500)	($107,500)	($107,500)	($107,500)	($430,000)
Beginning Cash	$54,131	$230,000	$54,375	$137,750	$290,375	$230,000
Ending Cash	$230,000	$54,375	$137,750	$290,375	$199,250	$199,250

Figure 9-1:
A quarterly forecast for ACME Distribution, Inc.

Making the Most of Your Projections

The previous sections of this chapter focus on actually producing a business plan and corresponding projection as opposed to utilizing the projections as an active management tool. Just like any other piece of financial information generated from the company, the real key lies in management being able to understand the information and then act on it. Producing a plan and projection that are never fully utilized is simply a waste of everyone's time. But with "Projection 101" under your belt, you can now turn your attention to working with more advanced forecasting techniques and concepts that can be utilized to achieve the plan.

The concepts presented in this section by no means require PhD-level thinking (like applying linear regression analysis to sales trends for the past 20 years). Rather, the goal here is to provide some additional forecasting tools, techniques, and strategies that can assist you in managing your business interests. We aim to enlighten you with forecasting strategies that provide the greatest value to your organization in terms of managing everyday challenges, stress, and growing pains.

Developing and utilizing financial projections should not be viewed as just an annual management process/function. Instead, forecasts should be managed proactively and adjusted as needed to adapt to changing business conditions. Staying actively connected and involved in the business planning process (including utilizing financial forecasts) is essential to remaining competitive in today's economic environment.

Getting familiar with some useful terms

Before we jump into an actual financial projection model, we review some basic terminology to help you "speak the language" (that is, accountant-ese or finance-ese) a little bit better. The following list is by no means all-inclusive; it's focused more on terminology that's used when evaluating financial forecasts (based on forward-looking information) as opposed to terminology applied to evaluating periodic financial statements (for example, calculating the current ratio):

✔ **Break-even:** The *break-even* point is the level of sales required to produce operating results with no profits or losses (that is, sales less costs of sales less expenses equals zero). For example, if a company has $50,000 a month in expenses and generates a gross margin on sales of 40 percent, it must generate $125,000 a month to break even. Or looking at the concept from the top down, sales of $125,000 would generate a gross profit of $50,000 (40 percent of $125,000), from which expenses are then subtracted, producing a profit of zero.

✔ **Burn rate:** The *burn rate* is the rate at which cash is burned or consumed in a business. For example, if a company's expenses are $100,000 per month and sales are $40,000 per month, it is losing, or *burning,* $60,000 per month. If the company has $600,000 in cash, then it basically has ten months left to operate.

✔ **Cap table:** A *cap table,* or *capitalization table,* simply offers a summary of who owns what portion of a company and in what structure. Ownership structures are a very sensitive and important issue with third-party financing sources.

✔ **Extending the runway:** The idea of *extending the runway* means that if you're forecasting your cash to run out in four months but a new source of cash won't be available for six months, a company must find a way to stretch its cash to reach the next funding date. The idea is to always conserve your cash resources and stretch every dollar as far and as long as possible.

✔ **Fume date:** Closely related to the burn rate, the *fume date* simply estimates what date a company will run out of cash and be left running on fumes (just like a car that's running on empty and can only make it a little longer).

✔ **Sustainable growth rate:** A company's *sustainable growth rate* is based on how quickly a company can grow with internal resources alone (that is, without securing external capital or cash to support future growth). This rate varies depending on the specific business and industry in which it operates, but when any company grows at rates in excess of 25 percent, supporting this growth with internal resources alone is very difficult. Hence, a breach of the sustainable growth rate indicates that external capital is most likely needed to support the company.

✔ **Dual bottom lines:** A concept that's becoming more and more important in today's socially responsible environment is that companies often measure their results on multiple fronts, also called *dual bottom lines.* For example, in addition to measuring how much profit the company generated, a company's results may also be measured on how much it returned to the community in terms of new jobs, charitable contributions, overall benefits to society, and so on.

When building financial projection models, make sure that your output in the models supports all bottom-line objectives. Everyone expects the output from a financial projection model to identify how much profit will be produced, but generating output reports and information such as the number of jobs created, how healthcare costs may be lowered (for a healthcare information technology company), and so on are also very useful. To a politician who went out of her way to promote your business by offering tax breaks, relaying job creation does wonders for everyone involved.

Treating forecasts as living, breathing management tools

The concept of a living projection model is based in the idea that in today's fiercely competitive marketplace, business models change much quicker than they did ten-plus years ago. Though the forecast prepared in the fourth quarter of the previous year looked reasonable, six months later the story can easily change. Any number of factors may occur, such as losing a key sales executive, having a competitor go out of business (opening up new opportunities), or experiencing a significant increase in the price of raw materials to produce your products, that can cause the best-prepared budgets to be useless by midyear. But if you understand two key forecasting practices, you can make sure that your forecasts continue to live and breathe throughout the year.

Recasting to avoid surprises

When you hear the term *recast* used, it generally means a company is going to update its original budgets or forecasts during some point of the year to update or revise the information through the end of the year. Companies are constantly under pressure to provide updated information on how they think the year will turn out.

In this economic environment, basically everyone is demanding updated information, so at the end of select periods (usually a month end or quarter end), the actual results for the company through that period are incorporated into the original forecast. Using the actual results through the cutoff period as the base starting point, the original forecast for the remainder of the year is then updated (based on business conditions that may have changed), so the operating results for the entire year are a combination of actual results and updated projected results and thus have been recast. Having access to updated information can greatly assist business owners and managers in properly directing the company and adapting to changing conditions, not to mention being able to provide timely updates to key external parties (on how the company is progressing).

Remember, nobody likes surprises (especially bad ones), and nothing will get an external party such as a bank or investor more fired up than management not being able to deliver information on the company's performance.

Using rolling forecasts

Rolling forecasts are similar to recast financial results with the exception that a rolling forecast always looks out over a period of time (for example, the next 12 months) from the most recent period end, whereas a recast is simply updating the original forecast during the current year to provide a revised outlook or forecast for the remainder of the current fiscal year. For example, if a company has a fiscal year-end of 12/31/10 and has prepared a projection for the fiscal year-end 12/31/11, an updated rolling 12-month forecast may be prepared for the period of 4/1/11 through 3/31/12 when the financial results are known for the first quarter ending 3/31/11. This way, management always has 12 months of projections available to work with.

Rolling forecasts tend to be utilized in companies operating in highly fluid or uncertain times that need to always look ahead a certain amount of time. However, more and more companies are utilizing rolling forecasts to better prepare for future uncertainties.

Understanding the difference between internal versus external projections

Businesses produce financial information for use by internal management and for external parties. Some businesses overlook the different needs of internal and external groups, and the company accountant may prepare financial statements from the internal accounting system and simply forward the same information to outside parties. Our thought about that approach is, to use the famous line from *Apollo 13,* "Houston, we have a problem."

The problem is that the information that's prepared for and delivered to external users (such as a financing source, taxing authorities, or company creditors) should not be the same as what's prepared for and utilized internally in the company. This is not to say that the information for external parties should be fabricated, misleading, or incorrect. The core information is still the same, but it's "conditioned" or formatted for delivery to the various parties in the most informative manner possible.

The following examples explain how a business can utilize the same information for different objectives:

✔ **Sales-driven versus accounting-driven budgets:** Companies often have more than one set of projections completed and used for different purposes. To date, we have yet to see a budget prepared based on sales and marketing information that is more conservative than a similar budget prepared based from operations or accounting information. By nature, sales and marketing personnel tend to be far more optimistic about the opportunities present than other segments of the business (which of course includes the ultraconservative accountants).

Rather than attempt to have these two groups battle it out over what forecast model is the most accurate, some businesses simply prepare two sets of projections. The marketing and sales–based projection can be used as a management and motivational tool, whereas a more-conservative projection can be used for delivery to external financing sources (thus ensuring "reasonable" expectations so the company isn't under enormous pressure to hit aggressive plans). Granted, this strategy has to be properly managed (and kept in balance), because one forecast shouldn't be drastically different from another. You don't want to have to defend management's integrity by explaining to external parties who happen to get their hands on both why the forecasts have a large difference.

✔ **Drilling down into the detail:** Information delivered to external parties should contain far less detail than what is utilized internally by management on a daily basis. This concept, of course, holds true for the forecasting process as well. The level and amount of detail at the base of the projection model often drills down to the core elements of your business. For example, the summary projection in Figure 9-1 displays corporate overhead expenses as one line item. This one line item can, in fact, be the summation of over 100 lines of data (or more) and capture everything from the cost of personnel in the accounting department to the current year's advertising budget. An outside party doesn't need (nor want) to see that level of detail because it tends to only confuse matters and lead to unnecessary questions.

However, by being able to drill down into the detail at any given time by using the internal information, you can kill two birds with one stone. Internally, you have the necessary detail to hold management team members responsible for expense and cost control. Externally, if needed you can provide real support for financial information presented in the budget, strengthening your credibility and giving your partners confidence that the business is being tightly managed.

Preparing and presenting different information internally and externally applies to a business's planning and projection documentation just like other critical operational and financial reporting. In this day and age of management transparency and accountability, you don't want to be left holding the bag on unkept forecasting promises made to external parties (especially investors thinking that they have the next Facebook on their hands). The summarized, final results aren't different, but rather the structure and level of detail you provide to different parties should be formatted accordingly.

Preparing multiple projection scenarios: The what-if analysis

A *what-if* analysis is just what it sounds like. That is, you consider what the impact on your business or the market will be if a particular something happens. For example, "If I can land this new account, what additional costs will I need to incur, and when, to support the account?" Utilizing the what-if projection technique is a highly effective business management strategy that can be applied to all levels of the forecasting process, from a single division to the company as a whole. Figure 9-2 presents the original forecast of ACME Distribution, Inc., from Figure 9-1 (the expected case) alongside two other scenarios, one of which is a worst-case scenario and the other a best-case scenario.

By having the ability to complete what-if projections, ACME provides itself with a better understanding of what business decisions need to be made in case different operating scenarios are realized.

Investing the time and effort into developing a projection model that's very flexible and adaptable and can easily incorporate changes to critical economic assumptions is invaluable. If you properly identify, manage, and incorporate critical economic drivers into the planning process, your company can quickly prepare and evaluate different operating scenarios with limited effort.

Low, medium, and high forecasting

A very worthwhile and valuable exercise to undertake each year is to prepare a complete set of projections by using a classic forecasting strategy referred to as *low, medium, and high* (or worst, expected, and best cases):

- ✔ The *low* forecast scenario is based on somewhat of a worst-case or reduced-expectation operating scenario.

- ✔ The *medium* case is based on a very comfortable and achievable operating scenario.

- ✔ The *high* case is based on an operating scenario that's basically best case, in which a number of events, transactions, and so on have to go right to hit the projection goals.

No set rules dictate what ranges should be use to determine the difference between the three operating scenarios. A good rule of thumb is that when a scenario triggers a ±20 percent change in critical operating results (such as revenue or net profit levels), a unique projection and operating scenario has been achieved that generally produces results that require a material or significant management adjustment to be undertaken. As highlighted in Figure 9-2, dramatic differences in the company's pre-tax profit occur between the different operating scenarios, which may lead management to develop a contingency plan in the worst case (to cut expenses or reduce personnel) to creating an added bonus plan if the best case is realized.

Arm forecasting

One additional scenario we often recommend that companies develop is the *Arm* version. Arm is short for Armageddon, and this scenario is basically when all hell breaks loose (as a number of companies experienced in 2008 and 2009 during the Great Recession). The point of the Arm version is to always have it available for disaster planning purposes in the event unforeseen "shocks" to the business operating model are realized (so that actions plans can be enacted to protect your business interests). Although you may never have to experience an Arm environment, the Great Recession and the devastating earthquake and tsunami in Japan in 2011 underscore just how invaluable these types of plans can be.

Summary Balance Sheet	Actual Year-End 1/1/15	Worst Case Year-End 1/1/16	Expected Cast Year-End 1/1/16	Best Case Year-End 1/1/16
Current Assets:				
Cash and Equivalents	$230,000	$67,613	$199,250	$125,039
Trade Receivables, Net	$705,000	$700,000	$937,500	$1,000,000
Inventory	$450,000	$425,000	$500,000	$600,000
Other Current Assets	$75,000	$75,000	$75,000	$100,000
Total Current Assets	$1,460,000	$1,267,613	$1,711,750	$1,825,039
Fixed & Other Assets:				
Property, Plant, and Equipment, Net	$1,340,000	$1,265,000	$1,315,000	$1,340,000
Other Assets	$470,000	$400,000	$400,000	$400,000
Total Fixed and Other Assets	$1,810,000	$1,665,000	$1,715,000	$1,740,000
Total Assets	$3,270,000	$2,932,613	$3,426,750	$3,565,039
Current Liabilities:				
Trade Payables	$385,000	$400,000	$425,000	$500,000
Accrued Liabilities	$215,000	$190,000	$200,000	$210,000
Line of Credit Borrowings	$350,000	$250,000	$250,000	$100,000
Current Portion of Long-Term Liabilities	$250,000	$250,000	$250,000	$250,000
Other Current Liabilities	$75,000	$75,000	$75,000	$75,000
Total Current Liabilities	$1,275,000	$1,165,000	$1,200,000	$1,135,000
Long-Term Liabilities:				
Notes Payable, Less Current Portion	$800,000	$600,000	$600,000	$600,000
Capital Leases, Less Current Portion	$100,000	$50,000	$50,000	$50,000
Subordinated Debt	$250,000	$250,000	$250,000	$250,000
Total Long-term Liabilities	$1,150,000	$900,000	$900,000	$900,000
Total Liabilities	$2,425,000	$2,065,000	$2,100,000	$2,035,000
Equity:				
Common Equity	$100,000	$100,000	$100,000	$100,000
Retained Earnings	$555,000	$745,000	$745,000	$745,000
Current Earnings	$190,000	$22,613	$481,750	$685,039
Total Equity	$845,000	$867,613	$1,326,750	$1,530,039
Total Liabilities & Equity	$3,270,000	$2,932,613	$3,426,750	$3,565,039

Summary Income Statement	Actual Year-End 1/1/15	Worst Case Year-End 1/1/16	Expected Cast Year-End 1/1/16	Best Case Year-End 1/1/16
Revenue	$8,043,750	$7,038,281	$9,000,000	$10,054,688
Costs of Goods Sold	$6,032,813	$5,454,668	$6,673,250	$7,289,648
Gross Profit	$2,010,937	$1,583,613	$2,326,750	$2,765,039
Gross Margin	25.00%	22.50%	25.85%	27.50%
Selling, General, and Administrative Expenses	$1,395,000	$1,250,000	$1,425,000	$1,550,000
Depreciation and Amortization Expense	$250,000	$225,000	$275,000	$300,000
Interest Expense	$125,938	$86,000	$145,000	$80,000
Other (Income) Expenses	$50,000	$0	$0	$0
Net Profit Before Tax	$190,000	$22,613	$481,750	$835,039
Income Tax Expense (Benefit)	$0	$0	$0	$150,000
Net Profit (Loss)	$190,000	$22,613	$481,750	$685,039

Summary Cash Flow Statement	Actual Year-End 1/1/15	Worst Case Year-End 1/1/16	Expected Cast Year-End 1/1/16	Best Case Year-End 1/1/16
Operating Cash Flow:				
Net Income (Loss)	$190,000	$22,613	$481,750	$685,039
Depreciation and Amortization Expense	$250,000	$225,000	$275,000	$300,000
Net Operating Cash Flow	$440,000	$247,613	$756,750	$985,039
Working Capital:				
(Increase) Decrease in Trade Receivables	($69,130)	$5,000	($232,500)	($295,000)
(Increase) Decrease in Inventory	($50,000)	$25,000	($50,000)	($150,000)
(Increase) Decrease in Other Current Assets	$200,000	$0	$0	($25,000)
Increase (Decrease) in Trade Payables	($115,000)	$15,000	$40,000	$115,000
Increase (Decrease) in Accrued Liabilities	($35,000)	($25,000)	($15,000)	($5,000)
Increase (Decrease) in Current Debt	$25,000	($100,000)	($100,000)	($250,000)
Increase (Decrease) in Other Current Liabilities	$0	$0	$0	$0
Net Working Capital Cash Flow	($44,130)	($80,000)	($357,500)	($610,000)
Financing Capital:				
Equity Contributions	$0	$0	$0	$0
Additions to Long-Term Debt	$0	$0	$0	$0
Deletions to Long-Term Debt	($250,000)	($250,000)	($250,000)	($250,000)
Fixed Asset Additions	$0	($100,000)	($200,000)	($250,000)
Change to Other Long-Term Assets	$30,000	$20,000	$20,000	$20,000
Change to Other Long-Term Liabilities	$0	$0	$0	$0
Net Financial Capital Cash Flow	($220,000)	($330,000)	($430,000)	($480,000)
Beginning Cash	$54,131	$230,000	$230,000	$230,000
Ending Cash	$230,000	$67,613	$199,250	$125,039

Figure 9-2:
What-if forecasts for ACME Distribution, Inc.

Integrating forecasts into the active management of your business

Thus far in this section of the chapter, we focus on making the most of financial forecasts from a forward-looking perspective as opposed to actively using forecasts on a periodic operating basis (with actual operating results). So we now turn our attention to incorporating projections with the active periodic management of a business by exploring three additional concepts: the variance analysis, operating plan implementation, and management discussion and analyses.

The variance analysis

An important step in integrating forecasts into operations is taking a look at the projection and comparing it to actual results for a period of time. This concept, called a *variance analysis,* is shown for ACME Distribution, Inc., in Figure 9-3. It presents a report that compares the budgeted results for the quarter against the company's actual results.

With a quick glance at the company's profitability, you could easily draw the conclusion that the company performed right in line with management's expectations, as the actual net loss of $100,100 is consistent with the forecast net loss of $98,125. But on further review, two problems appear. First, the company generated $1.585 million of revenue in the quarter compared to a forecast revenue level of $1.450 million. Yet when the company's gross margin is analyzed, the actual gross margin of 20.19 percent is well below the forecast gross margin of 22.50 percent. So all that effort to increase sales did not produce any improvement in gross profits earned. Obviously, management needs to understand what caused the gross margin to decrease (was it from lower sales prices, higher product costs, or a different product sales mix?).

The second issue is the fact that the company's trade accounts receivable balance was forecasted to reach $725,000 but actually amounted to $815,000, or $90,000 higher than expected. This difference appears to make sense in light of the increased revenue level, because higher sales generally translate into higher trade accounts receivable balances. But the issue to note is that the company had to borrow another $100,000 from the line of credit (forecast borrowings of $350,000 compared to actual borrowings of $450,000) to finance the increase in trade receivables (coming from higher sales), which adds interest expense and increases the leverage of the company.

Of critical importance, however, is that management needs to act on the information. If the market is looking for lower prices in general, then the company may want to revisit pricing strategies for the second through fourth quarters to take advantage of conditions that may allow it to improve the company's annual financial performance.

Summary Balance Sheet	Actual Quarter-End 4/1/15	Projected Quarter-End 4/1/15	Variance Quarter-End 4/1/15
Current Assets:			
Cash and Equivalents	$39,900	$54,375	$14,475
Trade Receivables, Net	$815,000	$725,000	($90,000)
Inventory	$555,000	$540,000	($15,000)
Other Current Assets	$75,000	$75,000	$0
Total Current Assets	$1,484,900	$1,394,375	($90,525)
Fixed and Other Assets:			
Property, Plant, and Equipment, Net	$1,325,000	$1,337,500	$12,500
Other Assets	$452,500	$452,500	$0
Total Fixed and Other Assets	$1,777,500	$1,790,000	$12,500
Total Assets	$3,262,400	$3,184,375	($78,025)
Current Liabilities:			
Trade Payables	$435,000	$450,000	$15,000
Accrued Liabilities	$220,000	$225,000	$5,000
Line of Credit Borrowings	$450,000	$350,000	($100,000)
Current Portion of Long-Term Liabilities	$250,000	$250,000	$0
Other Current Liabilities	$75,000	$75,000	$0
Total Current Liabilities	$1,430,000	$1,350,000	($80,000)
Long-Term Liabilities:			
Notes Payable, Less Current Portion	$750,000	$750,000	$0
Capital Leases, Less Current Portion	$87,500	$87,500	$0
Subordinated Debt	$250,000	$250,000	$0
Total Long-Term Liabilities	$1,087,500	$1,087,500	$0
Total Liabilities	$2,517,500	$2,437,500	($80,000)
Equity:			
Common Equity	$100,000	$100,000	$0
Retained Earnings	$745,000	$745,000	($0)
Current Earnings	($100,100)	($98,125)	$1,975
Total Equity	$744,900	$746,875	$1,975
Total Liabilities and Equity	$3,262,400	$3,184,375	($78,025)

Summary Income Statement	Actual Quarter-End 4/1/15	Projected Quarter-End 4/1/15	Variance Quarter-End 4/1/15
Revenue	$1,585,000	$1,450,000	$135,000
Costs of Goods Sold	$1,265,000	$1,123,750	($141,250)
Gross Profit	$320,000	$326,250	($6,250)
Gross Margin	20.19%	22.50%	-4.63%
Selling, General, and Administrative Expenses	$317,850	$325,000	$7,150
Depreciation and Amortization Expense	$64,750	$65,000	$250
Interest Expense	$37,500	$34,375	($3,125)
Other (Income) Expenses	$0	$0	$0
Net Profit Before Tax	($100,100)	($98,125)	($1,975)
Income Tax Expense (Benefit)	$0	$0	$0
Net Profit (Loss)	($100,100)	($98,125)	($1,975)

Summary Cash Flow Statement	Actual Quarter-End 4/1/15	Projected Quarter-End 4/1/15	Variance Quarter-End 4/1/15
Operating Cash Flow:			
Net Income (Loss)	($100,100)	($98,125)	$1,975
Depreciation and Amortization Expense	$64,750	$65,000	$250
Net Operating Cash Flow	($35,350)	($33,125)	$2,225
Working Capital:			
(Increase) Decrease in Trade Receivables	($110,000)	($20,000)	$90,000
(Increase) Decrease in Inventory	($105,000)	($90,000)	$15,000
(Increase) Decrease in Other Current Assets	$0	$0	$0
Increase (Decrease) in Trade Payables	$50,000	$65,000	$15,000
Increase (Decrease) in Accrued Liabilities	$5,000	$10,000	$5,000
Increase (Decrease) in Current Debt	$100,000	$0	($100,000)
Increase (Decrease) in Other Current Liabilities	$0	$0	$0
Net Working Capital Cash Flow	($60,000)	($35,000)	$25,000
Financing Capital:			
Equity Contributions	$0	$0	$0
Additions to Long-Term Debt	$0	$0	$0
Deletions to Long-Term Debt	($62,500)	($62,500)	$0
Fixed Asset Additions	($37,250)	($50,000)	($12,750)
Change to Other Long-Term Assets	$5,000	$5,000	$0
Change to Other Long-Term Liabilities	$0	$0	$0
Net Financial Capital Cash Flow	($94,750)	($107,500)	($12,750)
Beginning Cash	$230,000	$230,000	$0
Ending Cash	$39,900	$54,375	$14,475

Figure 9-3:
A variance analysis for ACME Distribution, Inc.

Budgets, financial statements, variance analyses, and other prepared statements are pointless if management is not prepared to respond to the information they provide.

Operating plan implementation

Beyond the variance report, another obvious use of the forecasts is to support the implementation of specific plans and action steps. For example, if a new production distribution facility is set to open in the third quarter of the year, then the staff to support this facility will need to be secured in the middle of the second quarter and then trained to ensure that they are ready when the new facility opens. The original budget for the new facility should also have accumulated and incorporated that info, but the idea is to turn the budget into a proactive working document (easily accessible for reference) rather than a onetime effort left on the shelf to die.

Management discussions and analyses

The budget plays an important part in helping businesses prepare a financial document that most companies ignore (either intentionally or out of ignorance): the MDOR *(management discussion of operating results),* or MDA *(management discussion and analysis).*

MDOR and MDA are essentially the same document and serve the same purpose, which is to provide a written narrative of how the company is performing. These documents translate financial information, results, and numbers into written words, strategies, plans, and events. Though this type of documentation sounds relative easy to complete, the MDOR and MDA can be very difficult to prepare because the translation process can be very difficult.

At the base of the MDOR and MDA, when explaining actual results versus planned, is a well-developed budget that provides a clear road map to understanding operating result variances. You may wonder why a business would bother putting together these difficult documents if they simply summarize information available elsewhere. We recommend them for the following two critical reasons:

✔ If you present financial information without explaining it, readers (whether internal or external) often come to their own conclusions about why the company is performing a certain way. More times than not, their conclusions are incorrect, which may lead to adverse decisions that negatively impact your business. Remember, assumptions are the mother of all you-know-whats, so the more you can do to eliminate assumptions from being made, the better.

✔ By being able to clearly relay your company's financial results, key parties (whether internal or external) will gain more confidence in your
management abilities, which gives your business more creditability.
This may not sound like much payoff for the work, but believe us when
we tell you that management integrity and creditability have saved more
than a few businesses. For financing sources, *credit decisions* are easy
and tend to be based on the financial information. But when a *business
decision* needs to be made, management integrity and creditability rise
to the surface.

Broadening the use of projections even further

When preparing projections, you must remember that the base data and
information accumulated (to prepare the budget) can be used to support
other business planning and management functions as well. For example,
a well-developed budget can be used not only to prepare forecast financial
statements but, in addition, to prepare the estimated taxable income or loss
of a company. For some companies, the difference between book and tax
income is small. However for others, the difference can be significant and
must be anticipated, as the following real world example demonstrates.

A large provider of personnel services elected to implement a strategy to self-
fund their workers' compensation insurance costs. The preliminary analysis
indicated that an average annual savings of 30 percent or more could be
achieved if properly managed. At the end of the third year of the self-funded
workers' compensation insurance program, the company had established
an accrued liability for over $1 million to account for potential future claims.
(That is, workers' compensation insurance claims for injuries sustained on the
job, which required subsequent payments to be made over a period of time).
In total, the claims amounted to $1.2 million, of which $200,000 was paid by
the end of the year and the expected additional payouts required for medical services, lost wages, and other damages amounted to another $1 million.
For book purposes, the $1 million represented an expense recorded in the
financial statements, which resulted in the company producing net income of
roughly zero dollars. For tax purposes, the IRS would not allow the expense
until the claims were actually paid, so the taxable income of the company was
$1 million (resulting in a tax liability of $400,000). If the company did not properly budget for this business event, it might have been in for a rude surprise,
as per the books the company made nothing yet owed $400,000 in taxes. You
can be assured that this is not the type of surprise an executive wants to experience on short notice.

The budget can be used for other purposes as well, ranging from preparing information for specialized needs from external parties (such as governmental agencies that require information to be prepared in a specific format) to training a new division manager on the basic economics of how his division should perform. The better the forecasts are designed and structured from the beginning, the more uses and value they provide your business down the road.

Chapter 10

Identifying and Securing External Sources of Capital

*O*ver the past 100 years, the face of the United States has been shaped by waves of industrial visionaries, technology giants, and innovative entrepreneurs who were in the right place at the right time. From Ford, Carnegie, Mellon, and Vanderbilt to Hewlett Packard, IBM, Google, and Facebook, the most prosperous companies have certain characteristics in common. The ultimate success of companies is based in a combination of the ability to secure all the essential ingredients needed to build a business (including leadership, vision, talent, planning, determination, and more) at the most opportune time, with a little luck, combined with the all-important element of securing the proper amount and type of capital (cash) to support the business concept.

Whether big or small, public or private, foreign or domestic, or 1 month new or 20 years old, securing and managing capital resources represents the lifeline of any company looking to operate in today's challenging economic climate. In this chapter you get a quick look at why capital is so important before delving into the details of one of the two types of capital, equity. We explain how equity works, what sources are available, and how you can go about securing them. And to make sure that your newly acquired capital works hard for you, we discuss how capital should be used and what you should know about the capital markets.

Getting a Grip on the Capital Concept

Securing capital for a company represents one of the most painstaking and time-consuming efforts a business undertakes. Getting a party interested in providing capital to your organization is one thing; actually receiving the commitment and securing the capital is an entirely different thing. Securing capital represents a full-time job requiring the undivided attention of a company's senior management team and ultimately the CEO, because that's where the buck stops.

Countless technical and/or theoretical definitions are available (to peruse at your leisure) on what capital actually is, but to keep it simple, when managing a business opportunity, you really only need to consider one expression to understand the real essence of capital: *It takes money to make money.* Launching any new business concept, from the aspiring entrepreneur designing a new software product from his home office to an executive of a multinational corporation looking to expand foreign distribution channels for new product introductions, requires capital (cash, money, greenbacks, or whatever you like to call it) as a basis to execute the business plan.

One of the most common reasons cited as to why businesses fail is a lack of capital, or inappropriately structured capital (to support the needs of the business). This problem not only applies to the more easily understandable business environment when continued losses consume all of a company's cash, but it also applies (maybe more importantly) when a company grows too fast and doesn't have enough capital or cash to support its growth. Companies can literally grow themselves right out of business if the growth isn't properly planned for and managed.

Business capital can basically be classified into one of two primary types: debt (loans that must be repaid), or equity (investments that should generate a return). This chapter explores some of the ways you can raise capital through equity. When these opportunities are paired with debt capital, available from banks and other lenders (and more fully overviewed in Chapter 11), a savvy and well-informed accountant can find plenty of potential sources to raise cash.

Deciding what form of capital, debt or equity, is most suitable for your company really depends on the company's stage in terms of its operating history, industry profile, profitability levels, asset structure, future growth prospects, and general capital requirements, all considered in relation to where the sources of capital lie. After exploring potential sources of capital in this chapter (on equity) and Chapter 11 (on debt), analyzing your company's financial condition in Chapter 7, and considering future requirements in Chapters 8 and 9, you'll be ready to answer this question and (hopefully) secure your financial future.

Keep in mind that capital should not be perceived as just the amount of cash on hand but rather the amount of financial resources available to support the execution of a business plan. This point is clearly illustrated throughout this chapter's discussion of raising/securing capital.

Understanding the Basics of Equity Capital

Equity-based capital is money provided to a company in the form of an investment in the business, which is looking for the generation of a return (such as a dividend being paid on stock you might own). This capital doesn't have set repayment terms but does have a right to future earnings. Unlike debt, equity investors may be provided dividends or distributions if profits and cash flows are available. For example, a software technology company requires approximately $2 million in capital to develop and launch a new Internet-based software solution. A niche venture capitalist group invests the required capital under the terms and conditions present in the equity offering, including what their percentage ownership in company will be, rights to future earnings, representation on the board of directors, preferred versus common equity status, conversion rights, antidilution provisions, and so on. Under this scenario, the company receiving the equity is not required to remit any payments to the capital source per a set repayment agreement, but it has given up a partial right to ownership (which can be even more costly).

Equity is best evaluated by understanding its two most important characteristics: preference and management influence.

Equity preference

Preference refers to the fact that certain types of equity have priority over other types in collecting earnings and, if needed, company assets. For example, a Series A preferred stock may be issued to investors that have an interest in making an equity investment but want to protect or prioritize their investments in relation to the common shareholders or another series of preferred stock. A Series B preferred stock may hold a lower preference to the Series A preferred stock in terms of asset liquidations but may have a slightly higher dividend yield attached or offered with a warrant that allows it to purchase common shares at a later date at a favorable price.

Actually, the features built into preferred stock are almost endless and can create a large number of different types of preferred stock (A through Z). For common equity, so too can preferences exist. Common stock Type A may have full voting rights and dividends (after the preferred shareholders receive their dividend), whereas a common stock Type B may only have rights to dividends and not voting. To list all the potential preferences and/or features built into equity instruments (including the ability to convert, antidilution provisions, cumulative versus noncumulative dividends, voting rights, acceleration clauses, liquidation criteria, and more) is well beyond the scope of this book.

The key point in understanding equity preferences is that equity investors attempt to secure as many preferences and features that protect their interests as possible. Though this strategy may be good for them, it may not be in the best interests of the company, and it may restrict the company's ability to operate farther down the road.

Equity and management influence

The concept of management influence is centered in the fact that when equity capital is raised, the provider of the capital is considered an owner or shareowner of the company. By its very nature, this involvement entitles the shareowner to have a say in the company's operations (unless otherwise restricted) with the ability to vote with the board of directors and on other critical matters (for example, on approving the company's external auditor or allocating equity to be distributed to company management). This management influence can be extended significantly when preferences are factored into the equation.

In the end, the old adage of "Money talks and you-know-what walks" really applies in today's economic environment as it relates to management influence. When investors with big money come to the show, they tend to have a significant influence on not only the composition of a company's board of directors but even on the actual management team running the business daily.

If you remember only one thing when raising equity capital, it should be this: Be prepared to co-manage the business with your new best friends — the equity investors — because for the business to run smoothly and efficiently, your dictatorship must give way to a democracy.

Starting to Look for Capital

In the movie *Jerry Maguire*, Cuba Gooding Jr. utters the now-somewhat-infamous line, "Show me the money." These four words sum up the capital-raising process as well as any, because until you have the money in hand, a business concept is really nothing more than the paper the business plan is written on. And as author Tage's dad (who is in fact the coauthor of this book) has always told him, that and one dollar should get you a cup of coffee.

To make that business plan worth something, you need to look at the potential sources of capital available to launch your new business, open a new product/service niche within a corporate conglomerate, or acquire a pesky competitor. The sources listed in this section are by no means all-inclusive, but they provide an overview of the variety of avenues available to raise capital and the pluses and minuses associated with each one.

Looking in the mirror

First up, the business founders need to look no farther than themselves to secure initial capital to launch or support a company. Their assistance may range from tapping their own savings to selling personal assets and holdings (to raise cash) to leveraging their creditworthiness with debt such as home equity loans, credit cards, and/or other sources. The bottom line is that just about every business venture starts with some type of initial capital or cash contribution being made by the founders.

Providing this preliminary *(seed)* capital is critical for two reasons. First, and most obviously, the new business venture needs cash to launch its operations, including covering the costs to legally form the company, supporting the initial operating expenses and payroll, and so on. Second, and just as important, most external capital sources want to see that the founders have actually invested some of their own hard-earned cash and effort into the business. If you haven't stepped up with the capital needed to launch a business, your lack of financial participation may raise a question about your real commitment to the business.

Retirement accounts, including 401(k)s, company-sponsored profit-sharing plans, IRAs, SEPs, and the like, are often considered as a source of cash by individuals when starting a business. Though tempting, a complete and full understanding of the risks and added costs associated with using these funds should be considered. For instance, significant additional tax burdens may arise from using these funds if not properly planned for and managed. And don't forget that this is your retirement money, so it should go without saying that tapping this capital source should be done with the utmost caution.

Sweat equity is the amount of time, effort, and energy an individual invests in a company in lieu of actual cash contributions. For example, if you work for free during the first year the business is formed but have a market worth of $100,000 in annual compensation, then that amount is considered sweat equity. Most likely, external capital sources are not going to assign significant value to this component, but it's a very important number to calculate and quantify when negotiating equity investments.

Turning to family, friends, and close business associates

Family, friends, and close business associates (or *FF&CBAs*) have been one of the primary capital sources to launch new business concepts since the beginning of time and will most likely continue to fill this role in the future. The involvement of FF&CBAs ranges from the founders of a business having mom and dad offer up the initial ante to a trusted business associate stepping in with the needed seed money to launch the company.

Generally, this type of capital tends to be for low dollar amounts, be geared toward equity as opposed to debt (given the uncertain nature of the business and higher risks present in terms of generating cash flow), and be provided to closely held and/or family operated businesses. However, debt can be effectively utilized with more mature businesses generating solid profitability with some type of security present (such as real estate).

The good news is that raising capital from FF&CBAs can often be completed quickly and without a significant amount of legal paperwork and/or similar investor creditability issues. The bad news is threefold:

- ✔ The amount of capital available from these sources is often restricted. Pulling together a couple of hundred thousand dollars is one thing, but when a business concept needs a million or two, not too many FF&CBAs have this type of liquidity available (unless maybe your last name is DuPont, Getty, Gates, or Buffett).

- ✔ The recent economic turmoil experienced in the United States from 2008 through 2010 has made this source of capital more difficult to access because personal wealth has eroded via decreasing real estate values, reductions in savings/investment values, and lost employment income, and many people are very nervous about protecting their nest egg. And given that traditional sources of capital (like from banks) have become scarce, many people among your FF&CBA may want to conserve cash for their own business interests.

- ✔ Having unsophisticated FF&CBAs provide capital to a business carries unforeseen risks and volatile emotional elements. Reporting back to a seasoned investor that a business concept didn't work and that his investment is worthless may not be the most pleasant task in the world, but at least the investor was aware of the risks. Telling your aunt and uncle that you've just blown through their nest egg may get your name replaced with something nasty when spoken at subsequent family gatherings. The costs of losing a family member's investment can be much greater than the actual amount of capital invested.

Be very wary of FF&CBA capital sources and the subjective costs that are often attached. Only FF&CBA sources who clearly understand the investment process and business in general, as well as can afford the potential loss, should be approached and evaluated as capital sources. Nothing is worse than having a business fail and then watching the family disintegrate as a result of the failed business.

Seeking Equity Sources of Capital

When your business has reached a point where external equity is needed to support its growth, a large number of private capital sources are available and generally fall into one of the four following primary sources: angel investors, venture capitalists, private equity groups, and other private investment groups.

These sources of private capital come in a variety shapes, sizes, and forms, but all tend to gravitate toward a common set of criteria:

- ✔ The dollar size of the capital commitment is generally larger than with FF&CBAs. These groups are comprised of highly trained and sophisticated professionals responsible for managing large pools of capital and, as such, frequently apply the concept of economy of scale (that is, they will spend the same amount of time and energy on evaluating an opportunity that needs $1 million of equity funding versus an opportunity that needs $10 million of equity money, with the latter providing a greater chance of turning into a much bigger and more valuable business).

- ✔ These groups tend to be more risk-based capital sources and look for higher returns from equity-driven transactions (as well as expect additional involvement in the management of the business, usually at the board level). These groups are comfortable making equity investments in relatively early-stage businesses without proven profitability (but with significant potential) or structuring risk-based debt facilities to support a higher-risk business opportunity (for example, the debt is secured by nothing more than goodwill). Just remember, higher investment returns will be expected for taking on the added risk.

- ✔ These groups are generally not looking to invest in a company with a revenue potential in the ballpark of only $5 million after five years (such as regionally based construction subcontracting company). With the types of capital these groups have available, the business opportunity must be relatively grand to pique their interest. Though you don't need to be the next Microsoft, you do need to provide a solid opportunity to produce in excess of $50 million in annual revenue (over a reasonable time), generate solid profits, and have an efficient exit strategy.

So the good news with private capital is that larger capital amounts are available, the groups are generally very sophisticated and can provide invaluable management support, and the capital is often equity based so that aspiring businesses in needs of large capital infusions have a resource. The bad news is that these groups tend to ask for (and receive) a higher ownership stake in the business and thus can exert a significant amount of management control and influence. In addition, these groups retain highly trained professionals who are very demanding when undertaking their due diligence.

Due diligence is the process by which a capital source evaluates, examines, tests, audits, and otherwise reviews the business information being provided from a company looking to secure capital. Or in other words, and for lack of a better comparison, due diligence is basically the equivalent of your business receiving a colonoscopy.

In the following sections, the ordering of these private capital sources is presented from most willing to assume and accept risk to least willing (with angel investors often taking on more risk and more-immature business opportunities and private equity groups looking for lower risk and more-mature business opportunities).

Angel investors

Angel investors typically are high-net-worth individuals that have ample financial resources to invest in new ventures. In addition, based on their past experiences or own curiosity, angel investors tend to have a strong interest in the business concept, product, technology, or service of the company seeking capital, and they're not afraid to invest in a business at more of a "conceptual" stage (that is, the early stage or before revenue is generated). Angel investment groups come in all shapes, sizes, and forms ranging from geographically based (for instance, a group of high-net-worth individuals who all live in the same city) to interest based (experts with a specific investment interest brought together virtually from around the globe). Capital availability from angel investors, however, tends to be lower than other private capital sources, with investment levels often in the six-figure to low-seven-figure range.

The very important term *accredited investor* (as defined by the Securities and Exchange Commission, or SEC) basically represents an individual who has the appropriate financial strength and business acumen to understand the risks of the investment and bear the brunt of any potential economic loss. The SEC has established a very clear set of tests and criteria to qualify investors as accredited, and you should follow these criteria when pursuing angel investors. The reason for this diligence is simple: If you raise capital from nonqualified parties, the risk of legal action against the owners of the business increases, especially if an investor complains. Trust us when we say that the last thing anyone wants to deal with is the combination of the capital source, the source's attorneys, and the SEC all pounding on the company at once.

Venture capitalists (VCs)

Next up in the risk-appetite order are venture capitalists, or VCs. VCs, similar to angel investors, come in groups of varying size and form but are generally aligned along a specific industry expertise or interest. For example, certain VCs have a strong interest and knowledge in the biotech industry, whereas others specialize in social media or green/clean energy.

Capital availability from VCs tends to come in much larger increments, with most VCs looking for investment minimums of $5 million (although some will go lower, depending on your industry and region). In addition to having funds to invest, VCs generally have other significant resources at their disposal, including decades of combined business management experience, in-depth industry knowledge, and well-developed contacts and business relationships. However, this level of funding and support carry with them higher levels of management involvement and much tighter due-diligence efforts.

Note: The *V* (or *venture* part of the name) in VC has become noticeably scarcer over the past decade, particularly since 2007. VCs are tending to hedge their risk and are looking for later-stage opportunities with proven management teams and solid revenue traction that are in need of working capital to support growth rather than innovate new products, technologies, or concepts. The days of VCs funding two guys in a garage with an idea are long gone.

VCs have significant resources at their disposal with professionals and experts available to address any issue, question, or concern that may arise. If your business isn't properly prepared to undertake the rigors of a detailed VC examination, then don't. If your presentation or pitch for capital fails, a VC is unlikely to give you a second chance.

Private equity groups (PEGs)

Private equity groups or (PEGs) offer sources of capital in a similar strategy to VCs in that they look for specific industries that they possess an expertise within. Capital availability from PEGs covers a wide range, with lower limits in the $5 to $10 million range and upper limits well into the hundreds of millions of dollars.

PEGs operate in just about every type of industry you can think of and tend to look for slightly different opportunities than VCs. Whereas a VC looks to invest in a newer concept with significant growth potential, a PEG tends to be more focused on mature businesses that have untapped potential that the PEG can help unlock. For example, a large regional distribution company may have reached its operating limit as a result of outgrowing the management team's capabilities and capital resources available. A PEG may recognize that by consolidating this operation with others, the combined operation (on a national or even global scale) can expand more efficiently and leverage all the acquired resources into a very large and highly profitable company.

PEGs can be attracted to untapped potential in financially sound businesses just as often as in troubled, financially weak, and/or poorly managed companies. PEGs may be able to unlock the economic value of many kinds of businesses just by bringing in new management and providing adequate capital.

Be very careful with how the *E* (or *equity* part of the name) in PEG is created. PEGs often use both equity and debt when structuring their deals in an effort to utilize the internal cash flow of a company to service the debt. As we note in Chapter 11, debt cuts both ways: It can greatly enhance an investment's return, but the added leverage can also increase the operating risk of the business. So though *E* was plentiful in the PEGs from 2003 through 2007 (when the economy was expanding), a number of PEGs experienced a very quick evaporation of *E* when the economy turned south in 2008.

Similar to VCs, PEGs have significant resources at their disposal with professionals and experts available to address any issue, question, or concern that may arise. So like a good Boy Scout, be prepared when working with PEGs.

Other private investment groups

In the United States, capital formation and deployment can be achieved relatively quickly and efficiently. When a new market opportunity presents itself, capital will find a way to exploit it (as long as the investment returns are appropriate). A case in point is how capital is moving to take advantage of the economic turmoil realized from 2008 through 2010. A variety of new private investment groups that can best be described as having a cross section of characteristics from VCs, PEGs, and lending sources have been formed to pursue opportunities in specific industries. For lack of a better term, I refer to these private investment groups as *pirate funds,* because they tend to look for promising but distressed situations and provide debt- and equity-based capital (with limited management support or involvement).

But although capital markets can form and deploy funding quickly, these types of investment groups also need to be approached with an added level of caution, because they tend to be very expensive when all their fees, costs, requirements, and demands are considered. This isn't to say that these groups are just looking to exploit the situation. A number of the groups are very well structured and provide invaluable resources. But understanding why these groups demand higher returns (in relation to the risks they take) and when they should be used is important.

For example, a business may need to secure $1 million of longer-term capital to execute a turnaround, pay off some pesky secured creditors (such as a bank), and provide working capital to cover short-term losses. A pirate fund may step in and provide this financing in the form of lower-priority debt at a relatively high interest rate, but which also carries an equity kicker to sweeten the deal and improve the investment return.

An *equity kicker,* a right or grant provided to a third party (providing higher-risk debt to a business) in the form of future upside earnings that may be realized from improved cash flows, the sale of a business, or the like, is usually provided to a third party as a way of improving the potential return on an investment in recognition of increased risks being taken. Taking the above example, if an investment group provides a $1 million loan to a business against inferior collateral (like intangible assets, such as goodwill, or intellectual property, such as patents or trade names), an interest rate in the mid to high teens (16 percent) should be expected along with a warrant attached to purchase 10 percent of the company at a very low price. So not only does the source providing the $1 million of capital earn 16 percent on the loan, but if the company is successful in executing its business plan and sells down the road for a handsome price, the investment group then also has an opportunity to participate in the increased value of the business. Numerous types of equity kickers are used, but the objective remains the same — to enhance an investment return in a high-risk transaction.

In terms of capital availability, these types of private investment groups have a significant bandwidth in deal size, which may range from as low as $500,000 to $1 million to the hundreds of millions of dollars. It just depends on the size of the investment fund and industry specialty.

Accessing Public Sources of Capital

Almost every business owner, professional, and manager is aware of the public markets for trading stocks and bonds, including the New York Stock Exchange, NASDAQ, and similar venues (that is, Wall Street). Instruments of both equity (such as the common stock of Microsoft) and debt (like United States Treasury Bills) are actively traded in these open markets. Though the allure of the public markets is very appealing to business owners and often is viewed as the end game ("I took my company public and now am worth X million dollars"), the reality of operating in a public market can be very different. As such, public capital sources have developed a unique set of qualifications in terms of making it the most appropriate capital source to pursue.

- ✔ **Think big.** Public markets are better suited for companies thinking in hundreds of millions or billions than in millions.

- ✔ **Think public.** Basically, all your company's information, financial records, activities, and so on will be available for public viewing. You must not only be prepared to disclose the information, but also make sure that the disclosure is prepared in the proper format.

- ✔ **Understand risk.** Are the returns and rewards for being public adequate in relation to the risks you and your business assume?

Public capital market's positive attributes include having access to extremely large capital levels that can tap the widest range of sources available (stretching the globe). As the national debt of the United States clearly displays, no deal is too big for public markets. The liquidity that public markets offer (allowing investments to be efficiently bought, sold, and traded), the ability to establish fair-market values almost instantaneously, and access to both debt and equity sources are also positive attributes.

But as everyone knows, no capital source is perfect, so there must be a downside to public capital as well:

- **Cost:** Staying in compliance with all the public reporting requirements can be extremely expensive and only continues to increase as investors demand more disclosures and the government looks to protect investors further (for example, with the Sarbanes-Oxley Act of 2003).

- **Management exposure:** Even when fraud isn't present, investors in public debt and equity instruments can turn into a company's worst nightmare when things aren't going as planned. The additional burden placed on the management team can be extensive and distract the company from actually running its business.

- **Misconception about liquidity:** Just because your company is publicly traded doesn't mean that it has liquidity. Stocks of smaller companies (with less than $100 million of market capitalization) are often not actively traded on the open market, which can make selling or buying a large block of stock more difficult (not to mention the scrutiny the company insiders, original founders, large equity owners, management, board members, officers, and similar parties receive when undertaking these transactions).

This discussion on public markets is fairly short, but the topic of accessing public capital markets could fill a book by itself. However, the long and short of public markets is fairly straightforward: Though plenty of small companies are publicly traded, public markets are generally best suited for the big boys of corporate America.

Putting Your Capital to Good Use

Raising or securing capital is without question one of the most difficult and time-consuming tasks the senior management team of a company undertakes. Preparing, packaging, marketing, negotiating, and closing the deal can easily consume 80 to 100 percent of an executive's time, depending on the stage of the company. For a start-up operation, chief executive officers (CEOs) and other senior executives often find themselves closing on one round of financing, resting for a day or two, and then starting the process all over again, looking for the next financing source. For chief financial officers (CFOs) of publicly traded companies, the majority of their time may be consumed in preparing information for the capital sources and markets and then managing the capital sources expectations, inquiries, and/or other needs. To a certain degree, managing the capital sources after the capital is secured can be even more challenging and difficult than raising the capital itself.

Managing this element of capital risks is somewhat intangible in nature because it's geared toward relationships and communication efforts as opposed to hard financial and accounting data. With that said, we now turn our attention toward the more tangible elements of managing capital risks, from both the accounting and financial perspectives. Check out Figure 10-1 to see these capital risks illustrated.

As you can see in Figure 10-1, all elements of this business are exactly the same, with the exception of how the business was capitalized. Under the equity scenario, a total of $1 million of capital was raised, all in the form of equity. Under the debt scenario, a total of $200,000 of equity was raised and $800,000 of debt was secured (of which $200,000 is due over the next 12 months and is thus classified as a current liability in the balance sheet). The income statements are exactly the same with the exception of the fact that the debt scenario has interest expense present.

The quick financial analysis highlights the key differences and indicates that, by using debt, the company was able to generate better returns for the equity owners in 2008 as follows:

- ✔ **Returns:** The debt scenario produces a return on equity of 16.65 percent compared to a return on equity of 11.84 percent with the equity scenario. The return on assets is almost identical for both scenarios.

- ✔ **Earnings:** The debt scenario generates earnings per share of roughly 4.5 times that of the equity scenario ($1.20 per share compared to $0.27 per share).

- ✔ **Leverage:** The only real downside to the debt scenario lies in the fact that this scenario has a much higher debt-to-equity ratio (1.09) compared to for the equity scenario (.34) in addition to having a debt service coverage ratio of approximately 1.16. Although using debt was beneficial in terms of enhancing returns, it also has placed the company in a higher risk status due to the amount of debt leverage used. This risk will be clearly illustrated when the next year's operating results are realized, as presented in Figure 10-2.

	Equity FYE 12/31/08	Debt FYE 12/31/08
Summary Balance Sheet		
Current Assets:		
Cash and Equivalents	$145,180	$116,380
Trade Receivables, Net	$750,000	$750,000
Inventory	$815,625	$815,625
Total Current Assets	$1,710,805	$1,682,005
Fixed and Other Assets:		
Property, Plant, and Equipment, Net	$1,250,000	$1,250,000
Other Assets	$75,000	$75,000
Total Fixed and Other Assets	$1,325,000	$1,325,000
Total Assets	$3,035,805	$3,007,005
Current Liabilities:		
Trade Payables	$611,719	$611,719
Accrued Liabilities	$30,586	$30,586
Line of Credit Borrowings	$0	$0
Current Portion of Long-Term Liabilities	$0	$200,000
Total Current Liabilities	$642,305	$842,305
Long-Term Liabilities:		
Notes Payable, Less Current Portion	$0	$600,000
Other Long-Term Liabilities	$125,000	$125,000
Total Long-Term Liabilities	$125,000	$725,000
Total Liabilities	$767,305	$1,567,305
Equity:		
Common and Preferred Equity, $1 Per Share	$1,000,000	$200,000
Retained Earnings	$1,000,000	$1,000,000
Current Earnings	$268,500	$239,700
Total Equity	$2,268,500	$1,439,700
Total Liabilities & Equity	$3,035,805	$3,007,005

	Equity FYE 12/31/08	Debt FYE 12/31/08
Summary Income Statement		
Revenue	$9,000,000	$9,000,000
Costs of Goods Sold	$6,525,000	$6,525,000
Gross Profit	$2,475,000	$2,475,000
Gross Margin	27.50%	27.50%
Selling, General, and Administrative Expenses	$2,000,000	$2,000,000
Interest Expense	$0	$48,000
Other (Income) Expenses	$27,500	$27,500
Net Profit Before Tax	$447,500	$399,500
Income Tax Expense (Benefit)	$179,000	$159,800
Net Profit (Loss)	$268,500	$239,700

	Equity FYE 12/31/08	Debt FYE 12/31/08
Quick Financial Analysis		
Debt-to-Equity Ratio	0.34	1.09
Debt Service Coverage Ratio	N/A	1.16
Return on Equity	11.84%	16.65%
Return on Assets	8.84%	7.97%
Earnings Per Share	$0.27	$1.20

Figure 10-1:
Unaudited financial statement comparison for a normal operating period.

Now we fast-forward to 2009 (as presented in Figure 10-2), during which time the company has gone from having a robust year (in 2008) with strong margins and profitability to now having to deal with the Great Recession driving sales lower by 25 percent and reducing gross margins as a result of having to lower prices (to stay competitive). Whereas the selling, general, and administrative expenses were reduced as result of the difficult times, the reduction wasn't enough to enable the debt company to generate a profit. Now the equity-financed company is able to generate a small profit and produce positive returns on assets and equity and the debt-financed company incurs a loss and negative returns.

Making matters even worse is that the debt-financed company may now be in violation of certain debt covenants and in default of the loan agreement. For example, the loan agreement may read that the company needs to maintain a debt service coverage ratio of at least 1 and/or produce profitable results on an annual basis (both common covenants for lending sources). Because the company has violated both, it is in technical default on the loan, which will require a fair amount of management attention moving forward.

And just to add a little more insult to injury, the real damage may not be realized until 2010 and beyond. While the equity-financed company has a strong balance sheet and ample cash to expand after the recession ends, the debt-financed company is stuck with restructuring its balance sheet to please its creditors. Thus, it may miss significant growth opportunities in 2010 and beyond, costing the company sales and profits.

In summary, debt- and equity-financing strategies cut both ways. Although debt-financing strategies can enhance returns, they also increase the company's operating risks by leveraging its assets. In good times, when profits and cash flows are ample and everyone's making a buck, debt-financing strategies look great. When the tide turns, profits dry up, and cash flows become restricted, debt financing can look like the evil stepchild that nobody wants around but which must be fed (usually at the expense of some good kids). Remember, debt-financing sources are focused on providing loans that generate sound returns and are repaid in a reasonable time frame. You won't get much sympathy from a bank if you ask them to suspend debt payments in order to keep a business unit open on the hopes of an eventual rebound.

Conversely, equity capital offers a chance to strengthen the balance sheet and help manage the company's operating risks through good times and bad. Maintaining a strong balance sheet can really provide a competitive weapon when expanding a business into new markets or exploring a unique business opportunity. However, having too much equity without being able to generate adequate returns can dampen investor enthusiasm and produce a rather restless group of shareholders and board members. Remember, equity-financing sources do not invest capital to watch it generate below-average returns. Equity capital, although representing a lower perceived risk to the company, is by its nature a higher-risk capital source (to the providers) and must produce a satisfactory investment return. If not, the equity capital will find an opportunity that does provide the necessary return.

Summary Balance Sheet	Equity FYE 12/31/09	Debt FYE 12/31/09
Current Assets:		
Cash and Equivalents	$876,027	$425,627
Trade Receivables, Net	$562,500	$562,500
Inventory	$632,813	$632,813
Total Current Assets	$2,071,340	$1,620,940
Fixed and Other Assets:		
Property, Plant, and Equipment, Net	$1,000,000	$1,000,000
Other Assets	$75,000	$75,000
Total Fixed and Other Assets	$1,075,000	$1,075,000
Total Assets	$3,146,340	$2,695,940
Current Liabilities:		
Trade Payables	$474,609	$474,609
Accrued Liabilities	$23,730	$23,730
Line of Credit Borrowings	$0	$0
Current Portion of Long-Term Liabilities	$0	$200,000
Total Current Liabilities	$498,340	$698,340
Long-Term Liabilities:		
Notes Payable, Less Current Portion	$0	$400,000
Other Long-Term Liabilities	$125,000	$125,000
Total Long-Term Liabilities	$125,000	$525,000
Total Liabilities	$623,340	$1,223,340
Equity:		
Common and Preferred Equity, $1 Per Share	$1,500,000	$500,000
Retained Earnings	$1,018,500	$989,700
Current Earnings	$4,500	($17,100)
Total Equity	$2,523,000	$1,472,600
Total Liabilities and Equity	$3,146,340	$2,695,940

Summary Income Statement	Equity FYE 12/31/09	Debt FYE 12/31/09
Revenue	$6,750,000	$6,750,000
Costs of Goods Sold	$5,062,500	$5,062,500
Gross Profit	$1,687,500	$1,687,500
Gross Margin	25.00%	25.00%
Selling, General, and Administrative Expenses	$1,600,000	$1,600,000
Interest Expense	$0	$36,000
Other (Income) Expenses	$80,000	$80,000
Net Profit Before Tax	$7,500	($28,500)
Income Tax Expense (Benefit)	$3,000	($11,400)
Net Profit (Loss)	$4,500	($17,100)

Quick Financial Analysis	Equity FYE 12/31/09	Debt FYE 12/31/09
Debt-to-Equity Ratio	0.25	0.83
Debt Service Coverage Ratio	N/A	0.08
Return on Equity	0.18%	-1.16%
Return on Assets	0.14%	-0.63%
Earnings Per Share	$0.00	-$0.03

Figure 10-2:
Unaudited financial statement comparison for a recession period.

Looking at the Reality of the Current Capital Markets

Raising capital really does represent the ultimate sale: You have to convince a capital source to actually believe in your business and then fork over the money. Terms such as *nerve-racking, frustrating, euphoric, riding a roller coaster* and the like become common in addition to the experiences of hair loss, stress, and joy. And the economic turmoil experienced across the globe from 2007 through 2010 has only made the capital-raising process even more challenging. So as a friendly reminder to help you with this challenge, we summarize ten key capital raising tips along with five critical realities of the capital markets.

Ten tips for raising capital

As you navigate the complicated job of raising capital, keep the following advice in mind:

- ✔ **Be prepared.** Always be prepared for anything and everything. Capital sources expect and demand the highest quality information, plans, and underlying support be made available when evaluating an investment opportunity.

- ✔ **Be persistent.** Capital sources are just looking for reasons to say no. The attributes of persistence and determination can't be emphasized enough when pursuing and securing capital.

- ✔ **Qualify the capital sources.** Make every effort to qualify your capital sources to ensure that the most appropriate avenue is pursued in relation to the operating status of your business. Don't waste your time or theirs, and by all means make sure that the capital source is capable and accredited to support the request.

- ✔ **Give yourself plenty of time.** Raising capital can be a painstakingly slow process, so make sure you plan well in advance and use one simple rule: If you need money in three months, plan on needing twice that long to obtain it.

- ✔ **Communicate.** Communication efforts are critical to successfully securing and managing capital. To keep capital sources happy, you absolutely must keep them up-to-date with all relevant information, good or bad.

- ✔ **Document and disclose.** Do not underestimate the importance of properly documenting all capital-raising activities, from the initial communications to final agreements. In addition, full and complete disclosures are a must in today's hostile economic environment and are often referred to as "representations and warranties." These disclosures include, but are not limited to, stating that the company has the rights to all intellectual property claimed as owned, no legal actions or lawsuits are present (and if they are present, they must be disclosed), is a company in good standing (has the right to legally conduct business), has executed the following material contracts or commitments, and on and on and on. Basically, representations and warranties cover just about every aspect of the business.

✔ **Keep your options open.** Having more than one financing option available is always helpful. Although it may not be feasible for every business, keeping more than one iron in the fire is important in this era of economic uncertainty.

✔ **Treat capital sources as partners.** Whether a business's source of capital is debt or equity, the party providing the capital represents a key partner to a company's current and future success. So by including the capital source in active and appropriate elements of the business, they are more likely to stay engaged, offer support, and advise to assist the company.

✔ **Have exit strategies.** Remember, all capital sources want their money back with a solid return at some point. Offer clear and reasonable exit strategies to assure the capital sources that a light will be present at the end of the tunnel (and that it's not a freight train barreling down the other direction).

✔ **Balance the risk/reward relationship.** To a capital source, equity investments carry more risk than debt investments, and as such the return realized on the investment must be higher. To a business, debt can expose the company to greater risks but also higher returns. The trick is to find the right balance between the two so returns are enhanced (with the equity source being happy) but not overleverage the company (which would place the entire livelihood of the business at risk). As with the so-called "stress tests" undertaken by banks in the United States in 2010 to evaluate how well they could hold up under adverse economic conditions, a similar stress test should be performed on your company to evaluate where its key tipping points may be.

Five realities of the current capital markets

As if capital sourcing wasn't difficult enough in the best of times, the current economic environment has made your job harder. Knowing the following unfortunate facts about today's capital markets will prepare you to deal with the current climate and reassure you that everyone is facing the same tall hurdles.

- **Longer lead times:** Plain and simple, securing capital takes much longer today than it did five to ten years ago. With fewer sources, added scrutiny, and increased regulations, all businesses should be prepared for a much longer sales or securing cycle.

- **More expensive:** Almost all forms of capital, debt or equity, are more expensive for most businesses than a decade ago. The current low-interest-rate environment should not be used as a basis when determining the cost of capital, because unless your company name is Apple, McDonald's, or Microsoft, access to cheap capital will not be available.

- **Fewer sources:** The Great Recession of 2007 through 2009 definitely thinned the herd in terms of available sources of capital. Bank failures were well documented, but other sources of capital, including VCs, PEGs, alternative lending sources, and even FF&CBAs, also saw contractions. There just aren't as many choices today compared to a decade ago.

- **Stringent underwriting:** As noted throughout this chapter, capital source underwriting and due-diligence efforts are as detailed, thorough, and intense as ever. The heightened concerns involving accountability and transparency have amplified the need for additional underwriting procedures.

- **Tighter reporting and management:** When capital is secured, you have to be prepared for much tighter management and reporting controls by the capital source. As the capital sources are under more pressure to manage their resources more efficiently, this requirement simply works down the food chain.

Chapter 11

Knowing When to Use Debt to Finance Your Business

*W*hen discussing the concept of debt in today's economy, a very serious and unfortunate misconception needs to be clarified. That is, contrary to popular belief, the term *debt* is not a four-letter word. Although the excesses of the debt housing binge have been well documented since the housing market started to crash in 2007 and conjure up numerous horror stories at the neighborhood barbeque, the crash really just highlighted how dangerous debt is — when used inappropriately.

If you remember one concept from this chapter, it should be this: Debt is most appropriately used when an asset is available to support the eventual repayment of the debt. Whether the asset is tangible (such as equipment used in a manufacturing process), paper based (such as a trade accounts receivable where a valid claim is present against a third party), or centered in the ability to reliably predict a positive cash-flow stream, the business must have a clearly identifiable asset that can, if needed, be validated by an independent third party.

The goal of this chapter is to pick up where Chapter 10 (on securing capital from equity sources) left off by beginning our discussion on debt with a more complete overview of its key attributes and characteristics.

Understanding the Basics of Debt Capital

Debt-based capital is money given to the business in the form of a loan. It represents a liability or obligation to a business because it's generally governed by set repayment terms as provided by the party extending credit and accompanied by a claim against specific assets. For example, suppose a bank lends $2 million to a company to purchase additional production equipment to support the expansion of a manufacturing facility. The bank establishes the terms and conditions of the debt agreement, including the interest rate (for instance, 8 percent), repayment term (say, 60 months), the periodic payment, collateral required, and other elements of the agreement. The company must adhere to these terms and conditions or run the risk of default.

But debt is not limited to just loans, leases, notes payable, and/or other similar agreements. Countless other sources of debt are used by a company to support daily operations. Examples of these sources include using payment terms (for example, due in 30 days) provided by vendors when purchasing products or services, leveraging customers to provide advances or deposits against future purchases, or remitting commissions to employees when the cash for a sale is received compared to when the actual sale is made.

Debt is best evaluated by understanding its two primary and critical characteristics: maturity and security.

Debt maturity

Debt maturity refers to the length of time the debt instrument has until the maturity date, which is the date the debt becomes due and payable. For example, in the case of trade accounts payable, vendors commonly extend credit terms of 30 days to their customers, which means payment is due within 30 days of receipt of the product or service. Any debt instrument requiring payment within one year or less is classified as *current (short-term)* in the balance sheet. Logic then dictates that *long-term debt* is any obligation with a payment due beyond one year. For example, mortgage loans provided by banks for real estate purchases are often structured over a 30-year period. Hence, the portion of the debt due past the first year is considered long term in nature.

Debt security

Debt security refers to the type of asset the debt is supported by or secured with. If a bank lends $2 million to support the expansion of a manufacturing facility, the bank takes a "secured position" in the assets acquired with the

$2 million loan. That is, the bank issues a public notice (generally through the issuance of a Uniform Commercial Code [UCC] document) that it has lent money to the manufacturing company and that it has a first right to the equipment financed in the case of a future default. This security provides the bank with additional comfort that if the company can't cover its debt service obligations, a tangible asset can be retrieved and liquidated to cover the outstanding obligation. Other forms of security also include intangible assets (like a patent or rights to intellectual property), inventory, trade accounts receivable, real estate, and future cash-flow streams (for example, a future annuity payment stream that guarantees X dollars to be paid each year).

You may assume, logically, that most organizations that provide credit to businesses prefer to be in a secured status to reduce the inherent risks present. However, for the majority of a company's transactions related to the periodic purchases of goods and services, this arrangement is logistically almost impossible due to the sheer volume of transactions being executed on a day-to-day basis (as filing paperwork with the state on a per-transaction basis to note a secured position is present is incredibly inefficient and would overwhelm the system).

Hence, the secured creditors are usually the ones focused on a company's infrequent or nonrecurring transactions, such as a bank. They tend to be associated with formal credit extension agreements (such as a lease or equipment loan), which are both relatively large from a dollars-committed standpoint and cover longer periods of time. Because the dollar amounts committed are large (and thus the risk is higher) and these transactions are less frequent, the secured creditors (such as a bank) are more than willing to prepare and file the necessary paperwork to "secure" their position with the asset they've loaned money against.

So in general, the majority of creditors actually turn out to be unsecured. This type of creditor tends to be the mass of vendors that provide basic goods and services to a company for general operating requirements. Examples of these vendors are professional service firms, utility and telecommunication companies, material suppliers, and general office services. Unsecured creditors obviously take on more risk in that a specific company asset is not pledged as collateral to support the repayment of the obligation. This risk is mitigated by the fact that unsecured creditors tend to extend credit with shorter repayment terms (for instance, the invoice is due on net 30-day terms) and in lower dollar amounts. In addition, if unsecured creditors are concerned about getting paid, then they may use other strategies including requiring the company to make a deposit or a prepayment.

When lenders refer to *security interest or position,* they're discussing the legal documentation (for example, a UCC) that's prepared and filed with the respective governmental authorities (usually a state commission) to publicly place on notice that the lenders have the first right to the asset to which they extended a loan against. This arrangement is very similar to a lender providing a first deed of trust against real estate to which it helped finance the purchase of. A similar process is used with business assets such as equipment, machines, inventory, trade accounts receivables, and other assets.

Other debt attributes

Beyond the maturity and security elements of debt are a number of additional attributes. Debt capital may involve the following distinctions and arrangements:

- ✔ **Personal guarantees:** A party outside the company guarantees the repayment of a debt, similar to how a cosigner on a debt instrument works.

- ✔ **Priority creditors:** Certain creditors to a business may maintain a priority status due to the type of obligation present, such as payroll taxes withheld for the IRS, which by law overrides almost all other liabilities.

- ✔ **Subordination agreements:** A creditor may specifically take a secondary position to a secured lender.

- ✔ **Default provisions:** In the event of a loan default, set provisions indicate what the remedies of the parties involved are.

- ✔ **Lending agreement covenants:** The business must perform at a certain level to avoid triggering a default.

Before you structure and execute any type of loan, lease, note payable, and/or set terms and conditions with a creditor, professional counsel should be secured and utilized to make sure that you clearly understand the agreement and risks present and protect your company's business interests.

Determining When Debt Is Most Appropriate

For almost any debt-based need, some type of lender is usually available in the market. On one end of the spectrum are traditional banks and credit unions, which tend to be the most conservative lenders but also provide some of the best rates. On the other end of the spectrum are investment funds that specialize in providing high-risk loans, but of course loans from these sources tend to carry the highest rates. And in between are a slew of lenders that all have a unique niche in the market, depending on the credit risks, and that carry interest rates appropriately matched to the associated risks.

Businesses often secure capital from more than one source on a periodic basis. For instance, risk-based capital (in the form of equity) may be secured to develop a new product and support the initial launch into the marketplace, whereas debt-based capital may be secured to support an increase in inventory and to carry trade accounts receivable as customers purchase the products. Not only are both forms of capital appropriate for this company's needs, but in addition the lenders may be more willing to step forward and provide the necessary capital knowing that another partner has made a commitment. The "herd" mentality holds true for capital sources because they view the opportunity in a more positive light (by assuming a higher degree of success) if they know that the right amount and types of capital have been secured.

Debt-based lenders, similar to equity sources discussed in Chapter 10, tend to look for a common (but different) set of characteristics when extending capital in the form of debt. Different lending sources give different weight to each characteristic in each unique business environment, but some definite deal killers apply to each. The three primary characteristics are discussed in the following sections.

When you can offer security or collateral

The business seeking a loan must offer primary and secondary sources of security or collateral (for example, a pledged asset or personal guarantee). If the amount of loan required is in excess of the collateral or security being pledged, then securing a loan will be very difficult (unless additional collateral is pledged).

The best scenario for securing a loan is a company that's highly profitable, has sound collateral, and offers a strong secondary repayment source. Of course, you may ask why debt would be needed in this scenario. The answer is that a company may want to use debt appropriately to enhance economic returns and results (because when all factors are considered, debt is cheaper than equity).

When business is stable

Lenders only want to get involved in stable business environments. The company must have been in business for an extended period of time, have a proven track record, and have a solid management team at the helm. This is not to say that businesses must generate a profit to secure debt financing, but it certainly helps expand the number of sources available and can help secure lower rates.

If the lending sources in any way, shape, or form become concerned with the credibility of the management team and/or stability of the business operation, then chances are that the lending source will pass on extending a loan. The last thing any lender wants to do is provide a loan and then, 90 days later, see the loan go into default and require collection actions.

When you have financial strength

Debt-capital sources are generally more conservative in nature than equity sources. Their goal is to ensure that the debt can be repaid, while generating an adequate return. Therefore, the company's ability to maintain solid financial returns and strong ratios is more important than its likelihood of doubling in size. Again, the same concept applies with financial strength as with business stability. The stronger the financial condition, the lower the interest rates. The weaker the financial condition, the higher the interest rates.

Some businesses, even if adequate collateral is available to secure the loan and no business credibility issues are present, may be just too financially "stressed" to extend a loan. In this situation, a lender may evaluate the company from its ability to survive a shock to the operating structure in terms of having enough financial resources to manage through turbulent times. If the lender becomes your last chance at survival, then its interest level generally falls off unless alternative financial resources can be secured to prop up the business.

Using Loans, Leases, and Other Sources of Debt

After you conclude that your business meets the security, stability, and financial strength requirements for appropriately using debt-based capital (discussed in "Determining When Debt Is Most Appropriate"), you can turn your attention to evaluating the different sources of debt and when each is generally used in a business.

No matter what source you choose, we can't stress enough the importance of qualifying the capital source. Nothing is worse than wasting your time in pursuing a loan that has no chance of being funded.

Borrowing from banks

Looking to secure capital from banks in the form of loans is one of the most tried and proven sources of capital. The old (and, yes, outdated) image of a business looking to grow and in need of a loan to expand, hire new employees, and increase sales and profitability has always been a mantra of the banks. Sorry to spoil the party, but we're here to explain why, due to the criteria they use to underwrite the loan, banks are not ideally suited to handle a good portion of business-loan needs in today's economy.

When a bank or any type of lender refers to *underwriting* a loan, it basically means the same concept of a private capital source performing due diligence. The lender undertakes a detailed review of the loan applicant's financial and business information to ensure that the borrower is credit worthy.

Banks do provide an important source of debt-based capital to some businesses, but they require five key criteria to be met before they consider providing a loan:

- ✓ **Positive earnings:** In most cases, a company must generate positive cash flow or earnings to secure a loan. Banks are cash-flow lenders, which basically means that for any type of debt they offer, internal cash flows must be adequate to repay the debt. So if a business has historical losses or is forecasting losses in the future, strike one.

- ✓ **Sound collateral:** Banks lend against assets to protect their loans. So every business looking to secure a bank loan needs to have sound collateral available (to repay the loan in case the business cannot). Generally, banks like to lend against the most liquid and best-performing assets, such as trade accounts receivable. They tend to be more cautious when asked to accept collateral such as inventory (which can become obsolete quickly and also carries the risk of simply disappearing from a business) and equipment (which can depreciate in value very quickly and is expensive to liquidate if needed). So the preference with banks is to lend primarily against trade receivables and, if needed, then offer reduced loans or lending facilities against higher risk assets such as inventory. If you don't have quality collateral or the right collateral, strike two.

- ✓ **Solid financial performance:** The strength of a company's balance sheet is just as important as positive earnings when requesting a loan. When a business has excessive leverage (too much debt compared to too little equity), its business risks increase and a bank's interest decreases. So if your business is too leveraged, strike three.

- ✓ **Secondary repayment:** For most smaller- to medium-size businesses (the vast majority operating in America), banks generally look for a secondary source of repayment to ensure that the debt gets paid. Or in other words, if internal cash flow is not adequate and the collateral (if liquidated) doesn't cover the debt obligation, the bank needs to turn to another source of repayment to cover the debt. This secondary source generally falls back on the personal assets of the company's owners, which may range from real estate to personal savings to retirement accounts to other business interests owned (by offering a personal guarantee). If no secondary repayment sources are available, strike four.

A personal guarantee (or PG) pretty much means what it implies. That is, if your business can't repay a loan, then the lender will pursue the assets of the individual who signed the PG to ensure that full payment is received. Needless to say, PGs should be executed with the utmost caution and understanding, but at the same time, you also keep an important concept in mind: If you elect to not execute a PG, then the bank views your reluctance as a sign that you, the owner or founder, do not have faith in the business. So why would a bank lend money if the owners aren't willing to stand behind the company (even if all the other criteria is met)?

✔ **Business plan:** To get a bank loan, your company needs a solid business plan with a highly experienced and credible management team. These requirements reassure the bank that their cash is being turned over to a third party who knows how to run a business and generate profits. Any plan that a bank reviews that is short on these items will certainly lead to strike five.

Since 2007, just about every bank (notice it's a four-letter word) has been maligned, fairly or not (and been referred to in the same sentence with just about every other unflattering four-letter word). The frustration with the banking industry, at both the personal and business levels, has been well documented and has really reshaped the banking industry's role in the capital markets. For example, prior to 2007, a bank might have been able to bend a little when extending credit to a good business that had some flaws (such as a relatively high debt-to-equity ratio). However, businesses are now being treated to a new normal that makes securing loans much more challenging. Banks still play a very important and vital role in the capital markets, but businesses must clearly understand when a bank can provide debt-based capital and when it cannot.

If your business meets the five criteria outlined previously, then approaching a bank is appropriate. Banks are always looking for A/A+ deals, and if your business qualifies, then taking advantage of this source of debt capital is advantageous because it usually carries far lower fees and interest rates than other forms of debt-based capital. However, if just one of the five criteria is not met, then banks may lose interest, so it's imperative that businesses understand the alternative forms of debt-based capital available. And if you fail two or more of the criteria, then bank financing options will likely be very limited, so the next step in evaluating securing financing is to explore the wonderful world of asset-based lending.

Making friends with asset-based lenders

Asset-based lending utilizes the same criteria as banks but with one critical difference. Asset-based lenders (ABLs) focus on the quality of the asset (such as trade accounts receivable or inventory) being offered as collateral first and the company's financial performance and strength second. In fact, ABLs often look past one or two years of poor financial performances and are more comfortable with weak balance sheets because they understand that businesses sometimes experience problems (look no farther than the 2009 recession and its impact on businesses). However, similar to banks, the need for sound collateral, solid secondary repayment support, and a well-developed business plan are essential to secure a loan.

But ABLs have a hidden benefit that a business should exploit when appropriate: ABLs may extend higher borrowing levels against certain assets than banks. For example, banks tend to be more conservative in nature and may only advance 75 percent against eligible trade accounts receivable, so if you have $1 million of eligible trade receivables, you can borrow a maximum of $750,000. If the collateral strength of the trade receivables is strong, an ABL may lend 80 or even 85 percent against the eligible trade receivables, which would allow a company to borrow $800,000 to $850,000. The additional borrowing availability may not seem like much, but when cash is tight, having an extra few dollars of liquidity available is invaluable.

So you may ask, why not skip the bank and simply secure financing from an ABL? Well, ABLs are more expensive. Period! From the interest rates charged on the loans to the fees assessed to manage the relationship, the cost of ABL-provided financing is much higher than traditional banks. As a general reference point, it's safe to say that ABLs will be about double what the bank costs "all in all" or when all costs, fees, and expenses are accounted for. (If bank-provided financing costs roughly 6 percent, then an ABL is around 12 percent). This source may appear expensive, but remember, an ABL absorbs additional risks with weaker companies and thus requires a higher rate of return.

Another downside of an ABL is that you need to be prepared to implement much tighter management reporting requirements than you would with a bank. Whereas a bank may require monthly reports and information, ABLs often look for weekly or, in some cases, daily reporting procedures to be implemented to properly track and manage the assets they're lending against.

Leasing as a source of capital

Leasing or renting an asset is an effective source of debt-based capital. The most common example is leasing office space. Instead of tying up cash in purchasing a building or investing in leasehold improvements, most companies simply execute a lease with a landlord.

An e-commerce retail company was growing rapidly and needed additional warehouse and distribution space for the company's products. Adjacent space was available but needed a number of improvements to be workable. Instead of making the improvements itself, the retail company negotiated with the landlord to make the improvements and then simply increased the rent proportionately to cover the additional costs. This arrangement allowed the retail company to utilize cash internally and finance the building improvements over the life of the lease (which was at a very reasonable rate).

Leases are most commonly structured with assets that have an extended life, such as buildings and capital equipment (like manufacturing equipment, furniture, computers, and autos). Structuring leases for capital equipment are also used extensively in the business community and provided by numerous financing or leasing companies. But before a business dives headfirst into leasing, the following key concepts and risks should be understood:

- ✔ **Risk of ownership:** Most equipment leases are structured to transfer the risk of ownership to the lessee, so insurance, property taxes, maintenance, and so on all fall on the shoulders of the party leasing the equipment. But in the same breath, remember that the leasing company has a secured interest in the asset being leased (to protect their interests). In other words, in most cases the leasing company retains legal title to the assets being leased. If the business defaults on terms of the lease, the owner (the lessor) can repossess the asset.

- ✔ **Real financing cost:** Understanding the internal cost of a lease in terms of the implied interest rate being charged is very important. Leasing companies use all types of tricks and tactics to improve their returns, including requiring payments to be made in advance (for example, on the first day of the month rather than the last), having the first and last months' lease payments made in advance, structuring fair-market value buyout options, and so on.

- ✔ **Used versus new equipment:** Leasing is best utilized when the equipment is new rather than used, because the interest rate charged and the amount of lease financing provided will be most favorable to the lessee. Attempting to secure lease financing on used equipment is both very difficult and expensive.

The bottom line in equipment leasing is the same with securing other forms of debt. The leasing companies generally take on higher levels of risk than a bank and, as such, demand higher returns (so leasing tends to be more expensive than other forms of debt). But though more expensive, leasing companies often extend leases based on 90 to 100 percent of the equipment's new value, so instead of having to place 20 percent down on the asset (with a traditional bank loan), more cash can be conserved inside the business when using leases.

In every debt-based financing decision, the borrower needs to make a critical decision based on the trade-off between higher financing costs and access to additional capital or cash. Or in other words, if the excess cash can be invested or used in the business to generate returns greater than the costs of the financing, then using more-expensive and flexible financing programs is appropriate. One mistake commonly made by businesses is that they're so consumed with making sure they get the lowest interest rate available that they don't consider the impact the loan facility may have on restricting available borrowing levels and access to cash. In a number of cases, paying a little extra for higher loan balances and/or access to cash is well worth the added expense.

Tapping government programs and the SBA

Government lending programs, at both the state and federal levels, are accessible for businesses. The most popular program at the federal level is provided through the Small Business Administration, or SBA, which offers programs geared toward real estate (for owner-occupied buildings) and general business working-capital requirements. Contrary to popular belief, the government is not handing out free cash (which we know is hard to believe) and in fact applies basically the same stringent underwriting criteria as the banks.

The government relies heavily on the banking industry to market and underwrite SBA loans. As such, the common perception that loans from the SBA are readily available and easy to obtain is a myth. In fact, securing an SBA loan can be more time consuming and challenging than a traditional bank loan.

In addition to the federal government's SBA program, various states also have lending programs to assist small businesses. The availability of these programs has declined over the years as state and local governments struggle with large budget deficits and limited financial resources. Turn to the later section "Leveraging Uncle Sam for Cash" for a more thorough discussion on tapping the government for cash.

Using other sources of debt-based capital

Numerous other forms of debt-based capital are available, and two common sources are particularly worth highlighting:

- ✔ **Factoring receivables:** When trade accounts receivable are factored, technically the receivable is sold to a third party who becomes the owner of the receivable (as cash is paid to the seller). Unlike banks and ABLs that lend against an asset (and thus the asset remains the property of the company), in this case, the asset is actually sold to a third party. When the customer pays, the cash goes to the factoring company and the transaction is completed. Factoring financing agreements are used in a wide range of industries, and as with all forms of debt financing, they carry both pros (high advance rates and quick turnarounds) and cons (they're relatively expensive).

Factoring trade accounts receivable involves selling an asset to a third party who then may notify your customer that the receivable has been sold (and where to properly remit payment). Needless to say, this may send a negative message to your customer in terms of the financial strength of your business (they may wonder, are you that desperate for cash?). When factoring agreements are used, you must properly communicate the transaction with customers to prevent misunderstandings or misinterpretations. The last thing you want to do is surprise your customers by introducing an unknown third party into the business relationship.

✔ **Subordinated debt:** Quite often, parties with a vested interest in a business may provide loans in the form of subordinated debt. The loan often comes from an owner or related third party. Subordinated debt has terms and conditions established just like other types of debt but is offered a lower security position in company assets than senior lenders. That is, if a company liquidates, the last creditors in the pecking order in terms of having claims against company assets are the subordinated debt holders.

Getting Creative with Capital

Banks, leasing companies, and other lenders are all viable and accessible sources of debt-based capital, with specific characteristics that give each source competitive strengths and weaknesses. However, the discussion of sources of capital wouldn't be complete if we didn't look a little deeper into some more-creative capital sources that can often be overlooked.

The number of creative capital sources is endless, so rather than attempt to cover every trick of the trade, we present a diversified list of examples to provide you with a sense of how businesses manufacture capital.

Generating internal cash flow

The primary concept of this book is educating business owners and managers on understanding, generating, and managing internal cash flow. To be quite honest, the best way to get capital is to look internally and manage business operations more efficiently to produce additional capital. Positive internal cash flow is both readily available and logistically much easier to secure. However, you need to keep in mind that positive internal cash flow must be managed and invested appropriately within the best interests of the company and its shareowners.

Leveraging unsecured creditors

Beyond generating additional cash from internal management efforts, a business is often afforded the opportunity to utilize creative forms of unsecured financing from vendors, partners, and customers. Following are three such examples:

- ✔ **Require customers to prepay 20 percent of their order as a requirement to start the production and future delivery process.** In addition, terms such as 20 percent down, 30 percent upon half completion, and the remainder due upon delivery can also be utilized. Companies that produce and sell customized products often use this strategy because active alternative markets are generally not present for "one of a kind" items.

- ✔ **Ask key product suppliers to grant extended terms from 30 days to 90 days during certain seasonal periods (for example, to support higher sales during the holiday season).** After the determined period, terms are brought back to 30 days when the cash flow from the increased sales catches up. Retailers often use this strategy during the holiday season as inventory levels are built up from October through November (with cash receipts realized in December and then used to repay the extended credit granted from its suppliers).

- ✔ **Work with a downstream customer to obtain funding to develop a new product or technology that can greatly improve the customer's future performance.** For example, a hardware technology company may need to ensure that software is available for use with its new products. Hence, a capital infusion into the software supplier to develop the technology for which it receives a royalty from future sales may be warranted.

Going after government aid, gifts, and grants

Governments, universities, and nonprofit organizations have resources available in the form of grants, low-interest-rate loans (with limited downside risk), incentive credits, gifts, and so on that are intended to be used for special interests or purposes. The general idea is to provide this capital to organizations that will use it in the best interest of the general public. For instance, biotechnology companies often secure research grants for work being completed on disease detection, prevention, and possible cures. Educational organizations may receive grants that help retrain a displaced group of workers or poorly educated work force.

Partnering up

A vast array of other creative capital sources is available to companies. In this section we summarize one such source, a partnership, in an example.

A software company was in the process of developing a new fraud-protection system for use in the banking system. Not only did the development of the system need to be capitalized, but the initial marketplace launch also required additional capital to ensure that the end customers, mainly banks, could review, test, evaluate, and implement the systems. Internally, the company didn't have enough capital to support this project, so they completed an acquisition of a sister company (which was related through partial common ownership) that was producing strong internal cash flows to support the project. The company issued its equity in exchange for all the assets of the target company (which in effect was the future cash-flow stream). This trade provided the company with enough ongoing cash flow (from the acquired businesses product sales) to both fund the system development and market it to the banks.

Leveraging Uncle Sam for Cash

This discussion on using debt to secure cash for your business ends most appropriately with tapping the government to assist with improving cash flows. However, before we dive into this topic and discuss specific strategies, two critical concepts should be noted.

First, we want to debunk the myth that the federal government simply hands out free cash. Yes, the bailouts provided to various banks, General Motors, and other companies during the Great Recession appeared to be rather generous, but these bailouts carried very specific terms and conditions and were due to extreme economic conditions. The federal government does have cash available for businesses, but as previously noted in the section "Tapping government programs and the SBA," it is looking to provide this cash to viable business operations with specific and somewhat strenuous terms and conditions.

Second, keep in mind that the strategies offered in this section of the chapter are fully endorsed and accepted by the federal government but carry a number of rules and regulations (the fine print). If you don't properly manage and comply with the rules, you can create unforeseen problems and headaches for your business.

You may wonder why we elected to incorporate a discussion on the impact of taxes in the chapter on using debt in a business. The simple answer is that taxes represent an expense and liability to a business (or debt), either short term or long-term in nature, and debt represents a source of cash for businesses. If tax obligations and liabilities can be managed more effectively, this in turn can help improve cash flows. But in order to capture the benefits of increased cash flows on the taxation front, the following four key points should be kept in mind:

- ✔ **Securing professional support:** Proper professional counsel, including CPAs, attorneys, and other taxation experts, should be secured and actively utilized to assist with appropriately managing tax liabilities and improving cash flows. Given the complexity of the tax laws, combined with how frequently tax rules and regulations are changed, high-quality tax professionals are usually worth their weight in gold. They often are aware of tax breaks, credits, and/or strategies that can save significant dollars.

- ✔ **Complying with all tax requirements:** Tax compliance can be a very frustrating, time- consuming, and expensive endeavor. But as the old saying goes, don't be penny-wise and pound-foolish. Skipping on the front end will ultimately cost far more down the road when the taxing authorities finally catch up to you.

- ✔ **Deferring tax obligations:** Most tax savings opportunities (and related improvements in cash flow) come from deferring tax liabilities rather than eliminating them altogether. Granted, tax credits represent a permanent method of reducing tax liabilities, but the vast majority of tax strategies, including utilizing the cash method to report taxable income, leveraging flow-through entities, and taking advantage of accelerated deductions, are based more on strategies of timing, offering the ability to delay paying the tax. Sometimes they also offer the possibility of deferring some taxable income to a future period when the tax rate may be lower.

- ✔ **Basing economic decisions on tax factors:** Business decisions should be based on sound economic and financial considerations first and tax factors a distant second. You always want to consider how you can structure business transactions to capture tax benefits, but the tax benefits should be the icing on the cake used to enhance the economic return (rather than the sole reason an economic return is even realized).

Four government-endorsed strategies to help improve cash flow

The number and variety of tax savings opportunities offered by the federal government are extensive and are generally designed to encourage or direct third parties toward undertaking a specific activity or transaction. For example, when the housing market and economy collapsed between 2007 and 2009, the government provided a first-time homebuyer tax credit to encourage the purchase of residential property. The government also encourages businesses to invest in various activities (such as research and development and alternative or clean energy) by providing a variety of tax credits. Of course, the majority of the opportunities are not applicable for most businesses, given the uniqueness of certain tax deductions, credits, and other savings opportunities. So rather than attempt to list every potential tax savings opportunity, we summarize the primary avenues available for small businesses to leverage Uncle Sam for some cash in the following four sections.

Reporting taxable income on a cash basis

One of the most common strategies utilized by small businesses to manage tax liabilities (and associated cash payments to the government) is electing to report taxable income by using cash-based as opposed to accrual-based accounting for profit. Most businesses are required to prepare periodic financial statements using generally accepted accounting principles (GAAP), which require financial information to be prepared on an accrual basis. (You can find out the details in Chapter 2.) Though this basis is without question the most appropriate method to prepare, report, analyze, and distribute the financial results of a business, the IRS allows companies that meet certain conditions to report taxable income on a cash basis.

What does this switch to cash basis mean? Well, to explain it as simply as possible, we look at the two main drivers that create differences between accrual- and cash-based taxable income — sales and expenses:

- ✓ **Sales:** Under the accrual method, sales are recognized and reported in the financial statements when fully earned, whether or not cash has been collected for the sale. Under the cash method, sales are only recognized and reported when cash is actually received.

- ✓ **Expenses:** What's good for the goose is good for the gander, so on the expense side of the accrual method, expenses also can be recognized and reported in the financial statements when fully incurred (with an obligation present), whether or not cash has been distributed to a third party. Under the cash method, expenses can only be recognized and reported when cash is actually distributed.

Figure 11-1 provides an example of how taxable income can be lowered by using the cash method as compared to the accrual method. The significance of using the cash method to report taxable income is that it allows for the deferral of tax obligations and payments to the government, which translates into more cash being retained in the business.

The IRS has a number of rules and regulations established to determine if a business qualifies to use cash-basis reporting. Thoroughly review these rules and regulations with help from professional counsel to make sure that your business qualifies to report taxable income using the cash method.

Description	Accrual Method	Adjustments	Cash Method
Revenue (A)	$2,500,000	$200,000	$2,300,000
Costs of Goods Sold (B)	$1,750,000	$75,000	$1,675,000
Gross Profit	$750,000	$125,000	$625,000
Corporate Overhead Expenses (B)	$500,000	$25,000	$475,000
Net Profit before Tax	$250,000	$100,000	$150,000
Income Tax Expense - 25% Rate	$62,500	n/a	$37,500
Deferral of Tax Obligation	n/a		$25,000

Figure 11-1:
The impact of cash-basis accounting reporting on taxable income.

A - The $200,000 trade accounts receivable increase at year-end has not been collected, so it does not need to be recognized as revenue in the current year using the cash method.

B - Of the $100,000 trade accounts payable increase at year-end, $75,000 relates to direct costs of good sold and $25,000 to corporate overhead. These expenses would not be allowed using cash method, because they were not paid as of the end of the year.

Remember that when using cash-based accounting to report taxable income, the taxes are not being *eliminated* but rather *deferred* or *delayed* to a future period, allowing a company to manage cash resources more efficiently and remit tax payments when cash is available. Eventually, income tax obligations will be realized when cash is received; so don't make a very common and often fatal mistake of spending the deferred taxable income inappropriately and having bare pockets when the tax bill comes due.

Structuring the business to impact cash resources

You can also manage income tax obligations and improve cash availability by utilizing the most appropriate legal structure to manage your business operations. Basically, IRS rules and regulations provide for the following two main types of legal structures when it comes to taxation:

> ✔ **Flow-through taxable entities:** Flow-through taxable entities allow taxable income or loss generated by the entity to be taxed not at the entity level but rather at the personal level when it flows through to the individual owners of the entity. So any tax liability and related cash requirement is an obligation of the individuals and not the legal entity. General partnerships, limited partnerships, limited liability companies, and subchapter S corporations are all flow-through entities.

✔ **Regular taxable entities:** Regular taxable entities, which include C corporations, among others, are taxed at the entity level with no impact on the individual owners. So any tax liability and related cash requirement is an obligation of the legal entity, not the individual owners.

So how exactly can the legal formation impact tax obligations and cash resources? An example can help explain. Two entrepreneurs coming out of Corporate America formed and launched a new technology business in the middle of the year. In the first six months of the year, both owners had worked and generated significant earnings that they were going to use to launch the business. They initially formed the company as a flow-through entity, so the losses from the new venture in the second half of the year, which amounted to over $200,000, flowed through to the owners' individual tax returns. The owners then could offset and reduce roughly $250,000 of regular earnings from the first half of the year.

The net effect was that their adjusted gross income was reduced to $50,000, which carried less than $5,000 of tax liabilities, compared to having to report $250,000 of gross income with resulting tax liabilities of over $60,000. By managing the legal form of the new company, they were able to reduce personal tax obligations, which resulted in increased cash availability (via not having to remit tax payments to the government). If the company had been formed as a regular C corporation (a non-flow-through entity), the loss in year one would have been "trapped" inside the legal entity and only available for use against future earnings of the company.

Flow-through entities can help lower and/or defer tax liabilities in countless other ways. The main point to understand is that the use of flow-through tax entities, if properly planned for and correctly structured, can enhance and improve cash flows by lowering or deferring income tax obligations. And as with all the topics presented on leveraging Uncle Sam, once again we can't emphasize enough the importance of securing proper professional counsel when evaluating the most appropriate legal form for your business.

As the old saying goes, "Never let the tax tail wag the economic dog," and you certainly shouldn't let the tax implications be your sole guide when deciding on what legal entity to utilize for your company. Numerous other factors may impact the economic viability of your company. For example, subchapter S corporations have restrictions on the number of parties that can own a portion of the company and must generally be individual persons (and not other legal entities, such as a C corporation). If your business is formed as a subchapter S corporation and is looking to secure an investment to fund operations, certain investors may be eliminated if they don't qualify.

A number of businesses formed initially as a tax-flow-through entity (such as a subchapter S corporation) later transition into a regular taxable entity (such as a C corporation) when business conditions dictate the need for change. This switch allows for these companies to maximize the benefits of being a tax-flow-through entity in the early years of the business (similar to the real-world example offered previously) and then transition into a regular taxable entity, which allows for more flexibility when securing financing. For most businesses, the transition from a subchapter S corporation to a regular C corporation is far easier and efficient than attempting to undertake the reverse.

Managing owner wages and business earnings

Another area that warrants a discussion on properly managing tax obligations to improve cash flows concerns how small businesses manage owner wages and business earnings. More specially, you want to consider the two basic strategies of estimating tax payments and reducing owner W-2 earnings.

Estimated tax payments

Most businesses (or the owners of the businesses, for flow-through entities) are required to make estimated taxes on a quarterly basis to cover anticipated income tax obligations throughout the year. For example, if a business anticipates generating $200,000 of taxable income throughout the year, it reasonably assumes that one-fourth, or $50,000, would be earned each quarter. If the business operates in a 25 percent federal government marginal tax bracket, then $12,500 is due each quarter.

Although this arrangement is relatively easy to understand, most businesses don't operate in a perfect utopia of guaranteed quarterly performances that will always produce a quarterly tax liability in equal amounts (plus or minus 5 percent). Rather, most businesses have to deal with issues that can create rather significant changes between quarterly operating performances (such as seasonal sales patterns, nonrecurring large projects, sales and expense timing in relation to cash receipts and disbursements, and so on).

So in order to properly manage estimated tax payments on a quarterly basis, the company's actual quarterly financial results should be used as the basis for calculating annualized net taxable income levels and resulting tax obligations. In other words, the quarter-by-quarter profit of the business may fluctuate widely. The busy season of the year may show large profits, which are offset by low profit numbers or even losses in other quarters. In short, the company may have relatively large swings in quarterly estimated payments. Be sure to properly calculate and document the financial results used as the basis for the estimated tax payments (in case an inquiry is ever made).

Don't overpay your estimated tax payments! Whether at the business or personal level, properly calculating and remitting estimated tax payments should be completed on a quarterly basis to avoid making the ever-so-popular statement, "I'm getting a big tax refund back." Not only have you let the government use your money at no cost, but you've also more than likely parked money with state governments that are strapped for cash and may take some time to issue a refund.

When possible, individuals should take advantage of the IRS's safe harbor rules. Though generally not available at the state level, the IRS provides for a simple way to pay estimated tax payments at the personal or individual on a quarterly basis. You take your previous-year tax obligation and multiply by 110 percent, and then use the resulting amount as the basis of your current-year tax obligation. For example, if your prior-year tax obligation was $20,000, you would multiply by 110 percent, which results in $22,000. As long as you make tax payments of $22,000 during the year, the IRS doesn't tack on penalties or interest charges if in fact you end up owing $40,000 in taxes that year. Granted, the difference or shortfall of $18,000 would still be due on the tax-reporting deadline, but by using the safe harbor rules, you've been able to defer paying the tax obligation and use that cash for a 6- to 12-month period for other purposes.

Using the safe harbor rules to keep cash in the business is generally most effective during a period of continued net earnings growth and increases in tax obligations because, in effect, the added income tax obligations are pushed out to the next year (for payment).

Owner W-2 earnings versus distributions of earnings

One decision every business must make is what compensation rate to set for senior management. In large companies, the decision is usually dictated by a number of factors, including the competition, board/shareholder approvals, and other factors. For smaller, closely held companies that are structured as pass-through entities, the decision is somewhat more arbitrary and is often influenced by tax savings opportunities (not to mention the performance of the company).

These types of companies often keep owners' taxable wages relatively low to deflate or reduce traditional W-2 wages to reduce the amount of Social Security and Medicare, taxes the company must pay. The current tax rules and regulations dictate that for regular W-2 wages, Social Security taxes (at a rate of 6.2 percent) are assessed on the first $106,800 (for 2011, unchanged from 2010) of W-2 wages with preliminary estimates of $110,100 being the base for 2012, whereas Medicare taxes (at a rate of 1.45 percent) are assessed on all W-2 wages. These taxes are important to understand, because they're not only withheld from the employee's pay but also matched by the company paying the wages. So if W-2 wages are deflated or reduced, the amount of taxes paid is reduced as well.

Figure 11-2 reflects the impact of using this strategy on total taxes paid, reduced tax expense, and increased cash flows:

Description	Low Wage Scenario #1	High Wage Scenario #2
Net Profit Before Owner W-2 Wages	$500,000	$500,000
Gross W-2 Owner Wages, One Owner	$100,000	$300,000
Net Company Profit, before Payroll Taxes	$400,000	$200,000
Total Payroll Tax Obligation:		
Social Security Taxes, Employee - 6.2% Base	$6,200	$6,622
Medicare Taxes, Employee - 1.45% Unlimited	$1,450	$4,350
Social Security Taxes, Employer - 6.2% Base	$6,200	$6,622
Medicare Taxes, Employer - 1.45% Unlimited	$1,450	$4,350
Total Payroll Tax Obligation	$15,300	$21,943
Net Company Profit, after Payroll Taxes	$392,350	$189,028
Gross W-2 Owner Wages	$100,000	$300,000
Total Individual Taxable Income	$492,350	$489,028
Marginal Tax Bracket/Tax Rate	35%	35%
Total Income Taxes Due	$172,323	$171,160
Total Payroll Tax Obligation:	$15,300	$21,943
Total Tax Obligation, Payroll and Income	$187,623	$193,103
Total Tax Savings		$5,481

Figure 11-2:
Comparison of owner wages and impact on net tax obligation.

The maximum wage level (or base) in 2010 subject to Social Security taxes as set by the IRS was $106,800. This base is adjusted each year by the IRS to account for inflation.

W-2 wages are treated as an expense to the company, which reduces taxable income. So if W-2 wages are reduced, taxable income is increased, which results in larger amounts of taxable income being passed through to the owners of the company. However, the savings from reduced Social Security and Medicare taxes are large enough to offset the increased tax on the net business income passed through. The owner's total income remains about the same whether earned as W-2 wages or passed through as taxable earnings from the company, but when applying a constant marginal tax rate, the strategy of reducing W-2 wages and increasing taxable income, as in the example in Figure 11-2, results in tax savings of $5,481.

This particular strategy can become very complex very quickly and contains a number of potential traps to unsuspecting business owners, so you should use it with an abundance of caution. However, when used at the optimal time (especially when a company is struggling with limited profits and tight cash flows), it can help lower tax liabilities and improve cash flows by directing more cash into the business as opposed to the government.

The W-2 wages can't be reduced to an amount that's unrealistically low for the job and that particular field, and the IRS is targeting owners who artificially deflate regular W-2 earnings to lower Social Security and Medicare taxes. For instance, if a partner in a law firm pays herself $80,000 a year in W-2 wages, with the going rate for similar paid professionals in other law firms at $300,000, not to mention that the partner's law firm generated taxable income of $1,000,000, the IRS will most likely challenge the W-2 wages paid (as being too low). The key in managing this issue is to make sure that the W-2 wages paid are reasonable, given the operating performance of the company and comparable wages earned by similar workers. Remember that the term *reasonable* provides for a fair amount of latitude, so again, if you're uncertain what is reasonable, consult professional counsel.

Finding hidden tax gems: Tax credits, accelerated deductions, and other incentives

The fourth government "hand-out" assists businesses with reducing expenses and improving cash flows by offering special tax credits, accelerated deductions, and other specialized incentives. We don't even attempt to summarize all the potential tax savings opportunities governments offer, because they could fill an entire book. Rather, we summarize these issues in three primary topics: tax credits, accelerated deductions, and other incentives:

- ✔ **Tax credits:** The most commonly used tax credits by businesses are offered for R&D (research and development) activities, clean and green investments (like solar power), and focused hiring in disadvantaged employment groups (such as the *WOTC,* or work opportunity tax credit). Tax credits are a great tool to utilize when available and appropriate because unlike tax deductions, tax credits represent a dollar-for-dollar offset of tax liabilities. For example, if a company has taxable income of $100,000 before claiming an accelerated deduction of $20,000, the company reports taxable income of $80,000. At a tax rate of 25 percent, the company then has a tax liability of $20,000. However, if a tax credit of $20,000 is obtained as a result of R&D efforts, quite a different result is achieved. Using the same $100,000 figure, which now represents the taxable income, and applying a 25 percent tax rate, the tax liability is $25,000. Then applying the tax credit of $20,000, the net tax liability is reduced to just $5,000. So it's no wonder why companies look to secure and utilize tax credits so aggressively.

✔ **Accelerated deductions:** The government aggressively encourages businesses to invest in new property, plant, and equipment by providing for accelerated deductions when qualified assets are purchased. The idea is that by providing an accelerated deduction, increased purchase activity in qualified assets will help stimulate the economy. The most common example of this encouragement is in equipment purchases. In a normal year, the IRS may allow a depreciation deduction of 20 percent of the equipment's purchase price in the first year, but during a targeted period (such as 2009, when the economy fell off a cliff), the deduction can be increased to 50 percent during the first year. For an asset that cost $100,000, the increased depreciation expense of $50,000 instead of $20,000 reduces taxable income by $30,000 and thus reduces the company's tax liability by an additional $7,500 (assuming a 25 percent tax rate).

The benefits of accelerated deductions are often maximized in a highly profitable operating year for a business. That is, if a company is in a high marginal tax bracket, say at 35 percent, the deduction saves far more taxes than if the company is in a low marginal tax bracket (say 15 percent). Proper tax planning becomes an important element of knowing when accelerated deductions give you the most bang for your buck.

✔ **Specialized incentives:** Government legislation is littered with all types of specialized incentives, awards, grants, and/or other types of windfalls that can be obtained if the right criteria are met. For example, the government supports a number of grant programs designed to encourage investments in desirable markets, such as the healthcare industry. The government also gives preferential treatment to women-, minority-, and disadvantaged-owned businesses in securing contracts when conducting business with the government.

The list of incentives at both the state and federal government levels is extensive, but we offer words of caution: To have any hope of securing specialized incentives, you must be very patient, persistent, and well prepared because the qualifications can sometimes be extremely rigid. Although the government generally has good intentions when providing incentives, remember that you're dealing with the largest bureaucracy in the world.

Don't forget the SALT: State and local taxation

Probably every Baby Boomer who has visited the doctor recently has been told three things: Exercise, watch your weight, and eat right (with a special emphasis on cutting down your salt consumption). Well, businesses may also want to reduce their SALT intake — that is, your state and local taxation. The fact of the matter is that with most states, counties, cities, and municipalities being strapped for cash, the exact opposite is happening. State and local governments are not only looking for ways to generate revenue from just about any source of SALT they can but also implementing policies to accelerate payments from these types of taxes.

We use the term SALT to refer to the plethora of taxes applied and administered at the state and local level, including property taxes, sales and use taxes, state income taxes, unclaimed property taxes, environment fees or taxes, new and expanded business licensing fees, employee head taxes, and the list goes on and on. Whether these expenses are actually called a *tax* or a *fee* doesn't change the fundamental principle: Your business is going to pay more.

The state of California now requires every business generating over $100,000 a year in revenue to complete an annual use-tax return. For a quick refresher course, *use taxes* are due from businesses that buy and consume tangible personal property that was acquired without paying sales tax (to the seller). For instance, a business may purchase technology equipment over the Internet from a supplier in Texas that's not required to collect and remit taxes in California (because it delivers the goods via a common carrier). So although the supplier isn't required to collect and remit the sales tax, the purchaser, or user, is required to report the purchase on a use-tax return and remit the appropriate tax to the state of California. It's probably not too hard to figure out why states are targeting this issue, given the explosion of Internet purchases and the loss of associated sales tax revenue.

The impact of SALT really hammers businesses on three fronts. First, existing tax rates, government-mandated fees, and so on are increasing. Second, new taxes and government-mandated fees are being created. And third, governments are looking for more ways to accelerate the collection of taxes and fees to "pull forward" these revenue sources into current budgetary years. Though we would love to summarize our discussion on SALT with ways to improve cash flows, our advice on SALT and cash flows is to make sure your business properly administers and complies with all SALT-related matters in your operating jurisdiction to avoid very nasty and problematic assessments.

In real estate, location, location, and location mean everything. For SALT, compliance, compliance, and compliance mean everything. With state and local governments pursuing every dollar they can (going as far as multiple states setting up tax-auditing groups in other states to ensure proper tax compliance), proactively managing this issue is imperative in order to avoid incurring added costs and management efforts to clean up old compliance issues (with will undoubtedly carry past penalties and interest charges, which aren't cheap).

The concept of nexus is very closely related to SALT. In the business world, *nexus* means that a company has established a business operating presence in another governmental jurisdiction, which in turn triggers the need to comply with all SALT reporting requirements there. Nexus can be established by having an office in that jurisdiction with employees or even by having simply a piece of property with no office or employees located there. Even if a company has only one employee covering the sales efforts of an entire state, nexus has been established. And remember, the state and local taxing authorities talk to one another, so if you're paying payroll taxes in a state, then the state is going to look for income tax returns, property tax returns, sales and use tax returns, and so on to be filed.

The pros and cons of debt

To help you remember how you can effectively use debt in a business as a source of capital of cash, look at debt from both ends of the spectrum: the pros and cons.

The advantages of using debt as a source of cash can be best summarized in following three attributes:

- **Flexibility:** Debt covers a broad spectrum of financing requirements, ranging from as little as $50,000 (a niche factoring or leasing company providing capital to small businesses) to billions of dollars (the world's largest banks providing financing for a multibillion-dollar public-company buyout). In addition, numerous sources of debt are available from the market, covering just about every type of risk scenario.

- **Management/ownership control:** Management and ownership control is not relinquished, because debt providers generally don't have a direct say in ongoing business matters.

- **Economic returns:** Economic returns can be enhanced when debt is used appropriately by leveraging this source of cash. Instead of being limited by the amount of equity (ownership) capital a business can raise, it can leverage or multiply its total capital by adding debt on top of the equity capital that should provide a larger base for sales and to earn more profit.

But unfortunately, you can't have your cake and eat it too when using debt, so here are the primary disadvantages when debt is used as a source of capital:

- **Secured interest:** Security in some form of asset, guarantee, or pledge is usually required, which places the business's assets (and potentially the personal assets of its owners) at risk. If the business defaults on the loan, these assets may have to be used to repay the debt if other means are not available to satisfy the obligation.

- **Debt must be repaid, with interest:** The debt must be repaid per the terms and conditions established, regardless of whether the company's performance allows for the repayment. Unlike equity investments, which tend to only generate a distribution of earnings or dividend if the company's performance dictates, debt repayment terms are rigid and must be adhered to. If not, the company suffers the wrath of its creditors demanding repayment.

- **Business restrictions:** Although direct management and ownership in a business is not sacrificed, debt sources often place restrictions on certain business activities (in the form of loan covenants), which may limit a company's ability to undertaken business transactions. Whether you like it or not, debt sources are partners that can influence management decisions.

Part IV
Managing Your Business with Cash Flow in Mind

"I'm not familiar with auditing terms. What do you think that means?"

In this part . . .

The chapters in this part of the book get down to day-to-day cash-flow matters that business managers have to deal with (or make sure that other employees in the business are doing well). Chapter 12 leads off with an in-depth discussion of fundamentals of bank accounts and the key features you should pay attention to. The chapter also provides valuable advice for managing cash in the digital, electronic-funds-transfer age and explains the importance of cash budgeting.

Chapter 13 discusses an unpleasant but necessary topic: preventing and minimizing cash losses from many kinds of embezzlement and fraud. Unfortunately, some customers, vendors, employees, and managers may seize any opportunity to steal from the business or otherwise take advantage of their positions for their personal benefit at a high cost to the business.

In Chapters 14 and 15, we shift to more positive topics. These two chapters explain improving cash flow in the basic cycles of selling and disbursements. These two fundamental business operations are often overlooked from the cash-flow point of view.

Chapter 12

Covering the Basics of Cash and Cash Activity

*Y*ou've probably heard the following clichés a thousand times over: "Cash is king," "He who has the gold makes the rules," and, in the infamous words of Warren Buffett, "When the tide goes out, we'll see who's left standing naked on the beach." But all these sayings are 100 percent accurate, because most businesses spend the better part of their lives either attempting to secure and create as much cash as possible (hopefully from the ability of generating real profits) or, after this goal is achieved, turning their attention to managing and protecting this invaluable and unique asset.

Looking at the uniqueness of cash from another perspective, a business works its tail off to increase and improve its cash levels, but after it does so, the business is going to then have to work its tail off attempting to keep other parties from grabbing it. Whether shareowners are looking for increased dividends, the government is looking for its share of tax receipts, vendors are wanting to be paid quicker, employees are feeling underappreciated (that is, underpaid), or management simply feels like all that cash is burning a hole in its pocket, the list of uses for perceived excess cash balances is endless.

Cash, just like every other business asset, must be properly managed, protected, and controlled by management. However, given the extremely liquid nature of this asset and the fact that cash can easily "disappear" without a trace, the types of controls required to properly manage and protect this asset take on an entirely different level of thinking and attention.

One theme that we hope to drive home in this chapter is that minding, controlling, and managing cash is basically a real-time event that requires active, timely, and appropriate (that is, senior-level) management involvement. Given the speed at which business moves in today's economy, gone are the good old days of evaluating a business's performance on a monthly basis. That system must be supplemented by very timely and highly relevant information reporting. And as part of that reporting, cash availability represents an invaluable internal management data point to evaluate a company's overall health and performance.

Managing the Unique Characteristics of Cash

When cash is evaluated from the perspective of reviewing the balance sheet, it really just looks like another business asset listed before trade receivables, inventory, and other assets. But when cash is really understood, its uniqueness begins to stand out based on the following characteristics. First, cash is very liquid and transportable (not to mention highly susceptible to fraud or theft). Second, cash really does represent the circle of life in a business as basically all business transactions either start or end with cash. Third, cash can be exchanged for basically any good or service required by a business. And fourth, cash not only represents the circle of life of a business but, more importantly, is also the lifeblood of all businesses, because it is imperative to maintain proper amounts of cash to support ongoing operations.

Understanding that cash ends up being one side of almost every transaction

One of the unique elements of cash (unlike trade accounts receivable or inventory) is that eventually it ends up being on one side of almost every business transaction executed. The following two examples explain how cash becomes a side of any transaction:

- **Sales cycle:** ACME Distribution, Inc., sells $10,000 worth of widgets to a customer on credit. The customer eventually remits payment. The series of entries shown in Figure 12-1 would occur in the accounting system.

- **Payables cycle:** ACME Distribution, Inc., purchases $6,000 of raw material to manufacture its widgets, initially receiving 30-day payment terms and then eventually pays the vendor in cash for the product (see Figure 12-2).

ACME Distribution, Inc. — The Trail of Cash

Account Description	Debit	Credit
To record the initial sale of products to a customer:		
Trade Accounts Receivable	$10,000	
Sales - Widgets		$10,000
To record receipt of the customer payment for the sale of widgets:		
Cash	$10,000	
Trade Accounts Receivable		$10,000

Figure 12-1: Recording the trail of cash for sales.

ACME Distribution, Inc. — The Trail of Cash

Account Description	Debit	Credit
To record the purchase of raw material to manufacture widgets:		
Inventory - Raw Material	$6,000	
Trade Accounts Payable		$6,000
To record the payment of the vendor invoice for the purchase of raw material:		
Trade Accounts Payable	$6,000	
Cash		$6,000

Figure 12-2: Recording the trail of cash for payables.

Although both of the examples are relatively simple, the point is that for most businesses cash represents the end game (either in the form of an eventual receipt or disbursement). In fact, when cash flows and balances are properly understood, they are the best management assessment tools available to capture the essence of a business's performance, and they offer a great benchmark on which to assess a company's health.

Certain transactions do not involve cash, such as recording depreciation expense on owned equipment or having to write off a trade receivable as bad debt that's uncollectable. However, these transactions tend to be less frequent in nature, are for lower dollar amounts (in total), and are generally accounted for at a specific point in time (for example, monthly or quarterly), so they tend to have a reduced role in the business's overall health. This is not to say that these types of transactions are not important to recognize in the financial statements, because full accrual-based financial statements produced by using GAAP require these types of transactions to be recorded. But the real economic value and "meat" of a business's viability should be based in transactions that eventually produce or consume cash.

Tuning in to the constant cash hum

Because basically all company transactions, in one form or another, end up in cash, cash creates a somewhat unique flow and rhythm depending on the specific attributes associated with your business. No two businesses are exactly the same, so the hum and rhythm of cash flows differ between businesses, but, as unique as businesses may be, most have to manage and understand three primary types of cash flows: routine, nonroutine, and shocks:

✔ **Routine cash flows:** Routine cash flows are generally driven from a company's internal normal operating cycle of selling products or services, collecting cash, purchasing materials or incurring expenses, and paying for these purchases or expenses (which includes the company's payroll). This type of cash flow tends to be very frequent (or routine, if you like, such as the restaurant serving the lunch crowd each day), highly predictable (the restaurant has a solid understanding of what the average ticket for each customer should be) and transacted in much higher volumes with a relatively low average transaction level. McDonalds offers a perfect example of routine cash flows because they have great data on when customers will make purchases, what they will buy, how much they will spend, and the volume of customers expected.

✔ **Nonroutine cash flows:** Nonroutine cash flows tend to be driven by a number of factors, including seasonal business trends, extraordinary events (such as acquiring a business), and/or timing-related events associated with the fiscal year-end of a business (like making estimated tax payments). For the most part, nonroutine cash flows can be anticipated and incorporated into the budgeting and forecasting process because though they're far less frequent in occurrence, they tend to occur in the same period during a given fiscal operating year. (For example, the final estimated tax payment for a regular C corporation using a fiscal year-end of December 31 falls in the last month of the year).

✔ **Shocks:** Even less routine than nonroutine cash flow is the occasional and cruel need for most businesses to manage sudden shocks to cash resources. Events that would fall into this category are natural disasters, potential adverse litigation outcomes, and a large and long-standing customer terminating a contract without warning. The good news associated with these events is that they are fairly rare. However, these events also tend to be very large and can significantly impact a company's cash position with little or no warning.

Having a properly structured and available lending facility to assist with managing the periodic uncertainties of cash flows is an extremely important tool (to have readily available) for most businesses. Unless you're the likes of Apple or IBM, sitting on literally billions of dollars of excess cash, you should always make sure your company has a rainy-day fund to tap in case of unexpected events. Working with financing sources (such as a bank or other lender) to make sure ample cash backs your rainy-day fund availability is a prudent management decision.

Deciding what a normal cash balance should be

It's the $10 million question: What should a normal cash balance be? Well, the answer to this question varies significantly based on the following four key operating issues.

Stage of business

Businesses just launching or starting up need a lot of available cash in order to cover projected operating expenses during the period prior to revenue being generated and converted to cash. For mature businesses with highly predictable revenue/sales patterns, cash availability can be lower because management has a much greater level of confidence related to periodic cash inflows and cash outflows.

The business stage also affects cash flow related to growth. For slower growth in more mature businesses (for example, a utility company), again, lower cash levels are needed. For rapidly expanding businesses (typically newer companies or businesses operating in highly competitive, rapidly changing, and/or innovative environments), higher cash availability is needed to support the anticipated growth.

Newly launched businesses must understand two key operating issues in order to determine how much cash is needed.

- ✔ First, the monthly cash burn rate (discussed in Chapter 7) indicates how fast the business is using up cash. For example, if your business generates $25,000 revenue and cash receipts but spends $100,000 a month to cover base operating expenses, your burn rate is $75,000 per month.

- ✔ Second, the revenue or selling cycle must be understood and managed to find out when cash will be received from eventual product or service sales. For some start-ups, this amount of time may be a little as six months, while for others (such as a biotechnology company developing a new drug), it may be ten years. Chapter 14 delves into the revenue cycle and how it can be managed to improve cash flows.

The selling cycle almost always takes longer than a company thinks. Business owners and entrepreneurs (who are often sales and marketing driven) are by nature optimistic and almost always think the market will accept their products or services in a very efficient and timely manner. So although optimism is welcome and encouraged, business plans should always double any best-case scenario time estimates for implementation to actual sales being realized.

By understanding these two critical issues, managers can determine the amount of cash needed to support the business operations over a set period of time. This number represents a base minimum level of cash the company needs to operate.

Type of business

Your business type has a significant impact on what's considered a normal cash balance. The cash resources needed for a retail business that sells directly to customers and generally doesn't generate trade receivables is very different from the cash resources needed for a construction company that builds bridges, highways, and other massive projects. For companies that are more affected by large projects, lengthy business decisions and operating cycles, and downstream influences (for example, a defense contractor waiting for Congress to approve a new military program), higher levels of cash are generally required to manage the ebb and flow of expenses versus receipts. For a long-standing fast food restaurant that deals only in cash, credit cards, and debit cards, the need for readily available cash tends to be reduced.

Access to cash

Although having available cash on the balance sheet is always important, having access to cash *when needed* is often far more valuable to a business. This access may come in the form of an established relationship with a lending facility you can tap when needed, or you may be able to access funds from investors who have committed funds to be released over a period of time. For companies with access to external available cash resources, lower levels of cash are required. For companies that don't have this luxury, higher levels of cash are needed.

Securing funding or cash for a business to operate is one of the most time-consuming, intensive, frustrating, and lengthy processes senior management undertakes. Planning for cash needs well in advance is absolutely critical to ensure that cash is available when needed. Prior to the Great Recession, which started in December 2007 (per the National Bureau of Economic Research), you could assume that planning three to six months in advance was sufficient (depending on where the cash was going to be secured from). Now you should double that estimate. With fewer sources of funding/cash available, more competition, and more stringent underwriting criteria, securing funding takes much longer in today's market.

Market stability

A company must always be evaluating its market and customer base to execute its business plan. In markets that are very stable and display a high level of predictability (for instance, we know X customers will purchase our products and pay in Y days, regardless of the state of the economy), operating risks are lower and thus cash balances can be kept lower. A good example of this market is liquor stores — whether times are good or bad, people tend to drink. On the opposite end of this spectrum are companies operating in markets that are highly competitive and fluid. For example, a video game manufacturer may have the best-selling title in the current year but miss the mark altogether in the next year. Ensuring that ample cash resources are available to adapt to rapidly changing market conditions is essential to a business's long-term strategic plan.

Your operating conditions

After you have a sense of where your business falls in the preceding four categories, you can go back to the original question of what a normal cash balance is. Obviously, the answer still varies on a business-by-business basis, but you can use the following three operating scenarios as general rules of thumb:

✔ **Mature/highly predictable business with stable markets and access to alternative sources of cash:** In this scenario, available cash balances can be lowered given the highly stable nature of the business. Many such companies use a three- to six-month operating expense metric to determine how much cash should be available. For example, if a company incurs $100,000 a month in operating expenses and always wants to have three months of cash on hand to cover every expense in the event that not one dime comes in from sale (highly unlikely), then the cash balance needed would be $300,000. Business types that fall into this scenario include grocery stores, gas stations, utility companies, larger retail operations (such as Walmart and McDonald's).

✔ **Older business operating in an unstable and evolving market with limited access to alternative sources of cash:** In this scenario, cash resources need to be increased to address a multitude of issues, including potentially having to support operating losses during a turnaround period, adapt marketing and sales strategies to changing markets and customers, and account for the fact that during the business turnaround phase, access to financing and cash will be limited. In this environment and using the operating expense metric, a minimum of 12 months of cash availability should be available and most likely more. The reason more money is better is that company turnarounds

• Usually take longer to implement than planned

• Cost more than anticipated

- Tend to be met with a large amount of skepticism from financing sources (that is, the source wants proof before it will provide financing, whereas you need financing in order to prove it)

So having extra cash available when operating in this environment is always recommended to help absorb the unforeseen roadblocks and speed bumps that will inevitably appear. If the monthly operating expense level if $100,000, then at least $1.2 million would be needed. A perfect example of a business operating in this environment was General Motors — and for that matter, the auto industry in its entirety. This industry underwent a major restructuring since 2008 and, if it wasn't for the United States Government, was going to fail due to large losses combined with limited access to capital.

✔ **Start-up or newly formed business penetrating a new market with no current revenue or real customers:** In this scenario, the operating expense metric needs to be at least 12 months, and in a number of circumstances should be closer to 2 years. So if a start-up company incurs $100,000 a month in operating expenses, it should have at least $1.2 million and maybe up to $2.4 million in available cash. The reason for this high level should be clearly evident — no real revenue is being generated (so no inflow of cash is occurring), and securing financing or cash from third parties often takes a long time (based in the fact that bank loans aren't available while a company is losing money, so equity needs to be secured, a much more time-consuming process).

The bottom line with cash availability is simple and straightforward: The higher the risk and business uncertainty, the higher level of available cash needed to support operations. One of the single biggest reasons small businesses fail is the lack of capital or, more specifically, the failure to develop a realistic business plan (ensuring that enough capital is available to execute the plan given multiple operating scenarios).

Can having too much cash be a problem?

The answer is yes, because too much cash indicates that the company isn't deploying assets in the most profitable manner possible. In today's economic environment, excess cash has limited earnings potential. Whether a company invests the cash in a bank CD (earning 1 to 2 percent) or United States T-bills or bonds (earning from less than 1 to 4 percent), the ability to generate any type of real earnings is limited, which is why you see shareowners of corporations always placing pressure on management with excess cash to either "use it or lose it." The goal is to redeploy internal earnings that sit in cash into business opportunities that can achieve much higher returns than 1 to 4 percent. And if that growth isn't possible, then management can at least increase dividends to return the excess cash to the shareowners (the rightful owners of the cash).

And one final thought that needs to be considered is that the available cash balances presented in this section are based on ideal levels. In today's economy, ideal is often far different from actual. Most strong, stable companies tend to have more cash than is needed, whereas most new and struggling companies tend to have far less cash than needed. The balance of this book is geared toward helping manage available cash to these ideal targets to ensure that your company has the necessary resources to prosper.

Implementing Fundamental Cash Management Practices

In one sense, cash is just like every other company asset. Similar to inventory, fixed assets, or patents, it needs to be proactively managed, controlled, and evaluated on a periodic basis to protect the economic interests of a company. On the other hand, cash represents a very unique and extremely liquid asset that requires additional management attention, not just from the standpoint that cash can quickly disappear due to fraud but, more important, because it truly represents the lifeblood of a business. This section focuses on the fundamental management issues associated with cash, from the beginning (setting up cash accounts) to the end (assessing and evaluating cash as an asset).

The same concept that applies with all other company assets also applies to cash. The goal is to utilize each company asset as efficiently as possible to improve operating results and increase the enterprise's economic value.

Establishing cash and bank accounts

When a business is initially formed, the first step usually undertaken (after the legal formation) is setting up bank and cash accounts. For the purposes of our discussion, bank and cash accounts are generally assumed to mean the same thing because for most companies the majority of business in cash is usually maintained in bank accounts. Even for businesses that maintain active on-hand cash balances (such as retail stores that need to have cash available to transact with consumers), the original source of this cash and the eventual destination are bank accounts.

In order to establish company bank accounts, you need to consider the type of bank accounts required, get approval for those accounts from the company's owners or governing board, and then determine who has signing authority (to make withdrawals and deposits). These subjects are discussed in the following sections.

Bank account types

First, a company must decide what types of bank accounts it requires to conduct business. The following types are most commonly used:

- ✔ **General operating account:** This account is used to process the majority of a business's normal and customary transactions, such as paying vendors and receiving customer payments. Thus the name *general*.

  Some companies establish a master general operating account and then establish smaller operating accounts for a business division or segment that needs to have ready access to a bank account to conduct business. For example, a recycling company that buys large amounts of material probably doesn't want to have cash on hand to purchase the items but yet needs to pay third parties on the spot. This company establishes a smaller operating account for this division, funded with lower cash levels, which can be used to pay third parties as needed. The account is then replenished periodically (in some cases, daily) based on the actual or anticipated needs. This type of structure represents a control procedure at two levels. First, it limits the amount of cash in an account that may be more susceptible to fraud (because normally this account has numerous check signers). Second, the division is forced to produce management information frequently in order to ensure that the bank account is properly funded.

- ✔ **Payroll account:** Quite often, businesses establish a separate bank account to process periodic payroll activity. Payroll-related activity is usually reviewed by a number of additional parties (like the human resource department, outside payroll processing services, and others). So to limit access to potentially confidential information, such as total company-wide cash levels, a payroll account is only funded with just enough cash to cover the next payroll.

- ✔ **Investment account:** Various names are used for this type of bank account, including *savings, money market, interest bearing,* and others, but the idea is always that when a company has excess cash balances, the cash is parked in an account that can generate interest earnings.

- ✔ **Restricted cash accounts:** A restricted cash account can be any number of different, unique bank accounts that hold cash for a particular use. It can be a certificate of deposit used as collateral (for example, a landlord may require a deposit on leased space, so instead of giving the landlord cash, the lessee makes a deposit with the bank and pledges it as collateral). It may be a trust account set up to segregate cash that can only be used for a specific purpose. For instance, a business was sold with 25 percent of the purchase price held back for one year to ensure that the company's performance met predetermined targets. When the company met those targets, the funds were released to the seller. The reason for the trust account was that the seller wanted to make sure the funds would be available.

The general rule of thumb is that the smaller the company, the fewer bank accounts needed. In some cases, the company may be so small (for instance, a one-location retail store with four employees) that all its banking needs can be addressed with one general bank account. However, managers at companies of all sizes should remember that the more cash is consolidated into fewer bank accounts, the higher the risk for large losses to occur. Thus, internal policies, procedures, and controls need to be that much tighter and stronger when fewer bank accounts are used.

Currently, the FDIC (Federal Deposit Insurance Corporation) insures bank accounts for up to $250,000. If your business has $400,000 in a bank account and the bank fails, your business is at risk for $150,000. Although cash losses such as those from failed banks are rare, all business owners need to understand that this risk does exist. Companies with large amounts of cash often diversify it across multiple banks and account types to help manage this concentration risk.

Bank account approval

After the number and type of bank accounts have been determined, the actual process of legally establishing the bank accounts must be undertaken. Companies are required to obtain proper approval from their governing board or membership group to legally open and operate a bank account. For a corporation with a board of directors, board authorization must be obtained in order to open and begin to use the bank account. Similar authorizations are also required for other business legal forms, such as LLCs, partnerships, and nonprofits. You can usually get a boilerplate form (for each legal entity type) from the bank to ensure that the proper language is used and documentation is prepared to establish a bank account.

Bank account signers

The following statement may seem unusual or even out of place coming from authors who are both accountants/financial professionals by training and trait, but we hope you will remember it above all else in this chapter:

The first and foremost control that needs to be placed on cash is that your senior-most accounting and financial personnel or staff *should not* be granted check-signing authority (or the ability to transfer funds outside of the company).

Why not, you ask? Well, in just about every business, the party most adept and qualified to commit fraud is the same party that's responsible for preparing the financial statements, reports, and/or other financial-based management tools used. So who is better situated and has the knowledge to commit fraud and hide it in the financial statements? The senior accounting and finance personnel! Don't allow the coyote to guard the hen house.

Of course, not all accounting and financial personnel are coyotes, and the intent of this statement is not to implicate them as being the primary source of fraud in a business. But we do want to reinforce a key financial control, segregation of duties, in which the objective is to separate the parties that prepare information from the parties that control/manage company assets to implement a simple yet very effective check and balance. The goal is to avoid being a victim of one of those classic stories we've all heard too often where the accountant of 20 years (you know, the little old bookkeeper), as reliable and dedicated as you could ever hope, has just made off with tens of thousands of your hard-earned dollars.

The last issue that needs to be addressed before opening an account is determining who in the business will have check-signing authority. Consider two key concepts when making this decision. First, the signers on the accounts should be independent from the parties preparing and processing the documentation requiring payments. The accounting department usually prepares and processes the documentation, so personnel in that department (the bookkeeper, controller, CFO, and others) should *not* have check-signing authority. This separation is an internal control to help protect company assets by reducing the opportunity for fraud. Second, the signers on the account should be in senior roles to ensure that proper review and approval are being completed before checks are signed.

Most companies employ a dual check-signing requirement when payments are above a certain level. For example, when payments exceed $10,000, two signatures are required to ensure that the expense is properly reviewed and approved. Getting two sets of eyes on large payments provides an additional level of control to safeguard company assets against large or material errors or irregularities.

Being a signer on a bank account represents a significant responsibility that carries with it additional exposure and potential liabilities. For example, if a company fails to remit payroll taxes, the IRS will look to all parties who were responsible for remitting the taxes to pursue collection efforts, which includes company officers, senior management, and potentially all signers on bank accounts. So before you choose parties to act as signers or accept this responsibility, think carefully, because this function is best left to the owners, officers, and/or senior management team (the parties within the business with the most to gain, the most at risk, and the most business experience).

Controlling cash and bank accounts

After the bank accounts have been established, the next order of business is to make sure proper controls have been established to protect and safeguard this business asset. The following list of basic cash and bank account controls outline the bare minimum of controls needed:

✔ **Securing bank instruments and documentation:** At all times, all bank instruments — account numbers, blank checks, facsimile signature stamps, statements, original agreements, and/or any other type of documentation — should be kept under lock and key, accessible only by authorized company personnel.

✔ **Performing periodic bank reconciliations:** On a periodic basis (usually monthly), an independent party should reconcile all bank account statements against the general ledger. In addition, a member of senior management should then review and approve the reconciliation.

✔ **Auditing and balancing cash activity:** In situations where cash is actively used in the business (like a retail business), a daily balancing of cash on hand against a sales report can control the physical handling of cash. The party handling the cash (for instance, a checkout employee) balances the cash in her drawer against a computer report generated for the period of time she worked to make sure that the cash sales reported agree with the cash in the draw (accounting for beginning balances and other adjustments). By implementing a frequent balancing procedure, any discrepancies can be quickly identified and addressed.

✔ **Monitoring petty cash:** Most companies have a small petty cash fund for use on discretionary purchases (like if the office manager wants to buy everyone lunch for a job well done). Although petty cash balances tend to be small, parties that have access to them tend to use the petty cash as their own personal slush fund. To manage this misuse, first, give access to petty cash only to responsible parties. Second, require that all disbursements from petty cash be supported by a receipt. And third, order a periodic audit/reconciliation of petty cash to make sure that leakage is not occurring.

✔ **Implementing flash reports:** *Flash reports,* high-frequency reports that provide a quick snapshot or summary of critical business information and results, are a very effective tool for managing and controlling cash. A simple example of flash reporting is having a sequenced bank report setup whereby all activity for a period of time (say, a week) is reported to management, independent of the accounting function. Managers can then review the report and, if needed, compare it against internal company information to determine if it's reasonable. Before the digital age, this type of control wasn't efficient to implement, but today pushing critical information out in a real-time fashion is easy and encouraged by banks to help prevent and detect fraud.

✔ **Limiting access to bank accounts and information:** In the digital era we all live and operate within, bank accounts and information are available at the touch of a button (just like about everything else). Keeping tight control on who has access to the bank account information and requiring passwords to be changed on a frequent basis are necessary controls.

✔ **Using other basic controls as relevant:** Other basic controls may be appropriate for your company, depending on what kind of business you engage in. For instance, many companies use lock-box accounts through which customers remit payments directly to a bank, which then receives the check, deposits it, and reports the payment information back to the company (to update the accounting records). This control prevents company personnel from handling (or mishandling) customer checks. Also, stop payments are basically used by most companies at one time or another to request that the bank stop payment on an issued check before it is cashed (or relieved from the bank account). These occur for various reasons (for example, a customer never received payment for invoices that were lost in the mail, so a new check is issued) but should be administered by the appropriate personnel.

The digital age has pushed banking into real time. Gone are the days of issuing checks and knowing that you have seven business days before they clear (to use the float or retain the luxury of issuing a stop-payment request on the check). Today, check information is captured and processed extremely quickly, so businesses must establish controls to make sure that when a check or payment is made, it is valid and has little or no chance of needing to be changed. These days, after the check or money has left the house, it isn't coming back.

Maximizing your business's cash

Generally, most businesses don't sit on large stockpiles of cash wondering what to do with their vast riches. But when excess cash does become available, you can use a number of strategies, including the four that follow, to help improve and enhance operating results:

✔ **Compensating balances:** Just about every business incurs bank fees in one fashion or another. One way to help reduce bank fees is by maintaining what's called a *compensating balance.* That is, if a general operating account (that doesn't earn any interest) is kept at a certain level, the bank calculates what the cash in the account would have earned and then credits your bank fees by this amount. These compensating balances can help reduce bank fees when slightly higher balances are kept in non-interest-bearing accounts (such as a general operating account or payroll account). To determine if a compensating balance agreement for your business makes sense, you should approach your bank and request that an analysis be completed. If it looks like it will save you money, then ask your friendly banker to set this service up.

Banks are constantly looking for new revenue sources, and bank fees have been a prime tool over the past three years. Today, banks charge for just about everything, ranging from issuing fees for online banking and electronic payments to charging for each check that clears. But remember, these fees are often negotiable, so don't be bashful about approaching the bank about reducing the fees. For strong customers, the banks make a significant amount of money from managing your cash and bank accounts, so requesting discounts on fees is reasonable.

✔ **Implementing sweep accounts/ZBAs (zero balance accounts):** Sweep accounts and ZBAs are often used by larger, slightly more sophisticated companies with multiple locations and bank accounts. A sweep account allows a business to "sweep" excess cash from multiple operating accounts into a centralized account. This sweeping event then usually produces excess cash, which can be used to either pay down borrowings on a line of credit (to reduce interest expense) or invested in a money-market account (to earn interest). In coordination with using a sweep account, ZBAs are frequently used as well. A ZBA basically keeps the balance of the account at zero per the bank. Any time a check or payment clears the account, money is swept in from the central account to cover the obligation. ZBAs provide the dual assistance of using internal cash as efficiently as possible and providing an additional internal control: Fraud and theft are less likely when the account appears to have zero cash available.

✔ **Leveraging the float:** A *cash float* occurs when a business issues checks on Friday that don't clear until the next Friday. In theory, the business has the use of these funds for a short period of time until the recipient actually cashes the checks. If $20,000 of checks have been issued but not yet cleared the bank, cash float explains why the company's cash balance per its books may state that $15,000 is available whereas the bank balance shows $35,000 available. Years ago, numerous businesses used this strategy to help finance their operations — they had using the float down to an art form. Today, using the float is more difficult. Given the advent of digital technology, check information is now captured much quicker and clears the issuing company's bank account must faster. However, in certain industries the float is alive and well and used actively to help finance business operations.

✔ **Using lock boxes:** As discussed in "Controlling cash and bank accounts," companies can use bank-provided lockboxes to process checks paid to the company and eliminate internal handling. Lockboxes also provide another advantage in that they can often result in customer's payments being received and processed more quickly (thus providing your business with the use of cash sooner). Although the processing may be only a day or two sooner, for larger companies, having access to the extra cash quicker can result in improved operating performances.

Understanding Cash in the Digital Age

The digital age has truly transformed how businesses operate in today's highly competitive business environment. The practice in the good old days of calling your accounting department to prepare a report and then providing a fax number to send the information has been replaced by accessing an *app* (or application) on your 4G cellphone or tablet computer that lets you obtain and manage critical business data (in as close to real time as possible). Okay, this example may be a slight exaggeration, as most businesses still operate by using the old brick-and-mortar method of e-mailing reports or files over the Internet for access in a computing environment. But the evolution and innovation of technology will without question push the distribution of accounting and financial information to an entirely new level over the next decade.

And yes, digital advances will have a profound impact on cash, both in terms of how cash payments and transactions are processed and, more important, in how cash and bank accounts need to be managed and controlled. In the digital age, when an electronic payment is processed, it basically is gone from your account at that moment, so if it is incorrect, you've just given cash to a third party (and out of your control). In the olden days, if a check was cut on Friday and did not clear the bank until the middle of the next week, you still had 72 hours to react and potentially place a stop payment on the check. If you let your guard down, just for a moment, cash can, per the words of Warden Norton in *The Shawshank Redemption,* "Vanish like a fart in the wind."

Most businesses rely on external professionals to support, maintain, and manage complex business issues (for example, taxation issues are usually best supported by a qualified and experienced CPA firm). Understanding cash in the digital age is one of those complex issues. The complexities surrounding electronic cash transactions are numerous. One of the best sources of advice and support for managing electronic cash transactions are banks, given their experience with and knowledge about processing just about every type of cash-based transaction used by businesses today. Your company should work closely with its primary bank to ensure that cash is both protected and managed as effectively as possible.

Moving and processing cash transactions electronically

With the exception of using cold, hard cash in a business transaction, the first thing to remember about cash is that basically every other type or form of cash payment, from wires to credit cards, represents an electronic transaction. Even the use of checks has moved into the electronic age; the critical information provided on a check, such as the payee, payer, amount, check number, date, and bank account information, is now often captured electronically by various parties involved in the process (from the end recipient to the banks processing the check).

Checking out forms of electronic payments

Table 12-1 summarizes the different types of electronic payments your business may use. In addition, various pros/uses and cons associated with each type of electronic payment are listed.

Table 12-1	Types of Electronic Payment	
Type of Payment	**Pros/Uses**	**Cons**
ACH (automated clearing house)	Most commonly used to support bulk or batch payment processing. Best suited for larger organizations with high volumes of payment transactions to process (like government-initiated payments for Social Security, which process millions of payments each month without actually issuing a check but uses ACH to credit the recipient's bank account).	A somewhat more-complicated system, basically administered by Federal Reserve Banks. Not well suited to individual electronic payments for infrequent or one-time payments, because it takes a little more effort to set up and establish the payment logistics.
EFT (electronic funds transfer), including direct deposits and electronic checks	Efficient, easy to use after established with the bank, and reduces expenses with traditional check writing. Often used with recurring disbursements (such as direct deposit for the weekly payroll).	Debits or reduces the payer's account immediately, reducing the ability to use the float. Added controls required to ensure that access is limited to appropriate personnel.
Wires (a form of electronic funds transfer)	Offers increased controls because each transaction tends to be individualized. Generally used for nonrecurring transactions and foreign-payment processing.	Same as the cons for EFT. In addition, extra fees are usually charged.

(continued)

Table 12-1 *(continued)*

Type of Payment	Pros/Uses	Cons
Credit cards	Offer ease of processing, an easy way to finance purchases, fraud protection and payment return services, and a chance to earn "points" (for example, for travel). They're widely accepted, and, on the receipt side, they accelerate customer payments.	For businesses that accept credit card payments: Fees range from 2 to 4 percent, liability is increased due to the need to keep information (like card numbers) confidential, establishing merchant accounts with financial institutions can be time consuming, and personal guarantees are required to protect against fraudulent charges.
Debit cards	Easy to use and, unlike credit cards, limit purchasers to spending only what's available in their checking account. Ideally suited to companies that sell to consumers and need to accept debit cards as an alternative form of payment.	Same as the cons for credit cards. In addition, has increased risks associated with giving other parties direct access to bank account. Generally not used extensively in the business community to process payments.

A number of new and innovative types of electronic payment processing are becoming imbedded in the mainstream including using PayPal and pre-paid (and rechargeable) debit cards, and, soon to be appearing at a store near you, swiping your cellphone to process payment. These forms of electronic payment are still emerging and tend to be based more in the BtoC ecommerce market (business to consumer) rather than BtoB (business to business). However, there can be no doubt that these forms of electronic payments will continue to grow in popularity, so adapting your business to accept these types of payments should be undertaken. (But be sure to work with only the most reputable third-party clearing companies and have a clear understanding of the fees charged.)

If your business hasn't already done so, now is the time to fully embrace the use of electronic cash. Developing and implementing the systems, controls, policies, and procedures to handle any form of electronic cash carries the following three critical advantages:

✔ **Reduced expenses:** Internal costs associated with security, supplies, mailings, and so on can be reduced.

✔ **Improved performance and efficiency:** Cash can generally be received and put to use quicker when electronic payment systems are properly implemented and utilized.

✔ **Lowering fraud:** When properly implemented and managed, electronic payments can reduce fraud by limiting the number of parties handling cash and by utilizing advanced fraud protection features available in the electronic environment.

Banks are starting to require businesses to implement fraud prevention tools to lower overall risks. Businesses may be held liable for fraudulent transactions if the bank has provided the tools necessary to prevent fraud but the business either doesn't elect to incorporate the tools or doesn't properly use the tools. Granted, this type of legal action is rare, but business owners need to be aware of the risks associated with not evolving with the market.

Considering the use of checks

The trend in business is definitely away from checks and toward electronic cash as a means to improve business efficiencies, reduce fraud, and lower business risks. In Corporate America, electronic cash has become the norm, so if you're looking to conduct any type of significant business with the Fortune 500 companies, be prepared to accept and remit by using electronic methods.

Even in the general population, the use of checks has greatly diminished over the past decade, with more customers using online electronic checks, debit cards, credit cards, and other forms of electronic cash (like PayPal) to process payments. Most small- to medium-size businesses will have to continue processing payments by check for the foreseeable future because some customers are still paying with checks. But the message is loud and clear: You'd better already be on the electronic-cash train, 'cause it has left the station.

Establishing cash controls in electronic-based accounting systems

Ten years ago, I would have titled this section of the book "Establishing cash controls in computer-based accounting systems," because the concepts of cloud computing, virtual companies, freely portable accounting systems, and the like really didn't exist. At the turn of the millennium, the world was really just being introduced to the dot-com boom-and-bust cycle and was busy working through Y2K issues, while social media, mobile networking, and cloud computing were concepts left for science fiction writers. What a difference ten years makes. Today, the dot-com era represents a distant memory (or for some, a forgettable nightmare) replaced by the world of instant mobile communication, cloud computing, and highly portable/on-demand information.

To begin this discussion on establishing controls over cash in an electronic environment, you need to understand that the same fundamentals of controls apply whether you're controlling cash in a traditional manual environment or in an electronic environment. (Refer to the earlier section "Controlling cash and bank accounts" for an overview of the fundamental practices.) Beyond these basic fundamentals, companies actively use the following additional controls, policies, and procedures to manage and protect cash in an electronic environment:

- **Access to and use of passwords:** Password protection in the digital age is absolutely critical to ensure that vital/confidential information is properly protected. Passwords should also limit who can access and manipulate company bank accounts and process payments. Require frequent password updates. In addition, your business should also set up logs or run reports that track logins, implementation of positive confirmation on password changes, and the location of the accessing computer or mobile source. Banks and financial institutions aggressively use algorithms to monitor and track unusual activity in bank accounts and credit cards, and your business should tap that source when the situation warrants.

- **Flash and exception reports (testing the system):** Various reporting tools are available to help manage and control bank accounts and cash levels. Just like a weekly sales flash report is generated to report on how the company performed during the past week, the same type of report can be generated to monitor cash levels (focusing on activity out of the norm). In addition, exception reporting can be used to identify any trends or activity that may indicate a problem. For example, management may want to be informed of any changes in employee compensation levels from the prior period (as provided by a payroll service) to ensure all changes were approved. With bank accounts, reports can be generated and provided that list any check over, say, $5,000 that cleared the bank account. Needless to say, these reports are unique to each business in terms of what information is critical and/or at the highest risk for fraud or mismanagement. Management should determine what information is needed and then develop and implement proactive tools to prevent problems from arising.

- **Positive pay and other bank tools:** Banks offer a number of tools and resources to help manage electronic cash transactions. One such tool that a number of companies use is most commonly referred to as *positive pay*. Positive pay reports to the bank all checks a company generated from its system in real time. Software sits on top of your company's accounting system and captures any check and payment information processed (so the bank has a record of what you approved). When checks or payments are presented to the bank for payment, the check is matched against the positive pay report to ensure that the check is valid. If not, the bank notifies your company of the discrepancy and the company indicates whether the check should be accepted or rejected. Other examples of bank management tools include using "push" reports (reports generated by the bank and pushed out to the customers) to notify customers of the latest electronic scams and fraud schemes and developing complex algorithms which track customer payment trends and credit card charges habits (to identify anything out of the ordinary which may indicate that fraud has been committed).

✔ **Advanced controls for checks:** While the electronic age continues to transform the movement of cash, the tried-and-true method of using checks isn't going away anytime soon. However, generating checks has evolved in the electronic age. Formerly, businesses would order preprinted checks from a supplier or the bank and then insert them into the printer when checks needed to processed. Today, blank check stock is received from the supplier, and when checks are printed, all the vital information is printed at the same time (such as the bank routing and account numbers, payee, payer, and check number). The check is printed with special MICR toner (that is, magnetically readable toner that the bank's computers can read and process) on special fraud-prevention paper (using watermarks and other distinctive features). Not only do these steps help with fraud prevention (because now a pre-printed check can't be stolen and filled out with fraudulent information), but they also improve the bank's efficiency in reading and processing checks (because all the information has been magnetically encoded).

An even further advancement in the check printing world is to use remote check printing. This feature allows a company to pay its vendor by processing a check payment that actually prints at the customer's site (on their printer), using a computer generated signature or fac-simile. This strategy is best used for larger relationships where frequent payments are made and carries numerous advantages including reduc-ing costs (no mailing required) and handling risks.

✔ **Using prepaid debit cards:** Prepaid debit cards are a growing form of control over electronic cash. One of their most common uses is for employee paychecks in cases where the employee doesn't have a bank account. Surprisingly, roughly 20 percent of the population doesn't use regular bank accounts and direct deposit but rather receives a live check, cashes it, and then pays bills with either cash or by purchasing money orders. Prepaid debit cards allow the employee to have his card "recharged" on the pay date so that the card carries a balance that can be spent. The card is safer than carrying cash because if the card is lost or stolen, it can be cancelled and another card issued (as long as the PIN is protected). Prepaid cards can also be used in a number of other areas, such as parents providing a set level of spending for their college student (usually quickly reached).

What should be clear from these bullet points is that working with your bank is very important in terms of implementing the proper controls, policies, and procedures to protect cash in an electronic environment. Fraud (including bad checks and credit card theft) remains a significant expense for banks and financial institutions, resulting in billions of dollars of losses over the years. And if fraud is costing the bank money, then it's costing you money, because the bank makes up for these losses or expenses by either charging your business higher fees or paying lower interest rates (on investable cash balances).

Managing and controlling cash in the electronic age requires a partnership between you, your bank, and critical customers and creditors. Your business needs to be proactive in implementing necessary controls because you can't assume that a bank is going to protect your interests at all times. The banks are smart, but the crooks are usually smarter (and often one step ahead when committing theft and fraud). Assuming that a third party is going to protect your business interests is often the source of unnecessary heartburn and the mother of all headaches.

Working with Cash as a Key Business Indicator

Chapters 8 and 9 of this book provide an in-depth discussion and overview of the business-planning process, including developing financial projection models — which, of course, includes forecasting critical cash information (that is, sources, uses, and available balances). Keep in mind that when budgeting cash, it tends to become a "forced" number in the financial forecasts. That is, after all other assumptions have been built into company projections and forecasts — items such as how long it will take to collect receivables, how much needs to be invested in fixed assets, whether the business will need to borrow from a bank this year, and so on — cash levels or balances are forced into the balance sheet so that it can balance. For example, a jewelry retailer will ramp inventory levels and gear up promotional efforts to support the holiday selling season which starts in mid to late November and runs through the end of the year. So cash balances tend to be very low at the end of October as the company has deployed cash for the benefit of the holiday season (so a low cash balance is expected or forced into the balance sheet). However, by the end of December, cash balances should reach extremely healthy levels as inventory has been reduced via high holiday sales levels (thus the high cash balance is forced into the balance sheet). The key isn't so much that cash balances went from extremely low levels in late October to the highest level of the year in late December but rather did the cash perform as expected against management's internal forecasts.

Of course, the forced cash balance may or may not be a desirable outcome; it may be too low or even negative (relative to the desired cash levels needed to operate a business). If cash levels are too low, your business should immediately view it as a red flag in terms of making sure management has a plan developed to address any potential cash squeezes that may occur.

Think ahead, very far ahead, when developing a plan to make sure that plenty of cash or access to cash will be available to support your business. In today's unsettled and competitive capital markets, securing cash from external sources (such as banks and investors) to support your business operations is a very time-consuming and lengthy process that can easily take three to six months or longer, depending on the source of the cash.

Knowing the seasonal ebb and flow of cash

Most financial projections prepared by businesses tend to follow a fairly similar pattern. Unless the economy is crashing (a la 2009), the goal for most businesses is to increase sales and improve profits. For example, a business unit may set a target of increasing sales by 15 percent for the year and profits by 20 percent in order to meet senior management's expectations. Instead of diving into all the fundamentals and strategies associated with preparing financial forecasts (covered extensively in Chapters 8 and 9), this section focuses on various seasonal factors and events (when viewed on an annual basis) that can significantly impact short-term cash flows and availability. Or looking at it from another perspective, if proper planning is not completed and adequate cash resources are not available to build inventory and promote sales (during a busy season), then sales will be negatively impacted (by not having the proper inventory available), which in turn will result in lower profits.

Very few if any businesses experience linear increases (or, for that matter, decreases) in sales, profitability, and cash flows over a 12-month period. This perfect world just doesn't exist for 99 percent of businesses, because they are always encountering events, transactions, external influences, and so on that have a material effect on cash flows and cash availability on a quarterly, monthly, or in some cases weekly basis. So because cash levels can vary significantly in a very short period of time, your business should always be prepared for trouble.

Recognizing the events that cause cash-flow variation

Although a number of factors and events can impact cash flows and availability over a year, most fall into one of the following three categories:

✔ **The four seasons:** A large number of companies build their business models around the four seasons of the calendar year, and changes in the season can significantly impact cash levels. For a jewelry company, the Christmas holiday rush, which last about six weeks a year, can produce as much as 35 percent of the entire sales for the year. In late October, just prior to the Christmas holiday season, cash levels decrease because cash has been spent on inventory that needs to be on the shelves for consumers to buy. However, in late December or early January, cash balances skyrocket due to the Christmas buying binge. To an uneducated party evaluating cash positions at these two points in time, the company looks to be in trouble in October, whereas at the end of December, the company looks to be very strong.

✔ **The government:** Rules and regulations established by the government can often create significant short-term impacts on cash flows and availability. A perfect example is the timing of quarterly estimated income tax payments. For regular C corporations, these tax payments fall on the 15th of the 4th, 6th, 9th, and 12th month of the corporation's fiscal year end. (For example, a calendar-year-ending fiscal year would make estimated payments on 4/15, 6/15, 9/15, and 12/15.) So for two months during the quarter, no estimated income tax payments are due, but in the third month, a large payment is made. Other examples of how the government can impact short-term cash flows and availability include unemployment insurance (due on the last day of the month following each calendar quarter end), remittances for sales and use taxes collected (which may vary from monthly to annually, depending on how much is due), and paying for licenses and permits in advance.

A very distinct trend is taking hold in states, cities, counties, and local municipalities in the United States. If you haven't heard, most of these entities are out of money. So not only are they looking for ways to increase revenues (for example, by raising sales tax rates), they are also looking for ways to accelerate payments (from businesses to governments). Paying more and quicker is a trend that you should anticipate to continue for years to come, so when creating a financial forecast, incorporate events that will accelerate the flow of cash from your business to the government.

✔ **The company itself:** Most businesses over a period of time develop specific policies, procedures, and operating structures that create peaks and valleys of cash flows and availability. Some companies may look to retool with new equipment during a particularly slow period. Other companies may accrue employee bonuses during the year and then pay them in a lump sum around Christmas of each year. Some companies may have a significant loan payment due as a result of a note payable executed three years earlier. The list of company-specific influences on cash are endless, but the same basic management concept applies to all: Managers who prepare the budget must have a clear understanding of these influences and must account for them in the annual budgeting process.

Staggering cash flow

Staggering is a practice that attempts to budget cash needs on a more even basis during the year. Staggering cash inflows and outflows to smooth them out on an annual basis can be a very effective management tool.

For example, if a business has to commit cash for new equipment purchases, it should plan to do it at a time when business won't be disrupted by the cash drain. The business can even out cash flows by budgeting for the purchase in a month that doesn't require other significant cash outlays (for example, not when the business has to build inventory levels to support seasonal sales and pay estimated taxes).

Business can also stagger cash flows when paying commissions. Rather than pay commissions when the sale has occurred, a number of companies pay commissions when the cash is actually received from the customer. Not only does this staggering help match the cash outflow with the cash inflow, but it also gives sales representatives an incentive to make sure that customers pay in a timely fashion.

Setting periodic cash level benchmarks

A very simple cycle to remember is that starting a business takes cash. The cash, when secured, is then deployed in the business via realizing expenses, investing in assets, generating sales, paying obligations, and hopefully producing net earnings or profit. The goal is to have the profits eventually turned back into cash so the cycle can start all over again. This cycle confirms the discussion at the beginning of this chapter about how basically all business transactions eventually end up in cash (either increasing or decreasing). So cash is a logical critical internal management benchmark on which to evaluate a company's performance. However, like most benchmarks, this one should be used with other critical benchmarks to properly evaluate a business's performance.

Businesses use all kinds of operating metrics as benchmarks to evaluate their performance. Classic examples include comparing a weekly sales report trending the last four weeks to a report from the like period for the prior year, calculating inventory turnover ratios for each company product and comparing the turns to the prior year, and so on. However, most small companies don't use cash benchmarks to help evaluate and manage their businesses. Seeing that most small businesses struggle with even putting together a statement of cash flows, it's no wonder that using cash as a critical benchmark is quite often overlooked.

When using cash as a benchmark, two underlying concepts are important to understand to extract the most value from this benchmark to assist in managing your business:

- ✔ **Use cash as a canary in the coal mine.** Cash is a great tool to use in the capacity of a canary in the coal mine (that is, as an early warning system), because if cash levels are significantly different than expected, it almost always indicates that a more significant issue or problem exists with the performance of other assets, liabilities, or the company's profitability.

  When cash benchmarks are established, they're generally based on either internal or external data points. External benchmarks (that is, comparing your business's cash to that of other businesses in the same industry) should be used with an abundance of caution. Even with companies operating in the same industry, capital structures, strategic business plans, and internal policies can differ greatly, having a significant impact on cash flows and cash availability. So although "best-in-class" external benchmarks for cash can be informative, avoid drawing conclusions based on this benchmark alone. Internal benchmarks are often much more informative. Cash benchmarks have the most value when they're driven from asking why cash balances or internal cash flows may be varying so significantly from budgeted levels.

- ✔ **Implement cash flash reporting at all costs.** Every business owner and manager needs to monitor operating performances with the use of information provided through reports. Traditional reports such as monthly financial statements or sales by product lines are helpful but incomplete. The implementation of high-frequency flash reporting is becoming more and more important for businesses so that key operating metrics can be monitored very closely. Cash is especially important to monitor frequently because having a solid handle on weekly (or in some cases, daily) cash inflows and outflows can highlight a problem much quicker (allowing management to respond faster) than waiting until the end of the month.

Chapter 13

Preventing Cash Losses from Embezzlement and Fraud

*W*hen the infamous bank robber Willie Sutton was asked why he robbed banks, he's reputed to have said, "Because that's where the money is!" The cash flows of a business are a natural target for schemers who see an opportunity to siphon off some cash from these streams of money. The grandfather and father-in-law of the authors — who was a very successful businessman — told us that there's a little bit of larceny in everyone's heart. Well, perhaps not everybody — but enough people that a business should be worried.

Making a profit is hard enough as it is. There's no excuse for letting some of your profit slip away because you didn't take appropriate precautions. You don't leave the keys in your car, do you? You lock your car and make it difficult to steal. Likewise, you shouldn't leave the keys to your business's cash flow lying around. This chapter discusses controls and preventive measures that a business should consider adopting in order to prevent and mitigate cash losses from dishonest schemes by employees, customers, and other parties it deals with.

This chapter is directed to business managers; it is not a detailed reference for accountants. The chapter takes the broader management view, whereas accountants take a narrower view. Accountants focus on preventing errors that may creep into the accounting system of the business and quickly detecting errors if they get by the first line of controls. In addition to these internal accounting controls, the accounting department typically has responsibility for many of the other controls discussed in this chapter, as we cover in the sections that deal with particular controls.

Setting the Stage for Protection

We start with the reasonable premise that the large majority of people are honest most of the time. You can argue that some people are entirely honest all the time, but realistically this assumption is too risky when running a business. In short, a business has to deal with the dishonesty of the few. A business cannot afford to assume that all the people it deals with are trustworthy all the time. Fraud against business is a fact of life. One function of business managers is to prevent fraud against their business, and it should go without saying that managers should not commit fraud on behalf of the business. (But some do, of course.)

A business is vulnerable to many kinds of fraud from many directions — customers who shoplift, employees who steal money and other assets from the business, vendors who overcharge, managers who accept kickbacks and bribes, and so on. The threat of fraud is ever present for all businesses, large and small. No one tells a business in advance that they intend to engage in fraud against the business, and compounding the problem is that many people who commit fraud are pretty good at concealing it.

So every business should institute and enforce internal controls that are effective in preventing fraud. An ounce of prevention is worth a pound of cure. Keep in mind the difference between controls designed primarily to stop fraud (such as employee theft) versus procedures designed to prevent errors from creeping into the accounting system. Both types of precautions are important. Even if it prevents theft, a business may lose money if it doesn't have accounting controls to ensure that its financial records are accurate, timely, and complete.

On the police TV series *Hill Street Blues,* the last thing the desk sergeant would tell the patrol officers before they went out to their beats each night was, "Be careful out there." Good advice too for a business and its internal controls!

Preventing loss with internal controls

The procedures and processes that a business uses to prevent cash losses from embezzlement, fraud, and other kinds of dishonesty go under the general term *internal controls. Internal* means that the controls are instituted and implemented by the business. Many internal controls are directed toward the business's own employees to discourage them from taking advantage of their positions of trust and authority in the business to embezzle money or to help others cheat the business.

Many internal controls are directed toward the outside parties that the business deals with, including customers (some who may shoplift) and vendors (some who may double bill the business for one purchase). In short, the term *internal controls* includes the whole range of preventive tactics and procedures used by a business to protect its cash flows and other assets.

Some businesses put the risk of cash losses from fraud near the bottom of their risk ranking. They downgrade these potential cash seepages to a low priority. Accordingly, they are likely to think that internal controls take too much time and cost too much. Most businesses, however, take the middle road and assume that certain basic internal controls are necessary and cost effective — because without the controls, the business would suffer far greater losses that the cost of the internal controls.

Some companies boldly assume that the company's internal controls are 100 percent effective in preventing all embezzlement and fraud. A more realistic approach is to assume that some theft or fraud can slip by the first line of internal controls. Therefore, a business should install an additional layer of internal controls that come into play after transactions and activities have taken place. These after-the-fact internal controls serve as safety valves to catch a problem before it gets too far out of hand. The principle of having both kinds of controls is to *deter and detect*.

Certain internal controls are designed such that two or more persons would have to collude to commit and conceal the fraud. Collusion may or may not be an effective deterrent. The deterrent value of collusion may be compromised when two persons have a personal relationship unbeknownst to the business — for example, the two may be in a sexual relationship, or one may be buying drugs from the other, or one may be a cousin of the other. The ultimate deterrent to fraud is knowing that you will be caught if you do it. Even so, desperate people still take their chances of being caught, so if the collusion requirement doesn't derail their plans, you can still try to detect them.

Recognizing the dual purpose of internal accounting controls

Many internal accounting controls consist of required forms that must be used and procedures that should be followed in authorizing and executing transactions and operations. A business's accounting department records the financial activities and transactions. So, naturally, the accounting department is put in charge of designing and enforcing many core internal controls. The accounting profession has a long history of involvement with internal controls.

Many accounting internal controls have both an accounting reliability purpose and an antifraud purpose. The business gets two for the price of one from these particular controls. For example, employees can be required to punch their timecards on a work clock as they start and end each day, or they can have their hours entered in a payroll log signed by their supervisor. This sort of internal control helps prevent employees from being paid for time they didn't work. Also, the procedure tells the accountant which expense account to charge for their work and produces a record of the transaction that helps eliminate (or at least minimize) errors in capturing, processing, storing, and retrieving wage data needed for financial records. The accounting system of a business keeps track of the large amount of information needed in operating a business, and these internal controls are designed to ensure the accuracy, completeness, and timeliness of information held in the accounting system.

Internal accounting controls need to be kept up-to-date with changes in a business's accounting system and procedures. For example, an entirely new set of internal controls had to be developed and installed as businesses converted to computer-based accounting systems. Before then, the word *hacker* referred to a poor golfer, or duffer, not software code breakers who pose very sinister threats to companies' computer systems. The transition to computer and Internet-based accounting systems brought about a whole new set of internal accounting controls, to say nothing of all the other internal controls a business had to install to protect its databases and communications.

Struggling with fraud committed by the business

There's fraud against a business, and then there's fraud *by* a business. The first type of fraud can be classified by who does it, and unfortunately, a business is vulnerable to all kinds of fraud attacks from virtually everyone it deals with. This side of the coin includes all kinds of schemes and scams by vendors, employees, customers, and even one or more of the business's own mid-level managers. The other side of the coin is the conscious behavior of the business itself that is sanctioned by top-level owner/managers.

Frankly, most discussions of business internal controls skirt around this sensitive issue. Most articles and books assume that the business is as honest as the day is long. The discussion frames the business as an innocent target of employees, customers, and others who want to steal its money or other assets. But the truth of the matter is that some companies carry on unethical practices as their normal course of business, including bribing government and regulatory officials, knowingly violating laws covering product and employee safety, failing to report information that is required to be disclosed, misleading employees regarding changes in their retirement plans, conspiring with competitors to fix prices and divide territories, advertising falsely, treating employees with discrimination, and so on.

Frauds perpetrated by businesses may very well be illegal under state and federal statutes and common law. Restitution for damages suffered from the fraud can be sought under the tort law system. The evidence is clear that many businesses deliberately and knowingly engage in fraudulent practices, and that their managers do not take action to stop it. Basically, managers are complicit in the fraud if they see fraud going on in the business but look the other way. The managers may not like it and not approve of it, but they often live with it due to unspoken pressure to follow the "three monkey" policy — see no evil, hear no evil, speak no evil.

The lenders and shareowners of a business should keep aware of the possibility of *financial reporting fraud.* The managers of a business may cook the books, resulting in seriously misleading financial reports. Independent CPA auditors test a company's internal accounting controls that are designed to prevent financial reporting fraud. However, audits don't catch all incidents of financial reporting fraud. This issue is beyond the scope of this chapter. For more on financial reporting fraud, refer to John A. Tracy's *How to Read a Financial Report,* 7th Edition (John Wiley & Sons, Inc.).

If you ask a CPA to audit your financial statements, the CPA may have to refuse you as a new client (or dump you if you're already a client) if your internal controls are inadequate. If your internal controls are too weak, the CPA auditor can't rely on your accounting records, from which your financial statements are prepared. And the CPA may have to withdraw from the engagement if the auditor discovers high-level management fraud. Both authors have worked on audits in which serious management fraud was discovered. Our CPA firm walked off the audit (and immediately sent a bill to the ex-client). CPAs cannot knowingly be associated with crooks and businesses that operate with seriously weak internal controls.

Even businesses that routinely engage in shady practices should implement internal controls. In fact, operating on the wrong side of the road may make the business more aware of the need for internal controls, and it makes the business more vulnerable to fraud. Employees, customers, and others the business deals with are not fools; they're generally aware of what's going on. And fraud begets fraud. If employees or people doing business with the company see fraudulent practices sanctioned by top-level managers, the natural inclination is to respond in kind, adopting an attitude of entitlement and doing some fraud of their own. And they may be very good at it.

In the following discussion of internal controls, we assume that the business is behaving ethically, that the people it conducts business with (employees, customers, and so on) are treated fairly, and that the managers have not cooked the books. We assume that the business is not facing a generally hostile or "let's get even" attitude on the part of its employees, customers, vendors, and so on. In other words, we assume that the business faces the normal sort of risks of cash losses from fraud that every business encounters. We don't discuss extraordinary safety measures that a business operating in a high-crime area may have to use (like armed guards at doors).

Putting Internal Controls to Work

In this section we discuss important steps and guideposts that apply to virtually all businesses in establishing and managing internal controls. You find out both what kinds of tools are available to protect your business and what particulars you need to consider when choosing and using them.

Because this chapter is directed to business managers, not accountants, we don't delve into the details of internal accounting controls. If you or your accountant wants to find out more about internal controls, we recommend that you go to the websites of the Institute of Internal Auditors (www. theiia.org) and the American Institute of Certified Public Accountants (www.aicpa.org). Both of these professional associations publish an extensive number of books on internal controls.

In this chapter, we use the term *fraud* in its most comprehensive sense; the word covers the waterfront. It includes all types of cheating, stealing, and dishonest behavior by anyone inside the business and by anyone outside that the business deals with. Examples range from petty theft and pilferage to diverting millions of dollars into the pockets of high-level executives. Fraud includes shoplifting by customers, kickbacks from vendors to a company's purchasing managers, embezzlements by trusted employees, padded expense reports submitted by salespersons, deliberate overcharging of customers, and so on. A comprehensive list of business fraud examples would fill an encyclopedia.

Going down the internal controls checklist

Businesses have a large and diverse toolbox of internal controls to choose from. The following sections provide a checklist for managers in deciding on internal controls for their business.

Watching over high-risk areas

Strong and tight controls are needed in high-risk areas. Managers should identify which areas of the business are the most vulnerable to fraud against the business. The most likely fraud points in a business usually include the following areas (some businesses have other high-risk areas, of course):

- Cash receipts and disbursements
- Payroll (including workers' compensation insurance fraud)
- Customer credit and collections, and writing off bad debts
- Purchasing and storage of inventory

Separating duties

Where practicable, two or more independent employees should be involved in the authorization, documentation, execution, and recording of transactions — especially in the high-risk areas. This arrangement is called *separation of duties,* and the idea is to force collusion of two or more persons to carry out and conceal a fraud. For instance, two or more signatures should be required on checks over a certain amount. For another example, the employee preparing the receiving reports for goods and materials delivered to the company should not have any authority for issuing a purchase order and should not make the accounting entries for purchases. Concentration of duties in the hands of one person invites trouble. Duties should be divided among two or more employees, even if it causes some loss of efficiency

Performing surprise audits

Making surprise counts, inspections, and reconciliations that employees cannot anticipate or plan for is very effective. Of course, the person or group doing these surprise audits should be independent of the employees who have responsibility for complying with the internal controls. For instance, a surprise count and inspection of products held in inventory may reveal missing products, unrecorded breakage and damage, products stored in the wrong locations, mislabeled products, or other problems. Such problems tend to get overlooked by busy employees, but inventory errors can also be evidence of theft. Many of these errors should be recorded as inventory losses but may not be if surprise audits are not done.

Letting employees blow the whistle

Encourage employees to report suspicions of fraud by anyone in the business (which has to be done anonymously in most situations). Admittedly, this policy is tricky. You're asking people to be whistle-blowers. Employees may not trust upper management; they may fear that they will face retaliation instead of being rewarded for revealing fraud. Employees generally don't like being spies on each other, but on the other hand they want the business to take action against any employees who are committing fraud.

The business has to adopt procedures to safeguard anonymity that are convincing to potential whistle-blowers. It also has to convince employees that they will not be ostracized if they report their suspicions. Frankly, a business may have to offer financial incentives to whistle-blowers to get them to take such a drastic action that could have serious repercussions over their future career with the company.

Leaving audit trails

Insist that good audit trails be created for all transactions. The documentation and recording of transactions should leave a clear path that can be followed back in time when necessary. Supporting documents should be organized in good order and should be retained for a reasonable period of time. The Internal Revenue Service (www.irs.gov) publishes recommended guidelines for records retention, which are a good point of reference for a business.

Limiting access to accounting records and end-of-year entries

Access to all accounting records should be strictly limited to accounting personnel, and no one other than the accounting staff should be allowed to make entries or changes in the accounting records of the business. Of course, managers and other employees may ask questions of the accounting staff, and they may ask for special reports on occasion. The accounting department can provide photocopies or scanned images of documents (purchase orders, sales invoices, and so on) in response to questions, but the accounting department should not let original source documents out of its possession.

Checking the background of new employees

Before any new employee is hired, management should have a thorough background check done on him, especially if he will be handling money and working in the high-fraud-risk areas of the business. Letters of reference from previous employers may not be enough. Databases are available to check on a person's credit history, driving record, criminal record, workers' compensation insurance claims, and life insurance rejection record, but private investigators may have to be used for a thorough background check.

A business should consider doing more extensive background and character checks when hiring mid- and high-level managers. Studies have found that many manager applicants falsify their résumés and list college degrees that they in fact have not earned, and any dishonesty could very well be a bad omen about future conduct.

Periodically reviewing internal controls

Consider having an independent assessment done on your internal controls by a CPA or other professional specialist. This step may reveal that certain critical controls are missing, or, conversely, that you're wasting money on ineffectual controls. If your business has an annual financial-report audit, the CPA auditor evaluates and tests your business's internal controls. But you may need a more extensive and critical evaluation of your internal controls that looks beyond the internal accounting controls. See the earlier section "Struggling with fraud committed by the business" for more on the benefits and possible consequences of hiring an outside CPA.

Appraising key assets regularly

You should schedule regular "checkups" of your business's receivables, inventory, and fixed assets. Generally speaking, over time these assets develop problems that are not dealt with in the daily hustle and bustle of activities and the time pressures on managers and other employees. Receivables may include seriously past-due balances, but these customers' credit may not have been suspended or terminated. Some products in inventory may not have had a sale in months or years. Some items in fixed assets may have been abandoned or sold off for scrap value, yet the assets are still on the books and being depreciated.

One principle of accounting is that losses from asset impairments (damage, aging, salability, abandonment, and so on) should be recorded as soon as the diminishment in value occurs. The affected assets should be written off or the recorded (book) value of the assets should be written down to recognize the loss of economic value to the business. The decrease in asset value is recorded as a loss, which reduces profit for the period, of course. Generally, fraud isn't lurking behind asset impairments — although it can be. In any case, high-level managers should approve and sign off on asset write-downs

Implementing computer controls

Computer hardware and software controls are extremely important, but most managers don't have the time or expertise to get into this area of internal controls. Obviously, passwords and firewalls should be used, and managers know about the possibility of hackers breaking into their computers, as well as the damage that viruses can cause. Every business should adopt strict internal controls over e-mail, downloading attachments, updating software, and so on.

If the business isn't large enough for its own IT (information technology) department, it has to bring in outside consultants. The business accounting and enterprise software packages available today generally have strong security features, but you can't be too careful. Extra precautions help deter fraud.

Curbing indifference to internal controls

Internal controls may look good on paper. However, the effectiveness of internal controls depends on how judiciously employees execute the controls day in and day out. Internal controls may be carried out in a slipshod and perfunctory manner. Managers often let it slide until something serious happens, but they should never tolerate a lackadaisical attitude regarding the performance of internal controls by employees.

Sometimes a manager may be tempted to intervene and override an internal control, not out of indifference but because bypassing the control will be more efficient or serve another purpose. This break in procedure, however well meant, sets an extremely bad example. And in fact in some cases it may be evidence of fraud by the manager.

Special rules for small businesses

The lament of many small business owners/managers is, "We're too small for internal controls." But even a relatively small business can enforce certain internal controls that are very effective. Here are basic guidelines for small business owners/managers:

✔ **Sign all checks:** The owner/manager should sign all checks, including payroll checks. This precaution forces the owner/manager to keep a close watch on the expenditures of the business. Under no conditions should the accountant, bookkeeper, or controller (chief accountant) of the business be given check-signing authority. These people can easily conceal fraud if they have check-writing authority.

✔ **Mandate long vacations:** The owner/manager should require that employees working in the high-risk areas (generally cash receipts and disbursements, receivables, and inventory) take vacations of two weeks or more and, furthermore, make sure that another employee carries out their duties while they're on vacation. To conceal many types of fraud, the guilty employee needs to maintain sole control and access over the accounts and other paperwork used in carrying out the fraud. Another person who fills in for the employee on vacation may spot something suspicious.

✔ **Get two sets of eyes on things:** Although separation of duties may not be practicable, owners/managers should consider implementing job sharing in which two or more employees are regularly assigned to one area of the business on alternate weeks or some other schedule. With this arrangement, the employees may notice if the other is committing fraud.

✔ **Watch out for questionable spending:** Without violating their privacy, owners/managers should keep watch on the lifestyles of employees. If the bookkeeper buys a new Mercedes every year and frequently is off to Las Vegas, you may ask where the money is coming from. The owners/managers know the employees' salaries, so they should be able to estimate what sort of lifestyles the employees can afford.

Considering some important details of internal control

Even when you know what internal controls you want to use, you must take care to implement them in ways that are legal, practical for the company, and effective. And you also need to know what to do if the controls fail and you have a case of fraud on your hands. The following sections address these important details that you may overlook in your eagerness to place controls and get back to business.

Considering legal implications

Pay careful attention to the legal aspects of internal controls and the enforcement of them. For example, controls should not violate the privacy rights of employees or customers (for example, no strip searches), and a business should be very careful in making accusations against an employee suspected of fraud. At the other extreme, the absence of basic controls can possibly expose a manager to legal responsibility on grounds of reckless disregard for protecting the company's assets. For example, a business may not have instituted controls that limit access to its inventory warehouse to authorized personnel only, with the result that almost anyone can enter the building and steal products without notice. The manager could be accused of neglecting to enforce a fundamental internal control for inventory. You may need to get a legal opinion on your internal controls, just to be safe.

Evaluating cost effectiveness

One obvious disadvantage of internal controls is their costs — not just in money but also in the time it takes employees to perform the internal controls. Internal controls are an example of "managing the negative," which means preventing bad things from happening as opposed to making good things happen. Rather than spending time on internal controls, employees could be making sales or doing productive activities. But putting it a more palatable way, internal controls are needed to manage certain unavoidable risks of doing business.

The mantra you often hear is that internal controls should be *cost effective*, meaning that the collective benefits of a company's internal controls should be greater than the sum of their costs. But measuring the cost of a particular internal control or the total cost of all internal controls isn't very practical, and the benefits of internal controls are difficult to estimate in any quantitative manner. In general, basic internal controls are absolutely necessary and worth the cost. In the last analysis, the manager has to make a judgment call on what level of internal controls to implement to achieve a reasonable balance between the costs and the benefits.

Hiding internal controls

Generally, internal controls should be as unobtrusive as possible to the outside parties the business deals with. Ideally, your customers and vendors should not take notice of them. If you're not very careful, internal controls can give the impression that you don't trust your employees, customers, or vendors. People are sensitive about accusations (real or imagined) that you think they may be crooks. Then again, people accept all kinds of internal controls, probably because they have become used to them. For example, bookstore customers hardly notice the small electronic chip placed in books, which is deactivated at the point of sale. On the other hand, bookstore customers probably would object to having to show a detailed receipt as they leave the store for all the books they have in their bag.

The exception to this rule is when a business wants to make an internal control obvious to help deter crime or to remind employees and customers that the business is watching them to help prevent fraud. For example, surveillance cameras may be positioned to make them clearly visible to customers at check-out counters. If you've been to Las Vegas, you probably noticed several internal controls in the casinos. But these controls are only the ones you can see. Casinos use many other internal controls they don't want you to see.

Don't forget about security measures

In addition to internal controls, most businesses need what are generally referred to as *security measures*. Some of these are obvious, such as locking the doors when the business is closed and limiting access to areas where products are stored. Other measures may or not be needed, such as security guards, surveillance cameras, motion detectors, ID cards for employees, security tags and devices on products, and so on. Generally, these controls are not under the authority of the accounting department. Larger businesses employ a director or chief of security. In a smaller business, the general manager may have to take on this duty.

Following procedure when fraud is discovered

The main advice offered in the professional literature on fraud against a business is to establish and vigilantly enforce preventive controls. The literature has considerably less advice to offer regarding what course of action managers should take when an instance of fraud is discovered, other than recommending that the manager plug the hole that allowed the fraud to happen. The range of options facing managers upon the discovery of fraud, assuming that the facts are indisputable, include

✔ Beginning an investigation, which may require legal advice regarding what you can and cannot do

✔ Immediately dismissing employees who commit fraud or putting the person on paid leave until a final decision is made

✔ Starting legal action, at least the preliminary steps

✔ If applicable, notifying the relevant government regulatory agency or law enforcement

Recognizing Limitations of Internal Controls

A good deal of business is done on the basis of trust. Internal controls can be looked at as a contradiction to this principle. On the other hand, in a game of poker among friends, no one takes offense at the custom of cutting the deck before dealing the cards. Most people see the need for internal controls by a business, at least up to a point. The previous sections of this chapter discuss the need for and various aspects of internal controls. In conclusion, this final section offers two final thoughts for managers: the need to maintain management control over internal controls, and ways of finding fraud that is not detected by the internal controls of the business.

Keeping internal controls under control

Many businesses, especially smaller companies, adopt the policy that some amount of fraud has to be absorbed as a cost of doing business and that instituting and enforcing an elaborate set of internal controls isn't worth the time or money. This mind-set reflects the fact that business by its very nature is a risky venture. Despite taking precautions, you can't protect against every risk a business faces. But on the other hand, a business invites trouble and becomes an attractive target if it doesn't have basic internal controls. Deciding how many different internal controls to put into effect is a tough call.

Internal controls aren't free. They take time and money to design, install, and use. Furthermore, some internal controls have serious side effects. Customers may resent certain internal controls, such as checking backpacks before entering a store, and take their business elsewhere. Employees may deeply resent entry and exit searches, which may contribute to low morale.

So even if your business can afford to implement every internal control you know of, remember that more is not always better. Limiting the business to a select number of most effective controls may provide a good balance of protection and customer and employee tolerance.

Finding fraud that slips through the net

Internal controls are not 100 percent foolproof. A disturbing amount of fraud still slips through these preventive measures. In part, these breakdowns in internal controls are the outcome of taking a calculated risk. A business may decide that certain controls are not worth the cost, which leaves the business vulnerable to certain types of fraud. Clever fraudsters can defeat even seemingly tight controls used by a business.

Internal controls should be designed to quickly detect a fraud if the first line of internal controls fails to prevent it. Of course, responding to this detection is like closing the barn door after the horse has escaped. Still, discovering what happened is critical in order to close the loophole.

In any case, how can you find out if fraud is taking place? Well, the managers or owners of the business may not discover it. Frauds are discovered in many ways, including the following:

- ✓ Alarms that call attention to suspicious activities may be raised in the normal internal reports to managers, such as unusually high inventory shrinkage for the period that has no obvious cause.

- ✓ An internal audit may find evidence of fraud.

- ✓ Employees may blow the whistle to expose fraud.

✔ Customers may give anonymous tips pointing out something wrong.

✔ Customer complaints may lead back to discovery of fraud.

✔ A vendor may notify someone that they have been asked for a kickback or some other under-the-table payment for selling to the business.

In financial statement audits, the CPA tests internal controls of the business. The auditor may find serious weaknesses in the internal controls system of the business, or instances of material fraud. In this situation, the CPA auditor is duty bound to communicate the findings to the audit committee or to other high-level executives of the business.

Large businesses have one tool of internal control that is not practical for smaller businesses — *internal auditing*. Most large businesses, and for that matter most large nonprofit organizations and governmental units, have internal auditing departments with broad powers to investigate any of the organization's operations and activities and report their findings to the highest levels in the organization. Small businesses can't afford to hire a full-time internal auditor. On the other hand, even a relatively small business should consider hiring a CPA to do an assessment of its internal controls and make suggestions for improvement. In fact, hiring a CPA for this job may even be of more value than having an independent CPA audit the business's financial statements.

Chapter 14

Managing the Selling Cycle to Improve Cash Flows

In This Chapter

▶ Looking at the big picture of the selling cycle

▶ Protecting cash in the sales cycle through basic controls

▶ Finding out some unconventional methods for improving cash flows from sales

▶ Seeing how lending agreements affect your selling cycle

*F*or most businesses, cash inflows are derived from two primary sources. First, as discussed in Chapters 10 and 11, cash or capital can be secured from external sources including investors, banks, and/or other lending sources. Transactions to secure this type of cash tend to be nonrecurring and focused on special needs or events (for example, securing seed capital when a business is first formed and launched or taking new loans to support a significant business expansion).

The second and more important source of cash is what's generated internally from the selling cycle. Unlike during the dot-com era of the late 1990s (when, for the briefest of moments, the markets discounted the importance of actually generating sales), businesses today do in fact need to generate real sales that can be quickly and efficiently turned into cash. This chapter focuses on how you can use the selling cycle to maximize cash inflows.

Generating cash from the selling cycle can and should be actively controlled and managed with internal resources. External sources of cash, which still must be managed, are often unpredictable and influenced by unforeseen or uncontrollable forces and events (which make them more difficult to manage and, thus, the predictability of securing cash from external sources is more challenging). Remember, proactive management of the selling cycle is a function that can be controlled internally and often can produce more-reliable sources of cash (than finding yourself always waiting on the decision of another party).

Understanding the Entire Selling Cycle: Start to Finish

The concept of the selling cycle can be looked at from many perspectives but basically boils down into one of two views: the accounting/financial perspective versus the strategic view. In this section we give you an overview of both.

The accounting/financial view

The accounting/financial perspective of the selling cycle is generally fairly narrow. In this view, the selling cycle typically starts when a "hard" transaction is executed — that is, when an actual sales order or contract is received from the customer and an agreement has been entered that stipulates terms and conditions of when the requested goods or services will be delivered and the need for any credit review and approval. After these items have been addressed, this accounting sales cycle continues through delivery of the goods or services and eventually collection of the balance due. In some cases, the accounting cycle can be as quick as less than one hour (just think of a customer purchasing products in Walmart) or may last six months or longer (say, in the case of a defense contractor such as Boeing building and delivering planes).

The key point with the accounting selling cycle is that it is very narrow in scope and doesn't properly capture the true or real amount of cash required to support the entire selling cycle (from customer identification through to customer retention).

The strategic view

The alter ego of the accounting/financial selling cycle is the strategic point of view, which looks at how a business operates and generates sales from the very beginning (conducting market research on target customers and developing a sales pipeline) to the very end (managing customers' expectations and providing additional support and service well after the sale).

Customers just don't magically appear when a business opens its doors and begin ordering goods and services. Instead, the process of identifying, courting, securing, managing, and retaining customers is a far more complex and management-intensive process than some people realize. For example, for a company like Boeing, the process of actually securing a contract from the Department of Defense to build planes can take years to finalize and will undoubtedly involve multiple parties within Boeing, including engineers (to support design requirements), legal personnel (to support contractual obligations), manufacturing employees (to address production capabilities), and even accountants (to quote and support overhead rate calculations).

Even a small retail business that opens in the local strip mall must develop an economically viable business model that ensures a product or service of value is offered at a competitive price to its target customers, reached via efficient marketing, promotional, and advertising efforts. So although a customer may enter this retail business, browse, and spend $100 on a product, all within a half hour, the time and effort required to actually bring that customer into the store more than likely took months and multiple times the amount of money spent during the first visit.

Why the sales cycle is the biggest consumer of cash

An old but very true saying in the restaurant business is that you always lose money on a customer's first visit because the profit generated off the first visit in no way even comes close to covering the costs of the entire selling cycle — accounting for all the costs incurred to get the customer in the door (the first time). This axiom really holds true for almost all businesses, because without repeat customers, failure is almost always guaranteed. Therefore, when a company develops its strategic business plan, it must understand the concept of the entire selling cycle to ensure that adequate cash resources are secured and managed from start to finish.

The sales cycle is a big consumer of cash because of the concept of *compounding:* the accumulation of all efforts of the sales cycle that must be completed in sequential steps, throughout which any delay in one element of the sales cycle slows down the entire sales cycle. The advertising campaign must wait until the product or service is developed into a commercially viable status. And this wait for the advertising campaign delays the point at which customers can be reached, which causes a lag to work its way through the entire sales cycle by delaying quotes, sales orders, goods or services delivery, invoicing, customer payments, and eventually, being able to generate repeat business from the customer. And all along the way and with basically every step, cash is being consumed, until that magical day when the first dollar is actually received (which is immediately framed and placed on display for everyone to see).

So when managing the sales cycle, utilize the following three strategies to help maximize cash flows derived from the selling cycle:

- ✔ Develop, implement, and manage proper policies, procedures, and controls throughout the entire selling cycle.

- ✔ Know your customers and your selling cycle inside and out.

✔ Remaining adaptable, flexible, and retaining some creativity when working with customers can go a long way to improve cash flows.

✔ Understand how cash can be generated or "manufactured" during the selling cycle through the windows and opportunities that present themselves.

You may wonder why we focus on the entire selling cycle so intently. Well, for almost every business we've ever worked with, the selling cycle always takes longer than the business's managers think it will. And mishandling the selling cycle and running out of cash is a good way to go belly up in a hurry. So with this warning in mind, the remainder of this chapter focuses on bringing in cash from the selling cycle quickly and possibly driving sales higher by turning your accounting function into a sales resource and tool.

Implementing Basic Controls in the Selling Process to Manage Cash

Every business has a selling cycle that's unique to that company. Some companies, such as retail stores or ecommerce sites, rely heavily on point-of-sale customer purchases (via accepting cash, credit cards, debit cards, or other forms of electronic payments) to realize the end of the selling cycle (at least from a cash perspective). Others, such as manufacturing companies or distributors, generally invoice or bill their customers, who then remit payments via checks or by using electronic forms of payments. But no matter the specifics of each sales cycle, all businesses must establish a standard set of basic sales controls to ensure that the entire selling cycle is optimized both from the net-profit and cash-flow-generation perspectives. In this section we walk you through these typical and necessary controls.

Qualifying the customer

The concept of qualifying customers goes well beyond simply identifying customers who will be able to pay for goods and services purchased. Rather, customers need to be evaluated from the broad perspective of how much profit they generate in relation to the amount of capital your company must invest to support them. For example, if you have a relatively small customer who demands frequent support and service, takes 60 days or more to pay, and is constantly looking for price discounts and/or other sales perks, the actual profitability from this customer may be quite low. Your business may prefer to work with other customers who generate you more earnings.

Another example of properly qualifying a customer is looking at the "reputation" risk associated with doing business with a specific customer (and the damage your business's image may sustain). Enron was considered one of the most successful businesses through the early 2000s, but when the company imploded, not only did a number of vendors lose money from not collecting receivables, but they also had to deal with the Enron association factor (was your business aware of and a party to the fraud?).

Businesses need to understand that the amount of invested capital required to support customers goes well beyond the simple calculation of determining how long it takes for the customer to pay (which we discuss in Chapter 5). The profitability of a customer encompasses numerous factors, which range from how the customer was initially obtained to what efforts are required to ensure that a repeat customer is present. Businesses really need to complete a more thorough review on potential customers by completing a number of steps as follows:

1. **After a customer has been identified, management should focus on whether the customer fits into the ideal business target or profile (established in the business plan) in terms of potential annual revenue levels, specialized product or service requests, and similar subjective factors.** Experience and industry knowledge are critical to supporting this process because, while the numbers are important, there's no replacing extensive experience (when qualifying customers).

2. **Management needs to evaluate the financial strength of the customer to assess whether they can even pay (by reviewing their financial statements and credit reports), and if they can, how long payment will take.** Also, establishing customer credit limits should be considered at this stage as well.

3. **With the customer identified as being valid and quantified as being viable, ongoing assessments of the customer's real economic return need to be completed.** For example, customers may play the partnership and "win-win" game at the start of the relationship, but if they are simply short-term, price-sensitive customers that will move to a new supplier at the drop of a hat (versus long-term, value-orientated customers), then the termination of the relationship needs to be considered.

These three steps are not meant to be all-inclusive of every step a business can take to qualify a customer, but the steps do highlight the basic logic in the qualification process. First, is the customer a proper fit in relation to the business plan? Second, is the customer's financial strength adequate to ensure that your business is paid? Third, does the customer really represent a valued long-term relationship or a pain in the butt who eats into operating margins (which usually can't be determined until the relationship has developed over a period of time)?

Customers can be disqualified for any number of reasons specific to a situation. For example, a large staffing company supported numerous customers from a wide variety of industries. As part of its business model, the staffing company paid workers' compensation insurance for all the workers it sent out to fill open positions at customer companies. Workers' compensation insurance is determined by numerous factors, one of which is a company's specific experience with losses. One of this staffing company's customers had a particularly bad safety record, which caused injuries to the temporary employees provided to the customer, impacting the workers' compensation rate for the entire company and increasing premiums for all employees. The staffing company had to terminate this customer, because its negative impact on the overall business was far greater than the profit generated from the single account.

Being prudent with credit review and approval

All businesses should implement proper policies, procedures, and controls for extending credit. Even retail businesses, which derive most of their sales from POS (point-of-sale) transactions, make sure to obtain proper credit approval by getting authorization for electronic forms of payments (credit and debit cards, PayPal, and sometimes even checks) before the sale is completed. However, for most businesses, a more formal and proactive credit review and approval process is required to ensure that after you make a sale, you actually get paid.

Establishing initial credit is one thing, but applying proper credit review and approval processes on an ongoing basis is something completely different. Credit defaults occur more often from a failure to continuously apply credit policies and procedures than from poor initial efforts. Remember, economic conditions can change quickly at both the macro and micro levels, so constant revisions and evaluations of customer credit are essential to limiting future losses.

The following sections cover basic credit review and approval policies and procedures that your business should use to prevent losses. We present the simpler efforts first and then move to more-extreme measures you may want to take.

Utilizing credit agencies and other external reporting/informational bureaus

A number of credit reporting agencies, such as Dun & Bradstreet, provide credit reports and other information on potential customers (for a price, of course). These sources are easily accessible and provide solid information and credit ratings on potential customers. The downside to these sources is that sometimes the data being provided can become stale, or outdated, because getting timely information from businesses can be a challenge and business conditions can change quickly. Credit agencies are an important tool, but they should be used as part of the entire credit process and not as a stand-alone resource.

Leveraging a network of local contacts and professional references is a great way not only to generate business but also, more importantly, to obtain market financial information on potential customers. Joining a trade organization in your business's region or niche with a specific market interest can be a great way to secure information on potential customers, because a number of trade organizations offer credit and business referral data. Better Business Bureaus are another external resource that can be tapped to support the credit review and approval process.

Processing internal credit applications and references

Businesses often utilize internal credit applications that request numerous pieces of information from customers, ranging from where they bank to how they're performing to who their largest creditors are. Whether this data is obtained from an actual credit application or through other means (customer websites, publicly reported financial data on file with government organizations, or other sources), your business should accumulate it for all customers and keep it up-to-date. Not only is this info essential to have in the event a customer defaults on payment obligations (to track down the customer and pursue collection efforts), but it can also provide vital information on the customer that your business may be able to mine to generate additional sales.

Your customers should always be willing to provide references, including banks or financial institutions they utilize or other suppliers they conduct business with, which your business can use as needed. References are not designed to obtain actual financial information but rather are geared more toward securing information on the nature of the relationship (such as easy to work with, professional, communicate well, and so on). When customers balk at providing references, the red flags should go up.

A customer data sheet can gather the same information as a credit application and may be viewed in a less hostile manner by the customer. Some customers view the process of applying for credit as an insult or waste of time, so rather than battling with the customer, developing a customer data sheet that's structured in a manner that emphasizes the long-term relationship and future sales potential may be received more favorably (and may help generate additional sales). It should be noted that the final decision to extend credit can be based on the credit application, the data sheet, both, or neither, because the final credit decision may take into account other considerations that are not disclosed in these documents. The idea with these documents is to support or enhance the credit decision process rather than to be used as the only source of information to make a credit decision.

Implementing the use of electronic forms of payments

When your business has concerns about a customer's creditworthiness, establishing multiple forms of electronic payment functionality is often very prudent. For instance, you may want to accept credit cards (including having a customer's credit card on file to charge if needed) and also set up ACH (automated clearing house) or EFT (electronic funds transfer) options such as PayPal to allow for processing payments in the new digital age. In some cases, credit card payments may not work given the size of the transaction being processed or the type of card the customer uses (for example, American Express is not accepted by your company), so having backup or alternative forms of receiving electronic payments is prudent. Even though your company may have to pay fees to process electronic payments, the fees pale in comparison to the time, effort, and losses realized from customers not paying.

The ability to process payments electronically not only assists with collection efforts and reduces bad debts but in addition may potentially increase sales. Larger corporations now basically insist that all their vendors accept electronic forms of payments. These payments may still take a while to receive (large corporations are notorious for slow payments), but by being able to accept electronic payments, your company may have the opportunity to expand business with certain customers.

Completing more-detailed financial reviews

In some situations you may require a more thorough credit evaluation of a customer, including a complete review of the customer's financial statements and operating performance. These types of efforts are generally reserved for customers who will be engaging in very large transactions and that in a sense may be more of a partner than a customer. Of course, each situation varies, but consider completing more-comprehensive financial reviews for customers who drive 10 percent or more of your annual revenue. The trade-off is the time, effort, and cost associated with completing a detailed review in relation to the value gained (or loss prevented) from undertaking this type of effort.

Obtaining collateral or guarantees (corporate or personal)

A credit-review and approval policy being used more and more by businesses is obtaining collateral and/or guarantees in exchange for extending credit. A very common form of guarantee relates to parent-subsidiary business structures where the parent company is financially solid with ample resources, but the subsidiary (the parent owns) is relatively young with a limited operating history. Under this scenario, a supplier to the subsidiary may request a parent guarantee for a year or two until the subsidiary's financial strength and operating history improves.

The Great Recession has changed the environment related to requesting collateral or guarantees, making them a more acceptable control against potential bad debts, especially for customers who have experienced financial difficulties, who demonstrate slow payment patterns, and/or who request a significant increase in credit. The good news with using this type of strategy is that payment is all but guaranteed (in one form or another) and your customer displays a commitment to the business relationship. The bad news is that this control is still considered an extreme measure, and to be quite honest, not many of your customers will happily provide collateral or offer a guarantee to receive credit. These types of requests can often rub the customer the wrong way. Another downside is that you'll generally require the involvement of professional counsel to make sure that the proper documentation is prepared and executed.

One strategy to consider when requesting collateral or guarantees is to allow the customer to remove these requirements when certain milestones are met. For instance, if a customer needs increased credit for only a 90-day period, the guarantee or collateral may only be required during this period. After the customer returns to normal credit and payment patterns, the collateral and/or guarantees can be removed. Displaying a willingness to work with customers provides the dual benefit of gaining loyalty and sending a message to your customer of being an astute business person.

Setting proper terms and conditions

While conducting the credit review and approval process, you want to simultaneously establish customer terms and conditions. For each customer, consider the following key questions and then clearly communicate your answers to the customer if you approve the credit request:

✔ **How much credit will your business extend?** The answer to this question depends on the credit review and approval process discussed in the preceding section and varies by company and with each customer. So a better way to skin this cat is to ask yourself another question: How much can my business afford to lose on a bad debt without damaging operations significantly? If your credit review and approval efforts were limited to the first two strategies noted in the previous section (relying on reports from credit agencies and internal credit applications and references), then a safe range of credit may be no more than 1 percent to 2 percent of your total sales. So if your business generates $10,000,000 a year in revenue, extending credit of $200,000 to a single customer would be reasonable.

For most businesses, diversifying the customer base so no more than one customer accounts for 2 percent to 3 percent of total revenue is difficult. Businesses tend to observe the 80/20 rule, which says that 80 percent of sales come from 20 percent of customers. With this reality in mind, businesses often extend credit levels well in excess of 5 percent of total company annual sales to support larger customers. If your business engages in significant credit extensions, be sure to undertake added credit review and approval processes to support and assess the added risks associated from potential large defaults.

✔ **What are the payment terms?** After the amount of credit has been determined, the actual payment terms need to be set. Probably the most common payment term utilized by businesses extending credit is *net 30,* which means that the customer has 30 days from the invoice date to pay. The variety of payment terms are extensive and are often tailored to the tendencies of a specific industry. However, the general rule of thumb is that for higher-credit-risk customers, payment terms are shorter and monitored very closely to limit potential losses. (In other words, keep these customers on a short leash.) For stronger, more-established customers, payment terms can be extended.

When establishing payment terms, make sure you understand the customer's paying habits and cycles to properly manage cash flows. Extremely large companies, including the biggest corporations operating in America, often leverage their supplier's payment terms. If you offer net 30, they will pay in net 60. If you offer a discount if they pay in 10 days, they will still take the discount if they don't pay for 45 days. Be prepared to make allowances for big customers. Of course, by stretching or changing the payment terms, you could easily assume that they have defaulted. Well, good luck in pursuing any action, because in the end, they will use their size and deep pockets to leverage payment terms to their liking. You may not consider it fair, but "it is what it is," and large corporations are going to leverage the relationship to their advantage.

✔ **Where will the customer take possession of the products sold?** Your business must determine which party is responsible for transporting products from your location to the customer. If you opt for *FOB (free on board)* at your company's dock, then the customer is responsible for either picking up the product from your dock/location or arranging for a common carrier to transport the goods. If you use the terms *FOB [the customer's dock/location],* then your business is responsible for shipping the goods to the customer. Although your business would probably like to determine the FOB status, in a number of cases (and especially with large customers), the customer will dictate this term.

Both strategies have pros and cons:

- For FOB your dock, you pass the shipping responsibility, risk of loss, fees, and so on to the customer at your dock. In addition, your business can invoice the customer earlier (rather than wait until receipt by the customer). The downside to this strategy is the customer service aspect, because this requirement may irritate the customer with having to manage additional tasks (for example, coordinating shipment).

- FOB customer's dock is a much more attractive proposition for the customer but requires more effort on your part to coordinate the shipment. Your business also assumes additional risk of loss (if something were to happen during the shipment) and must wait to invoice until the shipment has been received. In addition, the cost of shipment or freight may become an issue, because if the customer doesn't want to pay for the freight, you will most likely have to eat this expense.

✔ **What legal matters need to be disclosed?** Clearly stating all critical legal terms and conditions is very important in the terms of credit extension. Legal matters to address include when the risk of loss is transferred (for example, upon delivery or at final customer acceptance), any warranty information, return policies (including any restocking fees), and various other matters (which tend to be driven by the unique or specific issues associated with different industries).

Supplying CART — complete, accurate, reliable, and timely — invoices

One of the most tried-and-proven strategies resulting in improved cash flows from the selling cycle is as basic and as simple as it sounds: Apply the concept of *CART* by producing complete, accurate, reliable, and timely invoices. When invoices properly agree with and match the terms and conditions established in the original customer purchase orders (which represent your sales orders), you reduce the risk of customers rejecting the invoices for payment.

If the invoice isn't complete, accurate, and reliable, the customer's payable system kicks out the invoice and cycles it through an exception process within their accounting system to resolve the discrepancies. Customers that are experiencing financial difficulties may be eager to use inaccurate invoices as an opportunity to delay payments. In the end, the invoice will probably be approved and paid, but the delay may range from a couple of days to months (slowing down your cash flows).

As for the timely aspect, quickly producing and forwarding your invoice to your customer for processing should result in your business receiving speedier payments. So if you can process monthly invoices on the first of the following month and not wait until the fifth business day of the following month, then cash receipts should accelerate as well. To help the system run smoothly, develop a billing system that ensures the required information needed to bill customers in a timely manner is readily available (and doesn't take days to accumulate).

Reviewing the basic accounting and operational controls, policies, and procedures to ensure that your business produces CART invoices is beyond the scope of this chapter. However, you can take a big step in the right direction by making every effort to ensure that the terms and conditions set in the customer's purchase order, sales contract, or internal sales order generated are consistent with the invoice generated.

Managing past-due accounts and collection efforts

The final basic procedure of the selling cycle is management of the sale after it has occurred. Up to this point, the customer has been qualified, subjected to a credit review and approval process, given sale terms and conditions, and provided with a CART invoice. All these events occur prior to and at the point of actual sale — and, in some cases, after the point of sale (for example, a customer may be billed once a month for a number of purchases made during the month, which are accumulated on one invoice for easier reading and processing). Now we turn our attention to how past-due accounts can be managed to improve cash flows and limit losses.

Managing collection efforts is an ongoing and critical function that should be addressed on a periodic basis. A number of companies implement weekly reporting requirements that highlight all collection efforts, provide updates on how receivables are performing or trending, and note any significant problems that may be brewing. Building management discipline (periodic and timely review of receivable reports by the appropriate management team members) into your collection processes will enhance future results.

When customers delay payments, management needs to implement proactive efforts to collect the outstanding receivable. You can implement two strategies for collecting the balance due: internal efforts and external efforts.

Internal collection efforts

Internal collection efforts vary by company and situation, but all businesses should use the same basic steps to improve the collection results without impairing or damaging a customer relationship:

1. **Positive confirmation: Check that the customer received the invoice and verify all information, terms, and conditions.** If the customer claims not to have received the invoice, forward a copy via certified mail or e-mail. (If you e-mail, ask for positive confirmation of receipt by the customer.) When the customer has received the invoice, immediately confirm when it will be paid.

   Keeping open lines of communications and a professional and positive approach are very important. At the same time, firmly and clearly let the customer know that past-due invoices will not be tolerated. As the old saying goes, if you give an inch, they'll take a mile, so you must condition your customers to pay on time. To stay on top of potential problems, we recommend that you undertake positive confirmation efforts within seven days of the invoice becoming past due.

2. **Secondary contact: If the initial positive confirmation efforts are not fruitful, make an effort to work with the customer by establishing a payment plan, confirming when payments will be made, offering alternative methods for payment, and/or looking to resolve the outstanding balance due with other creative strategies (such as collateral).** You may attempt these more forceful and direct collection efforts from as soon as 14 days past due to as late as 60 days past due (depending on the customer). Regardless of when you begin offering various options, keep up constant customer contact. Remember, sometimes the best collection strategy is simply being a pest — but keep your pestering friendly and positive.

Get the sales representative who consummated the initial sale actively involved in the collection effort. This strategy can be very helpful for a couple of reasons. First, the sales representative has an established relationship with the customer and therefore can speak to contacts in a manner that may be more effective. Second, if the sales representative earns a commission based on when cash is received from the sale, then he or she has a vested financial interest to collect and will make collection a priority.

3. **Final contact: If payment still doesn't arrive, present the customer with an ultimatum to pay or suffer the consequences.** Consequences may include placing the customer on COD (cash on delivery) terms for future transactions, restricting future sales, turning over the account to a collection agency, and/or threatening legal action (a threat can sometimes be as fruitful as actually pursuing legal action). The idea with these consequences is to strongly encourage payment instead of pursuing a course that actually forces a payment.

When the point of final contact is reached, document your company's position and clearly relay it, with positive receipt confirmation, to the customer. If the customer begins to default on previously agreed-to payment plans (generally structured during the secondary contact stage), ceases communications, and/or undertakes a disinformation campaign, then it's time to raise the red flag and consider more-aggressive collection tactics (including moving from threatened legal action to actual legal action or turning the account over to a third-party collection agency to secure payment).

In summary, the consequences are really used as the first option in the final contact stage and is designed to strongly encourage payment (but not force payment). The second option then really becomes forced collection action, which is usually pursued in the form of retaining collection agencies (for smaller and more-routine matters) or attorneys (for larger and more-complex matters).

What if your customer goes bankrupt?

Most businesses that extend credit do so in an unsecured fashion, meaning that they don't obtain security in the customer's assets or take collateral. An unsecured position is generally the worst spot to be in when the customer experiences financial problems and can't pay everyone. The secured creditors and priority credits get paid first, and then whatever cash is left over gets divided up between the unsecured creditors. In bankruptcy proceedings, the unsecured creditors usually get hammered and receive (if they're lucky) 25 percent of the balance owed. So the trick to improving collection results is finding a way to move your claim from unsecured to priority.

One example of how a creditor was able to move up the priority ladder is a staffing company that provided staff and paid payroll of the staff to the company. The staffing company was able to move up the priority ladder by successfully claiming that 70 percent of their invoices to the company were for payroll and payroll taxes (and not general services). In bankruptcy proceedings, unpaid payroll and payroll taxes represent priority obligations that need to be paid before unsecured creditors are paid. So by moving up the priority ladder, the staffing company received 70 percent of their claim rather than the 10 percent it would have gotten otherwise from the trust of assets set aside for allocation to the various creditors (from liquidating the bankrupt company's assets). Although this example is somewhat unique, the primary point we want to drive home is that in order to move up the priority ladder, you must have a very strong case and set of circumstances to support why your claim should receive preference. Clearly, the dangers of being an unsecured creditor are significant in a bankruptcy proceeding, but options do exist (although limited) to improve your chances of collection outstanding balances due.

Document all collection efforts in writing with letters, e-mail, collection effort notes in an electronic system, or whatever other means available. Having a documented trail of collection efforts can greatly assist in the recovery effort, especially when third parties are secured to help resolve a dispute (because the party that is better prepared with quality supporting documentation generally receives more-favorable outcomes).

External collection efforts

Every company must determine at what point the collection effort must be turned over to external resources. That point may be 30 days past due, 60 days past due, or even longer (and is really dictated on a case-by-case basis, depending on the industry you operate within and potential unique issues with the customer). Be aware, though, that when external resources are used, the relationship with the customer will be damaged. In fact, when you employ external collection resources, you can pretty much kiss the customer goodbye.

External collection efforts are outside professional services and resources used to secure payment. Basically, external efforts boil down to the two following options:

✔ **Collection agencies:** Countless collection services are available to choose from when you need to retain a third party to secure payment. Most collection agencies work on a commission; if you don't get paid, they don't get paid. The good news with collection services is that they're very knowledgeable about their trade and have a wide range of resources available to help secure payment. Plus, the collection service takes care of the dirty work of playing the bad guy to collect money due. The bad news with collection services is that their fees can often exceed 25 percent of the amount collected, and their tactics tend not to be customer friendly.

Collection agencies offer a full range of services and are very competitive, so we recommend that you do some comparison shopping. Certain agencies may offer a broader range of services, including providing support on pursuing collections through taking actions to small claims court. When evaluating the effectiveness of collection agencies, consider the trade-off between price and range of collection tools.

✔ **Professional resources:** For larger or more-complex collection issues, securing professional resources in the form of legal and/or financial advice generally becomes a necessary step. Missteps with large or complex issues can often prove to be very costly, so protecting your business and financial interests with professional counsel needs to be evaluated from a cost-versus-benefit standpoint.

1. **The first step with securing professional resources is to determine if the cost of retaining professional counsel (such as an attorney) is reasonable compared to the expected payout from the customer.** If an attorney is going to cost $25,000 and the expected customer payment is, at best, $15,000, there's not much point in pursing this course of action.

2. **The second step is to determine if the matter is better resolved through an independent third-party settlement or arbitration proceeding (a qualified and independent third party agreed to by both parties to settle a matter) versus actually pursuing legal action in the form of a lawsuit.** Arbitration proceedings are commonly used in today's environment to avoid the added time, effort, and money it takes to actually take a collection case to court.

3. **The last step is to pursue a collection matter with an actual lawsuit (whether processed in small claims court or through regular court channels).** Needless to say, the lawsuit or "court" route should only be used with very large and complex collection matters (and really represents the exception rather than the rule).

When applying a cost-versus-benefit analysis on a collection issue, remember to incorporate all critical facts and data. For instance, if you're owed $100,000 but professional legal counsel is going to cost $25,000 to secure payment (in the form of representing your company in a settlement proceeding or law suit), you may quickly conclude that the $75,000 of net receipts is more than enough to pursue legal action and cover the $25,000 of costs. However, if you estimate that your company only has a 33 percent chance of collecting the balance due and that internal management resources will be consumed to support the process, the expected net receipts begin to drop considerably and may not be worth it.

Getting Creative to Improve Sales-Related Cash Flows

After you get a solid handle on the basics of cash flow in the sales cycle, addressed in previous sections of this chapter, you're ready to turn your attention to utilizing more-creative sales-cycle policies and procedures. On one hand, these procedures can accelerate or improve cash flow, but on the other hand, they do come with a price (usually in the form of added interest costs or one-time fees or charges). The list of ideas in this section is by no means complete, but it does provide a sampling of the types of strategies your company can use to accelerate the receipt of cash from the sales cycle.

Using discounts: The double-edged sword

A very commonly used payment term, net 30, gives customers 30 days from the invoice date to pay. This payment term is often expanded by providing the customer a discount such as *2 percent 10, net 30.* What this payment term means is that payment is due in 30 days but a 2 percent discount will be provided if it is paid within 10 days. This offer sounds great and can really improve cash flows, because if all invoices are paid within 10 days, receivable balances can be kept to a minimum. Another popular tactic is to offer *3 percent on receipt, net 30,* in which a 3 percent discount is offered if customers pay as soon as they receive the invoice (with payment otherwise due in full in 30 days).

But you can't have your cake and eat it too: Offering discounts brings two significant risks. First, larger customers may simply take the discount but still pay you in 30 to 45 days. They can use their leverage (banking on the fact that you don't want to lose a large customer) to extract the discount from your company even if they technically aren't abiding by the terms. Second, as highlighted in Table 14-1, offering discounts when translated into an effective interest rate can be very expensive indeed.

Table 14-1	The Cost of Providing Discounts		
Discount Terms Provided	*Discount Amount on Invoice of $1,000*	*Implicit Interest Rate If Customer Pays in 30 Days*	*Implicit Interest Rate If Customer Pays in 45 Days*
1% 10, net 30	$10	18.00%	10.29%
2% 10, net 30	$20	36.00%	20.57%
3% on receipt, net 30	$30	36.00%	24.00%

So before you jump headfirst into using discounts, think closely about the trade-offs that will be realized. Although the discounts are not reflected as interest expense in the financial statements, your business will need to reflect the customer discounts taken as a reduction from gross sales to reflect a net sales figure earned. In the above example, if a customer took a $20 discount for paying within ten days, then the company's net sales would be $980 (and not $1,000) so in effect, the company has realized a $20 expense to accelerate the receipt of cash.

Offering creative payment terms

Payment terms come in all shapes, sizes, and forms and may range from requiring prepayments or deposits (to cover a portion of a large project) to extending payment terms to two years or more (for example, in the case of payments made when a lawsuit is finally settled). The real battle with becoming creative with payment terms is the balancing act you must undertake between using these terms to improve cash flows while at the same time structuring terms to improve customer satisfaction and increase sales opportunities (which generally require longer payment terms).

The following three examples of creative payment strategies highlight various alternatives that address both objectives:

✔ **Covering out-of-pocket "hard costs" first:** When companies sell goods or services, the invoice to the customer should cover both the cost of providing the goods or services and a profit (if not, you're not going to be in business very long!). So one strategy to help manage risks is to structure dual payment terms that ensure your hard costs are paid within 30 days while letting your profit be paid with slightly more-favorable terms. This type of strategy is not appropriate to use for the masses, (such as a business that cannot separate hard costs from profits easily, or a high-volume, low-selling-price business such as a retailer), but it can be effective with larger or unique situations. Floating the profits can help manage your company's cash needs, while at the same time providing some flexibility to your customers.

An example of when this strategy may be appropriate is for a research and development project. The project may require additional external costs to be incurred as well as increasing the number of employees to support the project. These added hard costs can be quantified and billed to the customer in advance or early in the project, whereas the overhead and profit component of the project can be billed later.

✔ **Letting your customers pay when they get paid:** In some industries, such as construction, customers pay invoices from creditors when their own invoices are paid. In other words, "When I get paid, you get paid." So instead of extending an actual grace period for customers to pay (such as net 30 days), you may want to select a date for payment that you know relates to when your customer is getting paid (which generally you would obtain directly from your customer via verbal confirmation or in some cases, documentation in an executed contract noting when payments will be received). Proper coordination of payments should be pursued to avoid getting bumped to the next month.

✔ **Adjusting when the customer gets the products (and pays the bill):** A number of customers place blanket purchase orders to secure products over a period of time. In some cases, the purchase order requests the majority of the products be delivered over a short period of time (for example, by November 10 to support the holiday season). Although this arrangement may be ideal for the customer, the supplier can get trapped into delivering products in an unlevel manner. A strategy to help manage this requirement is requesting level loading delivery schedules with associated invoicing occurring at the same time. Instead of delivering 9,000 units of a 10,000-unit order over a 30-day period, a request could be made to deliver 2,000 units over five like periods and bill accordingly. This proposal can be further expanded by offering free storage and shipping in the event the customer doesn't have the capacity to accept the products until a specific date.

The variety of payment terms available for use are endless and often are heavily influenced by industry trends and norms. For example, consigned inventory programs are actively utilized in the jewelry industry in order to make sure that adequate product levels are on the store shelves for the critical shopping seasons. When the product is sold, then the supplier looks for payment within seven days. But remember, if your business uses creative payment terms, make sure that any lending facility established that advances funds against customer invoices is properly structured to account for these terms. For further information on this topic, refer to the section "Managing the Lending Agreement in Relation to Your Sales Cycle" later in this chapter.

Using deposits, advances, and prepayments

Companies have been using deposits, advances, and prepayment requirements for decades as a means to accelerate the receipt of cash and have the customers share in the risk (so to speak). Pre–Great Recession, this type of strategy worked well for a number of industries, including construction, defense, and research, in which it made perfect sense to receive a portion of the costs upfront to support a large project with a relatively long delivery timeline. The classic approach of requesting 30 percent down, 30 percent on achieving the first milestone, 30 percent on the second milestone, and 10 percent upon completion is a tried-and proven business strategy that continues to be used successfully throughout the economy.

But since the Great Recession of 2007 through 2009, the use of deposits, advances, and prepayments has taken on an entirely new meaning that goes well beyond the classic purpose of these payment tools. The reason for the increase in popularity is centered in the fact that traditional sources of credit from banks and other lenders have decreased as a result of tightened and much stricter underwriting standards (so businesses must look elsewhere for credit).

Arrangements these days offer new benefits, both for the customer and your business:

- ✔ **Benefits to the customer:** The largest and strongest corporations sit on mounds of cash — Apple alone has over $60 billion of cash, cash equivalents, and short-term investments. And these companies are probably earning no more than 2 percent on their cash balances. So one significant benefit to these companies is that by providing a substantial prepayment to a vendor (that is, your business), they may be able to secure a discount (say 5 to 10 percent). This return is higher than they'd get investing the cash, and with corporations always looking to reduce expenses, what better solution is available?

- ✔ **Benefits to your business:** Let's face it; America was spoiled rotten prior to the Great Recession, as credit was readily available and free flowing. That credit situation changed dramatically when the financial industry melted down in 2008 and 2009 as a result of the real estate market collapse. Today (contrary to what media is reporting), credit is still very tight and expensive for small businesses. So tapping a strong customer for cash upfront by providing a reasonable discount can not only strengthen the relationship with the customer but also provide a relatively cheap source of financing for your business.

If you're going to approach customers with this type of strategy, do so with the utmost caution in order to avoid the perception that your company is struggling financially. This strategy can quickly backfire if the customer's perception of the request is one of financial weakness (thus the customer needs to find another supplier) versus strategic value. Packaging the request or offer is of critical importance when using large prepayment requests. Proper packaging ideas tend to center around highlighting the benefit the customer will receive with committing upfront or prepayments including guaranteeing timely delivery, clearly noting how much upfront costs your business will be required to cover to support a project (which they did not have to initially cover), and related "benefits." The customer must be sold on the fact that providing a prepayment is truly in their best interests.

Prepayments, deposits, and advances can greatly improve a customer's "buy-in" and commitment to your business, because when customers have "skin in the game" (or in other words, have committed real money or capital to a specific endeavor or project), their interest and commitment levels tend to increase rather quickly. A very effective spin that businesses use to secure prepayments is the concept of sharing the risk. The point to make to your customer is very straightforward: "We're putting forth significant efforts and committing resources to meet your demands, so receiving a like commitment from you is more than reasonable".

Accepting alternative forms of payment

Over the past decade, electronic payment has clearly established itself as the new norm, so accepting electronic forms of payment is important for improving cash flows. Following is a review of the most common (and not so common) forms of payments your business may want to accept:

✔ **Checks:** Checks are still widely used today to process payments, but they continue to diminish in popularity. If your business still accepts checks (which most do), you can use two strategies to accelerate the speed at which your bank clears the check to your bank accounts (thus improving cash flows):

• If volumes are large enough, you can use a bank lockbox, which allows customer payments to be made directly to the bank, which can then process them sooner than if your company had to receive, process, and deposit the payments first. This strategy also provides an additional control procedure in that your internal staff doesn't handle vital financial documents, which could be lost, damaged, and/or stolen.

• Banks now support a very effective service that allows your business to scan customer checks on a special printer and automatically deposit them via electronic transmission of the key data. This strategy also improves speed, accuracy, and safety.

- ✔ **ACH (automated clearing house), EFT (electronic funds transfer), and wires:** Companies both small and large are using these types of electronic payments to conduct business (refer to Chapter 12 for a further discussion). Most companies rely on a "push" strategy in which the customer initiates the request to remit payment electronically and then pushes the payment to the vendor. A strategy that can improve cash flows is to request that your customers provide you the right to initiate and "pull" a payment from their bank accounts on a specific date and/or according to other predetermined criteria). Granted, most customers aren't overly receptive to this type of arrangement, but in certain cases (for example, if they have poor credit), it can be used to improve cash flows.

- ✔ **Credit, debit, and prepaid cards:** The use of credit, debit, and prepaid cards as a form of payment continues to expand throughout the country. If a business is operating in the retail industry, acceptance of credit, debit, and prepaid cards is absolutely essential (and these businesses should have a merchant account set up from day one).

  Businesses whose customers traditionally don't rely on cards to process payments are also looking at setting up merchant accounts to accept customer payments, because the customers' financing sources are changing these days. Small-business financing requirements ranging from $25,000 to $250,000 are now actively supported by credit card companies that base credit decisions on electronic credit scores, as opposed to being supported by the old brick-and-mortar method of obtaining a loan from a small community bank. Because your customers are likely to use a business credit card instead of cash obtained through a loan, your business needs to accept those credit cards. Even though a fee of between 2 to 3 percent must be absorbed to process a credit card transaction (by your business, because the party accepting credit card payments absorbs the fee), it beats having to track down the customer and pester them for payment.

Being sensitive to your customer's billing cutoff dates on credit cards can pay off. For example, if your customer's credit card has a billing cutoff date of the 24th of each month, charging the customer's card on the 25th can give the customer an extra 20 to 30 days to pay. Using this scenario, if a charge is made on the 24th, the customer is required to pay it by the 20th of the following month (or roughly 25 days in a normal grace period). By charging it on the 25th, the charge doesn't post to the credit card and appear on the statement until the next billing cycle, requiring payment 25 days after that. The benefit to the customer is that she receives an extra 25 days to pay the balance due basically interest free (assuming that the entire balance on the credit card is paid). The benefit to you as a business owner is that you can receive payment for the outstanding invoice (improving cash flow) before the end of the month to keep the trade accounts receivable aging in good shape (because it helps prevent invoices from getting older and increasing the days sales outstanding calculation).

✔ **Evolving electronic forms of payment:** The speed at which technology is moving in today's economy is nothing short of breathtaking. Seemingly just yesterday, PayPal established itself as a new and innovative method of processing payments; $71 billion total payment was processed in 2009. Today, the largest financial service companies in the country are teaming with Google and other technology companies to turn your cellphone into a payment-processing tool. Staying on top of these trends is extremely important to capture the benefit of both improved cash flows (by being able to accept every type of payment a customer is offering) and increased sales (because nobody wants to turn down a sale because a specific type of payment is not accepted).

✔ **Trades, offsets, and barters:** Due to the economic upheaval experienced in recent years, the use of trades, account offsets, and even barter transactions is expanding.

- *Trades* may be utilized when a customer has a specific asset of value and wants to exchange it for a balance due. As long as the asset is deemed valuable to your company, then getting something is better than nothing.

- *Account offsets* apply to customers and suppliers that conduct business back and forth. A customer may purchase goods or services from your business but at the same time also sell other items back to your business. In this case, account offsets can be used to simply net a balance due against a balance owed (avoiding the need to exchange cash).

  Unlike trades or account offsets (which tend to occur after the fact), *bartering* tends to occur before the transaction, with both parties agreeing to a predetermined deliverable. For example, a CPA firm may offer to complete an advertising company's annual income tax reporting requirements in exchange for the advertising company developing and launching a promotional campaign for the CPA firm. If barter transactions are used, just make sure that they are completed as an arm's-length transaction (a transaction completed at fair market value between two independent parties without any undue duress or coercion) and properly documented.

Utilizing trade, offset, and barter agreements can be effective, but remember to watch out for the tax man. In the eyes of the taxing authorities, these types of agreement represent arm's-length transactions that generate taxable sales and expenses. But unlike your business, the tax man does not like to accept alternative forms of payment, so be careful not to get trapped by accepting too many assets that can't be efficiently converted into cash.

Accepting other forms of currency, including gold and silver

Companies should be fully prepared to accept payment in the form of different world currencies ranging from the Japanese yen to the Chinese yuan to the European euro. Establish a proper banking relationship to facilitate the acceptance and conversion of global currencies into the almighty U.S. dollar.

Some companies are also finding that they may need to be prepared to accept payment in gold and silver. In 2011, Utah began allowing gold and silver to be legally recognized as a form of currency. Gold and silver have been out of favor over the past 100 or more years because

they have been viewed as being an inefficient method to conduct business. But the economic turmoil since 2007 has shaken the faith of people, business, and governments, and as a result, gold and silver have regained favor in terms of supporting transactions.

Although we're not prophesying a return to gold- and silver-based currency (highly unlikely), the development in Utah illustrates is how important it is to remain flexible and adaptable in accepting different forms of payments to improve sales, your business results, and cash flows.

Managing seasonality in the selling cycle

Almost all companies, in one form or another, have to manage seasonal selling issues with customers. If your business targets the youth clothing market, then be prepared to ramp up before the back-to-school selling season. For outdoor furniture, you need to gear up early in the calendar year so large customers have products on the floor in the spring for their customers to use in the summer.

The ebb and flow of seasonal selling cycles is a fact of life most companies simply have to live with, so rather than attempt to significantly influence or alter your customer's buying and paying habits (just to improve your internal cash flow), the burden on managing cash flows during the seasons really falls on your business. The following strategies can assist with managing impacts on cash flows from seasonal factors:

✔ **Securing additional financial support:** A widely used strategy in numerous industries is leveraging financing sources through the busy season to improve liquidity and cash availability. Whether your business has a lending agreement with built-in features to extend additional credit during the peak selling season or you secure and use specialized lending sources only during the peak season, working with lending sources is one of the most effective ways to support cash needs during this period. Factoring groups (see Chapter 11) can offer a flexible financial resource to support operations by structuring specialized seasonal lending programs to support your business (for example, predetermined customer accounts are targeted for factoring at set rates). The next section of this chapter delves into this issue in more detail.

✔ **Leveraging your vendors and employees:** Chapter 15 dives into this subject in more detail, but the general concept is that if your business has to manage seasonal peaks and valleys, so should your vendors and your employees. For example, you can request extended payment terms for a 90-day period from your vendors, and you can pay employee commissions on a cash-received-plus-15-days basis.

✔ **Business planning:** Cash and management resources tend to be stretched very thin running up to and during the seasonal sales crush. After the season ends and business returns to normal operating levels, with cash receipts at a peak (from collecting on seasonal sales), the opposite tends to occur. As such, business-planning efforts and associated infrastructure improvements or capital investments are best scheduled during this off-peak period in order to help smooth annual cash flows and to ensure that management has time to give those improvement and investments the proper amount of attention. Really, how many companies in the midst of a seasonal sales crunch want to implement a new computer information system?

Managing the Lending Agreement in Relation to Your Sales Cycle

A critical concept often overlooked by companies is the way your lending agreement is structured in relation to your sales cycle. Your setup can have a profound impact on improving cash availability and liquidity.

Lending agreements need to be structured in anticipation of the selling cycle and not adapted or adjusted during the selling cycle. Financing sources are notoriously more difficult to work with when a change is needed mid-stream and on short notice, because banks and other lending sources don't like surprises. So be a good Boy Scout by being prepared and planning well ahead to get the most out of your lending agreement. In this section we tell you how to prepare in advance and what to look for in a lending agreement.

Defining eligible receivables

Banks define *eligible receivables* as customer receivables that are available to borrow against, not the total receivables owed to a company. Following are the most common types of *ineligible* receivables:

✔ Receivables over 90 days past due (because the bank may think they're uncollectable)

✔ Foreign receivables

✔ Certain governmental receivables (for example, receivables generated from the federal government, which lending sources may not be able to legally obtain a secured interest in)

✔ Customer receivables with excess concentration levels

✔ Related or affiliated party receivables

✔ Cross-aged receivables (explained in the "Watching for hidden time bombs in your lending agreement" section of this chapter)

The goal for most businesses is to maximize the number of eligible receivables to maximize the amount of borrowing capacity. Of course, from a lender's perspective, the opposite holds true, as they tend to be more conservative (imagine that) and look to reduce eligible receivables.

In the context of receivables, the term *concentration* means that an inordinately high level of sales or receivables is associated with few customers or a single customer. Financing sources generally get nervous about high levels of concentration because if that customer encounters a problem, the risk of non-payment and defaulting on the lending agreement increases. Thus, you often see a provision in a lending agreement that states that any amount of receivables above 10 percent of the total receivables associated with one customer will be ineligible. So if total receivables are $1,500,000 and one customer comprises $300,000 of the balance (or 20 percent), $150,000 (the 10 percent over the 10 percent limit) is ineligible to borrow against.

Referring to the discussion on the credit review and approval process in "Implementing Basic Controls in the Selling Process to Manage Cash," the benefits of completing a more-thorough credit review flow through to the lending agreement. If the financing source can document and support that a large customer is financially sound, you can negotiate with the financing source to increase the concentration limit for the best and strongest customers (thus reducing ineligible receivables and increasing access to liquidity or cash) from say 10 percent to 15 or 20 percent. So the extra credit review and approval efforts has the dual benefit of providing more confidence in getting paid as well as structuring a strong lending arrangement.

Understanding advance rates and dilution

After you determine eligible receivables (and, hopefully, maximize them for your company), you next need to manage advance rates. The advance rate represents the maximum amount of borrowings that can be secured against the eligible receivables. A very typical advance rate is 80 percent, but this rate can be negotiated for your business needs or, conversely, may be lowered by the financing source if adverse trends develop, such as increasing levels of dilution or deteriorating collection rates. (In the later section "Driving a lending agreement to improve liquidity and access to cash," Figure 14-1 provides an example of how the advance rate works and how important it is to manage both eligible receivables and the advance rate to increase liquidity and access to cash.)

Dilution is a relatively simple ratio calculation all financing sources utilize to help determine advance rates. The denominator in the equation is sales figures over a period of time (such as a year). The numerator is the sum of all billing or invoice adjustments made during the same period for transactions such as sales returns, discounts offered, bad debts, billing adjustments, and other items. For example, if annual sales amount to $6,000,000 and the total of all returns, discounts, bad debts, and/or other adjustments is $400,000, the dilution rate is 6.67 percent ($400,000 ÷ $6,000,000 × 100). The general rule of thumb is that for each 5 percent increase in dilution, the advance rate is decreased by 5 percent (from a base rate of 80 percent). So in this situation, the advance rate is reduced to 75 percent because 6.67 percent is above the first 5 percent dilution increment.

Producing CART invoices is critical to getting the most out of your lending agreement. (If you need a reminder about CART, refer to the earlier section "Supplying CART — complete, accurate, reliable, and timely — invoices."). Lending sources don't like to see numerous adjustments and changes made to invoices after issuance. Changes make them nervous and raise questions about the strength of your internal policies and procedures. Something as simple as a billing address error (which requires the original invoice to be voided and a new invoice to be issued) increases the amount of adjustments as calculated by the bank, which in turn drives the numerator higher and the dilution rate higher (thus lowering the advance rate). Even if all other information is correct, this one simple adjustment shows up as a billing correction, which can influence the lending agreement.

Watching for hidden time bombs in your lending agreement

A number of other terms and conditions within your lending agreement need to be understood, and probably managed, to improve available liquidity. Following are some of the more common terms and conditions to be sensitive to and manage:

- **Cross-aging factor:** A term and condition usually buried within lending agreements that can be very nasty is a *cross-aging factor*. In its simplest form, a cross-aging factor is applied on a customer basis and states that if X percent of a customer's balance due is more than Y days old (60 or 90 days are common), then the entire receivable is ineligible to borrow against. Common cross-aging factors range from 20 to 25 percent, but note that if the test is applied and fails by even the slightest amount (20.1 percent past 60 days with the limit of 20 percent established), you get no margin for error (and the total of the receivable will be deemed ineligible).

You can probably see where we're going with this tip: Managing your slow-paying customers to somehow always having a cross-aging factor calculation of just below the limit established (say 18 percent compared to a 20-percent limit as set by the bank) can keep your eligible receivable levels higher and thus access to cash higher. By working closely with customers to make sure that just enough older invoices are paid and processing adjustments to older invoices in a timely fashion, you can meet the target. Just double check that the calculations are accurate and supportable, because the last thing your business needs is for a bank auditor to challenge your reporting.

✔ **Financial covenants:** Lending sources use financial covenants to ensure that the borrower's financial strength remains above predetermined levels to support the ability to repay the loan. These covenants come in all sizes, shapes, and forms and are generally based on the financial information presented by the borrower to secure the loan. Understand two key concepts about financial covenants:

- **If you violate a financial covenant, the lending relationship will become strained.** The normal reaction from the lending source is to tighten up your ability to borrow (restricting liquidity and cash availability).

- **You don't want to let the lending source dictate the financial covenants according to generic standards applied by banks and other lending sources.** Every business has a unique selling and operating cycle, which can result in widely varying financial performances between different times of the year. Lending sources tend to be relatively conservative and narrow minded when establishing financial covenants, so you need to educate them on expected business operating performances.

A bank wanted to establish a minimum quarterly profitability financial covenant for a staffing company requiring that a positive profit be realized each quarter. Given the seasonality of the staffing industry, with the first and fourth quarters being relatively poor and the second and third quarters being stronger, the covenant was changed to generating a positive profit on a rolling four-quarter basis. With these terms, a weaker quarter that produced a loss would not cause a violation of the covenant.

✔ **Reporting requirements:** Financing sources normally place a significant amount of reporting requirements in the primary loan agreement, including providing annual tax returns, monthly or quarterly financial statements, monthly borrowing base certificates, annual personal financial statements (for the owners of the business), trade receivable and payable agings, and other reports as deemed necessary. Complying with all reporting requirements is important to ensure that you maintain a healthy relationship with your lending sources.

In recent years, banks and other financing companies have come under increasing pressure from external auditors, examiners, the government, and/or other parties to improve the quality of the loans extended. One surefire way to cause problems and damage your ability to borrow is to fail to comply with all reporting requirements.

✔ **Other borrowing restrictions:** Quite often, financing sources place restrictions on the maximum amount of other loans that can be obtained while the current lending facility is in force. For example, a company may want to secure a loan (from another financing source) to purchase additional property and equipment that's not part of the lending agreement with the primary financing source. Assuming that this loan is below the amount established in the lending agreement, the company can secure the loan with no ramifications. If the loan is greater than the maximum amount established, a waiver from the primary lender needs to be obtained (to avoid defaulting on the agreement).

The problem with this type restriction is that it can limit the ability for a company to secure cash from other sources of nontrade debt (thus impairing a potential source of cash). Give careful consideration to structuring this term in the primary lending agreement.

✔ **Hidden fees and charges:** The list of additional fees and charges financing sources can think up is endless. To start, a loan-origination fee may be charged, which is nothing more than a percentage charge the financing source earns to originate the loan. A 1 percent loan-origination fee is very common — but remember that you can negotiate, so countering with 0.5 percent would not being unreasonable. Then be prepared to pay for a collateral exam completed by either the financing source or an external third party. In order to confirm the assets you intend to use as collateral are sound, they must be audited. Also be prepared to pay the legal fees incurred by the financing source to draft the agreement. So even before the loan is accessible, substantial expenses have already been racked up.

After you've closed, you may still incur fees. Say you're using 65 percent of the loan on average for the year. That's not bad, but be careful, because some loans incorporate an unused loan charge for the average amount of the loan not used during the year. Imagine that; you've done a great job minimizing the use of the loan and lower interest charges, but you still get stung with a fee to the financing source for just providing the commitment. And finally, to add insult to injury, if you secure a better lending facility before the initial term of the original loan expires, you can most likely expect an early termination or prepayment fee to be charged.

Financing sources have to compete for your business like everyone else, so when securing financing, get competitive bids. The hidden fees and charges are negotiable, so take advantage of opportunities to push back on pricing when presented. Remember, financing sources are going to get you coming and going, so any terms and conditions that can be structured to lower the overall cost of the loan should be pursued.

As the saying goes, the devil is in the details, especially for lending agreements. If you don't make an effort to read and understand all the terms and conditions (the fine print), something in the agreement will undoubtedly come back to bite you in the rear end.

Driving a lending agreement to improve liquidity and access to cash

Figure 14-1 displays a typical lending agreement, with limited-active management compared to a proactively managed and structured lending agreement in relation to a company's selling cycle. The impact on available borrowings and access to cash are significant, both in added cash available ($162,000) and as a percentage increase (15.76 percent).

For the purposes of Figure 14-1, limited-active management equates into the column titled standard bank terms, which basically means that the bank is setting the terms of the lending agreement based on their boilerplate offerings. The proactively managed column is headed by the description of company structured terms and basically indicates that the company has actively and aggressively negotiated with the bank to establish the terms and conditions of the lending agreement. This document would most likely be prepared by the company securing the financing to properly evaluate and compare what the bank is offering versus what the company needs (and has hopefully, successfully structured) and to evaluate if the added availability of cash would come at any additional costs.

The last section of the figure shows a simple analysis on the impact hidden fees and charges may have on the transaction. In this example, the company was able to reduce the loan origination fee from 1 percent to 0.5 percent, place a cap on examination and legal fees of $5,000 (versus higher actual), and remove the unused loan-commitment fee (which the financing source was attempting to charge at a rate of 0.25 percent for the year). These more-favorable terms helped reduce the hidden fees and charges by almost half, from roughly $21,000 to $11,000.

ACME Distribution, Inc. — Available Borrowing Capacity Comparison		
Description of Loan Provision	**Standard Bank Terms**	**Company Structured Terms**
Total Loan Facility	1,250,000	1,250,000
Total Accounts Receivables	1,500,000	1,500,000
Ineligible Receivables:		
Concentration Limitation, Bank 10% Company 15%	150,000	75,000
Cross-Aging Receivables, Bank 20% Company 30%	65,000	25,000
Total Ineligible Receivables	215,000	100,000
Advance Rate, During Peak Season	80.00%	85.00%
Borrowing Capacity	1,028,000	1,190,000
Increase in Borrowing Capacity, $	N/A	162,000
Increase in Borrowing Capacity, %	N/A	15.76%
Fees and Charges:		
Loan Origination Fee	12,500	6,250
Collateral Examination and Legal Fees	7,750	5,000
Unused Loan Commitment Fee	1,094	0
Early Termination Fee	0	0
Total Added Fees and Charges	21,344	11,250
Increase in Effective Loan Interest Rate	1.42%	0.75%

Figure 14-1:
Available
borrowing
capacity
comparison.

Chapter 15

Managing the Disbursement Cycle to Improve Cash Flows

In This Chapter

▶ Taking a look at what the disbursement cycle involves

▶ Using basic techniques to improve cash flow from the disbursement cycle

▶ Evaluating additional approaches to managing the disbursement cycle

▶ Hanging on to cash while compensating employees

C hapter 14 evaluates how a business can manage its relationship with customers throughout the selling cycle to improve cash flows and liquidity. In this chapter, we evaluate the exact opposite of the selling cycle — the disbursement (that is, expenditure) cycle. We explore how a business working with creditors can squeeze cash from the disbursement cycle. Throughout, we note numerous similarities between the two chapters, which of course is logical, because a business paying money from its disbursement cycle represents a part of someone else's selling cycle (in terms of receiving cash).

To gain a better understanding of the disbursement cycle in terms of how cash flows can be improved, first read Chapter 14 on the selling cycle so that you can simply think about those points from a different perspective. If discounts are offered to customers to accelerate payments, think of how your business can utilize any discounts being offered from suppliers to improve operating results. Or if a supplier is placing pressure on your business to pay obligations, confirm lending agreement terms to see how making just enough payments at the right time keeps their lending facility maximized.

Tracing the Entire Disbursement Cycle

The concept of the disbursement cycle can be looked at from the same two perspectives as the selling cycle: the accounting/financial view versus the strategic view.

The accounting/financial disbursement cycle generally starts when a commitment is made to purchase goods or services. For larger companies, the commitment is supported by the generation of a purchase order, which identifies the type, quantity, price, technical specifications, delivery dates, and other terms and conditions of the goods or services to be purchased.

For smaller companies without a formal purchase order system, another form of positive confirmation (such as an e-mail, fax, or even a simple phone call) is generally used to support the purchase request. The accounting/financial cycle then proceeds with the receipt of the goods or services purchased and then finishes when final payment is made. Similar to the sales accounting/financial cycle, the disbursement accounting/financial cycle is fairly narrow in scope and is based on "hard" transactional documentation.

From a strategic perspective, the disbursement cycle is much broader in scope and starts from the initial point of planning, running all the way through managing vendors and suppliers well after payments have been made. For example, a technology company that has developed a new accessory for a personal computer must develop a production plan that starts well before the first purchase order is ever issued. Suppliers must be identified and qualified as part of the overall production plan to ensure that forecast commitments can be satisfied (as the accessory is rolled out to the market). These suppliers may range from a manufacturer of a key component to an advertising firm retained to market the accessory.

On the tail end of the disbursement cycle, the management of vendors and suppliers continues well after their last invoice is paid, as invaluable business information is generated from managing the follow-up process proactively. Even after the primary thrust of the advertising and promotional campaign has been undertaken and the bills paid, the company can mine data related to customer purchasing trends, feedback, what worked, and what didn't work. Accumulating valuable business intelligence from vendors and suppliers is part of the ongoing and management-intensive disbursement process that extends well past the last invoice payment.

Looking at the disbursement cycle through the strategic view emphasizes how much cash is required and consumed well before the first purchase order is executed and well after the vendor/supplier is paid. If these cash requirements are not properly planned for, then you to will most likely experience the pain and suffering of not securing enough cash (or capital) to properly operate your business.

Taking Critical Steps in the Disbursement Cycle to Manage Cash

The most important difference between managing the selling cycle to improve cash flows compared to working the disbursement cycle for cash is also the simplest to understand: You control cash in the disbursements cycle, whereas your customer controls the cash in the selling cycle. This difference is no doubt significant, but in most other ways the cycles are very similar in the way they relate to establishing basic accounting policies, procedures, and controls to protect all business assets (including cash). The three critical steps explained in the following section — qualifying suppliers and vendors, establishing proper controls, and managing creditors — provide you with a better understanding of the basics of the disbursement cycle.

Qualifying suppliers and vendors

Good vendors and suppliers are essential to the ongoing profitable operations of your business. In fact, qualifying suppliers and vendors is just as important, if not more so, than qualifying customers. Whether a vendor provides a critical raw material component in the final finished good or simply sells your company the proper insurance coverage, you want that vendor to be reliable and provide the highest quality product or service.

Numerous resources and procedures are available to help you properly qualify suppliers and vendors. Following are some of the more popular strategies:

- ✔ **Request sample or trial runs.** Before a significant commitment is made with a vendor or supplier, companies often request a trial period, during which a reduced level of business is conducted so that both parties can properly evaluate the feasibility of a larger and longer relationship. The old saying of learning to walk before you run can definitely apply to new vendor relationships.

- ✔ **Tap industry and third-party references.** Countless resources are available for access from both trade and regional sources to obtain references on vendors and suppliers. From contacting the local Better Business Bureau (BBB) to reading online reviews to attending industry trade events, the basic concept always remains the same. Use available public and private resources to do your homework and follow through on references.

- ✔ **Put it in writing.** Making sure that clear and concise terms, conditions, and relationship expectations are established in advance serves a couple of purposes. First, both parties will be able to set expectations on which to operate and support the relationship. Second, you'll get a red flag if a vendor or supplier remains vague and noncommittal about relationship expectations.

> ✔ **Trust your instinct.** Successful business owners usually have a great instinct when it comes to establishing relationships with third parties, so always taking a moment to step back to assess a vendor or supplier is usually very helpful.

Don't be consumed with using price as the only decision point. Sure, a vendor or supplier may offer the best price, but if the product or service quality is substandard and delivery times are unreliable, the ultimate price your business may pay will be far greater than saving a few percentage points.

Establishing proper disbursement cycle controls

When establishing proper disbursement cycle controls, keep in mind the concept of CART (complete, accurate, reliable, and timely). Just like in the selling cycle, disbursement cycle failures, inefficiencies, and/or errors will ultimately have a negative impact on cash flows and cash availability (over the long run). Management should make the same effort in establishing proper disbursement-cycle controls, policies, and procedures as with the selling cycle, because cash leakage potential represents an even greater risk.

Establishing, implementing, and maintaining proper accounting policies, procedures, and controls varies by company and industry but should encompass the following basics:

> ✔ **Utilize a purchase-order system.** Although implementing a formal purchase-order system isn't practical for every business, using some sort of system that ensures proper review, approval, and authorizations for purchases of goods and services are made prior to making a firm commitment should be adhered to. The idea is to avoid errors and mistakes before they happen (which are often very costly) by making sure that the appropriate management team members approve and authorize transactions.

> Smaller businesses generally don't have resources available to implement a formal purchase-order system. But the lack of resources should not prevent even the smallest business from making sure that purchases or goods and/or services are properly approved and authorized. Senior management, and quite often the founder, president, and CEO, should explicitly instruct both internal employees and external vendors and suppliers that they (that is, senior management and others) are the only parties who can authorize purchases. Always establish and utilize a very simple internal policy that clearly relays authority levels.

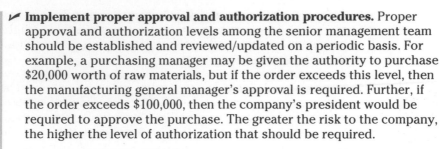

✔ **Implement proper approval and authorization procedures.** Proper approval and authorization levels among the senior management team should be established and reviewed/updated on a periodic basis. For example, a purchasing manager may be given the authority to purchase $20,000 worth of raw materials, but if the order exceeds this level, then the manufacturing general manager's approval is required. Further, if the order exceeds $100,000, then the company's president would be required to approve the purchase. The greater the risk to the company, the higher the level of authorization that should be required.

Business contracts related to real property leases, lending agreements, credit card processing, bank account access, and the like should almost always be executed by a legal officer of the company, because most third parties require an officer's signature to properly bind the contract. These types of financing-based agreements differ from more-traditional purchase agreements because the risks to both the company and third parties is far greater, which in turn requires the need for actual officer approvals and signatures.

✔ **Match, check, and verify.** Businesses should always make a concerted effort to match vendor and supplier invoices again original issued purchase orders (if utilized), receiving reports, executed contracts, and/or any other information available to ensure that the vendor invoice is correct. If you assume that every vendor or supplier invoice received is accurate, then you are going to be in for a rude awakening. Various sources estimates that two to four percent of all invoices contain errors, and in some industries such as healthcare, the error rate is closer to 30 to 40 percent.

✔ **Segregate duties.** If your business has the resources available, segregate different disbursement cycle functions among different employees. For instance, if material is received in the warehouse, have the warehouse staff be responsible for verifying the amount, quality, specifications, and so on of the material against the original purchase order. If correct, this information should then pass to the accounting department, which can verify the price on the vendor's invoice against the original purchase order and, if accurate, proceed to process the vendor invoice.

Smaller businesses may not have the luxury of having multiple departments that can assume different duties, so making sure that at least a couple of relatively independent parties are reviewing and approving vendor invoices will help improve accuracy, reduce errors, and avoid processing incorrect payments. For instance, an accounting manager may receive, review, and input a vendor invoice in the accounting system (for subsequent payment processing). When the invoice is selected for payment, a senior management team member with payment authority should review the invoice again prior to finalizing the payment.

> ✔ **Control the last line of defense — payment authorization.** Finally, the last line of defense for most businesses in the disbursement cycle is at the final check-signing stage (or, in this electronic age, before the send button is hit). A final review and approval of all disbursements should be undertaken by only the most senior management team members to ensure that when payments are processed, they are as accurate as possible.

One final thought we want to share, and a statement that may surprise you, is a warning to never allow your senior accounting and finance personnel to process payments. The reason why not is very logical when you ask yourself one simple question: "Who is best able to commit and conceal fraud in a business?" Everyone's heard the story about the bookkeeper of 30 years, so dedicated to the company and always so reliable and trustworthy until the unthinkable is discovered — the bookkeeper has been bilking the company over the years. By implementing a simple segregation of duty policy of requiring a senior manager independent of the accounting and finance group to review and process final payments, you can often be very effective in preventing your business from becoming a poster child for this kind of theft.

Managing external creditors

The overview of the accounting-based perspective of the disbursement cycle ends in the previous section, because after the vendor has been paid, the cycle is for the most part complete. But strategically, the management of external creditors, ranging from vendors and suppliers to lending sources such as banks, is an ongoing process with a direct impact on cash flows and cash availability.

Probably the most important component of managing external creditors is keeping lines of communication open. Speaking from experience, nothing is worse than failing to communicate with a bank and then delivering a very unwelcome financial or operating performance "surprise." The same can hold true for critical vendors as well, because if they are blindsided by unexpected events or requests, not only will they become nervous about getting paid but they also may feel somewhat slighted and change their attitude toward your business, shifting from being a partner (and willing to work with you) to being nothing more than another creditor. Be sure to communicate clearly and proactively about both good and bad news because creditors want to have an opportunity to proactively manage a potential problem, as well as to participate in your success.

But even with a solid communication plan in place, not all business information should be provided to the creditor, because the vast majority of the info is either irrelevant or confidential. Make sure that just the most appropriate and relevant business information is provided to the creditor. In addition, smaller and less-important creditors don't require the same type of communication effort and plan as key creditors do. For example, you're not going to provide the same information to the company watering the office plants as you do to the bank providing your financing.

Make a concerted effort to properly edit, cleanse, scrub, package, and/or prepare business information that will be distributed externally. There is a significant difference between financial and operational information used for internal management purposes and information distributed to external parties for review and evaluation. Externally provided information is usually presented in a more summarized format, focused on more general/macro-level issues, and avoids disclosing confidential data. Furthermore, a notice that the information is proprietary and confidential should always accompany it.

In the business world you often hear *NDA,* which stands for a nondisclosure agreement, and *CA,* which stands for confidentiality agreement. These agreements are used when confidential business information must be shared between parties in order to support a specific transaction or relationship. The basic idea with these agreements is to ensure that any information being shared between the parties remains confidential, and if one party violates the agreement, then damages may result. We recommend that you work with professional counsel (such as lawyers) to draft these agreements when critical and confidential business information is shared.

Establishing open lines of communications between your business and its vendors and suppliers is a great way to harvest invaluable and, to a certain extent, nonpublic market and industry information. Chances are, one of your suppliers also supports one of your competitors, so although the supplier may not intentionally disclose useful information, it never hurts to keep your ears and eyes open to information that may be of keen interest.

Communication with and management of creditors is often critical to your own business's health. In one situation, a large contractor relied on multiple suppliers and vendors to source products for an end product sold to the government. One supplier of critical importance (this supplier provided a highly technical component that could not be readily provided by other parties) experienced financial difficulties and began to experience delivery problems. By having strong communications between the parties, delivery problems were averted because the contractor was able to step in and provide additional financial support (to ensure no disruption to the supply chain). If the contractor had not stepped forward, a single component, comprising less than 2 percent of the total end product, would have caused significant delivery delays and resulted in reduced cash flows (as without product delivery, no customer payments would be received).

Getting Creative to Improve Cash Flows from the Disbursement Cycle

Most businesses don't have the luxury of General Motors (having Uncle Sam available with billions of dollars of emergency cash) and banks (structuring TARP, or Troubled Asset Relief Program, to provide emergency liquidity during the financial crisis of the Great Recession) or of being too big to fail (we just had to make reference to that term at least once in the book). Rather, most businesses have to operate under the context of TSTC — too small to care. The government really never came running to the thousands of struggling small businesses with any type of financial rescue program. When faced with economic difficulty, the majority of businesses have to buckle down and return to their entrepreneurial roots not only to develop a survival strategy but also to identify new and creative ways to generate cash. Within these cases, a primary target is squarely placed on the disbursement cycle. Honestly, if your sales have decreased and your customers are taking longer to pay, then what better way to generate cash than turning about and taking longer to pay your own vendors?

When utilizing more-creative strategies to improve cash flows from the disbursement cycle, understand the following two key concepts:

✔ First, being creative *does not* mean being dishonest or manipulative. In fact, when creative strategies are used to improve cash flow from the disbursement cycle, just the opposite occurs, as working with vendors and suppliers (to improve cash flows) requires the utmost management and business credibility.

✔ Second, using creative disbursement-cycle strategies to improve cash flows almost always comes at a cost. It may be an outright interest charge from the vendor, a higher lease payment, increased material costs, or something else, but in one form or another, an added cost is going to be present. The key is understanding the trade-off between improving cash flows and the increased cost.

Leaning on vendors and suppliers

When looking for ways to generate additional cash from the disbursement cycle, the starting point is with your vendors and suppliers that have provided goods or services to your business and are now looking for payment. Vendors and suppliers are in business, too, have most likely experienced some form of past cash-flow problems (and have felt your pain), and they don't want to lose you as a customer. Therefore, you should have some room for negotiation.

supplier is to the business. The lower the grade, well, those vendors and suppliers will get paid when cash becomes available.

Here we present a simple A-through-D grading system, but companies may use number schemes, color-coding, and/or other measurement systems as preferred.

- **Grade A:** These vendors represent the highest level of importance in terms of keeping the lights on, the doors open, and ensuring that sales continue to be made. In addition, these vendors tend to retain leverage on your business in one fashion or another. A critical product component supplier, bank or financing company, and landlord tend to fall into this group.

- **Grade B:** Grade B vendors tend to have a number of similarities to the grade A vendors but can be pushed around a little bit (for example, you can ask for another 15 to 30 days to pay) and don't have quite as much leverage (because replacement vendors are available, for instance). Noncritical product component suppliers and some professional service providers tend to fall into this group.

- **Grade C:** The grade C vendors are the first group that can really be stretched on the payment front, because they don't provide essential and/or critical goods or services to the company (that is, they aren't needed on a daily basis to operate). An example of a grade C vendor is a temporary staffing company that your business no longer needs but that has past-due bills outstanding.

- **Grade D or F (if you like):** At the bottom of the barrel are the grade D or F vendors. These vendors tend to have no leverage, provide goods and services that are not needed, and really have no long-term strategic importance to the business. As much as these vendors would hate to admit it, they fall into the prime category of potentially receiving a "haircut" or "cram down" when payments are made. An example of these vendors is an advertising agency (supporting a terminated promotional campaign) or a material supplier for a discontinued product line.

The terms *haircut* and *cram down* essentially mean that the vendor, supplier, or even a creditor is not going to receive 100 percent of the balance they're owed. Haircuts are usually voluntary, in that the creditor understands that a loss will be realized and works toward achieving the best outcome possible (for example, 70 percent on the dollar). A cram down tends to be delivered in a harsher context via the debtor "cramming down" a settlement to the creditor. Call it what you may, if you believe that your business is graded as a D or F by one of your customers, be prepared to settle for what you can and move on with life. Although you will most likely never know what "grade" your business has been assigned, astute business owners can usually quickly figure out where they fall on the food chain in terms of determining just how valuable they are to their customer.

The grading of vendors and suppliers is highly confidential information that should be guarded very closely internally. Nothing is worse than letting this information slip out to vendors and suppliers and then having to respond to the angry C and D rated vendors and suppliers.

Floating along

Years ago, in the good old business days when most payments were processed via check and the banks hadn't fully embraced digital technology, a tried-and-proven method of improving cash flow was to use the *float*. For example, a company would process vendor payments on Friday of each week and drop the checks in the mail (of course, after the last post office pickup of the day). Vendors would then receive payment early the following week, deposit the funds in their bank accounts, and wait for the banks to clear the checks, which could result in a payment taking as long as a week to transfer from the business to vendors. The issuing company therefore had a little extra time (a week) to work on customer payments to cover outstanding checks. This strategy truly defined the old saying, "The check's in the mail."

Now welcome to the 21st century. Between the advances in technology and the adoption of electronic payment processing, the float has almost entirely disappeared in terms of having any type of material impact on cash flows. A week of float has now turned into a day of float as modern technology greatly improves payment-processing efficiency as well as helping to reduce fraud.

But float strategies are still available for creative companies, just in a different capacity. A prime example of using the float relates to processing payments with credit cards. If your business regularly pays certain vendors by using credit cards, you can realize benefits by setting payments to occur one day after the billing cutoff date. If your business's credit card has a cutoff date on the 20th of each month (due on the 15th of the next month), processing a vendor payment on the 22nd rolls this charge into the next billing cycle and provides another 30+ days to pay.

Utilizing the credit card payment cutoff date doesn't mean that a higher credit balance is available. Rather, the goal is to simply buy an extra 30 to 40 days of interest-free financing to support your business operations. Of course, this strategy assumes (and it's a big assumption) that discipline is maintained and credit card balances are paid in full each month. If not, the interest charges on the outstanding credit card balances can quickly turn this strategy into a money-losing event.

This tip may be overkill, but we recommend getting to know your vendor payment-processing habits and trends in order to try to identify which vendors still are slow to deposit/process payments and which utilize the most advanced techniques to quickly process payments. For some businesses, every little bit of cash flow helps.

Creating cash from inventory

Manufacturing, stocking, maintaining, purchasing, and managing inventory is often one of the worst offending areas within a business in terms of consuming excess cash. Left unattended, inventory quickly becomes the ultimate black hole in terms of sucking cash right off the balance sheet. Proactive management of inventory (that is, actively managing inventory product lines to identify and reduce or eliminate slow-moving, obsolete, and/or poor-performing items to improve inventory turnover rates) is without question the best strategy available to avoid incurring additional risk of loss with both obsolete inventory and tied-up cash. However, alternative strategies are also available to help turn inventory into cash (as described in the following two real-world examples).

A manufacturer of high technology products required fairly expensive raw materials and chemicals in the production process. In order to improve availability and reliability of certain key products, a primary vendor agreed to store the inventory on the manufacturer's site, which was accessed on an "as needed" basis. When the raw material was accessed and used, a report was generated once a week, invoices produced, and the manufacturer was provided net 30 days to pay. This strategy worked well for the vendor because the manufacturer was a large customer that it wanted to provide the highest value service to. In addition, the vendor had excess financial resources available to support this strategy. For the manufacturer, not having to purchase, warehouse, and manage this raw material provided the ultimate opportunity to utilize a JIT inventory strategy. (If you missed it, the earlier section "Using JIT payment strategies" describes the JIT concept.)

Here's another helpful example: A jewelry retailer required a large amount of inventory in the form of precious metals and stones to ensure that enough products were on the store shelves for the all-important holiday selling season. A primary supplier of precious stones agreed to consign the stones over half a karat and accept 14-day payment terms after the consigned inventory was sold. By consigning the inventory, the supplier technically remained the legal owner of the large stones but, at the same time, made sure that its large stones were available for sale (improving operating results). For the jewelry retailer, having the right product available at the right time improved its operating results as well.

These inventory strategies by no means represent a complete listing of all the options available. However, when using these types of strategies, remember the key point: There's no such thing as a free lunch. If your business is going to use these types of strategies, somewhere and somehow, your vendors or suppliers will build in added costs in the price of the materials to compensate for your business using their cash and assets.

Tapping vendor-provided financing

Probably the most common type of credit extended from vendors and suppliers is *net 30,* which means that the payment is due within 30 days of the invoice date. Countless other vendor credit terms are available and range from due in advance (for rent payments) to net 90 days or more (to support seasonal sales). Following are two more opportunities available to tap vendor-provided financing to improve cash flows:

✔ **Insurance:** Insurance premiums for general liability, umbrella, auto, directors and officers, and other forms of annual coverage requirements are usually billed 100 percent in advance (for the entire year). Inquiring with the broker or insurance company about financing options is worthwhile, though, because for financial strong companies, very attractive payment plans are often available. (For example, you may get 20 percent down with the balance due in nine equal installments at 4 percent per annum).

✔ **Leasehold improvements:** Most businesses at one point or another lease real property to support their operations. As the business evolves, expands, and/or market conditions change, updates to the leased space may be required. If the landlord doesn't want to make these leasehold improvements or updates on his nickel (which is most often the case), you will be responsible for paying for the leasehold improvements. One strategy to consider is to go back to the landlord and ask whether he will absorb the leasehold improvement costs and then adjust the rental rate moving forward. If the increase is reasonable, then instead of coming out of pocket from day one to cover the leasehold improvement costs, the costs can be amortized over the life of the lease.

For larger and more-infrequent transactions, it never hurts to ask about financing options. Most larger, astute, and savvy vendors and suppliers will already be working with third-party financing sources to make your life (as their customer) as easy as possible.

Leveraging Your Employees for Cash

The majority of this chapter has been focused on managing the disbursement cycle to improve cash flows from the perspective of external third parties such as material suppliers, corporate vendors, and professional service providers. At this point, we want to explore how companies leverage their employees and manage the payroll and compensation cycle to improve cash flows without violating the plethora of rules, regulations, and laws designed to protect employees.

Federal and state laws alike have been designed to protect employees and ensure that they are paid in a timely manner (in addition to ensuring that all payroll taxes and other payroll associated obligations are paid in a timely manner as well). Although opportunities are present to leverage the payroll and compensation cycle to improve cash flows, they aren't numerous given the relatively stringent regulatory environment.

Timing commissions and bonuses

One of the most effective and legitimate strategies used by businesses to properly match cash receipts with disbursements is to structure commission and bonus plans in a consistent manner with the receipt of cash from sales.

- ✔ **Commissions:** The simplest strategy to use with commissions is to defer the payment of any sales commission earned until the cash has been received from the customer. For instance, if a sales representative generated $100,000 in sales in April and earns a 5 percent commission on all sales, the commission of $5,000 would be recognized as an expense in April by accruing the obligation due. However, if the customer doesn't pay until June, then the commission of $5,000 isn't paid until June as well (to match the cash receipt with the payment of the commission). This strategy can be further leveraged to improve cash flows by implementing a policy such as paying all commissions on the 10th day of the month following customer payment. So if the customer doesn't pay until June, the commission could actually be delayed until July 10.

  Structuring a commission plan that remits commissions when the customer pays encourages the sales representatives to stay actively engaged with the customer to ensure that payments are received (because if the customer doesn't get paid, the sales representative doesn't either).

- ✔ **Bonuses:** Bonus plans are generally tied to specific business goals and objectives established for a company's operating performance overall (as opposed to a commission paid on sales). To maximize cash flows, the ideal scenario is to pay bonuses during a period of the year when cash balances are usually higher (for example, 90 days after the company's primary selling season so that sales can turn into cash from customer payments) and/or to pay the bonuses after the operating period on which the bonus is based has been properly evaluated (to ensure that an accurate bonus is calculated and paid).

All compensation plans that include bonuses, commissions, and/or other similar types of payouts should be properly structured and approved by either an internal human resources department or by external professional counsel. The last thing any business needs is to run afoul of state or federal laws pertaining to employee compensation.

Connecting compensation to performance

It should go without saying that all compensation plans need to be structured with a clear correlation between objectives and rewards. A perfect example of this link is the classic sales compensation and commission plan whereby a sales representative earns 5 percent of all sales generated up to $1,000,000 and then 6 percent on all sales above $1,000,000. The company's objective is to drive sales, and the reward is a higher commission for the sales representative. But this type of simple compensation structure has gotten more than a few businesses in trouble because although sales were being driven, the company forgot to ask whether the sales were profitable and collections were being received.

A more relevant and worthwhile sales representative compensation and commission plan expands on the above base program by adding the following features:

✔ All sales commissions are paid when cash is received, for cash received within 90 days of the invoice date. Commission payment is then matched with the actual receipt of cash and also ensures that customers pay within a timely manner (by keeping the sales representative engaged).

✔ The base minimum gross margin required on all sales is 20 percent. For sales that generate a gross margin of less than 20 percent, no commission is earned (unless approved by management). The goal with this requirement is to keep the sales representative focused on selling profitable goods or services and avoiding the trap of "buying" sales by offering deep discounts or special deals.

This sales commission example is very basic and is offered merely to highlight the types of compensation plan features and structuring options that can be utilized to achieve desired results (which for a business is generating profits and for an employee is earning fair and reasonable compensation). The key issue is that compensation plans need to be properly aligned with business operating objectives to produce the desired results.

The sales compensation and commission plan example provided is based on a *top-line approach,* which looks at the top line of the income statement (which is first revenue or sales) and then the next critical line of gross profit.

The top line — in this case, net revenue — can be used as the basis to calculate a commission for an individual sales representative that produced $2 million in sales and earns a 5 percent commission, or $100,000. The top line can also be used to calculate a bonus for the sales and marketing team, such as paying a bonus of 3 percent if the company's top line exceeds $10 million for the year (thus providing $300,000 to be split between the team in the form of a bonus). Top-line compensation programs represent only a portion of most businesses' employee compensation because in addition to top-line commissions, bottom-line bonuses — that focus on the last lines of the income statement, which are typically net profits — are also widely used by businesses.

The same logic applied to structuring commission programs also applies to structuring bonus programs, as a clear correlation between the reward being offered and the desired business objective needs to be developed. In addition, identifying what method will be used to measure the bottom line should be incorporated into the bonus program (for the benefit of all parties). One of the most common methods employed is to simply structure the financial measurements based on GAAP (generally accepted accounting principles). It's both reliable and independent.

Don't be consumed with structuring bonus programs strictly on the income statement alone. For senior management, keeping the business on sound financial footing with a solid balance sheet and strong cash flows is just as important as generating high profit levels. The higher the level of senior management, the more broad-based the objectives should be, factoring in data from all financial statements, including both quantitative and qualitative targets. Remember, one of senior management's primary responsibilities is to think strategically, which usually involves developing and implementing long-term business plans. So senior management should be incentivized appropriately for achieving critical objectives that don't necessarily contribute to current-year profits but lay the foundation for higher profits three years down the road.

Utilizing noncash forms of equity compensation for employees

A number of noncash forms of compensation are available for use by employers that can supplement the employee's earning potential over the long run. One of the most widely used forms of a noncash-compensation program is an incentive stock-option plan. Diving into the details of stock-option plans is well beyond the scope of this book, but the general idea is to provide employees with a grant of stock options (which represent equity ownership in the company) that they can earn or vest over a period of time.

Start-up companies often use stock-option plans for a number of reasons, including to attract high-quality employees. Because the start-up company doesn't have the resources to match cash-compensation programs of larger businesses, they sweeten the pot with offers of equity. Start-ups may also use stock-option plans as a means to conserve cash (trading cash compensation for potential equity appreciation at a later date) and to make sure that the employee stays committed to the company for an extended period (as the stock-option grant is earned over a period of, say, three to five years). For employees, the trade-off is usually straightforward in that lower near-term compensation is earned with the hope that the start-up becomes the next Google and stockholders will exit with millions.

If your company is considering implementing an incentive stock-option plan, obtain proper legal counsel to ensure that it's structured and managed correctly. The technicalities with these types of plans are significant and best left to the experts.

Another type of noncash equity compensation is often referred to as *phantom equity.* Under these plans, an employee is provided upside earnings potential upon a future event being achieved (and is compensated at that time). For example, a key employee may be provided a phantom-equity incentive of 2 percent of the company's value when it is sold. The advantage to the business owners is that they don't actually have to give up any equity (thus having another shareowner with voting and other rights to account for). The advantage to the employee is that she has an incentive plan with significant upside when the event is realized (although some tax disadvantages are present). The variety of colors and flavors with phantom-equity plans are extensive, but they all provide the employee with significant earnings potential upside (like an incentive stock-option plan) but without actually issuing equity. Withholding equity may be particularly favorable for businesses that are family owned, tightly controlled, structured as subchapter S corporations, and/or have other ownership structures that limit the ability to issue equity.

Providing equity in lieu of cash compensation can be expensive. Companies need to understand that although cash can be conserved, giving up equity represents a real cost of conducting business. The trade-offs of giving up ownership interests in exchange for securing the employee need to be carefully evaluated.

Checking out other benefit strategies and ideas

Finally, a couple of other employee-compensation strategies may be relevant in terms of improving cash flows, controlling expenses, and reducing the risk of fraud.

✔ **Use it or lose it vacation policies:** Encouraging all employees to use accrued vacation within a certain time period or lose it can help improve cash flow by limiting the potential of having to actually pay accrued vacation balances if the employee leaves. The idea is to avoid building up multiple years of accrued vacation by strongly encouraging employees to take vacation (thus reducing outstanding balances). In addition, having employees take vacation achieves a significant internal control by providing an opportunity to have another independent employee cover the workload of the employee on vacation. This employee brings a fresh set of eyes to the job, which can uncover fraud, waste, and/or other inefficiencies.

✔ **Employee allowances versus expense reports:** Employers for years have used allowances as an additional form of employee compensation to cover directly incurred expenses for such items as mileage, auto, travel, phones, and so on. Although relatively easy to administer, using allowances also creates problems for the employee and employer alike. Employees are generally required to report allowances as earned income on their tax returns, because the IRS tends to view allowances as additional compensation. For the employer, allowances tend to be paid at the same time as payroll (thus accelerated) and may be inflating expenses (because employees may be taking advantage of the allowance if their actual direct costs are much lower).

To manage this issue, requiring employees to prepare and submit expense reports not only keeps the employee honest with expenses but also can buy the employer a little time in remitting payment (for instance, employees must submit expense reports within 10 days after the month end and will be paid on the 25th of the following month). Furthermore, direct reimbursements of employee expenses from an expense report is generally not considered additional income to the employee by the IRS.

Part V
The Part of Tens

"But rather than me just sitting here talking, why don't we watch this video of me sitting here talking?"

In this part . . .

The Part of Tens contains a couple shorter chapters. Chapter 16 summarizes the top ten keys for managing cash flow in small businesses. Chapter 17 offers ten true stories of cash-flow woes, based on author Tage's business and financial consulting experience. Only the names are omitted to protect the innocent.

Chapter 16

Ten Keys to Managing Cash Flows in a Small Business

In This Chapter

▶ Understanding *all* the financial statements

▶ Managing your business's critical cycles

▶ Protecting cash and cash-producing assets

*I*f cash could talk, it might quote Tony Montana in the movie *Scarface,* who states, "I always tell the truth, even when I lie." Even when the income statement and balance sheet are "lying" (that is, misrepresenting the facts), the cash-flow statement always tells the truth about the state of the business's cash. Simply put, the cash-flow statement is one of the best management tools to help determine if your income statement and balance sheets are lying.

We've said it before, but it's worth mentioning again here: In the black, but where's the green? Translation: Just because your company generates a profit doesn't mean it's generating positive cash flow.

So with this relatively simple but extremely important concept in mind, this chapter provides you with ten tips for managing cash flow so your business always has enough cash available when opportunities occur or disasters strike. These tips have all been discussed in the book and range from the basics of understanding your financial statements to the importance of managing your critical cash inflow and outflow cycles to working with the wonderful world of financing sources, but they all circle back to Tony Montana's quote. That is, if the cash-flow statement displays relatively poor cash flow but large profits, then chances are your business may have an issue (some asset or liability is consuming cash) to address in the balance sheet and income statement.

Respect and Understand Financial Statements

Small businesses are notorious for not maintaining proper accounting books and records. According to some surveys, 25 percent of businesses don't even maintain accounting records (let alone produce financial statements), a number that still stuns us. And when financial statements are produced, most small businesses generally tend to focus on the income statement first and foremost. They may then take a crack at the balance sheet (sometimes without a clue as to what it's really saying), but most business managers leave the statement of cash flows for the bean counters to deal with.

The bottom line for small businesses is simple. If you don't make an effort to prepare, review, and completely understand your financial statements, then you need to ask yourself why you're in business in the first place. And this especially holds true for the statement of cash flows, because an abundance of invaluable information is available from this most commonly overlooked and mismanaged financial statement.

You know your mom was right when she constantly harped on you to always eat your fruits and vegetables. So if you must, think of all the financial statements as fruits and vegetables. Although you may not want to eat them, in the end, you will be stronger and extremely thankful you did. You can get started understanding all three important financial documents in Chapter 3.

Plan, Do Projections, and Plan Some More

Proper planning is essential to the launch, growth, management, and ultimate success of your business as measured by the ability to generate profits and, just as important, to avoid running out of cash. Dedicating resources to this all-important function cannot be underestimated in today's rapidly changing and complex marketplace. Having access to sound financial plans structured for different operating scenarios is an absolute must.

During the planning process, keep in mind these two critical elements:

> ✔ **Planning is an ongoing and constantly changing and evolving process.** Treat the business plan as a living, breathing tool that is constantly changing and needs constant attention as market conditions shift. The ability to adapt and remain flexible to changing market conditions has never been more critical than in today's fiercely competitive global marketplace.

> ✔ **Financial planning starts with identifying, obtaining, and evaluating reliable business, operational, and market data and information (both from internal and external sources).** Yes, you may be surprised that the authors of this book (both being accountants) acknowledge the importance of accumulating nonfinancial and accounting data first, but we're not dealing with "the chicken or the egg" riddle — data must come before any financial forecasts or projections can be completed. Reliable internal and external data and information are the basis of any sound business plan and forecast.

Chapters 8 and 9 walk you through the background work necessary for planning, help you create a viable business plan, and provide the basis for building best in class projection models.

Focus on Capital and Cash: The Lifeblood of Any Business

You must secure the proper amount, type, and structure of capital to provide your business with the necessary financial resources to execute the business plan. One of the most common reasons small businesses fail is that they lack adequate cash or capital, not only to survive difficult times, but also (and more important) to prosper during growth opportunities. Although having a war chest to tap during down times is important, having the proper amount and type of capital available to support a rapid-growth period is even more critical, because although surviving is nice, most companies are in business to create wealth and value to the owners. Face it; in a capitalist economic system, wealth creation is of paramount importance, and wealth is created most often by not treading water and staying afloat but by riding the monster wave when it arrives. So be prepared. Raising capital has been and will continue to be one of the most critical and time-consuming tasks business owners and managers ever undertake, and its importance should never be underestimated.

Remember, one of the greatest losses a small business can realize is that of lost opportunity, which has its roots in not being prepared to properly capitalize on market opportunities. The harsh reality is that this great loss is never accounted for or presented in any way, shape, or form on the business's financial statements. Rather, missed market and business opportunities lurk in the background, haunting the business owner, manager, or entrepreneur with the torturous thought, "Imagine what I could have achieved!" Chapters 10 and 11 can help you understand how to secure capital as needed so you won't ever have to face this regret.

Understand Your Selling Cycle

From an accounting perspective, the selling cycle basically commences with the initiation of a sales order, which then turns into the issuance of an invoice, which, of course, eventually results in the receipt of payment. The accounting cycle, although relatively easy to define, is only one element of the entire selling cycle that starts with conducting proper planning and market research and doesn't end until the customer's needs are completely satisfied (to ensure the customer returns). The length of the complete selling cycle is often much longer than the aspiring entrepreneur projects and/or wants to believe. And if not properly managed, the selling cycle generally becomes one of the largest consumers of cash in a business (as sales goals and objectives are not met, capital is depleted more rapidly than forecasted, and management's creditability is impaired). Without fail, almost every aspiring business owner, at one point or another, will experience delays in the selling cycle.

The selling cycle involves more than selling a product or service and collecting the cash. Rather, the selling cycle in its entirety spans the time from the very start of the process when a product or service is first visualized and developed (that customers may actually purchase) to supporting customers after the sale and developing additional products or services that may be in demand (thus completing the circle). The lesson learned from understanding the complete selling cycle can and should also be applied to almost any business function, from raising capital to securing management to developing new products. Make sure you apply the concept of the selling cycle to every aspect of your business to ensure that you develop proper plans and secure capital resources to handle the inevitable bumps in the road that will come. Chapter 14 can help you on your way.

Manage Your Disbursements Cycle

The selling cycle is generally the largest consumer of cash for most businesses. To counteract this cash consumption machine, businesses need to understand that the disbursement cycle (managing expenditures and cash payments to vendors, employees, and other creditors) can be leveraged and managed to be a primary source of cash for your business. You may be thinking, "What, have the authors lost it? Everyone knows that sales produce cash and disbursements consume cash!" Well, at the end of each of these cycles, your objection is absolutely correct, but in 90 percent of the activity and transactions that occur prior to the end of each cycle, you can manage things to alter how cash is consumed and generated. Chapters 14 and 15 offer detailed tips on how to improve cash flows, ranging from structuring customer payment terms to entice customers to pay quicker to developing relationships with vendors and understanding how much time you can really buy before you have to pay outstanding invoices, to approaching financing sources on how to squeeze more money from lending agreements.

When at all possible, invoke one of the most important accrual-based accounting principles — the matching principle. That is, similar to properly matching revenue and expenses to ensure that an accurate measurement of a business's profit or loss is obtained, you should be able to match cash inflows and outflows. This effective management tool is used in a wide range of environments and is best understood by taking a closer look at paying sales commissions. Generally, sales representatives earn commissions when sales occur. If the commission is paid in the same month the sale is recorded (regardless of if the customer has paid), then cash outflows may be accelerated. However, if the commission is paid when the customer pays, the cash inflow from the customer is matched with the cash outflow to the sales representative.

Be Creative to Generate Cash

Small businesses must continually (and quickly) innovate, create, adapt, and adjust to have a chance at competing against the corporate behemoths that dominate so many markets. Deep pockets are a luxury that most small businesses generally don't have, as sitting on mounds of cash is a problem that most companies would love to have but few will ever experience. To stay afloat, small businesses should apply to accounting the same business creativity they use when developing new products or services, figuring out how to reach customers more efficiently, or structuring employee compensation plans to retain the best talent available.

The following three areas offer significant opportunities for creativity when looking to improve cash flows:

- ✔ **Turn your assets over quicker.** Assets consume cash. The quicker you can turn over assets, the quicker they turn into cash. It's as simple as that.

- ✔ **Leverage your vendors, suppliers, and financing sources.** These businesses are your vendors, but, more important, you are their customer. They don't want to lose your business, so placing just the right amount of leverage on these groups can result in enhanced cash flows because liabilities offer a source of cash. Looking at it from another perspective, if a vendor offers your company 30-day payment terms that you can stretch into 45 days, in effect, you have 15 extra days to remit payment (and thus keep cash with your company longer).

✔ **Manage external sources of cash proactively.** You can proactively manage your relationships with banks, leasing companies, and even the federal government to ensure that cash is made available when needed. If you give an inch with these groups, they most likely will take a mile, so be sure your business takes the lead with managing these types of external parties.

Balance the Balance Sheet

Many businesses overlook the concept of properly managing the financial structure of their balance sheet, which has gotten more than a few businesses in trouble. Your business needs to strike a proper balance between making sure that current assets (on the left side of the balances sheet) are financed or supported with current liabilities (on the right side of the balance sheet) and making sure that long-term assets are financed (again, on the left side of the balance sheet) or supported with long-term sources of capital (such as a five-year note payable or equity). Every business should strive to achieve a financial condition that ensures constant maintenance of adequate levels of both solvency (the ability to pay all just debts) and liquidity (the ability to quickly access cash to support business operations).

For a case study on how to fail at financing, look no farther than the federal government. The problem is not only that the federal government is running enormous deficits that it's funding with debt, but also that the composition of the debt in relation to the federal government's expenditures is out of balance (and problematic). The federal government is currently utilizing more and more short-term treasury bills (30, 90, or 180 days until maturity) to finance long-term structural expenditures (such as the military). Although implementing this strategy helps reduce interest expense (because the interest rates on short-term debt are less than 1 percent compared to ten-year rates of closer to 3 percent), this type of imbalance increases potential financing risks down the road: If short-term rates rise or market conditions change dramatically (and selling the debt becomes more difficult), access to cash to fund ongoing government operations may become a very big problem, very quickly.

Understand External Capital Markets

Business owners love to quote two old sayings when it comes to banks: Banks always have money available to lend when you don't need it, and banks love to say yes, yes, yes, yes — and then, when it's time to make the commitment, *no!* To be fair, these statements also apply to basically all types of external sources of capital, ranging from investors to alternative lending sources. The following key concepts help you understand how to prepare for and deal with external sources of cash or capital:

✔ **Think well ahead.** In today's economic climate, it takes a long time to identify external sources of capital (because fewer choices are available) and to secure them (because the review or underwriting process is very stringent, not to mention that more businesses are competing for capital). So plan well ahead to make sure that you'll have cash available when needed, because it's not a process you can rush.

✔ **Think expensive.** For the biggest companies, like Apple and McDonald's, money is still cheap (in fact, extremely cheap). For the balance of the business community, money is expensive (often very expensive). Being realistic on how expensive money is and what source is most appropriate for your business should be understood from the beginning so that you can avoid sticker shock and properly plan for financing related costs (making sure that your projections are as accurate as possible and that cash will be available to meet loan obligations).

✔ **Think colonoscopy.** Examinations, reviews, audits, evaluations, due diligence — however you refer to it, the bottom line is that when you pursue external capital, the process undertaken to verify your business's information is going to be very detailed, broad, time consuming, and lengthy. So if you're not properly prepared for the underwriting process, then don't bother, because the end result will be easily predictable.

Also think *internal* by scrubbing the balance sheet to find hidden cash and sources of capital. When appropriate, external sources of capital should be pursued to secure cash to finance a business (and we discuss these sources and scenarios in Chapters 10 and 11). But businesses need to remember that countless internal sources of cash may be available to support the operation and maybe, just maybe, alleviate the need for loans or outside investments.

Protect Cash at All Times

Cash represents an asset just like trade accounts receivables, inventory, and equipment, and like those assets it must be controlled, managed, and protected at all times. However, cash has a very unique characteristic unlike these other assets that makes it highly susceptible to additional risk of loss: Cash is an extremely liquid and marketable asset.

Most assets require a series of transactions or steps in order to be converted into cash. Sometimes those steps can protect businesses from fraud. For example, if theft occurs with inventory, it first must be taken from the business and then converted into cash from some type of fraudulent transaction. Furthermore, the party purchasing the inventory usually knows that the transaction isn't legitimate and will deeply discount their purchase to account for increased risk. So inventory that may sell for $100 in a store and has a cost of $50 may actually only sell for $20 in this type of environment. Needless to say, $20 isn't much of an incentive to steal the item. The problem with cash, however, is that it doesn't require a conversion transaction, and when it's stolen, it retains its face value.

So the basic rule of thumb for all assets (and particularly cash) is that with a higher level of convertibility and net-realizable face value, the higher the level of controls, policies, procedures, and management attention that needs to be applied.

Advances in the digital or Internet age have had significant influences on the management of cash, both positive and negative. Although improving business efficiencies and lowering the risk of handling actual cash receipts (including checks), they have also opened the door to an entirely new type of electronic fraud and theft. Utilizing technology to manage cash receipts and disbursements is definitely the wave of the future, but it should be accompanied by the appropriate accounting policies, procedures, and controls to manage the increased risks.

Always Think of CART

If you remember one acronym from this book, remember CART — complete, accurate, reliable, and timely. Your company's financial and accounting information system needs to produce complete, accurate, reliable, and timely financial information, reports, data, and so on, which management can use to make informed business decisions. Without CART, a business cannot function properly, nor can it make informed and timely business decisions. Furthermore, CART is essential to improving cash flows because a direct correlation links improved CART and improved cash flows.

Without producing CART invoices for your customers, payments will be delayed. Without having CART financial statements or reports, your chances of securing a loan from a bank will be significantly impaired. And without providing CART data to shareowners or the board of directors, you can kiss your job goodbye (and your ability to generate positive cash flow).

Chapter 17

Ten Tales of Cash-Flow Woes

In This Chapter

▶ Consuming cash in underperforming assets

▶ Utilizing loans, debt, and liabilities incorrectly

▶ Being caught off guard by changing market conditions

▶ Making management mishaps, mistakes, and mayhem

Time and time again, business gurus write articles and reports on the most common reasons small businesses fail. At the top of the list, you almost always find the issue of undercapitalization, or lack of enough cash to support the operating strategy. This chapter provides ten other tales of how companies got into to severe cash-flow crunches by not attending to critical accounting, financial, and operational issues properly.

An underlying trend with almost every cash-flow woe is poor management. Yes, the economy crashed, but management in many cases was not prepared. Yes, market conditions changed, but management often didn't understand the competitive forces to begin with. The point is that just as poor management can make a difficult situation even worse, solid management can help offset the damage of a number of cash-flow sins.

Misunderstanding Trade Account Receivables

The number of cash-flow woes that can be attributed to mismanaging trade accounts receivable are endless. One specific, extremely problematic issue we've encountered over the years is centered in what a business considers a legitimate trade receivable, because financing sources don't lend against receivables with certain characteristics. Examples of problem receivables include federal government sales, foreign sales, related/affiliated party sales, concentrated sales, receivables subject to future discounts/adjustments, and others. (See Chapters 11 and 14 for further information on why these types of receivables present lending problems.) These receivables may be completely legitimate and eventually be collected, but from a financing source's perspective, they're too risky to lend against. The following examples demonstrate how businesses can go wrong with accounts receivable:

- A professional service firm was pursuing a large contract that it felt assured of receiving. Although it hadn't obtained a signed contract, it established billing jobs and codes to capture the initial work and invoice the customer. When the contract fell through, the invoices became uncollectible, which resulted in the receivables being written off and the company taking a loss. Furthermore, when the receivable dropped from the borrowing facility (that is, the receivable extended past 90 days from the original due date before it was written off, which made the receivable no longer eligible to borrow against), access to available cash was reduced because the company couldn't use this receivable as collateral to borrow against.

- A medical device distribution company sold various medical equipment and supplies to customers throughout the country. The company's standard practice was to match any competitor price if pressured by customers. An audit of the business determined that the average discount offered and subsequent billing adjustment was 20 percent. Prior to the audit, the financing source had been lending at a rate of 80 percent against eligible receivables. Subsequent to the audit, the lending rate was reduced to 65 percent as a result of the high billing discounts and adjustments provided to the customers. In order to remain in compliance with the lending facility, the company had to pay down the line of credit, which reduced cash levels very quickly.

Always obtain a true understanding of the real value of your trade receivables by making sure that proper reserves are established for potential bad debts, product returns, and/or other billing adjustments. Establish proper reserves in a prudent and objective manner based on analyzing reliable sales and trade receivables data, reports, and information to calculate correct reserve amounts. Don't trick yourself into believing that 100 percent of all customer invoices will eventually be received — we have yet to see a business achieve this objective.

Letting Good Inventory Go Bad

The reality of the economy is that industries and markets can move so fast that today's highly successful products can quickly become obsolete in less than six months. Just ask anyone operating in the consumer electronics business, such as Apple, Sony, or RIMM, because without a constant product-development and market-introduction strategy, these companies can move from Hero to Zero in the blink of an eye.

Of course, the consumer electronics market isn't the only industry that can suffer from inventory obsolescence issues. The distribution company in the following example learned that lesson quickly.

A distributor of both domestic and imported picture and mirror framing and molding products had operated a successful business for over 25 years. The company amassed a large inventory of specialty and unique products sold primarily to niche framing and molding retail shops located throughout the country. Unfortunately, two events occurred that quickly turned good inventory into worthless wood:

✔ First, the company never properly evaluated and managed specific inventory lines or items in relation to how quickly the products were turning over into sales. In some cases, the company had over a two-year supply of certain products.

✔ Second, the company's customer market was dramatically reshaped over a ten-year period as the smaller niche retail stores it relied on for the majority of its revenue decreased from an estimated 40,000 shops to less than 15,000 due to competition by big box retailers (such as Michaels).

In the end, the company's inventory problem created two cash problems: Cash was used to purchase inventory that was taking more than a year to sell, and having the excess inventory required storage, maintenance, and administrative support, which resulted in higher operating expenses. In this situation, for every $100 of inventory owned, these added costs amounted to 10 percent annually. And finally, to add insult to injury, the inventory's value wasn't even 50 percent of the original cost due to styles changing and storage-related damage.

One of the simplest ways to avoid these types of inventory-management problems is to generate frequent inventory performance reports by product line and SKU (or individual product) to determine how quickly products are selling, what gross margins are being generated, and other potential trending information. If management stays on top of these reports, inventory problems can quickly be identified with corrective action taken (such as simply reducing purchases of slow-moving items).

Improperly Investing in Soft Assets

When the term *soft assets* is used, it usually refers to some type of intellectual property such as patents, trademarks, trade names, publications, trade secrets, and/or some other type of proprietary business asset that generates earnings (or cash flows). For example, the formula of Coca-Cola is one of the most valuable and highly guarded assets in the world, but yet no tangible or hard asset is present. However, soft assets can quickly turn into cash-guzzling machines, as the following situation highlights.

A sports nutrition company developed and sold a highly successful muscle-building nutrient that produced strong revenues and profits (as well as cash flows). To leverage this success, the company elected to develop and publish a bimonthly fitness magazine, which required significant cash investments upfront to produce all the content needed for the magazine (as well as to publish the initial edition of tens of thousands of copies). A cash problem arose before one dollar of cash was actually received from subscription or rack sales, and a total of only four editions were produced and published. The problem was that the parties handling both the subscription and rack sales used magazine sales remittance strategies (customary in the industry) that stretched the end customer sales (the point at which a consumer would purchase a magazine from a retailer such as a grocery store) out roughly eight months. If the consumer purchased the magazine for $5 in March, the company didn't receive actual payment for their share until November. To compound this problem, in an attempt to keep from overloading readers with endless amounts of advertising, the fitness magazine didn't secure advertising revenue from third parties in the original editions.

Needless to say, the company's mismanagement of both the receivables cycle and advertising potential in the magazine quickly changed (via watching cash levels quickly fall) after this painful cash lesson was learned.

Soft assets can have a double-negative impact on cash. First, an investment in the soft asset needs to be made (which consumes cash). And second, cash receipts driven from soft-asset-generated sales can often take much longer to materialize than a more traditional manufacturing or service-based business.

Falling into the Taxable Income Trap

The number of potential problems and pitfalls with taxes are so extensive that providing a complete discussion would warrant an entire book. However, one tax trap has created grief more than a few times. The distribution of taxable income from flow-through entities (that is, subchapter S corporations, limited liability companies, and partnerships) has a negative impact on personal income tax obligations all too often.

A manufacturing company aggressively used tax incentives, including accelerated depreciation on equipment purchases and the cash method, when reporting taxable income for a number of years. During these years, book income was positive but taxable income was neutral to negative. Cash balances built during these years were subsequently distributed to the owners who, in turn, used the majority of the cash for personal expenditures. Eventually, the business's reportable sizable taxable earnings as accelerated depreciation deductions were eliminated and the benefit of the cash method of reporting flattened out. When the business reported the taxable income, which flowed through to the owners, the owners had not set aside the appropriate amount of cash from the earlier years to cover the tax liabilities. To pay the bill, they tapped the business for cash, which produced two negative side effects. First, cash the business needed to reinvest and support growth was not available. Second, when the cash was distributed to the owners, it had the effect of reducing the business's net equity, triggering a subsequent increase in its debt-to-equity ratio (because debt remained constant but equity decreased), creating a covenant default with a bank loan.

Entities that are legally structured to allow taxable income to flow through to owners don't report income tax expense and aren't obligated to report income tax obligations. Rather, these responsibilities fall on the owners of the business. Business managers and owners must always have a clear understanding of any potential income tax obligations that are outstanding and take care to reserve the appropriate amount of cash for these obligations (at either the company or individual level). Remember, most tax rules and regulations are structured to enable a company to defer income taxes, not eliminate or avoid income taxes, so eventually cash will be required.

Given the complexity of tax issues that most business have to operate under (at the federal, state, and local levels), securing professional tax assistance is essential to avoid getting some nasty surprises down the road. The tax environment is only going to get worse and more complicated as every government entity expands its search for tax revenue, so staying on top of tax issues early and complying with all rules and regulations should be a top priority.

Misapplying Available Debt-Based Capital

The best way to highlight how misapplying available debt-based capital can wreak havoc on a business's available cash is with the following two rather simple but devastating real-world examples:

- A wholesale food producer secured a working capital line of credit to support anticipated receivables growth from recently acquired large customers. The line of credit was designed to be used to purchase raw materials and finance increases in trade receivables. The company elected to draw on the line of credit to invest in property leasehold improvements and repay some old debt. Unfortunately, when the growth opportunity arrived, the company had used its remaining cash and available borrowing capacity on the line of credit and didn't have any liquidity left to purchase raw materials and support new orders. Needless to say, the discussion between the bank and the company was very lively, and the management team immediately lost credibility with the bank. So the wholesale food producer missed out on a wonderful growth opportunity.

✔ Company X was profitable, with strong earnings and a solid balance sheet. The founders of Company X then became part owners in a new business operation that required periodic cash infusions to support its launch and subsequent growth. Company X advanced or loaned cash to the new company, which used the money for general operating purposes. As you may have guessed, Company X then found itself in need of the cash to cover various obligations, but the new business was unable to repay (because it was sunk in start-up costs and other illiquid assets). Not much longer after this, the ownership of the companies changed dramatically as trust between the owners disintegrated.

Just because cash is available doesn't mean that your company has a green light to spend it, loan it, distribute it, or use it in another capacity. Exercise extreme caution and care with excess cash because it has a tendency to disappear very quickly.

Failing to Prepare for the Economic Hard Landing

We doubt that many businesses want to revisit the problems created courtesy of the Great Recession (from late 2007 through early 2010). In fact, most companies would just as soon block this time period from memory, given the severity of the economic contraction. But a number of invaluable lessons were learned during this period that relate to managing cash and liquidity. Following are two of these critical items:

✔ **Companies that didn't maintain a strong balance sheet with ample liquidity quickly became casualties.** The combination of both the speed and depth of the economic contraction caught a number of businesses off guard. As for speed, businesses witnessed sales evaporate in a matter of months, not years. The depth of the economic contraction also stunned businesses, as expected 10 to 15 percent revenue reductions experienced over a 12- to 18-month period (in a normal recession) were replaced by 30-plus percent sales decreases experienced over a 6- to 12-month period. The bottom line is that businesses simply couldn't adjust and adapt their economic operating models fast enough, which resulted in significant negative operating losses (translating into large cash losses as well).

✔ **Companies without multiple operating plans to cover potential disaster scenarios had to scramble quickly and redeploy business resources just to survive.** Business managers and owners tend to become very complacent when economic times are more robust. Added bonuses are paid, questionable asset investments are made (based on assuming that growth will continue), cash that may in fact be needed down the road is used to repay debt, and so on. But economic "hard landings" can quickly underscore how important it is to have multiple operating plans and forecasts available to support timely business decision making. Companies learned that they should have multiple operating plans/projection models ready to go in the event that rapid and rash decisions have to be made. Simply having the "expected" operating case to work with was not nearly adequate, because what most companies needed was access to a "disaster" plan in order to properly evaluate and implement the choices available.

As we write this book, Corporate America (that is, the Fortune 500) sits on over $2 trillion of cash with record earnings being reported over the past year. Hardly the type of statistics you'd expect coming out of what's considered the second worst economic contraction America has experienced, but representative of how financially strong these companies are and how well they plan. Or as Warren Buffett stated, "When the tide goes out, we'll see who's left standing naked on the beach." For businesses that were fully clothed (having solid plans and being well prepared with strong balance sheets and high liquidity), when the tide went out, the pain was far less severe and recoveries were very robust. And the market quickly disposed of businesses that found themselves wearing nothing but their birthday suit during this same period.

Getting Left in the Cold by Changing Market Conditions

The economy goes through natural periods of expansion and contraction, which can be very painful (as summarized in the preceding section). In addition, competitive forces throughout the economy are constantly reshaping industries, whether or not the overall economy is growing or contracting. During the Great Recession, most industries were contracting, yet pawnshops saw an increase in demand. And today, the technology industry is expanding by leaps and bounds, but certain niches within the industry are looking at the end. (For example, are DVD players even needed anymore?). The following example illustrates how even a very mature industry can be reshaped by competitive market forces.

A single-branded oil and gas distributer operated a family-owned business serving a secondary market (that is, not a major market in a metropolitan area such as Atlanta or Chicago but a smaller, rural market with a wider geographical reach). Over the years, a number of large oil and gas suppliers determined that supporting the secondary markets was far more efficient if the local distributors began carrying multiple brands to improve their operating efficiency (such that delivery equipment could then be used at a 90-plus percent efficiency ratio). After this strategy was enacted, the multibranded local distributors then passed on lower costs to their retail customers, who could then

charge a lower price for gas and oil. This change placed significant competitive pressure on retail customers supplied by the single-branded distributor
and forced price decreases as well. In the end, the single-branded distributor's
operating performance moved from generating profits to producing losses,
which drained the company's cash reserves and ultimately forced its sale (at a
deep discount).

Making Overly Optimistic Sales Forecasts

We harp on our concerns about the selling cycle throughout this book, and
here we once again call out a way that this cycle can drain cash.

Back in the 1990s when the dot-com craze was in full swing, a number of companies built business plans for delivering products or services through stand-
alone, electronic kiosks. To provide a frame of reference, these kiosks looked
and operated somewhat like Redbox (which distributes DVDs) and Coinstar
(which counts coins and exchanges them for cash or gift certificates) but
suffered the following fatal flaws as a result of not understanding the selling
cycle adequately:

- ✔ **Unreliable kiosks:** Every selling cycle needs to ensure not only that
  sales are made but also that the customer experience and the service
  provided guarantee repeat business. In this case, the kiosks proved to
  be unreliable, which turned customers off very quickly. Improvements
  were made, but by that time, customers were lost and the economic
  model no longer worked because management had underestimated the
  amount of repairs and maintenance needed to ensure properly operating kiosks.

- ✔ **Unrealistic volume expectations:** Even when the kiosks worked and
  were rolled out on time and customers purchased products, the miss
  in the selling cycle was on volume, because transactions took longer to
  process and customer participation rates were lower than anticipated.
  With a relatively high fixed operating cost, the kiosks could not generate
  enough profit to cover expenses and thus drained the company of its
  remaining cash.

- ✔ **Inability to compete in technologies and pricing:** Kiosks that were
  based on the distribution of information were quickly displaced by
  more-efficient and reliable competing technologies that generally provided a better product at a lower price.

Remember, the selling cycle can drain cash in countless ways, ranging from purchase timing to volumes to price to product/service reliability. Understanding all critical aspects of the selling cycle is essential to calculating just how much cash will be consumed.

Robbing Peter to Pay Paul

Small-business owners are by nature entrepreneurs and, generally, forever optimists. Their spirit is often best measured in the satisfaction they receive from providing a product or service of value to the market and not just based in the amount of money they make. Although this trait is admirable, it can also be a flaw because entrepreneurs often stop at nothing to see their ideas succeed and business survive for decades. Engaging in business and ensuring its ultimate survival, at any cost without looking at the big picture, is where the blacks and whites of running a business often turn gray and transaction legitimacy comes into question. Business owners often become some consumed in whether they *can* do something (which in this case means keeping the business afloat by overstepping critical boundaries) that they forget to ask the more important question related to whether they *should* be doing this.

A manufacturing company experienced a sharp downturn in sales as a result of a number of confluencing factors. The company developed a turnaround plan but had run out of cash, so it began using partial, advance, and pre-billing strategies to process invoices before the products were actually shipped. Instead of waiting to access cash against the receivable when the complete shipment and sale occurred (30 days in the future), they robbed the future by accessing the cash today to pay current outstanding obligations. These invoices were provided to the manufacturing company's financing source, which in turn advanced cash (assuming a valid receivable was present) to finance the company's turnaround. The company initially intended to use this strategy as a stop-gap measure on a limited basis. In the end, the strategy was used much longer and more extensively than planned. Eventually, the problem was rectified, but the impact on cash (not to mention management credibility) was significant, because cash was repeatedly pulled forward and used for historical needs with nothing left to support future needs.

Business owners typically want to believe the best about their businesses, so although their intent is not to commit fraud, they often undertake small accounting "adjustments" to buy another week or month — a practice that can soon accumulate into a major problem. By robbing Peter (accelerating a sale set for the next month to the current month) to pay Paul (using the sale to meet a current target), all you do is make the next month's targets even more challenging to achieve. And if this practice continues for a long period of time, eventually the weight of the problem implodes on the business. Forming strong boards of directors or advisory boards that actively participate in the business can help provide the proper insight and guidance to avoid falling into this trap.

Growing Yourself Out of Business

Companies that simply grow themselves out of business are a good example of the dangers of equating profits with cash flow. In one particular case, entrepreneurs launched an ecommerce-based retail business that specialized in selling consumer goods. The company was highly successful as measured by annual revenue growth, which in year one was less than $500,000 but exploded to over $12 million in five years. The primary problem this company faced was that the suppliers of the consumer goods generally required payments upon delivery (to secure the best pricing) for products that would be marketed over a period of 6 to 12 months (as a result of seasonality sales strategies). The company assumed that financing would be available from either primary or secondary lending sources (to support the growth), but given the nature of the product, the age of the company, and the status of the financial information, securing external financing proved to be a significant challenge.

This cash-flow tale of caution doesn't end too badly: The company continued to operate profitability albeit at a much lower growth rate. But the cash-flow woe does highlight the importance of securing proper amounts and types of financing to support rapid-growth scenarios.

Rapidly growing industries or markets are going to attract the interest of numerous competitors. By not having a plan in place with the proper amount of capital or cash, companies leave the door open to bigger and stronger competitors that will take market share and may ultimately force smaller and weaker businesses out of the market.

Index

• F •

• T •